3D VISUAL COMMUNICATIONS

3D VISUAL COMMUNICATIONS

Guan-Ming Su
Dolby Labs, California, USA

Yu-Chi Lai
National Taiwan University of Science and Technology, Taiwan

Andres Kwasinski
Rochester Institute of Technology, New York, USA

Haohong Wang
TCL Research America, California, USA

WILEY

A John Wiley & Sons, Ltd., Publication

10 0681235 3

Library of Congress Cataloging-in-Publication Data

Su, Guan-Ming.
  3D visual communications / Guan-Ming Su, Yu-Chi Lai, Andres Kwasinski, Haohong Wang.
    pages cm
  Includes bibliographical references and index.
  ISBN 978-1-119-96070-6 (cloth)
1. Multimedia communications. 2. Three-dimensional display systems. I. Lai, Yu-Chi. II. Kwasinski, Andres.
III. Wang, Haohong, 1973- IV. Title. V. Title: Three dimensional visual communications.
  TK5105.15.S83 2013
  006.7–dc23
                                                                                    2012031377

A catalogue record for this book is available from the British Library.

ISBN: 978-1-119-96070-6
Typeset in 10/12pt Times by Laserwords Private Limited, Chennai, India
Printed and bound in Malaysia by Vivar Printing Sdn Bhd

Contents

Preface   **ix**
About the Authors   **xiii**

1   **Introduction**   **1**
1.1   Why 3D Communications?   1
1.2   End-to-End 3D Visual Ecosystem   3
       1.2.1   3D Modeling and Representation   5
       1.2.2   3D Content Creation   6
       1.2.3   3D Video Compression   7
       1.2.4   3D Content Delivery   8
       1.2.5   3D Display   9
       1.2.6   3D QoE   9
1.3   3D Visual Communications   10
1.4   Challenges and Opportunities   11
       References   15

2   **3D Graphics and Rendering**   **17**
2.1   3DTV Content Processing Procedure   19
2.2   3D Scene Representation with Explicit Geometry – Geometry Based
       Representation   22
       2.2.1   Surface Based Representation   23
       2.2.2   Point Based Representation   37
       2.2.3   Point Based Construction   38
       2.2.4   Point Based Compression and Encoding for Transmission   38
       2.2.5   Point Based Rendering: Splatting   39
       2.2.6   Volumetric Representation   40
       2.2.7   Volumetric Construction   40
       2.2.8   Volumetric Compression and Encoding for Transmission   41
       2.2.9   Volumetric Rendering   42
2.3   3D Scene Representation without Geometry – Image-Based
       Representation   43
       2.3.1   Plenoptic Function   43
       2.3.2   Single Texture Representation   46
       2.3.3   Multiple Texture Representation   48
       2.3.4   Image Based Animation   51

2.4   3D Scene Representation with Implicit Geometry – Depth-Image-Based
       Representation   51
       2.4.1   History of Depth-Image-Based Representation   52
       2.4.2   Fundamental Concept Depth-Image-Based Representation   53
       2.4.3   Depth Construction   56
       2.4.4   Depth-Image-Based Animation   57
       References   57

3   3D Display Systems   63
3.1   Depth Cues and Applications to 3D Display   63
       3.1.1   Monocular Depth Cues   63
       3.1.2   Binocular Depth Cues   64
3.2   Stereoscopic Display   65
       3.2.1   Wavelength Division (Color) Multiplexing   65
       3.2.2   Polarization Multiplexing   69
       3.2.3   Time Multiplexing   69
3.3   Autostereoscopic Display   71
       3.3.1   Occlusion-Based Approach   71
       3.3.2   Refraction-Based Approach   75
3.4   Multi-View System   78
       3.4.1   Head Tracking Enabled Multi-View Display   79
       3.4.2   Automultiscopic   79
3.5   Recent Advances in Hologram System Study   83
       References   84

4   3D Content Creation   85
4.1   3D Scene Modeling and Creation   85
       4.1.1   Geometry-Based Modeling   86
       4.1.2   Image-Based Modeling   86
       4.1.3   Hybrid Approaches   87
4.2   3D Content Capturing   87
       4.2.1   Stereo Camera   87
       4.2.2   Depth Camera   88
       4.2.3   Multi-View Camera   88
       4.2.4   3D Capturing with Monoscopic Camera   89
4.3   2D-to-3D Video Conversion   101
       4.3.1   Automatic 2D-to-3D Conversion   103
       4.3.2   Interactive 2D-to-3D Conversion   111
       4.3.3   Showcase of 3D Conversion System Design   112
4.4   3D Multi-View Generation   125
       References   126

5   3D Video Coding and Standards   129
5.1   Fundamentals of Video Coding   129
5.2   Two-View Stereo Video Coding   142
       5.2.1   Individual View Coding   142
       5.2.2   Inter-View Prediction Stereo Video Coding   143

5.3	Frame-Compatible Stereo Coding	144
	5.3.1 Half-Resolution Frame-Compatible Stereo Coding	144
	5.3.2 Full-Resolution Frame-Compatible Layer Approach	146
5.4	Video Plus Depth Coding	148
5.5	Multiple View Coding	156
5.6	Multi-View Video Plus Depth (MVD) Video	160
5.7	Layered Depth Video (LDV)	163
5.8	MPEG-4 BIFS and AFX	165
5.9	Free-View Point Video	166
	References	167
6	**Communication Networks**	**171**
6.1	IP Networks	171
	6.1.1 Packet Networks	171
	6.1.2 Layered Network Protocols Architecture	172
6.2	Wireless Communications	174
	6.2.1 Modulation	175
	6.2.2 The Wireless Channel	177
	6.2.3 Adaptive Modulation and Coding	191
6.3	Wireless Networking	193
6.4	4G Standards and Systems	193
	6.4.1 Evolved Universal Terrestrial Radio Access Network (E-UTRAN)	195
	6.4.2 Evolved Packet Core (EPC)	200
	6.4.3 Long Term Evolution-Advance (LTE-A)	201
	6.4.4 IEEE 802.16 – WiMAX	202
	References	203
7	**Quality of Experience**	**205**
7.1	3D Artifacts	205
	7.1.1 Fundamentals of 3D Human Visual System	205
	7.1.2 Coordinate Transform for Camera and Display System	206
	7.1.3 Keystone Distortion	211
	7.1.4 Depth-Plane Curvature	212
	7.1.5 Shear Distortion	212
	7.1.6 Puppet-Theater Effect	213
	7.1.7 Cardboard Effect	215
	7.1.8 Asymmetries in Stereo Camera Rig	216
	7.1.9 Crosstalk	217
	7.1.10 Picket-Fence Effect and Lattice Artifacts	217
	7.1.11 Hybrid DCT Lossy Compression Artifact	218
	7.1.12 Depth Map Bleeding and Depth Ringing	219
	7.1.13 Artifacts Introduced by Unreliable Communication Networks	219
	7.1.14 Artifacts from New View Synthesis	219
	7.1.15 Summary of 3D Artifacts	220
7.2	QoE Measurement	220
	7.2.1 Subjective Evaluations	222
	7.2.2 2D Image and Video QoE Measurement	226

	7.2.3	*3D Video HVS Based QoE Measurement*	235
	7.2.4	*Postscript on Quality of Assessment*	246
7.3	QoE Oriented System Design		247
	7.3.1	*Focus Cues and Perceptual Distortions*	247
	7.3.2	*Visual Fatigue*	249
	References		250

8   3D Video over Networks   259
8.1	Transmission-Induced Error	259
8.2	Error Resilience	267
8.3	Error Concealment	270
8.4	Unequal Error Protection	275
8.5	Multiple Description Coding	279
8.6	Cross-Layer Design	282
	References	286

9   3D Applications   289
9.1	Glass-Less Two-View Systems		289
	9.1.1	*Spatially Multiplexed Systems*	290
	9.1.2	*Temporally Multiplexed Systems*	290
9.2	3D Capture and Display Systems		291
9.3	Two-View Gaming Systems		294
9.4	3D Mobile		298
	9.4.1	*HTC EVO 3D*	298
	9.4.2	*Mobile 3D Perception*	299
9.5	Augmented Reality		302
	9.5.1	*Medical Visualization*	304
	9.5.2	*Mobile Phone Applications*	306
	References		309

10   Advanced 3D Video Streaming Applications   313
10.1	Rate Control in Adaptive Streaming		313
	10.1.1	*Fundamentals of Rate Control*	313
	10.1.2	*Two-View Stereo Video Streaming*	318
	10.1.3	*MVC Streaming*	318
	10.1.4	*MVD Streaming*	319
10.2	Multi-View Video View Switching		321
10.3	Peer-to-Peer 3D Video Streaming		325
10.4	3D Video Broadcasting		328
10.5	3D Video over 4G Networks		329
	References		331

Index   335

Preface

As the Avatar 3D movie experience swept the world in 2010, 3D visual content has become the most eye-catching spot in the consumer electronics products. This 3D visual wave has spread to 3DTV, Blu-ray, PC, mobile, and gaming industries, as the 3D visual system provides sufficient depth cues for end users to acquire better understanding of the geometric structure of the captured scenes, and nonverbal signals and cues in visual conversation. In addition, 3D visual systems enable observers to recognize the physical layout and location for each object with immersive viewing experiences and natural user interaction, which also makes it an important topic for both academic and industrial researchers.

Living in an era of widespread mobility and networking, where almost all consumer electronic devices are endpoints of the wireless/wired networks, the deployment of 3D visual representation will significantly challenge the network bandwidth as well as the computational capability of terminal points. In other words, the data volume received in an endpoint required to generate 3D views will be many times that of a single view in a 2D system, and hence the new view generation process sets a higher requirement for the endpoint's computational capability. Emerging 4G communication systems fit very well into the timing of 3D visual communications by significantly improving the bandwidth as well as introducing many new features designed specifically for high-volume data communications.

In this book, we aim to provide comprehensive coverage of major theories and practices involved in the lifecycle of a 3D visual content delivery system. The book presents technologies used in an end-to-end 3D visual communication system, including the fundamentals of 3D visual representation, the latest 3D video coding techniques, communication infrastructure and networks in 3D communications, and 3D quality of experience.

This book targets professionals involved in the research, design, and development of 3D visual coding and 3D visual transmission systems and technologies. It provides essential reading for students, engineers, and academic and industrial researchers. This book is a comprehensive reference for learning all aspects of 3D graphics and video coding, content creation and display, and communications and networking.

Organization of the book

This book is organized as three parts:

- principles of 3D visual systems: 3D graphics and rending, 3D display, and 3D content creation are all well covered

- visual communication: fundamental technologies used in 3D video coding and communication system, and the quality of experience. There are discussions on various 3D video coding formats and different communication systems, to evaluate the advantages of each system
- advances and applications of 3D visual communication

Chapter 1 overviews the whole end-to-end 3D video ecosystem, in which we cover key components in the pipeline: the 3D source coding, pre-processing, communication system, post-processing, and system-level design. We highlight the challenges and opportunities for 3D visual communication systems to give readers a big picture of the 3D visual content deployment technology, and point out which specific chapters relate to the listed advanced application scenarios.

3D scene representations are the bridging technology for the entire 3D visual pipeline from creation to visualization. Different 3D scene representations exhibit different characteristics and the selections should be chosen according to the requirement of the targeted applications. Various techniques can be categorized according to the amount of geometric information used in the 3D representation spectrum; at one extreme is the simplest form via rendering without referring to any geometry, and the other end uses geometrical description. Both extremes of the technology have their own advantages and disadvantages. Therefore, hybrid methods, rendering with implicit geometries, are proposed to combine the advantages and disadvantages of both ends of the technology spectrum to better support the needs of stereoscopic applications. In Chapter 2, a detailed discussion about three main categories for 3D scene representations is given.

In Chapter 3, we introduce the display technologies that allow the end users to perceive 3D objects. 3D displays are the direct interfaces between the virtual world and human eyes and these play an important role in reconstructing 3D scenes. We first describe the fundamentals of the human visual system (HVS) and discuss depth cues. Having this background, we introduce the simplest scenario to support stereoscopic technologies (two-view only) with aided glasses. Then, the common stereoscopic technologies without aided glasses are presented. Display technologies to support multiple views simultaneously are addressed to cover the head-tracking-enabled multi-view display, occlusion-based and reflection-based multi-view system. At the end of this chapter, we will briefly discuss the holographic system.

In Chapter 4, we look at 3D content creation methods, from 3D modeling and representation, capturing, 2D to 3D conversion and, to 3D multi-view generation. We showcase three practical examples that are adopted in industrial 3D creation process to provide a clear picture of how things work together in a real 3D creation system.

It has been observed that 3D content has significantly higher storage requirements compared to their 2D counterparts. Introducing compression technologies to reduce the required storage size and alleviate transmission bandwidth is very important for deploying 3D applications. In Chapter 5, we introduce 3D video coding and related standards. We will first cover the fundamental concepts and methods used in conventional 2D video codecs, especially the state-of-the-art H.264 compression method and the recent development of next generation video codec standards. With common coding knowledge, we first introduce two-view video coding methods which have been exploited in the past decade. Several methods, including individual two-view coding, simple inter-view prediction stereo video coding, and the latest efforts on frame-compatible stereo coding, are presented. Research on the depth information to reconstruct the 3D scene has brought some improvements and the 3D video coding can benefit from introducing depth information into the coded bit stream. We describe how to utilize and compress the depth information in the video-plus-depth coding system. Supporting multi-view video sequence compression is an important topic as multi-view systems provide a more immersive viewing experience. We will introduce the H.264 multiple view coding (MVC) for this particular application. More advanced technologies to further reduce the bit rate for multi-view systems, such as the multi-view video plus depth coding and layered depth video coding system, are introduced. At the end of this chapter, the efforts on the 3D representation in MPEG-4, such as binary format for scenes (BIFS) and animation framework extension (AFX), are presented. The ultimate goal for 3D video system, namely, the free viewpoint system, is also briefly discussed.

In Chapter 6, we present a review of the most important topics in communication networks that are relevant to the subject matter of this book. We start by describing the main architecture of packet networks with a focus on those based on the Internet protocol (IP) networks. Here we describe the layered organization of network protocols. After this, we turn our focus to wireless communications, describing the main components of digital wireless communications systems followed by a presentation of modulation techniques, the characteristics of the wireless channels, and adaptive modulation and coding. These topics are then applied in the description of wireless networks and we conclude with a study of fourth generation (4G) cellular wireless standards and systems.

To make 3D viewing systems more competitive relative to 2D systems, the quality of experience (QoE) shown from 3D systems should provide better performance than from 2D systems. Among different 3D systems, it is also important to have a systematic way to compare and summarize the advances and assess the disadvantages. In Chapter 7, we discuss the quality of experience in 3D systems. We first present the 3D artifacts which may be induced throughout the whole content life cycle: content capture, content creation, content compression, content delivery, and content display. In the second part, we address how to measure the quality of experience for 3D systems subjectively and objectively. With those requirements in mind, we discuss the important factors to design a comfortable and high-quality 3D system.

Chapter 8 addresses the main issue encountered when transmitting 3D video over a channel: that of dealing with errors introduced during the communication process. The chapter starts by presenting the effects of transmission-induced errors following by a discussion of techniques to counter these errors, such as the error resilience, error concealment, unequal error protection, and multiple description coding. The chapter concludes with a discussion of cross-layer approaches.

Developing 3D stereoscopic applications has become really popular in the software industry. 3D stereoscopic research and applications are advancing rapidly due to the commercial need and the popularity of 3D stereoscopic products. Therefore, Chapter 9 gives a short discussion of commercially available products and technologies for application development. The discussed topics include commercially available glass-less two-view systems, depth adaptation capturing and displaying systems, two-view gaming systems, mobile 3D systems and perception, and 3D augmented reality systems.

In the final chapter, we introduce the state-of-the-art technologies for delivering compressed 3D content over communication channels. Subject to limited bandwidth constraints in the existing communication infrastructure, the bit rate of the compressed video data needs to be controlled to fit in the allowed bandwidth. Consequently, the coding parameters in the video codec need to be adjusted to achieve the required bit rate. In this chapter, we first review different popular 2D video rate control methods, and then discuss how to extend the rate control methods to different 3D video streaming scenarios. For the multi-view system, changing the viewing angle from one point to another point to observe a 3D scene (view switching) is a key feature to enable the immersive viewing experience. We address the challenges and the corresponding solutions for 3D view switching. In the third part of this chapter, we discuss the peer-to-peer 3D video streaming services. As the required bandwidth for 3D visual communication service poses a heavy bandwidth requirement on centralized streaming systems, the peer-to-peer paradigm shows great potential for penetrating the 3D video streaming market. After this, we cover 3D video broadcasting and 3D video communication over 4G cellular networks.

Acknowledgements

We would like to thank a few of the great many people whose contributions were instrumental in taking this book from an initial suggestion to a final product. First, we would like to express our gratitude to Dr. Chi-Yuan Yao for his help on collecting and sketching the content in Sections 9.1 and 9.2 and help with finishing Chapter 9 in time. We also thank him for his input on scene representation because of his deep domain knowledge in the field of computer geometry. We would like to thank Dr. Peng Yin and Dr. Taoran Lu for their help in enriching the introduction of HEVC. We also thank Mr. Dobromir Todorov for help in rendering figures used in Chapters 2 and 9. Finally, the authors appreciate the many contributions and sacrifices that our families have made to this effort. Guan-Ming Su would like to thanks his wife Jing-Wen's unlimited support and understanding during the writing process; and also would like to dedicate this book to his parents. Yu-Chi Lai would like to thank his family for their support of his work. Andres Kwasinski would like to thank his wife Mariela and daughters Victoria and Emma for their support, without which this work would not have been possible. Andres would also like to thank all the members of the Department of Computer Engineering at the Rochester Institute of Technology. Haohong Wang would like to thank his wife Xin Lu, son Nicholas and daughter Isabelle for their kind supports as always, especially for those weekends and nights that he had to be separated from them to work on this book at the office. The dedication of this book to our families is a sincere but inadequate recognition of all their contributions to our work.

About the Authors

Guan-Ming Su received the BSE degree in Electrical Engineering from National Taiwan University, Taipei, Taiwan, in 1996 and the MS and PhD degrees in Electrical Engineering from the University of Maryland, College Park, U.S.A., in 2001 and 2006, respectively. He is currently with Dolby Labs, Sunnyvale, CA. Prior to this he has been with the R&D Department, Qualcomm, Inc., San Diego, CA; ESS Technology, Fremont, CA; and Marvell Semiconductor, Inc., Santa Clara, CA. His research interests are multimedia communications and multimedia signal processing. He is the inventor of 15 U.S. patents and pending applications. Dr Su is an associate editor of Journal of Communications; guest editor in Journal of Communications special issue on Multimedia Communications, Networking, and Applications; and Director of review board and R-Letter in IEEE Multimedia Communications Technical Committee. He serves as the Publicity Co-Chair of IEEE GLOBECOM 2010, International Liaison Chair in IEEE ICME 2011, Technical Program Track Co-Chair in ICCCN 2011, and TPC Co-Chair in ICNC 2013. He is a Senior member of IEEE.

Yu-Chi Lai received the B.S. from National Taiwan University, Taipei, R.O.C., in 1996 in Electrical Engineering Department. He received his M.S. and Ph.D. degrees from University of Wisconsin–Madison in 2003 and 2009 respectively in Electrical and Computer Engineering. He received his M.S. and Ph.D. degrees from University of Wisconsin–Madison in 2004 and 2010 respectively in Computer Science. He is currently an assistant professor in NTUST. His research focus is on the area of computer graphics, computer vision, multimedia, and human-computer interaction. Due to his personal interesting, he is interested in industrial projects and he currently also cooperates with IGS to develop useful and interesting computer game technologies and NMA to develop animation technologies.

Andres Kwasinski received in 1992 his diploma in Electrical Engineering from the Buenos Aires Institute of Technology, Buenos Aires, Argentina, and, in 2000 and 2004 respectively, the M.S. and Ph.D. degrees in Electrical and Computer Engineering from the University of Maryland, College Park, Maryland. He is currently an Assistant Professor at the Department of Computer Engineering, Rochester Institute of Technology, Rochester, New York. Prior to this, he was with the Wireless Infrastructure group at Texas Instruments Inc., working on WiMAX and LTE technology, and with the University of Maryland, where he was a postdoctoral Research Associate. Dr. Kwasinski is a Senior Member of the IEEE, an Area Editor for the IEEE Signal Processing Magazine and Editor for the IEEE Transactions on Wireless Communications. He has been in the Organizing Committee for the 2010 IEEE GLOBECOM, 2011 and 2012 IEEE ICCCN, 2012 ICNC and 2013 IEEE ICME conferences. Between 2010 and 2012 he chaired the Interest Group on Distributed and Sensor Networks for Mobile Media Computing and Applications within the IEEE Multimedia Communications Technical Committee. His research interests are in the area of multimedia wireless communications and networking, cross layer designs, cognitive and cooperative networking, digital signal processing and speech, image and video processing for signal compression and communication, and signal processing for non-intrusive forensic analysis of speech communication systems.

Haohong Wang received the B.S. degree in computer science and the M.Eng. degree in computer applications both from Nanjing University, China, the M.S. degree in computer science from University of New Mexico, and the Ph.D. degree in Electrical and computer engineering from Northwestern University, Evanston, USA. He is currently the General Manager of TCL Research America, TCL Corporation, at Santa Clara, California, in charge of the overall corporate research activities in North America with research teams located at fourplaces. Prior to that he held various technical and management positions at AT&T, Catapult Communications, Qualcomm, Marvell, TTE and Cisco. Dr. Wang's research involves the areas of multimedia processing and communications, mobile sensing and data mining. He has published more than 50 articles in peer-reviewed journals and International conferences. He is the inventor of more than 40 U.S. patents and pending applications. He is the co-author of 4G Wireless Video Communications (John Wiley & Sons, 2009), and Computer Graphics (1997).

Dr. Wang is the Editor-in-Chief of the Journal of Communications, a member of the Steering Committee of IEEE Transactions on Multimedia, and an editor of IEEE Communications Surveys & Tutorials. He has been serving as an editor or guest editor for many IEEE and ACM journals and magazines. He chairs the IEEE Technical Committee on Human Perception in Vision, Graphics and Multimedia, and was the Chair of the IEEE Multimedia Communications Technical Committee. He is an elected member of the IEEE Visual Signal Processing and Communications Technical Committee, and IEEE Multimedia and Systems Applications Technical Committee. Dr. Wang has chaired more than dozen of International conferences, which includes the IEEE GLOBECOM 2010 (Miami) as the Technical Program Chair, and IEEE ICME 2011 (Barcelona) and IEEE ICCCN 2011 (Maui) as the General Chair.

1

Introduction

1.1 Why 3D Communications?

Thanks to the great advancement of hardware, software, and algorithms in the past decade, our daily life has become a major digital content producer. Nowadays, people can easily share their own pieces of artwork on the network with each other. Furthermore, with the latest development in 3D capturing, signal processing technologies, and display devices, as well as the emergence of 4G wireless networks with very high bandwidth, coverage, and capacity, and many advanced features such as quality of service (QoS), low latency, and high mobility, 3D communication has become an extremely popular topic. It seems that the current trend is closely aligned with the expected roadmap for reality video over wireless, estimated by Japanese wireless industry peers in 2005 (as shown in Figure 1.1), according to which the expected deployment timing of stereo/multi-view/hologram video is around the same time as the 4G wireless networks deployment. Among those 3D video representation formats, the stereoscopic and multi-view 3D videos are more mature and the coding approaches have been standardized in Moving Picture Experts Group (MPEG) as "video-plus-depth" (V+D) and the Joint Video Team (JVT) Multi-view Video Coding (MVC) standard, respectively. The coding efficiency study shows that coded V+D video only takes about 1.2 times bit rate compared to the monoscopic video (i.e., the traditional 2D video). Clearly, the higher reality requirements would require larger volumes of data to be delivered over the network, and more services and usage scenarios to challenge the wireless network infrastructures and protocols.

From a 3D point of view, reconstructing a scene remotely and/or reproducibly as being presented face-to-face has always been a dream through human history. The desire for such technologies has been pictured in many movies, such as *Star Trek*'s Holodeck, *Star Wars*' Jedi council meeting, *The Matrix*'s matrix, and *Avatar*'s Pandora. The key technologies to enable such a system involve many complex components, such as a capture system to describe and record the scene, a content distribution system to store/transmit the recorded scene, and a scene reproduction system to show the captured scenes to end users. Over the past several decades, we have witnessed the success of many applications, such as television broadcasting systems in analog (e.g., NTSC, PAL) and digital (e.g., ATSC, DVB) format, and home entertainment system in VHS, DVD, and Blu-ray format.

3D Visual Communications, First Edition. Guan-Ming Su, Yu-Chi Lai, Andres Kwasinski and Haohong Wang.
© 2013 John Wiley & Sons, Ltd. Published 2013 by John Wiley & Sons, Ltd.

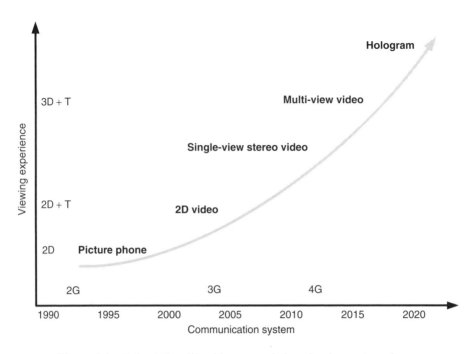

Figure 1.1   Estimated reality video over wireless development roadmap.

Although those systems have served for many years and advanced in many respects to give better viewing experiences, end users still feel that the scene reconstruction has its major limitation: the scene presentation is on a 2D plane, which significantly differs from the familiar three-dimensional view of our daily life. In a real 3D world, humans can observe objects and scenes from different angles to acquire a better understanding of the geometry of the watched scenes, and nonverbal signals and cues in visual conversation. Besides, humans can perceive the depth of different objects in a 3D environment so as to recognize the physical layout and location for each object. Furthermore, 3D visual systems can provide immersive viewing experience and higher interaction. Unfortunately, the existing traditional 2D visual systems cannot provide those enriched viewing experiences.

The earliest attempt to construct a 3D image was via the anaglyph stereo approach which was demonstrated by W. Rollmann in 1853 and J. C. D'Almeida in 1858 and patented in 1891 by Louis Ducos du Hauron. In 1922, the earliest confirmed 3D film was premiered at the Ambassador Hotel Theater in Los Angeles and was also projected in the red/green anaglyph format. In 1936, Edwin H. Land invented the polarizing sheet and demonstrated 3D photography using polarizing sheet at the Waldorf-Astoria Hotel. The first 3D golden era was between 1952 and 1955, owing to the introduction of color stereoscopy. Several golden eras have been seen since then. However, there are many factors affecting the popularity and success of 3D visual systems, including the 3D visual and content distribution technologies, the viewing experience, the end-to-end ecosystem, and competition from improved 2D systems. Recently, 3D scene reconstruction algorithms have achieved great improvement, which enables us to reconstruct a 3D scene from a 2D one and from stereoscope images, and the corresponding hardware can support the heavy computation at a reasonable cost, and the underlying communication systems have advanced to provide sufficient bandwidth to distribute the 3D content. Therefore, 3D visual communication systems have again drawn considerable attention from both academia and industry.

In this book, we discuss the details of the major technologies involved in the entire end-to-end 3D video ecosystem. More specifically, we address the following important topics and the corresponding opportunities:

- the lifecycle of the 3D video content through the end-to-end 3D video communication framework,
- the 3D content creation process to construct a 3D visual experience,
- the different representations and compression formats for 3D scenes/data for content distribution. Each format has its own advantages and disadvantages. System designers can choose the appropriate solution for given the system resources, such as computation complexity and communication system capacity. Also, understanding the unequal importance of different syntaxes, decoding dependencies, and content redundancies in 3D visual data representation and coding can help system designers to adopt corresponding error resilient methods, error concealment approaches, suitable unequal error protection, and customized dynamic resource allocation to improve the system performance,
- the advanced communication systems, such as 4G networks, to support transmission of 3D visual content. Being familiar with those network features can help the system designer to design schedulers and resource allocation schemes for 3D visual data transmission over 4G networks. Also, we can efficiently utilize the QoS mechanisms supported in 4G networks for 3D visual communications,
- the effective 3D visual data transmission and network architectures to deliver 3D video services and their related innovative features,
- the 3D visual experience for typical users, the factors that impact on the user experiences, and 3D quality of experience (QoE) metrics from source, network, and receiver points of view. Understanding the factors affecting 3D QoE is very important and it helps the system designer to design a QoE optimized 3D visual communications system to satisfy 3D visual immersive expectations,
- the opportunities of advanced 3D visual communication applications and services, for example, how to design the source/relay/receiver side of an end-to-end 3D visual communication system to take advantage of new concepts of computing, such as green computing, cloud computing, and distributed/collaborated computing, and how to apply scalability concepts to handle 3D visual communications given the heterogeneous 3D terminals in the networks is an important topic.

1.2   End-to-End 3D Visual Ecosystem

As shown by the past experience and lessons learned from the development and innovation of visual systems, the key driving force is all about how to enrich the user experiences, or so-called QoE. The 3D visual system also faces the same issues. Although a 3D visual system provides a dramatic new user experience after traditional 2D systems, the QoE concept has to be considered at every stage of the communication system pipeline during system design and optimization work to ensure the worthwhileness of moving from 2D to

3D. There are many factors affecting the QoE, such as errors in multidimensional signal processing, lack of information, packet loss, and optical errors in display. Improperly addressing QoE issues will result in visual artifacts (objectively and subjectively), visual discomfort, fatigue, and other things that degrade the intended 3D viewing experiences.

An end-to-end 3D visual communication pipeline consists of the content creation, 3D representation, data compression, transmission, decompression, post-processing, and 3D display stages, which also reflects the lifecycle of a 3D video content in the system. We illustrate the whole pipeline and the corresponding major issues in Figure 1.2. In addition, we also show the possible feedback information from later stages to earlier stages for possible improvement of 3D scene reconstruction.

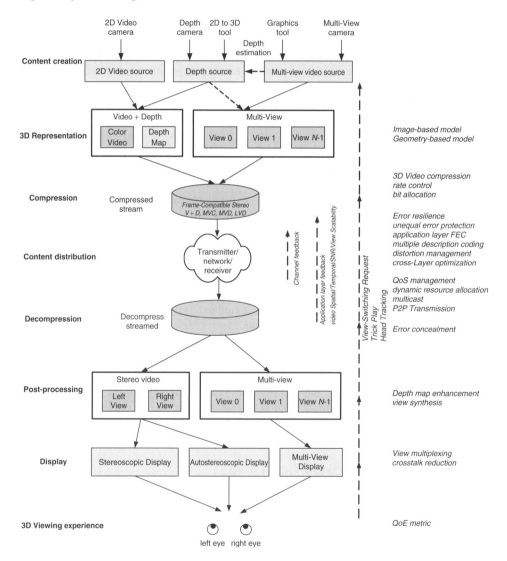

Figure 1.2   End-to-end 3D visual ecosystem.

The first stage of the whole pipeline is the content creation. The goal of the content creation stage is to produce 3D content based on various data sources or data generation devices. There are three typical ways of data acquisition which result in different types of data formats. The first is to use a traditional 2D video camera, which captures 2D images; the image can be derived for 3D data representation in the later stage of the pipeline. The second type is to use a depth video camera to measure the depth of each pixel corresponding to its counterpart color image. The registration of depth and 2D color image may be needed if sensors are not aligned. Note that in some depth cameras, the spatial resolution is lower than that of a 2D color camera. The depth image can also be derived from a 2D image with 2D-to-3D conversion tools; often the obtained depth does not have a satisfactory precision and thus causes QoE issues. The third type is to use an N-view video camera, which consists of an array of 2D video cameras located at different positions around one scene and all cameras are synchronized to capture video simultaneously, to generate N-view video. Using graphical tools to model and create 3D scene is another approach which could be time consuming, but it is popular nowadays to combine both graphical and video capturing and processing methods in the 3D content creation.

In the next stage, the collected video/depth data will be processed and transformed into 3D representation formats for different targeted applications. For example, the depth image source can be used in image plus depth rendering or processed for N-view application. Since the amount of acquired/processed/transformed 3D scene is rather large compared to single-view video data, there is a strong need to compress the 3D scene data. On the other hand, applying traditional 2D video coding schemes separately to each view or each different data type is inefficient as there exist certain representation/coding redundancies among neighboring views and different data types. Therefore, a dedicated compression format is needed at the compression stage to achieve better coding efficiency. In the content distribution stage, the packet loss during data delivery plays an important role in the final QoE, especially for streaming services. Although certain error concealment algorithms adopted in the existing 2D decoding and post-processing stages may alleviate this problem, directly applying the solution developed for 2D video system may not be sufficient. This is because the 3D video coding introduces more coding dependencies, and thus error concealment is much more complex compared to that in 2D systems. Besides, the inter-view alignment requirement in 3D video systems also adds plenty of difficulties which do not exist in 2D scenarios. The occlusion issue is often handled at the post-processing stage, and the packet loss will make the occlusion post-processing even more difficult. There are also some other application layer approaches to relieve the negative impact of packet loss, such as resilient coding and unequal error protection (UEP), and those technologies can be incorporated into the design of the 3D visual communication system to enrich the final QoE. At the final stage of this 3D visual ecosystem, the decoded and processed 3D visual data will be displayed on its targeted 3D display. Depending on the type of 3D display, each display has its unique characteristics of artifacts and encounters different QoE issues.

1.2.1 3D Modeling and Representation

3D scene modeling and representation is the bridging technology between the content creation, transmission, and display stages of a 3D visual system. The 3D scene modeling and representation approaches can be classified into three main categories: geometry-based modeling, image based modeling, and hybrid modeling. Geometry-based representation typically uses polygon meshes (called surface-based modeling), 2D/3D points (called point-based modeling), or voxels (called volume-based modeling) to construct a 3D scene. The main advantage is that, once geometry information is available, the 3D scene can be rendered from any viewpoint and view direction without any limitation, which meets the requirement for a free-viewpoint 3D video system. The main disadvantage is in the computational cost of rendering and storing, which depends on the scene complexity, that is the total number of triangles used to describe the 3D world. In addition, geometry-based representation is generally an approximation to the 3D world. Although there are offline photorealistic rendering algorithms to generate views matching our perception of the real world, the existing algorithms using graphics pipeline still cannot produce realistic views on the fly.

The image based modeling goes to the other extreme, not using any 3D geometry, but using a set of images captured by a number of cameras with predesigned positions and settings. This approach tends to generate high quality virtual view synthesis without the effort of 3D scene reconstruction. The computation complexity via image based representation is proportional to the number of pixels in the reference and output images, but in general not to the geometric complexity such as triangle counts. However, the synthesis ability of image based representation has limitations on the range of view change and the quality depends on the scene depth variation, the resolution of each view, and the number of views. The challenge for this approach is that a tremendous amount of image data needs to be stored, transferred, and processed in order to achieve a good quality synthesized view, otherwise interpolation and occlusion artifacts will appear in the synthesized image due to lack of source data.

The hybrid approach can leverage these two representation methods to find a compromise between the two extremes according to given constraints. By adding geometric information into image based representation, the disocclusion and resolution problem can be relieved. Similarly, adding image information captured from the real world into geometry-based representation can reduce the rendering cost and storage. As an example, using multiple images and corresponding depth maps to represent 3D scene is a popular method (called depth image based representation), in which the depth maps are the geometric modeling component, but this hybrid representation can reduce the storage and processing of many extra images to achieve the same high-quality synthesized view as the image based approach. All these methods are demonstrated in detail in Chapters 2 and 4.

1.2.2 3D Content Creation

Other than graphical modeling approaches, the 3D content can be captured by various processes with different types of cameras. The stereo camera or depth camera simultaneously captures video and associated per-pixel depth or disparity information; the multi-view camera captures multiple images simultaneously from various angles, then multi-view matching (or correspondence) process is required to generate the disparity map for each pair of cameras, and then the 3D structure can be estimated from these disparity maps. The most challenging scenario is to capture 3D content from a normal 2D (or monoscopic) camera, which lacks of disparity or depth information, and where a

2D-to-3D conversion algorithm has to be triggered to generate an estimated depth map and thus the left and right views. The depth map can be derived from various types of depth cues, such as the linear perspective property of a 3D scene, the relationship between object surface structure and the rendered image brightness according to specific shading models, occlusion of objections, and so on. For complicated scenes, the interactive 2D-to-3D conversion, or offline conversion, tends to be adopted, that is, human interaction is required at certain stages of the processing flow, which could be in object segmentation, object selection, object shape or depth adjustment, object occlusion order specification, and so on. In Chapter 4, a few 2D-to-3D conversation systems are showcased to give details of the whole process flow.

1.2.3 3D Video Compression

Owing to the huge amount of 3D video data, there is a strong need to develop efficient 3D video compression methods. The 3D video compression technology has been developed for more than a decade and there have been many formats proposed. Most 3D video compression formats are built on state-of-the-art video codecs, such as H.264. The compression technology is often a tradeoff between the acceptable level of computation complexity and affordable budget in the communication bandwidth. In order to reuse the existing broadcast infrastructure originally designed for 2D video coding and transmission, almost all current 3D broadcasting solutions are based on a frame-compatible format via spatial subsampling approach, that is, the original left and right views are subsampled into half resolution and then embedded into a single video frame for compression and transmission over the infrastructure as with 2D video, and at the decoder side the demultiplexing and interpolation are conducted to reconstruct the dual views. The subsampling and merging can be done by either (a) side-by-side format, proposed by Sensio, RealD, and adopted by Samsung, Panasonic, Sony, Toshiba, JVC, and DirectTV (b) over/under format, proposed by Comcast, or (c) checkerboard format. A mixed-resolution approach is proposed, which is based on the binocular suppression theory showing that the same subjective perception quality can be achieved when one view has a reduced resolution. The mixed-resolution method first subsamples each view to a different resolution and then compresses each view independently.

Undoubtedly, the frame-compatible format is very simple to implement without changing the existing video codec system and underlying communication infrastructure. However, the correlation between left and right views has not been fully exploited, and the approach is mainly oriented to the two-view scenario but not to the multi-view 3D scenario. During the past decade, researchers have also investigated 3D compression from the coding perspective and 3D video can be represented in the following formats: two-view stereo video, video-plus-depth (V+D), multi-view video coding (MVC), multi-view video-plus-depth (MVD), and layered depth video (LDV). The depth map is often encoded via existing a 2D color video codec, which is designed to optimize the coding efficiency of the natural images. It is noted that depth map shows different characteristics from natural color image. Researchers have proposed several methods to improve the depth-based 3D video compression. In nowadays, free-viewpoint 3D attracts a lot of attention, in which the system allows end users to change the view position and angle to enrich their immersive experience. Hybrid approaches combining geometry-based and image based representation are typically used to render the 3D scene for free-viewpoint TV. In Chapter 5, we discuss V+D, MVC, MVD, and LDV.

1.2.4 3D Content Delivery

Transmitting compressed 3D video bit streams over networks have more challenges than with conventional 2D video. From the video compression system point of view, the state-of-the-art 3D video codec introduces more decoding dependency to reduce the required bit rate due to the exploitation of the inter-view and synthesis prediction. Therefore, the existing mono-view video transmission scheme cannot be applied directly to these advanced 3D formats. From the communication system perspective, the 3D video bit stream needs more bandwidth to carry more views than the mono-view video. The evolution of cellular communications into 4G wireless network results in significant improvements of bandwidth and reliability. The end mobile user can benefit from the improved network infrastructure and error control to enjoy a 3D video experience. On the other hand, the wireless transmission often suffers frequent packet/bit errors; the highly bit-by-bit decoding-dependent 3D video stream is vulnerable to those errors. It is important to incorporate error correction and concealment techniques, as well as the design of an error resilient source coding algorithm to increase the robustness of transmitting 3D video bit streams over wireless environments. Since most 3D video formats are built up on existing 2D video codec, many techniques developed for 2D video systems can be extended or adapted to consider properties of 3D video. One technique that offers numerous opportunities for this approach is unequal error protection. Depending on the relative importance of the bit stream segments, different portions of the 3DTV bit stream are protected with different strengths of forward error control (FEC) codes. Taking the stereoscopic video streaming as an example, a UEP scheme can be used to divide the stream into three layers of different importance: intra-coded left-view frames (the most important ones), left-view predictive coded frames, and right-view frames encoded from both intra-coded and predictive left-view frames (the least valuable ones). For error concealment techniques, we can also draw from properties inherent to 3D video. Taking video plus depth format as an example, we can utilize the correlation between video and depth information to do error concealment. The multiple-description coding (MDC) is also a promising technology for 3D video transmission. The MDC framework will encode the video in several independent descriptions. When only one description is received, it can be decoded to obtain a lower-quality representation. When more than one description is received, they can be combined to obtain a representation of the source with better quality. The final quality depends on the number of descriptions successfully received. A simple way to apply multiple-description coding technology on 3D stereoscopic video is to associate one description with the right view and one with the left view. Another way of implementing multiple-description coding for 3D stereoscopic video and multi-view video consists of independently encoding one view and encoding the second view predicted with respect to the independently encoded view. This later approach can also be considered as a two-layer, base plus enhancement, encoding. This methodology can also be applied to V+D and MVD, where the enhancement layer is the depth information. Different strategies for advanced 3D video delivery over different content delivery path will be discussed in Chapters 8 and 10. Several 3D applications will be dealt with in Chapter 9.

1.2.5 3D Display

To perceive a 3D scene by the human visual system (HVS), the display system is designed to present sufficient depth information for each object such that HVS can reconstruct each object's 3D positions. The HVS recognizes objects' depth from the real 3D world through the depth cues. Therefore, the success of a 3D display depends on how well the depth cues are provided, such that HVS can observe a 3D scene. In general, depending on how many viewpoints are provided, the depth cues can be classified into monocular, binocular, and multi-ocular categories. The current 3DTV systems that consumers can buy in retail stores are all based on stereoscopic 3D technology with binocular depth cues. This stereoscopic display will multiplex two views at the display side and the viewers need to wear special glasses to de-multiplex the signal to get the left and right view. Several multiplexing/de-multiplexing approaches have been proposed and implemented in 3D displays, including wavelength division (color) multiplexing, polarization multiplexing, and time multiplexing.

For 3D systems without aided glasses, called auto-stereoscopic display (AS-D), the display system uses optical elements such as parallax barriers (occlusion-based approach) or lenticular lenses (refraction-based approach) to guide the two-view images to the left and right eyes of the viewer in order to generate the realistic 3D sense. In other words, the multiplexing and de-multiplexing process is removed compared to the stereoscopic display. Mobile 3DTV is an example of an AS-D product that we have seen in the market. The N-view AS-D 3DTVs or PC/laptop monitors have been in demos for many years by Philips, Sharp, Samsung, LG, Alioscopy, and so on, in which it explores the stereopsis of 3D space for multiple viewers without the need of glasses. However, the visual quality of these solutions still has lots of room to improve. To fully enrich the immersive visual experience, end users would want to interactively control the viewpoint, which is called free-viewpoint 3DTV (FVT). In a typical FVT system, the viewer's head and gaze are tracked to generate the viewing position and directions and thus to calculate images directed to the viewer's eyes. To render free-viewpoint video, the 3D scene needs to be synthesized and rendered from the source data in order to support the seamless view generation during the viewpoint changing.

To achieve full visual reality, holographic 3D display is a type of device to reconstruct the optical wave field such that the reconstructed 3D light beam can be seen as the physical presentation of the original object. The difference between conventional photography and holography is that photography can only record amplitude information for an object but holography attempts to record both the amplitude and phase information. Knowing that current image recoding systems can only record the amplitude information, holography needs a way to transform the phase information such that it can be recorded in an amplitude-based recoding system. For more details on 3D displays and their theory behind them, readers can refer to Chapter 3.

1.2.6 3D QoE

Although 3D video brings a brand new viewing experience, it does not necessarily increase the perceived quality if the 3D system is not carefully designed and evaluated. The 3D quality of experience refers to how humans perceive the 3D visual information, including the traditional 2D color/texture information and the additional perception of depth and visual comfort factors. As the evaluation criteria to measure the QoE of 3D systems is still in its early stages, QoE-optimized 3D visual communications systems still remain an open research area. At the current stage, the efforts to address 3D QoE are considering the fidelity and comfort aspects. 3D fidelity evaluates the unique 3D artifacts generated and propagated through the whole 3D visual processing pipeline, and comfort refers to the visual fatigue and discomfort to the viewers induced by the perceived 3D scene.

In general, stereoscopic artifacts can be categorized as structure, color, motion, and binocular. Structure artifacts characterize those that affect human perception on image structures such as boundaries and textures, and include tiling/blocking artifacts, aliasing, staircase effect, ringing, blurring, false edge, mosaic patterns, jitter, flickering, and geometric distortion. The color category represents artifacts that affect the color accuracy, with examples including mosquito noise, smearing, chromatic aberration, cross-color artifacts, color bleeding, and rainbow artifacts. The motion category includes artifacts that affect the motion vision, such as motion blur and motion judder. Binocular artifacts represent those that affect the stereoscopic perception of the 3D world, for example, keystone distortion, cardboard effect, depth plane curvature, shear distortion, puppet theater effect, ghosting, perspective rivalry, crosstalk, depth bleeding, and depth ringing. Note that AS-D suffers more crosstalk artifacts than stereoscopic scenarios. This is mainly caused by imperfect separation of the left and right view images and is perceived as ghosting artifacts. The magnitude of crosstalk is affected by two factors: observing position between display and the observer and the quality of the optical filter in the display. The extreme case of crosstalk is the pseudoscopic (reversed stereo) image where the left eye sees the image representing the right view and the right eye sees the image representing the left view.

Free-viewpoint 3D systems have more distinctive artifacts due to the need of synthesizing new views from 3D scene representations. In a highly constrained environment camera parameters can be calibrated precisely and, as a result, visual artifacts in view synthesis arise principally from an inexact geometric representation of the scene. In an unconstrained environment where the lighting conditions and background are not fixed and the videos may have different resolution and levels of motion blur, the ambiguity in the input data and inaccuracies in calibration and matting cause significant deviation in a reconstructed view from the true view of the scene.

Visual fatigue refers to a decrease in the performance of the human vision system, which can be objectively measured; however, its subjective counterpart, visual discomfort, is hard to quantify. These factors affect whether end users enjoy the entire 3D experience and are willing to purchase 3D consumer electronic devices. In Chapter 7, more details on QoE topics will be discussed.

1.3   3D Visual Communications

Living in an era of widespread mobility and networking, where almost all consumer electronic devices are endpoints of the wireless/wired networks, the deployment of 3D visual representation will significantly challenge the network bandwidth as well as the computational capability of terminal points. In other words, the data volume received in an endpoint required to generate 3D views will be many times greater than that in a single view of a 2D system, and hence the new view generation process sets a higher requirement for the endpoint's computational capability. The emerging 4G networks can significantly improve the bandwidth as well as include many new features designed specifically for high-volume data communications, which fit well into the timing of 3D visual communications. The two main 4G standards are 3GPP LTE (long-term evolution) [1] and IEEE 802.16m WiMAX (sometimes called WiMAX 2) [2]. Both standards provide features in the physical layer achieving high data rates and low latency based on orthogonal frequency-division multiplexing (OFDM) technology with adaptive modulation and coding (AMC) and multiple transmit/receive antenna (MIMO) support. In the upper communication layers, 4G networks support all-IP architectures and allow the uplink scheduler at the base station to learn the buffer status for the associated mobile devices by offering several quality of service (QoS) mechanisms to establish connections with different scheduling types and priorities.

In general, as the technologies, infrastructures and terminals evolving in wireless system (as shown in Figure 1.3) from 1G, 2G, 3G to 4G and from wireless LAN to broadband wireless access to 4G, the 4G system would contain all the standards that the earlier generations had implemented. Among the few technologies that are currently considered for 4G are 3GPP LTE, and WiMAX. Among the few technologies that are currently considered for 4G are 3GPP LTE and WiMAX. The details about the 4G networks will be presented in Chapter 6. We will discuss 3D over LTE and WiMAX in Chapter 10.

1.4   Challenges and Opportunities

As 3D visual communication has become one of the main focus research areas for the coming decade, we emphasize some potential research directions in this chapter. Streaming 3D video over 4G wireless networks has become a feasible and practicable application.

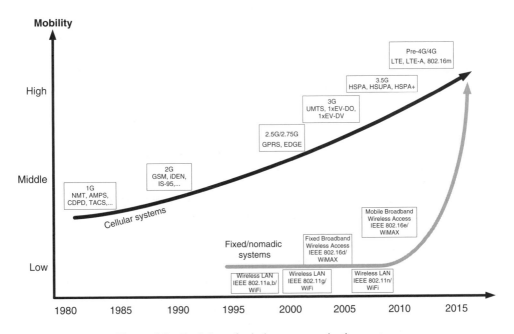

Figure 1.3   Evolving of wireless communication system.

4G wireless network standards include mechanisms to establish connections with different scheduling types and priorities, which support, for example, traffic with guaranteed maximum and minimum traffic rates. Also, the standards include different mechanisms that allow the uplink scheduler at the base station to learn the status of the buffers at the mobiles. Since the resource allocation mechanism is not yet specified in 4G wireless communication standard, it is an important topic to jointly consider the design of schedulers and resource allocation mechanisms with the QoS-related mechanisms in the standard to meet the final users' QoE requirement. The combination of the flexibility offered by 4G physical layer technologies, such as OFDM and AMC, and 4G features at higher layers, such as QoS support for heterogeneous services and all-IP, results in a framework that is suitable for delivery of 3D video services which require high bit rates, low latencies, and the feasibility to deploy adaptive application layer adjustment, such as unequal error protection, that can tailor the error control and transmission parameters to the very different requirements exhibited by the different components of 3D video streams.

As there is such a great flexibility in the 3D video service over 4G network applications, the major challenge becomes how to efficiently utilize system resources supplied in different layers to maximize users' 3D viewing experience. From the perspective of the communication system, the allocation of system resources for a cross-layer designed framework is both constrained across different communication layers and constrained among users who are simultaneously sharing the same spectrum [3]. From the perspective of 3D video QoE, real-time 3D video transmission has further delay constraints for real-time playback, minimal requirement for binocular quality, more coding parameters with more decoding dependency to consider, and limited computation complexity on the mobile side. Moreover, the allocation of system resources should be conducted dynamically to reflect the time-varying characteristics of the channel condition and the time-heterogeneity of the video source. To acquire up-to-date information on system resource availability, the resource allocator often accrues extra computation costs and communication overhead depending on the accuracy and frequency. A formal way to resolve the resource allocation problem is to formulate a 3D over 4G network as a cross-layer optimization problem to maximize user QoE subject to system QoS constraints. The problem we often encountered is how to develop a good model to link/map between system QoS and user QoE. Also, we often have to deal with resources having both continuous and integer-valued parameters. The overall optimization problem may also have nonlinear or/and nonconvex objective functions/constraints, and many local optima may exist in the feasible range. Thus, obtaining the optimal solution is often NP hard. How to choose the parameter sets in different layers as the optimization search space and how to develop fast solvers to attain optimal/suboptimal values in real time remain challenging issues.

As there are more and more applications with high bandwidth requirement, and these services increase the demands on the 4G networks. A growing tendency toward increasing network capacity is to include architectures that tend to reduce the range of the radio links, thus improving the quality of the link (data rate and reliability) and increasing spatial reuse. In WiMAX, the solution is proposed by adopting the use of multi-hop networks. The other solution with an analogous rationale is to introduce the use of femtocells [4]. Femtocells are base stations, typically installed at a home or office, which operate with low power within a licensed spectrum to service a reduced number of users. Work in femtocells was initiated for 3G networks and it focused on addressing the main challenges when implementing this technology: interference mitigation, management ease of configuration, and integration with the macrocell network. The progress achieved with 3G networks is being carried over to 4G systems, for both LTE and WiMAX. With the popularity of femtocells, 3D streaming over femtocells (or as the first/last mile) will become an important service. Therefore, there is a strong need to study how to efficiently allocate resources and conduct rate control.

In the multiuser video communications scenario, a single base station may serve several users, receiving the same 3D video program but requesting different views in free-viewpoint systems or multi-view video plus depth systems. As the information received by different users is highly correlated, it is not efficient to stream the video in a simulcast fashion. A more efficient way to utilize the communication resource is to jointly consider the correlation among all users' received 3D video programs and send only a subset of the video streams corresponding to a selection of views. The views actually transmitted are chosen in such a way that they can be used to synthesize the intermediate views. How to maximize all users' QoE by selecting the representative views and choosing the video encoding parameters and network parameters to meet different users' viewing preferences under different channel conditions becomes an important issue.

Most of the approaches in a 3D video communications pipeline take advantage of intrinsic correlation among different views. In networks of many users receiving 3D video streams, the view being received by one user could serve other users by providing the same view, if needed, or a view that could be used to synthesize a virtual view. This scenario could arise in multimedia social networks based on video streaming through peer-to-peer (P2P) network architecture. Some recent publications have studied techniques that address incentive mechanisms in multimedia live streaming P2P networks to enable the cooperation of users to establish a distributed, scalable, and robust platform. These techniques, nevertheless, fall into an area of incipient research for which still more work is needed. In the future, the properties of 3D video make it an application area that could benefit from techniques to incentivize the collaboration between users.

The features and quality offered by 4G systems result in an ecosystem where it is expected that users' equipment will present vastly heterogeneous capabilities. In such a background, scalability and universal 3D access become rich fields with plenty of potential and opportunities. With the introduction of 3D video services – in addition to the traditional spatial, temporal, and quality scalabilities – video streams will need to offer scalability in the number of views. For this to be realizable, it will be necessary to design algorithms that select views in a hierarchy consistent with scalability properties and that are able to scale up in a number of views by interpolation procedures. Considering scalability from the bandwidth perspective, it is also important to realize the challenges for 3D streaming services over low bit-rate network. Under a strict bit-rate budget constraint, the coding artifacts (e.g., blocking/ringing artifacts) due to a higher compression ratio become much more severe and degrade the binocular quality. Furthermore, channel resources for error protection are limited such that channel-induced distortion could further decrease the final 3D viewing experience. A joint rate control and error protection mechanism should be carefully designed to preserve/maximize objects with critical binocular quality (such as foreground objects) to remedy the coding artifacts and channel error. On the other hand, in order to achieve universal 3D access, 3D video analysis and abstraction techniques will attract more attention, as well as the transmission of 3D abstract data.

The development of distributed source coding paves the way for 3D video transmission over wireless network. Distributed source coding solution tries to resolve the problem of lossy source compression with side information. When applying this concept to video coding, this technique can be summarized as transmitting both a coarse description of the video source and extra data that completes the representation of the source, which is compressed using a distributed source coding technique (also known as Wiener–Ziv coding). The coarse description contains side information that is used to decode the extra data and obtain a representation of the reconstructed video. The main property exploited by the distributed video coding system is the correlation between the distributed source-coded data and the side information. The coarse description of the video can be either a highly compressed frame or an intra-predictive frame. In the latter case, the combination of the distributed source-coded data with the side information is able to recover the time evolution of the video sequence. Distributed video coding is a technique of interest for wireless video transmission because there is a duality between the distributed source-coded data and error correcting redundancy that results in an inherent resiliency for the compressed video stream.

We can extend the principle of distributed video coding to multi-view 3D video, since we can exploit the redundancies already present in mono-view video and add the new ones in multi-view video. Taking the simplest scenario consisting of two views, we can encode one view using distributed video coding and use the second view as side information. The other way to construct such a system is to deploy the distributed video coding for both views and use the implicit correlation between the two views to extract their time-dependent difference as side information. For a more generic setting involving more than two views, the multi-view video structure can be exploited by generating the side information from a combination of inter-view texture correlation and time-dependent motion correlation. Owing to the distributed nature, it is possible to combine the distributed 3D video coding with the use of relay nodes enabled with cooperative communications. Such a combination of distributed video coding and cooperative communications sets up a flexible framework that can be applied in a variety of ways. For example, different types of data in the multi-view video (or even V+D) can be via different channels/paths. Even more, if the relay is equipped with high computation ability, it can perform different application layer processing, such as transcoding/video post-processing/error concealment/view synthesis, to facilitate the 3D visual communication.

We often rely on the objective measurement, such as throughput, goodput, and mean-squared-error (MSE), to evaluate the system resource utilization from communication layer to 3D video application layer. One of the reasons is that the selected objective measurement simplifies the problem formulation by excluding the highly nonlinear HVS factors and the optimal solutions exist in the formulated linear/nonlinear continuous/integer optimization problem. However, the final 3D video quality is evaluated by the human eyes; and the objective measurement does not always align with what human beings perceive. In other words, understanding the 3D human vision system and quantifying the QoE becomes extremely important. More specifically, we need to find the critical features and statistics which affect the 3D QoE and an effective objective measurement for 3D QoE that reflects subjective measurement. It is also important to have a quantitative measurement mechanism to evaluate the impact of distortion caused in each stage of the 3D communication pipeline to the end-to-end 3D QoE. Having those QoE metric will enables the QoE-based optimized framework for 3D visual communications.

References

1. D. Astely, E. Dahlman, A. Furuskar, Y. Jading Y, M. Lindstrom, and S. Parkvall, "LTE: the evolution of mobile broadband," *IEEE Communications Magazine*, vol. 47, no. 4, pp. 44–51, April 2009.
2. S. Ahmadi, "An overview of next-generation mobile WiMAX technology." *IEEE Communications Magazine*, vol.47, no. 6, pp. 84–98, June 2009.
3. G.-M. Su, Z. Han, M. Wu and K. J. R. Liu, "Multiuser cross-layer resource allocation for video transmission over wireless networks," *IEEE Network Magazine, Special Issue on Multimedia over Broadband Wireless Networks* 2006; vol. 20, no. 2, pp. 21–27.
4. V. Chandrasekhar, J. Andrews, A. Gatherer, "Femtocell networks: a survey," *IEEE Communications Magazine*, vol. 46, no. 9, pp. 59–67, September 2008.

2

3D Graphics and Rendering

With the advance of technology, stereoscopic 3DTV is now available and popular in the current electronics market. The fundamental concept of a 3DTV system is to deliver stereoscopic 3D perception of the world to viewers while watching streams of 2D videos. These 2D videos are sent to each eye separately and later the brain fuses them together to generate the perception of the world. In other words, 3DTV delivers the content of a 3D scene to consumers' 3D displayable devices for generating 3D perception to viewers. The 3D content may be virtual (synthesized by computers) or realistic (captured from real scenes) and can be transmitted in various ways and forms according to the types of the scene, the level of required realism, the type of applications, the available bandwidth of the transmission channel, and so on. The representations of the 3D scenes is the bridging technology among the procedures of scene extraction, modeling, transmission, and viewing for a 3DTV framework. However, the requirements of scene representations in each procedure are often very different and even sometimes conflicting (e.g., transmission rate versus visual quality). To achieve these different requirements, different 3D scene representation techniques are available and generally categorized into three fundamental classes according to whether geometric models are used or not:

1. **Rendering with explicit geometry:** The first category is rendering with explicit geometry which has direct 3D information. It is also called a geometry-based representation and can be roughly divided into two different categories:
   (a) **Surface-based representations:** This category, which includes polygon meshes, nonuniform rational B-spline (NURBS), subdivision and point-based modeling, is popular due to its generality, extensive support by current hardware, and enriched interactivity. However, the ability to provide realistic rendering is the largest limitation to meet the requirement of 3DTV.
   (b) **Volume-based representations:** They have the ability to encapsulate neighborhood information which is important for parallel processing the reconstruction of surfaces for multi-view algorithms. However, the largest issue is the trade-offs between resolution and memory usage or transmission bandwidth.
   More details will be given in Section 2.2

3D Visual Communications, First Edition. Guan-Ming Su, Yu-Chi Lai, Andres Kwasinski and Haohong Wang.
© 2013 John Wiley & Sons, Ltd. Published 2013 by John Wiley & Sons, Ltd.

2. **Rendering with no geometry:** These representations use no geometry information but only 2D images or videos to represent the 3D scene and are also called image-based or texture-based representations. The representations encode the different views in a single image or video or in a set of images or videos. Without geometry, the sampling must be very dense, or the possible motion is restricted. Examples in this category include [1–4]. The main advantage is the inherent realism because the represented images and videos are captured from the real world. In other words it can easily give viewers the sense of realism. However, the memory and/or the transmission rate of this type of representation is a serious issue. In addition, the provided interactivity has its own limitation. More details will be discussed in Section 2.3 and Chapter 5.

3. **Rendering with implicit geometry:** This category relies on positional correspondences across a small number of images to render new views. The methods are also called depth-image-based representations. The term *implicit* implies that the geometry is not directly available. The representatives include [5–9]. Depth-image-based methods can be viewed as a hybrid of the geometry-based and image-based representations in order to gain the advantages of both categories and alleviate the disadvantages of both categories. Depth-image-based representations are appropriate for free-view 3DTV applications, since they can generate the virtual views easily. They are currently the popular choice for stereoscopic representations. More details will be discussed in Section 2.4 and Chapter 5.

Figure 2.1 is a diagram which shows the representation spectrum, ranging from one extreme, geometry-based representations, to the other, image-based representations. In this chapter, we provide a short description of these important techniques and approaches which could be used for 3D scene representations. In addition, we also provide a short discussion about the pros and cons of each method.

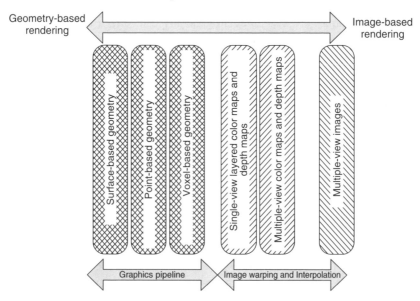

Figure 2.1 This shows the categorization of scene representations for 3D applications and 3DTV systems.

2.1   3DTV Content Processing Procedure

Stereoscopic 3DTV has to provide each eye with a separate 2D video stream for the perception of the 3D world. The easiest way to represent the 3D content is to prepare the whole set of videos for all possible views. However, this representation requires high bandwidth and may not be suitable for interactively viewing the scene. Additionally, naked-eye free-view 3DTV will appear in the market soon and this kind of equipment will require multiple views for creating the sense of seeing the 3D world from different viewpoints. Thus, we must first understand the pipeline of 3DTV processing procedure which involves four basic tasks: representation, transmission, animation, and rendering as shown in Figure 2.2.

1. **Representation**
   A real world scene contains moving objects with different shapes and complexities. Generally, the best choice of representation scheme depends on the requirement of

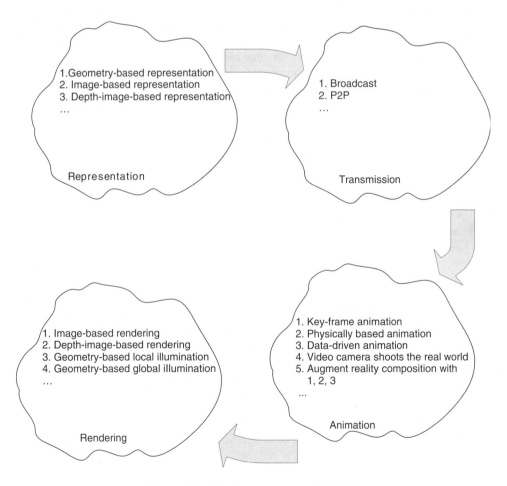

Figure 2.2   Content processing of 3DTV.

the applications including the properties of the scene, such as the complexity, appearance and motion the transmission speed, the requirement of realism, and interactivity. A typical example is to show a view of realistic scenery to an end user such as a view of the Grand Canyon. Since the requirement of the application is realistic, the scene is static and comprised geometries are generally far away, a set of captured images, that is, image-based representations, are probably the best choice. However, in a 3D online urban shooting game, proper interactivity is the main requirement and realism can be sacrificed. In this situation, the geometry-based representation is the best choice. In the literature, there are different ways to represent the 3D content in the scene. Section 2.2 gives a more detailed description of several representative geometry-based techniques used in computer graphics to represent the 3DTV content. Section 2.3 gives a more detailed description of several representative image-based techniques to represent the 3DTV content. Section 2.4 gives a more detailed description of depth-image-based techniques used to represent 3DTV content.

2. **Transmission**

The main purpose of a 3DTV system is to transmit stereoscopic content to viewers. In order to generate realistic perception, transmitting all representations in the original form requires really high bandwidth. Even the traditional TV requires a proper 2D video codec to compress 2D video streams for giving high fidelity to viewers. Therefore, the content of 3DTV must be properly encoded to enable efficient transmission. If the content is transmitted through a computer network using a wired or wireless path, the delay and uncertainty in the transmission network can cause extra problems. Instead of showing entirely blackout content on screen owing to network traffic, progressivity tackles this problem by differentiating layers/priorities of streams and lets the receivers get baseline content decoded from the low bit rate portion of the streams to generate a coarse-quality perception. This is important for user experience. Therefore, a short discussion about compression will be presented for each geometry-based representation, and Chapter 5 will discuss the encoding methods for image-based and depth-image-based representations.

3. **Animation**

The objects in the world generally move around. Interactive free-view 3DTV allows viewers to change the viewpoints interactively and even interact with the content. Thus, the representation must have methods to represent the moving objects. Geometry-based representations are originally developed for the need in computer-aided design and computer animation software. Therefore, the animation techniques [10] mainly focus on the geometry-based representation. They are mainly divided into three categories: key-frame, data-driven, and physically-based methods. Key-frame methods allow the user to set up the key frames and the algorithms compute the in-between positions, orientations, and other properties automatically, using proper interpolation techniques such as linear interpolation [10]. The user is also allowed to edit the in-between results. The controlled parameters can be almost anything such as polygon vertex positions, joint angles, muscle contraction values, colors, and camera parameters. Data-driven methods are similar to the concept of image-based and depth-image-based methods to capture the movement of real objects and then use the captured data to perform the animation. The most popular ones include motion capture and facial expression capture.

Since the world object follows the physics in the real world, physically-based methods simulate the interaction among objects with external forces, such as air resistance and gravity, and the constraints existing on the objects, such as the constraint imposed on a roller coaster car on a track. The representatives are [11–13]. Thus, physically-based techniques basically construct the rules which can be physical rules or behavioral rules and then follow the rules to update the behavior of the objects in the scene. However, these techniques are computationally expensive, since the simulations involve numerical computation including integration, solving the partial differential equations, and so on. Thus, the physically-based techniques are generally offline. All three methods mentioned are first designed for offline animation. However, interactivity becomes more and more important and so the three techniques are accelerated by certain simplification and modification to make it look visually correct to human beings. This makes real-time interactivity with the geometry-based representations possible. Currently, the geometry-based representation provides the proper interaction for interactive 3DTV systems.

Image-based and depth-image-based representations capture a dynamic scene in the real world in videos and depth maps. When the system requires to set up the proper scenery and animation, the shooter can manipulate the character and move the objects in the designed and desired way. The shooting cameras are set up in a designed configuration. This shooting configuration allows the control of all possible view positions and directions. After capturing, view manipulation and editing the content are the only really proper operations on the data although there are a large number of researchers focusing on creating new content by concatenating or adopting parts of existing videos. For image-based and depth-image-based representations, augmented reality focuses on putting virtual objects in a real scene and computing the interaction of the object with the scene through a display device. However, the interactivity to the content is still not possible for image-based and depth-image-based algorithms. There is still a large amount of research focusing on adding interaction into these two categories of representations.

4. **Rendering**

The rendering is mainly on the receiver side. When the receiver receives the data transmitted from the 3DTV producing system, it must synthesize the new view from the data. Image-based representations fundamentally pick up the video streams from the nearest camera configuration and interpolate the content accordingly (see Chapter 5 and Section 2.3 for more details). Depth-image-based representations use a similar method to synthesize new views but with additional depth information. With the help of the depth information, the interpolation can be more precise and the artifact can be reduced (see Chapter 5 and Section 2.3 for more details). The rendering literature for the geometry-based representation is enormous. Fundamentally, they can be categorized into two groups:

(a) **Local illumination** only considers the relationship between the shading point and the light sources.

(b) **Global illumination** must take into account not only the light which comes directly from a light source (direct illumination), but also subsequent cases in which light rays from the same source are reflected by other surfaces in the scene (indirect illumination).

According to the requirement of each procedure, the representations will have different requirements to fulfill and can be analyzed in terms of generality, accuracy, perceptual quality, level of detail scalability, progressivity, compression, editing, animation, and compatibility.

- *Generality*: This means the ability of a representation to handle different types of topology and geometry. Generality is extremely important because real-world objects can have extremely complex shapes. It is important to choose a representation when system designers start to plan an application since the possible construction procedures are determined by the chosen representation.
- *Accuracy and perceptual quality*: These two properties are important especially for applications whose main concern is realism. Ideally, it is preferred to have a representation which can give viewers all the fine details of the world and generate perceptually smooth results, that is, the result must contain little aliasing at the same time. These two properties are the main concern during the representation and construction procedure and they are a trade-off to the efficiency.
- *Level of detail (LoD) scalability*: This addresses the ability to use a complete description of a 3D content to generate quality-reduced or simplified versions. This property enables the usage of less powerful rendering engines to generate a reduced quality view of the world. The choice of LoD techniques is important for all procedures especially in transmission.
- *Progressivity*: This property refers to the ability to progressively transmit and visualize a highly detailed 3D content. Note that LoD scalability is different from progressivity because progressivity means incremental detail representation. Progressive modeling schemes give a decoder or viewer the ability to construct a 3D scene from a partial bit stream. This is related to the transmission and rendering procedure.
- *Compression*: This addresses the efficiency of storing and transmitting 3D models. In addition to statistical de-correlation of data, the compactness of a representation is an important issue of compression. This is mainly related to the transmission stage.
- *Editing*: This refers to the ability to change, deform, and edit the shape and topology of the 3D content. This ability is important for interactive 3DTV applications. This is mainly related to the animation stage.
- *Compatibility*: This property address the availability of hardware support to render a specific representation. This is mainly related to the rendering stage.

2.2 3D Scene Representation with Explicit Geometry – Geometry Based Representation

Geometry-based representations have been the fundamental form to represent 3D objects in the world for decades. Since the dawn of computer graphics, real world objects have been represented using geometric 3D surfaces with associated textures mapped onto them and then the surfaces are rasterized to generate the virtual view using graphics hardware. More sophisticated attributes such as appearance properties can be assigned and used to synthesize more realistic views as well. Point-based representations use a set of discrete samples on the surface to represent the geometry. The sophisticated attributes can be recorded with the surface sample. The sampling density can also be adjusted according to need. In addition, volumetric representation is developed as another branch of geometry-based representations. Volumetric techniques extend the concept of a set of 2D pixels representing a set of unit patches in an image to a set of 3D voxels representing a set of unit volumes of the 3D scene.

Fundamentally, the object can be created by three different methods: manual creation through a user interface such as Maya, results from physical simulation, and results from examination such as MRI or CT scan.

Animation describes the transformation of the objects including the rigid transformation and deformation. Geometry-based representations are generally easier to be manipulated than the image-based representation and the depth-image-based representation. Additionally, all animation techniques developed in computer graphics are for geometry-based representations and interested readers can refer to the book written by Parent et al. [10] and this section will not give any further discussion on geometry-based animation.

The rendering process is generally time-consuming and, therefore, there are a large number of acceleration methods to synthesize new views from the set of representations. Currently, graphics hardware has been designed to accelerate the rendering of surface-based representations, and state-of-the-art PC graphics cards have the ability to render highly complex scenes with an impressive quality in terms of refresh rate, levels of detail, spatial resolution, pre-production of motion, and accuracy of textures. These developments in the graphics pipeline give us the possibility of rendering objects in different representations from any viewpoint and direction using the same infrastructure. The achievable performance is good for real-time applications for providing the necessary interactivity. All these fit the need of an interactive 3DTV system to allow users to control the view position and direction efficiently and independently without affecting the rendering algorithm.

There are several limitations in geometry-based representations when applying them to a 3DTV system. These limitations are that the cost of content creation is high since the real world object is generally complex and the model is an approximation with a trade-off between complexity and errors; and the rendering cost depends on the geometric complexity and the synthesized views are still not close to the realism we have come to expect. In this section, we provide a comparative description of various techniques and approaches which constitute the state-of-the-art geometry-based representations in computer graphics.

2.2.1 Surface Based Representation

Objects in the world are generally closed, that is, an object is completely enclosed by a surface. Viewers can only see the surface of most objects and cannot see their interior. Therefore, they can be represented by the outside boundary surface and the representation is called the surface-based representation, which is one of the popular forms in computer graphics. The polygonal mesh is one type of surface-based representations and is used as the basic primitive for the graphics hardware pipeline. The advantage of the surface-based representation is its generality, and it can be used to represent almost all objects. However, the limitation is that the surface-based representation is only an approximation to the original model and potentially requires a huge number of primitives to represent a complex object.

NURBS stands for nonuniform rational B-spline surfaces and is another popular form. The representation uses a set of control points and a two-parameter basis function to represent any point on the surface. The stored data, consisting of their coefficients, is compact, and the resolution can be infinite and adjustable according to the need in precision and the affordable computation speed. The main limitations are the requirement of extra computational process to approximate the surface on the receiver side and its requirement of complexity to represent fine surface detail.

Subdivision surfaces represent an object by recursively subdividing each face of an arbitrary polygonal mesh. The subdivision process allows the sender to send the fundamental polygonal mesh across the channel and reconstruct the surface in desired detail according to the computational ability of the receiver side. However, the limitation is similar to NURBS in keeping the surface detail through the subdivision process, and the extra cost for subdivision.

We will give an introductory description of each representation. Then, a short description of the creation and rendering generally to surface-based representations is also given.

2.2.1.1 Polygonal Mesh Representations

Polygonal meshes are the most popular and common representations for 3D objects in computer graphics. The representation is also the fundamental primitive for graphics hardware pipeline techniques. The main advantage is that the representation can represent any object with almost no topological restrictions. The representation can be adjusted according to the requirement of realism and better approximation. However, those high-precision polygon meshes generally contains millions of polygons. This leads to the main disadvantage that storing, transmitting, and rendering objects with millions of polygons is very expensive. This also leads to a large amount of research in mesh simplification and compression and the results give flexible representations for expressing different levels of detail and progressive quality.

A polygonal mesh represents the surface of a real world object in computer graphics through a collection of vertices, edges, and faces. A vertex is a point in the 3D space which stores the information such as location, color, normal, and texture coordinates. An edge is a link between two vertices. A face is a closed set of edges on the same plane such as a triangle which has three edges and a quadrilateral which has four edges. In other words, a face consists of a set of vertices on the same plane to form a closed loop. A polygonal mesh consists of a set of connected faces. The relationship among vertex, edge and face is illustrated in Figure 2.3. Generally, triangles are the fundamental primitives for any renderer. Some renderers may support quadrilaterals or other simple convex polygons. However, commercially available graphics hardware only supports triangles and quadrilaterals. Generally, triangles and quadrilaterals are good for representing the shape of an object. A surface presents a set of triangles that logically have the same properties or work under the same set of actions. For example, triangles which have the same appearance under the same lighting condition are grouped together to use the same shading information to simulate the appearance of objects. Because of its popularity, different representations are proposed for the need of different applications and goals.

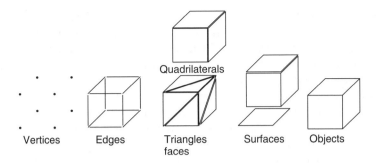

Figure 2.3 The elements for representing an object by polygonal meshes.

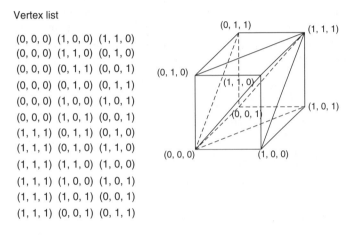

Figure 2.4 A cube is represented with a vertex-vertex mesh.

The representations vary with the methods for storing the polygonal data including vertices, edges, and faces and the following are the most commonly used ones:

1. **Vertex-vertex meshes**

   An object can be viewed as a set of vertices connected to other vertices. Both the edge and face information are implicitly encoded in this representation. This is the simplest representation and is used in DirectX and OpenGL but is not optimized for mesh operations since the face and edge information is implicit because any operation related to faces or edges has to traverse the vertices. Figure 2.4 shows a simple example of a cube represented using a vertex-vertex mesh. This representation uses relatively less storage space and is efficient for shape morphing.

2. **Face-vertex meshes**

   The representations store a list of vertices and a set of faces consisting of indices to the referred vertices. It is an improvement on vertex-vertex meshes for giving explicit information about the vertices of a face and the faces surrounding a vertex. Therefore, they are more appropriate for certain mesh operations. This is the most common mesh representation in computer graphics and is generally accepted as the input to the modern graphics hardware. For rendering, the face list is usually transmitted to a graphics processing unit (GPU) as a set of indices to vertices, and the vertices are sent as position/color/normal structures (only position is given). This has the benefit that changes in shape, but not topology, can be dynamically updated by simply resending the vertex data without updating the face connectivity. Figure 2.5 shows the face-vertex mesh of a cube. However, the downside is that the edge information is still implicit, that is, a search through all surrounding faces of a given face is still needed, and other dynamic operations such as splitting or merging a face are also difficult.

3. **Corner-table meshes**

   The representation stores a set of vertices in a predefined table. A special order to traverse the table implicitly defines the polygonal mesh. This is the essential concept for the "triangle fan" used in graphics hardware rendering. Figure 2.6 demonstrates an example of a cube. The representation is more compact than a vertex-vertex mesh and more efficient for retrieving polygons. However, it is harder to represent a surface in a single corner-table mesh and thus multiple corner-table meshes are required.

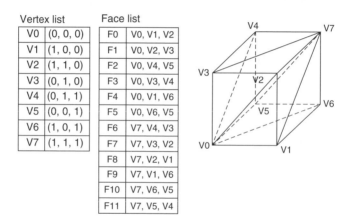

Figure 2.5 A cube is represented with a face-vertex mesh.

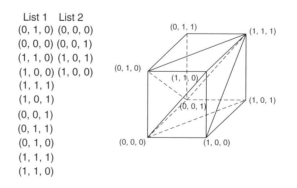

Figure 2.6 A cube is represented with a corner-table mesh.

4. **Winged-edge meshes**

   This is an extension to face-vertex meshes. Extra edge information includes the index of two edge vertices, the index of the neighboring two faces, and the index of four (clockwise and counterclockwise) edges that touch it. This representation allows traversing the surfaces and edges in constant time but requires more space to store this extra information. Figure 2.7 shows the winged-edge mesh of a cube.

5. **Half-edge meshes**

   This representation uses a similar concept to a winged-edge mesh but instead of creating an edge table, edge traversal information is recorded in the extra edge traversal information with each vertex. This makes it more space efficient. Figure 2.8 shows the half-edge mesh of the cube.

6. **Quad-edge meshes**

   This is also a variant of winged-edge meshes. It realizes that a face can be easily recognized by one of its edge and the four edges connected to the face edge. Therefore, the representation only stores vertices and edges with indices to the end vertices and four connected edges. Memory requirements are similar to half-edge meshes. Figure 2.9 shows the quad-edge mesh of a cube.

The representations discussed above have their own pros and cons. A detailed discussion can be found in [14]. Generally, the type of applications, the performance requirement, the size of the data and the operations to be performed affect the choice of representation. In addition, texturing techniques are important to add more lighting details to generate the realistic appearance of objects in computer graphics. Texture techniques can be viewed

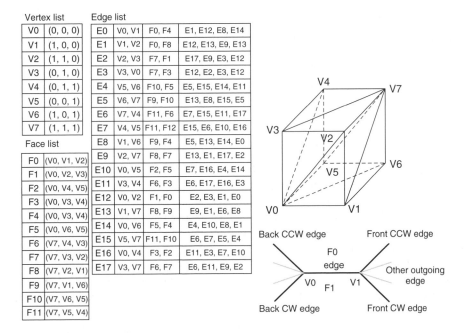

Figure 2.7 A cube is represented with a winged-edge mesh.

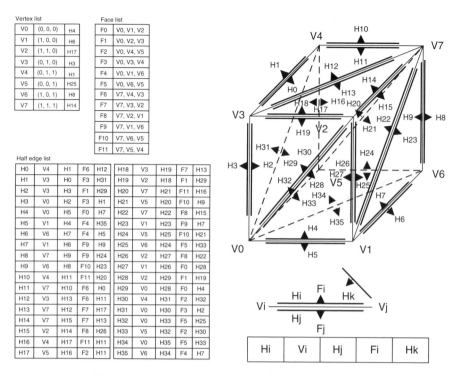

Figure 2.8 A cube represented by half-edge meshes.

as wrapping a sheet of 2D detail paper onto different parts of the mesh and generally require some form of texture coordinates to generate proper wrapping. How to apply the texture techniques is also an important consideration when choosing a representation for an application. As a result, there are more variants existing for different applications and still no dominant representation exists. It is still an active research field.

2.2.1.2 Polygonal Construction

One category of construction methods for surface-based representations are those generated manually by users. Currently, there is a large range of animation software such as Maya, 3DS Max, and Blender, and computer-aided design (CAD) software such as Autocad available. All of them have the ability to generate polygonal meshes, NURBS surfaces, and subdivision surfaces. 3D animation software gives users the ability to make 3D animations, models, and images and is frequently used for the production of animations, development of games, design of commercial advertisements, and visualization of architecture. They are especially important for movie special effects. CAD tools are used to create the basic geometry for physical simulation and for creating architectural blueprints and product profiles. For example, Abaqus is for mechanical and thermal simulation. All these tools can be used to generate really complex geometry-based objects and also have extra ability to generate different sorts of animations.

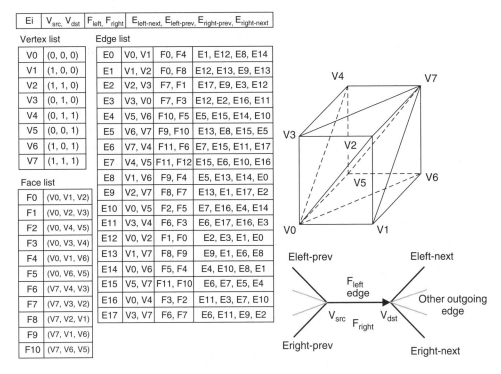

Ei	V_{src}, V_{dst}	F_{left}, F_{right}	$E_{left-next}$, $E_{left-prev}$, $E_{right-prev}$, $E_{right-next}$

Vertex list

V0	(0, 0, 0)
V1	(1, 0, 0)
V2	(1, 1, 0)
V3	(0, 1, 0)
V4	(0, 1, 1)
V5	(0, 0, 1)
V6	(1, 0, 1)
V7	(1, 1, 1)

Face list

F0	(V0, V1, V2)
F1	(V0, V2, V3)
F2	(V0, V4, V5)
F3	(V0, V3, V4)
F4	(V0, V1, V6)
F5	(V0, V6, V5)
F6	(V7, V4, V3)
F7	(V7, V3, V2)
F8	(V7, V2, V1)
F9	(V7, V1, V6)
F10	(V7, V6, V5)

Edge list

E0	V0, V1	F0, F4	E1, E12, E8, E14
E1	V1, V2	F0, F8	E12, E13, E9, E13
E2	V2, V3	F7, F1	E17, E9, E3, E12
E3	V3, V0	F7, F3	E12, E2, E16, E11
E4	V5, V6	F10, F5	E5, E15, E14, E10
E5	V6, V7	F9, F10	E13, E8, E15, E5
E6	V7, V4	F11, F6	E7, E15, E11, E17
E7	V4, V5	F11, F12	E15, E6, E10, E16
E8	V1, V6	F9, F4	E5, E13, E14, E0
E9	V2, V7	F8, F7	E13, E1, E17, E2
E10	V0, V5	F2, F5	E7, E16, E4, E14
E11	V3, V4	F6, F3	E6, E17, E16, E3
E12	V0, V2	F1, F0	E2, E3, E1, E0
E13	V1, V7	F8, F9	E9, E1, E6, E8
E14	V0, V6	F5, F4	E4, E10, E8, E1
E15	V5, V7	F11, F10	E6, E7, E5, E4
E16	V0, V4	F3, F2	E11, E3, E7, E10
E17	V3, V7	F6, F7	E6, E11, E9, E2

Figure 2.9   A cube represented by a quad-edge mesh.

Another category of methods to construct geometry-based objects is to use a 3D scanner to create a set of samples on the surface of the subject. These samples can be used to create the surface-based representations through a reconstruction procedure. 3D scanners are directly related to depth-image-based content construction. 3D scanners are similar to photographical cameras in terms of a cone-like field of view and collecting information from visible surfaces. In addition to collecting color information, they collect the distance information. In other words the "image" produced by a 3D scanner describes the distance from the scanner to the sample on the visible surface. Generally, a single scan cannot produce a complete model of the world. Multiple scans are needed to obtain all necessary geometrical information for the world. The system requires a common reference and a registration process to combine the result of all scans. The whole process is known as the 3D scanning pipeline [15]. There are different technologies available and they are generally categorized as contact, noncontact active, and noncontact passive 3D scanners [16].

2.2.1.3   Compression and Encoding for Transmission

The number of polygons grows really fast with the advance in the 3D model scanned technology and the requirement for realism. It is hard to transmit and store the entire mesh without compression or simplification. Simplification is useful in order to make storage, transmission, computation, and display more efficient. A compact approximation of a shape can reduce disk and memory requirements and can also speed up network transmission. There are a large number of different simplification or compression methods such as vertex clustering, incremental decimation, resampling, edge collapse, vertex removal, half edge collapse, and so on. Mesh simplification is still an active research field in computer graphics. There is still no algorithm which is better than all others, but the following will only give a short introduction to edge collapse and its reverse operation, vertex splitting because they are popular choices and also the applications for progressivity. We use examples to illustrate the concept of simplification and the ability to progressively deliver a polygonal mesh for coarse-to-fine transmission. Interested readers can refer to [17] for more details.

An example of the edge collapse process is shown in Figure 2.10. First, one edge in the polygonal mesh is picked up according to some global or local error metric which measures the approximation error or the degree of visual fidelity. Then, the end points of the edge are merged into a single vertex and the position of the vertex is updated according to the neighboring vertices. Finally, the faces are updated. Vertex splitting is the reverse of the edge collapse by recording the information necessary to reverse the edge-collapse operation including which vertex is most newly formed and the information of the two merged vertices. Then the collapsed edge can be recovered. In other words, edge collapse is to remove the detail from a polygonal mesh, and vertex split is to recover the details and to increase the accuracy.

A progressive mesh (PM) scheme [18] uses edge collapse and vertex split to achieve the delivery of details in progressive order. In the PM scheme, edge collapse is applied to a fine detailed triangular mesh for creation of a coarser mesh and the resulting coarse mesh can be reconstructed through a sequence of vertex-split refinement operations. Each intermediate mesh along the coarsening sequence corresponds to an LoD approximation. This scheme can automatically support the need of progressive transmission. However, the collapsing criteria are generally based on the global error metric which estimates the degree of approximation to the original model and thus the scheme cannot guarantee smooth transition between consecutive levels. Hoppe et al. [19] proposed a partial fix by incorporating a view-dependent information into the error metric for coarsening the mesh according to visual quality.

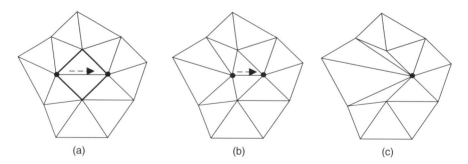

(a)   (b)   (c)

Figure 2.10 The edge collapse process. (a) This is the original mesh. (b) The vertices in the collapse pair move close to each other. (c) Two vertices become one and the connectivity is adjusted to form the new mesh.

There are several variants proposed to relieve the limitation of the original PM scheme. The progressive forest split (PFS) [20, 21] and compressed progressive meshes (CPM) [22, 23] consider several meshes at the same time to form a more space-efficient PM scheme. Progressive time-varying meshes [24] further address the extra dimension of time by considering the deforming meshes at different moments of time. Thus, when considering which edge to collapse, the error metric will take all frames into account and then make the decision. Note that these progressive mesh algorithms are not the most compression-efficient algorithm as extra aided information is needed for progressivity. However, they are important for coarse-to-fine transmission because they allow viewers to get the sense of the viewing scene via a coarse view and the quality can be improved gradually. In addition, during the congestion in the network, the coarse model can still help the transition instead of hanging there without showing anything on the screen.

2.2.1.4   Polygonal Mesh Rendering

Rendering is the process of generating an image of a scene as the result of the interaction between light and the environment. Currently, the popular choice of rendering algorithms is a simple method involving only local information such as the Phong illumination model [25], which is an approximation to the rendering equation [26], or it can be a really complex method involving all objects in the scene such as ray tracing, path tracing and photon mapping.

According to the information involved, the rendering algorithms are generally categorized into:

1. **Local illumination**
   The local illumination method only considers the relationship between the shading point and light sources and does not take the interaction of light with the environment into account such as object-to-object light interactions (reflections, transmissions etc.). They are only approximations to the direct illumination from light sources on the surface points without considering the occlusion effects. A graphics pipeline generally computes the lighting at each vertex and then uses interpolation techniques such as flat shading, Gouraud shading [27], or Phong shading [25], to fill in the color in each pixel in the scanning line order. Researchers develop advanced techniques such as texture mapping [1, 28], environment mapping [29], and bump mapping [30], to add realism into the rendering results. Generally these techniques are not computationally intensive when compared to global illumination algorithms discussed next and can be implemented in real time on GPUs. Local illumination only involves the lighting computation at each vertex of all primitives in the scene and then the color in each pixel can be computed according to the lighting computations in these vertices. Through careful observation, the lighting computation at each vertex and the color computation at each pixel are independent of those computations for other vertices and pixels. Therefore, the local illumination can be structured as a pipeline to quickly process the computations for vertices and primitives. This pipeline is generally called a graphics pipeline. The process of image generation is called rendering or rasterization with a graphics pipeline which is the most important and popular method of generating images in computer graphics. Generally, primitives used in a graphics pipeline are polygonal

meshes and thus surface-based representations will be transformed to a polygonal mesh and then the graphics pipeline is used for rendering.

2. **Global illumination**

Global illumination simulates inter-object lighting effects such as reflections and refractions to render more realistic images. However, the computational cost is generally very high.

- **Radiosity** [31] can generate a new view by solving the diffuse reflection problem using energy equilibrium equations and is important for rendering interiors in a building and appropriate for architectural walk-throughs. However, the materials allowed to be used in radiosity are limited to diffuse-only materials. This limitation makes it unsuitable for simulating most scenes in the world.

- **Ray tracing algorithms** [32, 33] trace the view with rays sent from the camera through each pixel and recursively calculate the intersections of these rays with the scene objects and compute the contribution of light on the intersection points. They can handle specular reflection and refraction. There is a category called photorealistic rendering algorithms. They combine the ray tracing and statistical Monte Carlo methods to estimate the intensity in each pixel. There are several representative algorithms including path tracing [26], bidirectional ray tracing [34, 35], photon mapping [36], and so on. Photon mapping, proposed by Jensen et al. [36], is a two-pass algorithm. The first pass is photon distribution which starts to trace light from light sources to simulate reflections and refractions of light for photons. The second pass is photon collection which is similar to a ray tracing procedure to compute the light contribution at each intersection point according to the photon distribution. The advantage of this algorithm is that it works for arbitrary geometric representations, including parametric and implicit surfaces, and calculates the ray-surface intersections on demand.

The rendering methods are multivarious in the literature. It is not the focus of this book. Interested readers can refer to [37, 38] for more details.

2.2.1.5 Non-uniform Rational B-spline Surface (NURBS) Representations

Polygonal meshes are unorganized representations of surfaces and the approximation error cannot be estimated beforehand. Instead of polygonal meshes, NURBS can describe many shapes without loss of mathematical exactness. NURBS has long been a popular choice in computer aided design (CAD), computer aided manufacturing (CAM), and computer animation because the representations are easily manipulated and with controllable smoothness. NURBS generally defines a patch using a basis function defined by two parameters, u and v. The basis function defines a mapping of a 2D region into the 3D Euclidean space and is usually expressed as the tensor product of some piecewise-polynomial basis functions (B-splines). The patch is specified by a set of 3D control points and two knot vectors to control two parameters, u and v, of the B-spline basis functions. A point on a NURBS patch can be computed as following:

$$S(uv) = \frac{\sum_{i=1}^{n} \sum_{j=1}^{m} B_{ip}(u) B_{jq}(v) w_{ij} \mathbf{C}_{ij}}{\sum_{i=1}^{n} \sum_{j=1}^{m} B_{ip}(u) B_{jq}(v) w_{ij}} \tag{2.1}$$

where B is the B-spline basis functions, $\mathbf{C}$ is the set of control points for the patch, p and q are degrees (orders) of the surface in u and v directions respectively, and w is the weight for the corresponding control point. Generally, NURBS partitions the entire parameterization domain into subintervals with two known sequences, $U = \{u_1, u_2, \cdots, u_n\}$ and $V = \{v_1, v_2, \cdots, v_m\}$, which are two nondecreasing sets of real numbers. Furthermore, the knot vectors can be nonuniform, that is, the interval between two consecutive knots can be different inside a knot vector. The B-spline basis functions $B(u, v)$ are defined over these knot sequences and can be calculated in a recursive manner. Equation (2.1) associates each knot in a knot sequence with a control point and a basis function. One of the key characteristics of a NURBS patch is that its shape is primarily determined by the positions of its control points. Hence, the influence of each control point is local and this characteristic allows the application to adjust the shape locally by moving only individual control points, without affecting the overall shape of the surface. In addition, the knot vectors can control the shape and smoothness of a NURBS patch. The weight of a control point may make the effect of one control point on a patch different from another. And the weight is a ratio function between two B-spline basis functions and this is why NURBS is rational. Tensor-product uniform B-spline surfaces can be treated as a special case of NURBS with uniform knot vectors and equally weighted control points by setting the denominator to be 1. Interested readers can refer to [39] for mathematical description of NURBS and to [40] for an introduction to the functionality of NURBS in practice.

The main advantages of NURBS is its controllable smoothness within a patch, that is, the continuity can be controlled by the degree of the B-spline basis function. However, mathematical definition of NURBS, which is a tensor product surface, makes it only be able to represent planar, cylindrical, or toroidal topologies. To overcome this topological limitation, a set of NURBS patches can be stitched together to represent an arbitrarily topological surface. Actually, stitching a set of NURBS patches together seamlessly is one of the challenges in the modeling process and generally requires human intervention. There is one solution proposed by Eck et al. [41], but their method is limited to uniform B-splines or to force all patches to have the same knot vector and the same order. This limitation makes it not general to handle all NURBS.

Built-in smoothness is the main advantage of NURBS but this also leads to one of its major drawbacks which is its inefficiency in representing fine surface detail. In order to add a single control point into a patch, an entire column or row of control points must be split to preserve the desired quadrilateral grid structure in the parameter space. A built-in continuity setting may propagate the modification in a control point into the entire surface to generate global effects. The usage of the displacement map [42] is one solution to resolve this problem. The displacement map is a texture storing the fine detail of a model and used to add detail during the rendering process. This scheme is also useful for separating detail from coarser fundamental surface for animation and editing. Another solution is to use a hierarchical NURBS [43]. They work better for editing and refining by providing a valuable coarse manipulation fundamental surface but are hard to generalize for arbitrary complexity and topology.

Infinite resolution is another advantage of NURBS. However, a NURBS patch in practice is tessellated into a polygonal meshes before rendering. Generally, tessellation is achieved by producing a grid of sample points on the parameter space, and then evaluating the position of each sample point accordingly, and linking sample points according to the neighboring information in the parameter space. The density of sampling points can be controlled according to the desired level of detail for the application. However, this built-in LoD does not imply a real incremental LoD representation. A NURBS surface is a compact representation and its LoD hierarchy can be constructed only if the complete representation is available.

2.2.1.6 NURBS Construction

Generally, animation and model software discussed in the previous subsection also provide the tools for creating NURBS. Another commonly used construction method is to fit a NURBS to a polygonal mesh and the method is called surface fitting. The fitting process can be considered as a constrained optimization to construct the surface patchwork and the parameterization. However, they generally either have serious topological limitations [43, 44] or suffer from parameterization distortion, and computational complexity [41]. These limitations can be relieved by human interaction in both patch placement and B-spline patch fitting [42].

2.2.1.7 NURBS Compression and Encoding for Transmission

Since NURBS uses a finite set of control points and a basis function to represent the surface, the representation is compact and is good for transmission. The resolution or precision can be controlled in the receiver side according to the computational ability supported in the receiver end. Therefore progressivity is also supported naturally in this structure.

2.2.1.8 NURBS Rendering

When rendering, generally NURBS surfaces are first transformed to polygonal meshes with proper precision, and then global illumination and local illumination methods for polygonal meshes can be applied directly to generate the images and videos. The downside of this is an extra step for transformation. Additionally, the intersection of a ray with NURBS surfaces can be directly computed and thus ray tracing based methods can be directly used to render the NURBS surfaces.

2.2.1.9 Subdivision Surface Representations

Pixar uses subdivision algorithms in their main production and this has given the technique renewed attention in the past decade as a possible alternative to NURBS and polygonal meshes. The subdivision representation provides an infrastructure to represent a compromise of arbitrary topology and any fine detail with a more controllable smoothness. The basic idea of subdivision is to construct a surface from an arbitrary initial polygonal mesh by recursively subdividing each face in the mesh. When the process is done appropriately, the limited surface to this sequence of successive subdivision will be a smooth surface. For example, Stam [45] proved that the limited surface of the well-known

Catmull Clark subdivision scheme can be represented by a bicubic B-spline surface. In the literature, subdivision schemes can be categorized into the following three criteria:

1. the pattern of the refinement rule including vertex insertion [46, 47] and corner cutting [48].
2. the type of generated meshes including triangular meshes [47, 49] and quadrilateral meshes [46, 50].
3. the time of refinement schemes including approximating schemes [46, 49] and interpolating schemes [47, 49].

The refinement rule decides how to subdivide the original polygonal meshes. On the one hand, the vertex insertion scheme inserts three new vertices into each triangle as shown in Figure 2.11 and splits the triangle into four subfaces. The inserted vertices are then repositioned according to the refinement scheme.

On the other hand, the corner cutting scheme inserts extra vertices into each edge and the position of the inserted vertex is updated according to the subdivision scheme. Then the original vertices are removed and the connections of all inserted vertices are reconstructed accordingly. Figure 2.12 shows a simple example.

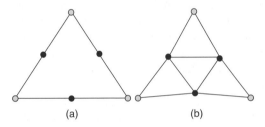

(a)   (b)

Figure 2.11   (a) The relative positions to the original three vertices drawn as gray dots and the insertion vertices drawn as black dots. (b) The result after applying the subdivision scheme to all inserted vertices.

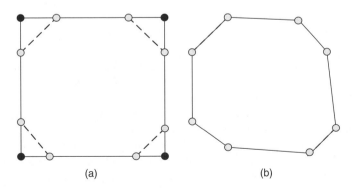

(a)   (b)

Figure 2.12   (a) The relative positions to the original vertices drawn as black dots and the insertion vertices drawn as gray dots. (b) The result after applying the subdivision scheme to all inserted vertices.

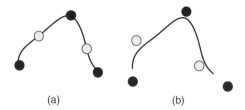

Figure 2.13   (a) An example result after applying the interpolation scheme. (b) An example result after applying the approximate scheme. The black dots represent the original vertices and the gray dots represent the new inserted vertices.

Refinement schemes compute the position and other properties of the newly inserted vertices. Approximating schemes mean that the limited surface after subdivision is only an approximation to the initial mesh, that is, after subdivision, the newly generated control points are not on the limited surface (see Figure 2.13b). Interpolating schemes mean that after subdivision the control points of the original mesh and the new generated control points are interpolated on the limited surface (see Figure 2.13a). Interpolating schemes provide the advantage of controlling the limit of subdivision in a more intuitive way and the approximating scheme can provide a higher quality of surface in fewer iterations of subdivision. For example, the loop subdivision scheme [49] uses vertex insertion and subdivides the triangular meshes using an approximating scheme. The main advantage of subdivision schemes is the smoothness, even with irregular settings [51], and Stam [45] proves that the limit of subdivision can be computed mathematically without explicitly applying subdivision recursion.

Another advantage of subdivision is to provide a method to build a multi-resolution mesh pyramid similar to the concept of the image pyramid. The pyramid provides the freedom to coarsen a given mesh and then refine it later to recover exactly the same mesh with the same connectivity, geometry, and parameterization. The coarsening process is equal to reversing the subdivision process, that is, repeatedly smoothing and downsampling. This is achieved by using an intermediate representation above the current representation in the subdivision hierarchy. Zorin et al. [52] and Lee et al. [53] propose that the geometrical information lost due to smoothing and downsampling is encoded into the subdivision process using the difference as detail offsets. The lost details can be recovered smoothly at any time through the subdivision process and the detail is independent of the others. The detailed mesh can be recovered from the coarse mesh by repeatedly subdividing the coarse mesh to add the detail. This also automatically provides a mechanism for progressive transmission and rendering [54, 55].

Note that since subdivision representations provide the guarantee of smoothness, they must deal with irregular meshes. Generally, the subdivision schemes divide vertices into two categories: regular and extraordinary. Extraordinary vertices are identified as vertices whose valence is other than six for the triangular case and four for the quadrilateral case. In order to guarantee smoothness, there will be a different refinement scheme for extraordinary vertices and the scheme generally depends on the vertices' valences such as [47].

2.2.1.10 Subdivision Construction

Subdivision is first developed because of the need in modeling, animation, and mechanical applications. Therefore, manual construction by a user is the main source of subdivision surfaces. The construction starts from creation of the base mesh using animation or modeling software and then a set of user interfaces is also provided to the users to set up constraints and select subdivision schemes and parameters to create the desired surface.

2.2.1.11 Subdivision Compression and Encoding for Transmission

The subdivision is constructed from a base mesh using a refinement scheme iteratively to subdivide the base mesh to the desired resolution, and thus the transmission of the subdivision can be done by sending the base mesh and the choice of refinement scheme and its associated parameters. Then the refinement of the base mesh to the desired resolution can be achieved in the receiver side. If necessary, the base mesh can be compressed one step further to minimize the amount of data transferred. According to the discussion in previous paragraph, multi-resolution analysis also allows the construction of an efficient progressive representation which encodes the original mesh with a coarse mesh and a sequence of wavelet coefficients which express the detailed offsets between successive levels. Therefore progressivity is supported naturally.

2.2.1.12 Subdivision Rendering

Generally, to synthesize a view of a subdivision object, the representation must first be transformed to a polygonal mesh at the desired resolution. Then the local illumination and global illumination scheme can be applied to generate the result.

2.2.2 Point Based Representation

Meshes represent the surfaces enclosing the objects. The information needed for a polygonal representation is generally large and complex. Thus, an efficient representation is proposed to only record sample points on the surface with the surface properties such as normal and material information. The representation is called point-based modeling including surface points [6, 56], particles [57], or surfels [4] which denote dimensionless space points. Figure 2.14a shows an example of point-based representations of the main building of Chiang Kai-shek Memorial Hall in Taipei.

The representations use simpler display primitives for surface representations. This set of points sampled from the surface contains no topology or connectivity information. In other words the set of points does not have a fixed continuity class nor are they limited to a certain topology as other surface representations. Hence, they can represent any shape with arbitrary topology and complexity. Point-based modeling was first proposed by Levoy et al. [6] to represent those phenomena that are difficult to model with polygons, such as smoke, fire, and water. With the recent advances in scanning technologies, the scanned 3D polygonal meshes can approximate real world objects to high accuracy but their triangle

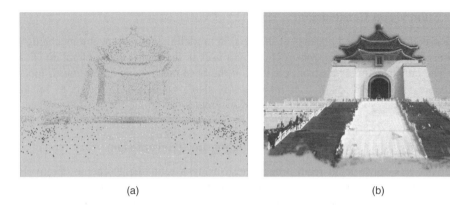

(a)   (b)

Figure 2.14   (a) A set of point samples of the main building in Chiang Kai-shek Memorial Hall. (b) The splatting algorithm is applied to render the point samples of the main building.

counts are huge and become processing bottlenecks with current graphics technology. Thus, point-based representation has regained attention recently. In addition, Pixar also proposed extending the point-based idea for micropolygons to accelerate the rendering process needed in animation production. This is because rendering a large number of triangles realistically becomes a huge issue in terms of its inefficiency. The projected size of a primitive in a highly detailed complex polygonal model onto the image plane during the rendering process is often smaller than the size of a pixel in the screen image. At this moment, the rasterization of polygonal meshes becomes unnecessarily costly. Therefore rendering individual points is more efficient in this situation.

2.2.3   Point Based Construction

3D scanners are popular for surface-based representations. Many scanners first probe the object to create a set of sample points on the object surface and then a reconstruction method is applied. The set of sample points can be used as the point-based representation of the object. Another method creates a set of surface points by sampling a surface representation. The most crucial problem in sampling is how to distribute the sample points on the surface. For example, each patch can have a uniform number of samples or a number of samples proportional to its area or according to its curvature, and so on. Then the samples in each patch are distributed uniformly in the 2D space. Generally, the distribution scheme can be adjusted according to the needs of application.

2.2.4   Point Based Compression and Encoding for Transmission

Generally, point-based modeling can be more efficient with regard to storage and memory in the process of progressive modeling when compared to polygonal meshes because point-based modeling only needs the information related to samples but need not store the extra structural information such as connectivity. However, low-resolution approximations of point sets do not generally produce realistic rendering results and easily generate holes in the process. Therefore, progressivity is important for adjusting resolution for different displays and different transmission speeds. The first idea that comes to mind is to apply filtering techniques in a similar manner to the construction of image pyramids. Thus, the point set sampled on a regular grid can easily support progressive transmission/ visualization and LoD scalability. Thus Yemez et al. [58, 59] proposed a progressive point-based modeling method based on an octree volumetric structure. Their method works as follows: the method first voxelizes the surface in octree volumetric representation and then hierarchical point sets are uniformly sampled on the surface according to the hierarchical voxel in the octree structure which will be discussed later. With the octree hierarchical structure, the samples can also be encoded in a similar hierarchical order and the viewer can reconstruct the surface information progressively.

Spherical hierarchy is another type of progressive point-based modeling and the visualization of the point set is rendered using splatting as discussed below. The algorithm uses different sizes of spheres to represent the hierarchy and the region enclosed by each volume. All those points located in the sphere belong to the same node and thus the algorithm can construct the tree structure, too. Since splatting is the main rendering method and will be discussed in the next section, the rendering technique allows the progressive transmission to render the point sets in different levels with different parameters. There are several other progressive schemes proposed after that. All these are based on hierarchical data structures [7, 58, 60, 61].

2.2.5 Point Based Rendering: Splatting

The simplest way to render the point-based representation is to reconstruct the polygonal surface as mentioned in the construction section of polygonal meshes. And then the global illumination and local illumination algorithms for polygonal meshes can be used to synthesize the view.

There is another group of methods called splatting which is carefully designed to achieve high visual quality at a speed of millions of points per second without the need for special hardware support [4, 7, 62–64] (see Figure 2.14b). Splatting renders a point using a small oriented tangential patch, and the shape and size of the patch can vary according to the design of the algorithms and the local density of points. The shape and size of the patch defining the kernel function of reconstruction. The shading or color of the patch is the original sampled color modulated by the kernel function. The kernel function can be a Gaussian function or non-Gaussian kernels can be used [65]. The choice of the kernel function is basically the trade-off between rendering quality and performance. One must note that when the points sampled in the object space are projected onto the image space, the projected points do not coincide with the regular grid of the image coordinate. As a result, if the projected process is not handled properly, visual artifacts such as aliasing, undersampling, and holes might appear. Gaussian circular splatting usually performs well. Other more sophisticated non-Gaussian kernels could also be used at the cost of an increase in rendering time [65]. Even without special hardware support, current splatting techniques can achieve very high quality when rendering point-based surface models at a speed of millions of points per second.

2.2.6 Volumetric Representation

A real world object always contains a volume. Thus, the general representation should be constructed from this concept. This representation refers to parameterizing the reconstruction volume in the world reference frame. The fundamental representation is to use a unit volume called a voxel which is defined in a regular grid in the world frame. In other words a voxel corresponds to the smallest representable amount of space [66]. This is similar to the pixel which is used as a basic unit in 2D image space to represent the information in an image. The fundamental information in a voxel encodes the existence of the object which records whether the voxel is inside or outside a valid object. Empty voxels are typically not associated with any information other than a Boolean flag indicating that they are vacant. In addition, the data associated with the objects, such as color, normal, and transmission index, can also be added into each voxel. Since the voxel records the existence and object attributes, the resolution of the voxel also determines the precision of the representation. Figure 2.15 shows a teapot represented by a set of voxels. Generally, straightforward implementation of a voxel space is through a volume buffer [9] or cuberille [67] which employs a 3D array of cubic cells.

Volumetric representations are good structures for multi-view stereo techniques which reconstruct a 3D scene from multiple images taken simultaneously from different viewpoints. The representations are valuable to provide a common reference framework for the images taken from multiple viewpoints [68–70]. In addition, they also include neighborhood information. In other words, the representation provides direct access to neighboring voxels. This is efficient for the computation of stereo algorithms such as space carving [71] and voxel coloring [72] approaches, where the reconstruction result is obtained implicitly by detecting the empty voxels. The representation also can help compute local geometric properties (e.g., curvature [73]), as well as for noise-filtering of the reconstruction results.

2.2.7 Volumetric Construction

There are mainly three different methods to generate volumetric data: 3D object or medical scanning (such as CT and MRI), physical simulation, and voxelization, that is, transformation from a polygonal mesh. The first category creates the 3D content via the depth-image-based representations. The second category is the product of physical

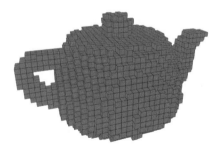

Figure 2.15   A teapot represented with voxels of a uniform size.

simulation for generating animation or mechanical design for fluid such as smoke, water, and fire as discussed in the previous animation section. The third is to transform a polygonal mesh into a volumetric representation and the procedure is called voxelization. Kaufman et al. [74] proposed the first voxelization algorithm. Generally, volumetric data stores properties of an object in a set of regular 3D grids. Voxelization strategies can be classified based on how to describe the existence of a model as surface voxelization [75–77] which uses the existence of a voxel to describe the boundary and solid voxelization [78–80] which describes the existence of the boundary and interior of the entire model. Another common classification is based on how the existence of a voxel is represented and can be described as binary [81–83] and non binary [75, 80, 83–87] voxelization approaches. The latter can be further divided into filtered voxelization [80, 87], multivalued voxelization [83, 84], object identification voxelization [75] and distance transform [85, 86]. A large amount of previous work focuses on the sampling theory involved in voxelization and rendering to generate high rendering quality by introducing well-defined filters. Thanks to the advance in GPU technology. With its powerful flexibility and programmability, real-time GPU voxelization becomes possible. Chen [88] presented a slicing-based voxelization algorithm to slice the underlying model in the frame buffer by setting appropriate clipping planes in each pass and extracting each slice of the model to form a volumetric representation. There are later several improvements [81–83, 89–92] proposed to enhance the computation efficiency and enrich the rendering effects.

2.2.8 *Volumetric Compression and Encoding for Transmission*

Although the unit-sized volumetric representation can approximate any object to any desired accuracy, it might be quite memory-inefficient in several conditions. One condition is where the objects only occupy a small portion of the world. The objects contain complex details and thus the size of the voxel for representing the detail needs to be small, that is, the required number of voxels to represent the world is huge. The representation wastes a large amount of memory for empty space. If possible, a representation should use a large volume to represent the major part of the object and a small volume to represent the detailed part of the object. A common implementation of the above idea is called an octree [93]. Their idea starts from a coarse resolution, and the coarse representation is used to detect the large empty regions and large occupied regions. Then for those regions with mixed occupied and empty regions, the volume is subdivided into eight parts of equal size. The process recursively subdivide volumes into eight parts with an equal size and terminates at a predefined resolution. The proper data structure to represent this concept is a tree that grows in depth and whose nodes correspond to occupied voxels. Octrees can exhibit greater memory efficiency over uniform-sized voxel representation and provide the advantage of both data compression and ease of implementation. At the same time, the structure also provides progressivity by first sending the coarse structure in the top levels and then progressively sending the details in the lower levels.

Because of the compression and progressivity, there are several works proposed to improve the limitation of the original octree methods. These researches include linear octrees [94], PM-octrees [95], kD-trees [96], and interval trees [97]. Conceptually, the kD-tree, a binary space-partitioning tree, is similar to the octree except that each subdivision is binary and segments the volume by a plane of arbitrary orientation. The subdivision also terminates at a predetermined threshold of spatial resolution or height. This representation can provide better memory efficiency than unit-volume representations and better flexibility than octrees. However, the limitation is that the representation is not compatible with a regular parameterization which facilitates transmission and rendering. The compression and progressivity of volumetric representations is still an active research topic.

2.2.9 Volumetric Rendering

The main advantage of volumetric representations is their linear access time, and this property makes rendering new views efficiently and the rendering cost is independent of the complexity of the object. There are already GPU-based Z-buffer rendering algorithms [46] for synthesizing new views from volumetric representations.

Furthermore, volumetric representations can be transformed to meshes first and then the meshes are rendered with the graphics pipeline or global illumination algorithms. The easiest way to render a volumetric representation is to render each voxel as a cube. The polygonal cubes are rendered with a graphics pipeline but the rendering results for those cubes which are close to the viewpoint are generally not smooth and cause poor visualization. Instead of using polygonal cubes, polygonal meshes transformed from volumetric representations can produce smoother result and are the designed primitives for the commodity graphics architecture. Therefore, there are researches such as the marching cube [98] to generate better polygonal meshes from volumetric representations in more efficient ways. However, the resulting meshes are not optimized for memory usage, and geometrical structure is still shaped as an arrangement of cubes. This causes undesired artifacts in the rendering results.

When a light ray passes through a medium, the energy of the ray is absorbed by the medium along the path. Ray marching is a volume rendering algorithm built based on this concept. The ray casting process in ray marching is illustrated in Figure 2.16. When rendering a view, the algorithm shoots out a ray through the center of each pixel. The ray traverses through several voxels and the opacity and color of the voxel are accumulated to get the final color and opacity as follows:

$$C = \sum_{i=1}^{N} C_i \prod_{j=0}^{i-1} (1 - A_j) \tag{2.2}$$

$$A = 1 - \prod_{j=1}^{N} (1 - A_j) \tag{2.3}$$

where C and A are the color and opacity of the pixel, C_i and A_i are the color and opacity of the voxel i along the ray path, and N is the total number of voxels along the ray path. The contribution of the color from the voxel is weighted with the transparency product; in other words, those voxels that show up later in the path will contribute little. When the ray shoots out of the volume or the transparency product reach zero, the accumulation is finished. A view can be synthesized by tracing all view rays as described previously.

There are more volume rendering techniques. Interested readers could refer to [37] for more details.

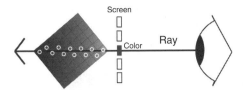

Figure 2.16 Schematic diagram of volume ray casting. A ray is cast from the eye passing through a pixel. The ray will continue to traverse through the object, and the color and transparency of voxels along the path will be accumulated to compute the color of the pixel.

2.3 3D Scene Representation without Geometry – Image-Based Representation

Geometry-based representations use geometry primitives to represent objects in the scene, the content being transmitted from the sender to the receiver, and the receiver synthesizes the views by rasterizing the primitives with computer graphics techniques. However, the need of advanced graphics hardware for rendering and the lack of realism in the synthesized views make these geometry-based methods not appropriate for 3DTV systems. Instead, original TV systems capture the real world in a single-planar-view high-definition video stream and the video can deliver realism to viewers. Thus researchers propose to extend the idea to capture the real world in a set of videos and then synthesize new views from these sets of videos in the receiver side to deliver the reality to the consumer. This idea is called image-based representation. The image-based representations are categorized into:

1. single texture techniques: a single texture can represent the appearance of an object or the entire world by a single and connected surface such as a cylinder or a plane.
2. multiple texture techniques: a multiple texture representation refers to using a set of original camera views to represent a 3D scene.

In the following, we will first give a mathematical description of the process, namely, the plenoptic function, and then we will discuss image-based representations.

2.3.1 Plenoptic Function

3DTV should be able to deliver the image content to each eye separately. Thus, we should first describe what our eyes can see, that is, what information about the world the light delivers to each eye. A dense set of light rays with various intensities at different frequencies fills the 3D space. The set of rays passing through a point in the space is mathematically described as a pencil. If a theoretical pinhole is positioned at a given point as shown in Figure 2.17, the pencil of rays reaching the retina will form an image. One eye can be simply described as a pinhole camera with the assumption that the aperture is infinitely small. Therefore, pictures can be described as capturing partial of rays in the world as shown in Figure 2.18. Let us continue this line of thought to consider the necessary parameters for describing these lighting effects. First, when the image taken

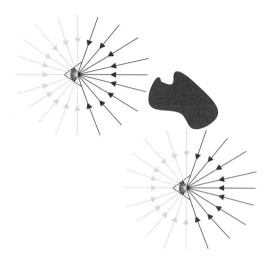

Figure 2.17 The plenoptic function describes the information available to an observer at any point in space and time. This shows two schematic eyes, which one should consider to have punctated pupils, gathering pencils of light rays. A real observer cannot see the light rays coming from behind, but the plenoptic function does include these rays.

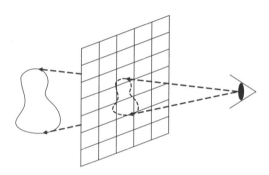

Figure 2.18 The image captures all the light rays shot from an object passing through the image.

by a pinhole camera is a gray-scale image, it gives us the averaging intensity of light over the wavelength of the visible spectrum passing through a single viewpoint at a single moment of time. In other words, it describes the intensity distribution of light rays passing through the lens and the distribution is denoted as I. The spherical coordinates, $I(\theta, \phi)$, or the Cartesian coordinates of a picture plane, $I(x, y)$, may be used to parameterize this distribution. (Figure 2.19; see discussion below).

The concept can be extended to a color image by adding an extra parameter to the intensity variation with wavelength, λ, and the description becomes $I(\theta, \phi, \lambda)$. Extending to a color video and the equation becomes $I(\theta, \phi, \lambda, t)$ by adding the time dimension, t. The equation above is used to describe the light information arrived at one point which is a specific world position. In order to describe the light arriving at any point in the world,

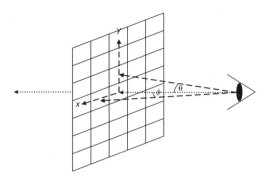

Figure 2.19   The image information available from a single viewing position is defined by the pencil of light rays passing through the pupil. The rays may be parameterized in angular coordinates or in Cartesian coordinates. The Cartesian approach is commonly used in computer vision and computer graphics, but the angular approach can more easily represent the full sphere of optical information impinging on a point in space.

the distribution function must be able to describe the observable light intensity at every viewing position (P_x, P_y, P_z) and the description becomes $I(P_x, P_y, P_z, \theta, \phi, \lambda, t)$. This is a 7D function describing all view rays at all possible positions, at all possible moments and at all possible wavelengths. Therefore, the function allows reconstruction of all possible views in the world. The function is called the plenoptic function [99] and is the fundamental equation which can be used to describe the light intensity to reach each eye. It is also fundamental for all discussion in this section. In other words the plenoptic function implicitly contains all possible spatial-temporal views of the world (neglecting the polarization and instantaneous phase of the incoming light). Since the direction of gaze implicitly aligns with the orientation of the eye, the plenoptic function need not contain the specifications of the three viewing angles. According to the plenoptic function, some rays behind the eye may be blocked. The plenoptic function is intended to describe all the optical information potentially available at each point in space, as if the hypothetical eye had a 360 degree field of view. Figure 2.17 shows two possible examples from this function, with the eye placed at different positions in a scene. Thus, the plenoptic function can be measured by placing an ideal pinhole camera at all possible positions, (P_x, P_y, P_z), to record the intensity of the light rays arriving at all possible direction, (θ, ϕ), in terms of all wavelengths, λ, at every time t. The simplest setting is to let the pinhole camera always look at the z-axis of the world. The resulting function takes the form:

$$i = I\left(P_x, P_y, P_z, \theta, \phi, \lambda, t\right) \qquad (2.4)$$

where (P_x, P_y, P_z) is any position in 3D space, (θ, ϕ) is the arriving direction, t is the measurement moment, and λ is the frequency of the measurement. Thus, the equation describes the intensity of light rays with frequency, λ, reaching the position of (P_x, P_y, P_z) at the direction of (θ, ϕ) at time t. (θ, ϕ) is hard to define in the 3D space. Therefore, alternatively, the ray direction may be parameterized as the passing image (x, y) coordinates, where x and y are the spatial coordinates of an imaginary picture plane erected at a unit distance from the pupil. This is a commonly adopted approach in the graphics and vision community. The newly parameterized equations becomes:

$$i = I\left(P_x, P_y, P_z, x, y, \lambda, t\right) \tag{2.5}$$

where (P_x, P_y, P_z) is any position in 3D space, (x, y) is the pixel position in the image, t is the measurement moment, and λ is the frequency of the measurement. Thus, the equation describes the intensity of light rays with frequency, λ, reaching the position of (P_x, P_y, P_z) through the pixel of (x, y) at time t.

These two parameterization methods have their own advantages and disadvantages. The spherical parameterization more easily describes the fact that the light passes through a given position in 3D space from all directions at any moment of time. All directions are the same. However, the Cartesian parameterization is more familiar to users and more suitable to the current architecture and picture format and thus the following discussion will follow the Cartesian parameterization.

The plenoptic function is an idealized concept and cannot really be used to describe all possible rays in the world. Obviously it is impossible to record all this 7D light information from every possible point of view, for every wavelength, at every moment of time in the world, but the significance of the plenoptic function is to link the physical objects in the world with their corresponding images taken by a pinhole camera.

Image-based representation is to record the sparse sampling of the plenoptic function in a set of videos and try to synthesize the new view from the set of samples. Image-based rendering uses the view interpolation technique to reconstruct the plenoptic function [99] from the existing views.

The problem becomes how to recover the plenoptic function to allow us to synthesize the view from the set of images. Texturing 3D geometric objects is essential for realistic rendering in 3DTV applications. The texture of a real object is usually extracted from a set of images that capture the surface of the object from various angles. These images can either be processed and merged into a single texture representation or stored separately to be used as multi-textures.

2.3.2 Single Texture Representation

Single texture representation may use a single connected area or several isolated areas to represent the appearance of the surfaces in the scene or the object surface. The single connected area can be a 2D plane or a spherical surface and the true object surface is transformed to the representation. The connected representation is easily coded and transmitted along with the surface geometry information and eventually mapped onto the surfaces during rendering. They can be compressed more efficiently due to the high correlation among neighboring pixels but they cannot be generalized to represent objects with arbitrary topology. Therefore, Hndrik et al. [100] propose the usage of several isolated areas for each part of a 3D object. Figure 2.20 gives an example of using a texture atlas in a single texture for modeling the appearance of an object with no topology limitation. However, the compression is less efficient because of limited correlation. The representation of both methods must be static in terms of different lighting and reflection effects during navigation, which is a limitation of these representations. There are a

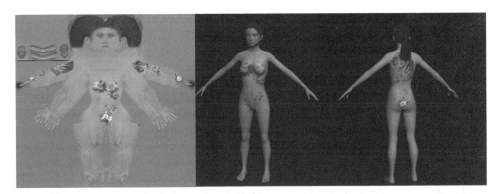

Figure 2.20 This demonstrates a concept of single object with multiple patches. The girl's body is textured with two patches of texture.

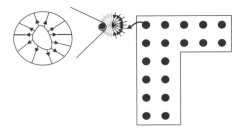

Figure 2.21 This demonstrates the grid points for an indoor scene of QuickTime VR. The black dots at the right are the positions of bubbles which represent the looking outward views. The bubble points may contain a hot point for interesting objects as shown in the left corner represented by looking inward views.

large number of applications available in computer graphics and computer vision. In the followings, we give two famous examples that apply this concept:

1. **QuickTime VR**

   As shown in Figure 2.21, there are two possible viewing situations: looking outward and looking inward.

   - **Looking outward** condition assumes that all interesting objects are far away and thus the center view can be used to approximate the view.
   - **Looking inward** assumes that the object is at the center and the blocking condition does not happen.

   This concept is good for a navigation system in a closed environment such as a museum. The first step is to lay down a grid for a possible hub in the possible navigation areas. After laying down the grid points, at each point a set of images will be taken using a panoramic tripod to ensure the seamless stitching. In addition the designers also lay down the hot spots for the interesting objects which are taken using a sphere looking inward method. Then the bubbles and hot spots are oriented and recorded in the disk space in the QuickTime format. During navigation, the users use the control means to hop around the grid points and allow changes of the view direction. The grid position is used to retrieve the proper bubbles and the direction is used to synthesize the new view from the bubble for navigation. When the user would like to see the hot spot, the inward sphere texture is extracted and the view direction of the user is also used to synthesize the new views. Basically, the construction of image-based representations uses a special camera setting. For QuickTime VR applications, the looking outward configuration uses a camera array with several cameras looking out as shown in Figure 2.22b and the inward texture is captured with an infrastructure with a camera to shoot for the object with proper lighting for the entire shooting process as shown in Figure 2.22a. The idea is to use one camera to capture a part of the entire hemispherical view of the world. All images captured by the camera array are combined with stitching algorithms [101–104] and commercial applications [105–107]. Interested readers can refer to [104] for more details about the stitching methods.

2. **Google street**

   This is an extension to QuickTime VR. In addition to laying down a grid in the space, Google lays down the grid points in the world using a set of special equipment which consists of a car, a panorama camera and a GPS. The panorama camera sits on the top of a car and the car is driven on the street in a city. The GPS and the city map are incorporated to lay down the grid points and align all the bubbles together in the world. During navigation, the user is walking on the destination path which is the vehicle's driving path. In addition to hopping between the bubbles, the system uses the zoom-in and zoom-out synthesis to simulate the driving effects.

2.3.3 Multiple Texture Representation

Texture mapping means that a colored pixel map is assigned to the 3D surface. The simplest way is to assign a single still image as the texture. However, this leads to poor rendering results. In reality, natural materials look different from different viewing angles depending on reflectance properties, micro-structures, and lighting conditions. It is not possible to reproduce these properties by a single texture that looks the same from any direction. The promising solutions are to incorporate it with image-based rendering. The idea is to describe the real world by a set of images from multiple views instead of

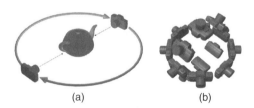

(a)   (b)

Figure 2.22 (a) This shows an object shooting scheme which consists of a camera rotating around the object and a set of light sources to provide consistent lighting conditions during shooting. (b) This shows a bubble shooting camera array whose cameras shoot outward to capture the entire world.

graphical 3D models. View-dependent texture mapping, depending on the actual view direction, is a realistic texture which can reproduce natural appearance calculated from the available original views. Multiple texture techniques give objects that include the environmental effects as they appear in the original camera view. Surface light fields combine a classical 3D mesh representation with the concept of a light-field rendering. In computer graphics, multiple texturing is a technique which can add environmental and illumination effects to generate a more realistic appearance of an object. These effects include reflections, refractions, caustics, color bleeding and so on. Each special effect is represented as an artificially generated texture and is auxiliary to the original texture of the object. However, multiple texturing refers to a set of images of a 3D object taken from the original camera views in mutli-camera scenarios in computer vision [108]. In other words, the set of images is the sampling representative of the plenoptic function described previously. The view of the object is to synthesize the result from the set of samples. Hence, the quality of the rendered result mainly depends on the number of camera views, resolution of the images, and the interpolation strategy between original views. In the following, we discuss two popular techniques in the computer graphics community and possibly important for the 3DTV system:

1. **Light field or lumigraph**
   The radiance of a light ray passing through two points will be the same if there are no occlusion objects between the two points. Thus, we can enclose the objects with two planes as shown in Figure 2.23. The light ray can be expressed as (u, v, s, t). This simple representation is called a light field or lumigraph, which is a 4D simplification of the plenoptic function as described in Equation (2.5). The light field [109] and the lumigraph [110] are developed independently. Generally, the light fields are often sampled by using large camera arrays consisting of 4×4 or 5×5 cameras arranged in a simple plane. This results in a set of high resolution camera views from these cameras. Virtual views are synthesized from the parameterized representation shown in Figure 2.23 that uses coordinates of the intersection points of light rays with two known surfaces. The views in the center are interpolated linearly [109] or using the basis interpolation method [110]. This method is originally designed for capturing all lighting effects of static objects and can be easily extended to include the time dimension, which is essential for 3DTV applications by recording the videos from each

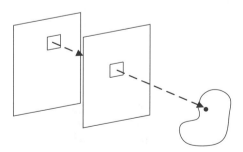

Figure 2.23   This demonstrates the parametrization in a light field. Two planes (u, v) and (s, t) are used to parameterize all possible rays shot from the object in a space.

camera instead of images. The most critical problem for dynamic light field methods is the large volume of data. Thus, efficient data compression is important for the success of the algorithm [111, 112]. However, the research direction in light field rendering leans toward using more sparsely arranged cameras and additional scene information, such as geometric proxies; this obviously leads to other scene representation methods.

2. **Multiple view images**

   Generally a 3DTV system only provides different view directions in the horizontal direction but not in the vertical direction because of the general environment setting. Thus, the general camera is lined up along a baseline which is the line passing through all camera centers as shown in Figure 2.24. All cameras are synchronized to take the shots in videos. The videos are delivered to the receiver side. Rendering is first to position the virtual camera and project the virtual camera view in the coordinate where the original camera array takes. For the rendering of a particular display view, the closest view is selected out of the N available camera views as a first step. Then, the virtual view is synthesized from the two closest cameras by view morphing. The virtual view is then de-rectified such that it fits into the 3D display geometry again. However, using interpolation of color information from multiple views to synthesize new views results in a disocclusion recovery problem as shown in Figure 2.25. Since two views see different scene points, a point in an object observed by one camera may not be observed by another camera, which results in the occlusion of objects. In order to overcome this occlusion problem, more views must be added to remove the possibility of occlusion. Theoretically, if the number of views provided goes to infinity, the quality of the synthesized view will be improved accordingly. The main

Figure 2.24 A simple diagram of a line camera array. All the view directions of the cameras are parallel to each other and the camera centers are on a line.

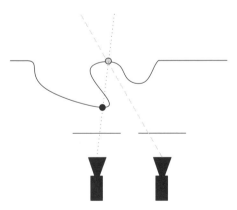

Figure 2.25 An example of occlusion when two parallel cameras shot at the scene. The point shown in gray can be seen by the right camera but cannot be seen by the left camera.

advantage of the multi-view video method is a realistic synthesized view with high quality without the need for 3D scene reconstruction. In addition, the rendering time is proportional to the number of pixels synthesized in the output images, the number of reference images, and the number of pixels from each reference image checked, and it is independent of the complexity of geometry such as primitive count in the polygonal case. This makes photorealistic rendering of a natural scene in real time possible without the need for expensive computation for rendering millions of polygons. However, this method has limitations in the possible range of changes in view direction and movement, and the quality of synthesized view depends on the number of captured views, the resolution of each view, and the scene depth variation. This leads to the need for plenty of original view images, that is, a large number of cameras has to be set up to achieve high-performance rendering, and plenty of image data needs to be processed. Therefore, conversely, if the number of cameras used is too low, interpolation and occlusion artifacts will appear in the synthesized image, possibly affecting the quality. The number of views needed to overcome the quality and occlusion problem in multi-view video methods makes the graphics community data, add some geometry information with depth data, as well as adding more flexibility in rendering and interpolation. The video-plus-depth method will be described in the next section.

2.3.4 Image Based Animation

Image-based representations give the reality of the world to the viewers by directly capturing the real world, but this also causes the largest limitation on dynamically animating the content. This is because, when the content in the images are shot, the lighting conditions, object relations, and other rendering conditions are fixed at that moment. Therefore, the reasonable and plausible animation to the content is to manipulate the viewing position, direction, and other viewing conditions using proper interpolation of the textures. This is because a camera is generally modeled as a point and does not affect any lighting condition, that is, changing viewing condition does not affect the content in the texture. However, even with this limitation, image-based representations can still satisfy the need for free view 3DTV systems. Interactivity for future 3DTV systems may require further interaction with the content. Generally, the interaction with the content is still difficult and therefore the main research focus is on adding virtual objects into the texture and rendering with image-based and geometry-based algorithms. The interaction and rendering technique is categorized as augmented reality. Interested readers can refer to [113] for more details.

2.4 3D Scene Representation with Implicit Geometry – Depth-Image-Based Representation

In the previous two sections, we study the geometry-based and image-based representations of 3D scenes. However, we also learn the limitations in each category. Rendering the geometry-based scenes in real time requires expensive hardware and the achieved level of realism is still far below human expectation. Image-based methods encounter the synthesized artifacts problem during the new stereoscopic view generation process, which limits the interactivity. Knowing the pros and cons of each representation, 3D scene representations with implicit geometry (known as depth-image-based representations) are proposed to take advantages from both geometry-based and image-based representations. In other words, it's a hybrid method to include the necessary information from both methods to synthesize new views for 3DTV systems. In this section, we briefly introduce the general concept of depth-image-based representations and provide an overview of depth construction methods which serve as the fundamentals in depth-image-based representations. The details about the construction will be given in Chapter 4 and the compression and encoding and rendering detail will be discussed in Chapter 5.

2.4.1 History of Depth-Image-Based Representation

In early 1990s, all the proposed 3DTV systems were based on the concept of delivering stereoscopic videos, that is, capturing, transmitting, and displaying two separate video streams to two eyes. As a result, the display geometry must be suitable for capturing stereo videos and vice versa. The cameraman must consider display properties, viewing conditions, and other related factors [109] during the shooting process. For example, when shooting two separate videos, the cameraman must consider whether human visual systems can merge these two separate views into a stereoscopic view. All these constraints make 3D production extremely complicated. Therefore, researchers concluded that it is necessary to separate the capturing and display geometry processes by using new technologies from computer vision, 3D video processing, and image-based rendering. However, image-based rendering has limitations in the size of transferred data and the artifacts in the synthesized views. Thus, the European PANORAMA project proposed to use an implicit geometry-based stereo adaptation and demonstrated the feasibility and the potential of implicit geometry-based systems in 1998. Originally PANORAMA was designed for stereoscopic video conferencing. Later, ATTEST proposed to use the same depth-image-based concept for fulfilling the requirements of a 3DTV processing pipeline. The ATTEST system transmits both regular image videos and depth map videos providing the implicit geometry information using a Z-value for each pixel. The data format is often called depth-image-based representation (see Figure 2.26). At the receiver end, depth-image-based rendering (DIBR) techniques are used to synthesize the two stereoscopic images. The ATTEST system demonstrates the major advantages of depth-image-based 3DTV systems over image-based 3DTV systems. These advantages include the ability to adapt for different viewing conditions, user preferences, and the properties of a 3D display device, efficient compression capabilities and the backward compatibility to the current 2D services for digital video broadcast (DVB). The following two reasons make the depth image-based representations a widely accepted technology for 3DTV systems:

- the compatibility to the existing DVB infrastructure
- the flexibility in terms of interoperability and scalability.

This trend is shown at IBC 2003 in Amsterdam, SIGGRAPH 2004 in Los Angeles [24] and IFA 2005 in Berlin [114]. Additionally, MPEG also formed a group to standardize the depth image-based format needed in 3DTV [115]. Clearly, there are more groups targeting the market of near-future 3DTV services. The Digital Cinema Technology

(a)   (b)

Figure 2.26   This demonstrates an example of image and depth maps of a real scene computed with [116].

Committee (DC28) of the Society of Motion Picture and Television Engineers (SMPTE) also standardized the format for 3DTV [117] and this pushed the publication of Avatar and the popularity of 3D movies since 2010. The advances in DVB and 3DTV hardware technologies, especially in the auto-stereoscopic 3D displays, make interactive 3DTV become future innovative entertainment services. Thus, all these demonstrate that the depth image-based representation is a strong candidate used in the video-stream representation for 3DTV systems.

2.4.2   Fundamental Concept Depth-Image-Based Representation

The main idea is to decouple the camera and the display geometry by deriving depth maps from capturing videos or images. This color and geometry decoupling strategy gives the high flexibility and adaptability at the receiver side. Fundamentally, the depth information can be estimated from a given stereo or multi-view video and will be shortly previewed in this section. More details will be discussed in Chapter 4. The color and depth information is delivered to the receiver and used to resynthesize a virtual stereo pair according to the viewer's condition and preference. This gives the perfect adaptability for display properties and related viewing conditions. Therefore, currently 3D content representations are usually based on the distribution of a single video plus the corresponding depth map for the central view to the receiver [118, 119]. The delivered content gives us the flexibility to compose stereoscopic images in real time at the receiver side. This concept also provides the backward compatibility to the original DVB system by encoding the monoscopic color video stream and the auxiliary depth information using the standard MPEG video coding tools [5, 120, 121] and the new MPEG H.264/AVC standard [5]. This allows 3DTV services to be built on the conventional 2D DVB system with a minor transmission overhead of about 10% for depth maps. It also means that the stereoscopic imagery is only generated during rendering at the receiver side and this allows for adapting the depth experience to different 3D displays and viewing conditions as well as to the user individual preferences [119]. An image can be generated by sampling the color for each pixel when looking through the pixel and intersecting the scene and then recording the image as shown in Figure 2.26. At the sampling points the color is gained according to the color appearance at that point and then all color information is recorded in a color map. The depth map is an extension to the color map. Additionally, the depth map is to record the depth information which is the value of the distance from the intersection point projected to the z-axis in the camera coordinate. Figure. 2.27 demonstrates the concept of synthesizing a new view at the receiver side for a virtual stereo setup used for view and display adaptation. As shown in Figure 2.27 the black dot is the real scene point in the original view, and the image in the new view can be synthesized by projecting the black dot into the new view.

According to the discussion in the previous paragraphs, disocclusion or exposure [122, 123] is an inherent drawback in the depth image-based representations. Disocclusion happens as shown in Fig 2.25 when the areas which are occluded in the original view become visible in the virtual views. Since the information about the originally hidden parts is missed from the transmitted monoscopic color videos and depth maps, the missing regions must be filled in with some smart mechanisms. These mechanisms include preprocessing (smoothing) the original depth data with a 2D Gaussian low-pass filter in order to avoid the appearance of holes, or interpolation from neighborhood pixels around the hole. For synthesized views with a relatively small amount of parallax [119], the filtering and interpolation methods can generate perceptually acceptable results. However, when depth effects are large or head-motion parallax (HMP) is involved, the image quality is generally not good enough. Thus, similar to multi-view coding (MVC), some systems proposed to use multiple depth image-based representations to overcome this limitation. In Chapter 5, we will discuss potential solutions to transmit this information efficiently.

2.4.2.1   Layer Depth Images

Depth-image-based representations can synthesize new views with high fidelity with a limited number of views transmitted through the network. However, color and depth information of all these views is transmitted at the same time, so the data rate will be huge. As a result, the concept of layered depth images (LDI) is proposed by Shade et al. [9] to solve this issue. Figure 2.28 shows a schematic example of different representations

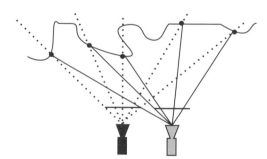

Figure 2.27   This illustrates the concept of the depth-image-based representation. The black camera represents the original view and black dots denote the scene position captured by the original camera. The gray camera represents the virtual view and all black dots are projected onto the image plane of the virtual camera.

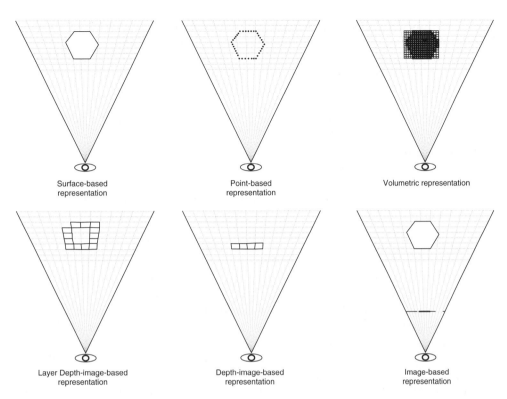

Figure 2.28 This uses a hexagon as an example to illustrate the concepts and data recorded for surface-based (discussed in Section 2.2.1), point-based (Section 2.2.2), volume-based (Section 2.2.6), layer-depth image-based (Section 2.4.2.1), depth-image-based (Section 2.4), and image-based (Section 2.3) representations. In the surface-based representation, six edges are represented as solid lines are used in the top-left. In the point-based representation, a set of points is represented as solid dots along the six edges in the top-middle. In the volume-based representation, a set of voxels is represented as solid-line squares inside the hexagon in the top-right. In the layer-depth representation, a set of intersections is represented as solid-line quadrilaterals along the intersection of view rays from the eye and all hexagon edges in the bottom-left. The intersections are recorded in the link list for each pixel with the values of color and depth. In the depth-image-based representation, a set of pixels is represented as solid-line quadrilaterals along the intersection of view rays and the front-face edges of the hexagon in the bottom-middle. The intersections are recorded at each pixel with the values of color and depth. In the image-based representation, a set of pixels is represented as a solid line on the image plane in the bottom-right.

discussed previously in this section to compare the difference. A 3D scene (or object) in LDI is represented using a texture grid whose pixels contain a set of depth values from the main view and projected from the other view and the corresponding color information. The center of all views is generally chosen as the reference view and the depth plus image of the other views would be projected into this view. After projection, the depth of each projection point is compared against the reference depth value. If the depth value is larger than the reference, the projected point is behind the current reference point and LDI will record this extra projection point's depth and color information. In this way, LDI can record the difference between projection and the camera result as residual information. This residual information consists of disoccluded information, and is therefore mainly concentrated along depth discontinuities of foreground objects as well as image boundary data in both side views. When the compressed streams are received, the view synthesis consists of the following two fundamental steps:

1. **Layer projection:** the central view is projected onto the intermediate view to synthesize the new view using DIBR.
2. **Intermediate view enhancement:** fill the holes and cracks and filter the foreground objects to provide a natural appearance.

In this way, instead of sending all the images and depths, we only need to send one complete image and depth plus a residual depth and image information. This can reduce the amount of data transmitted [124]. The algorithms particularly take care of aspects of interoperability and multi-view adaptation for different baseline geometries used in multi-view capturing and rendering for 3DTV systems. There are more advanced solutions for creation of depth maps and depth image-based rendering related to multi-view adaptation needed in 3DTV system.

Similar to multiple-view depth-image-based methods, the number of original views and camera settings decides the navigation range and synthesized quality. Because LDI can save a large amount of storage space, layered depth video [114, 125, 126] is proposed to reduce the raw data rate for 3DTV drastically. On the other hand, since LDI is an extension to depth-image-based representations, reliable dense-depth extraction is still a problem in LDI. There is another serious boundary problem which often arises at depth discontinuities such as object boundaries or corners. Alpha-matting blends the depth values along the object boundary. When the discontinuity regions are identified, alpha-matting can be applied over those regions to significantly improve the output [127]. Therefore, to deploy a LDI-based representation, it is better to add an extra step, layer extraction, before the layer projection step. The layer extraction step uses edge detection to separate the image into reliable regions such as foreground, background, and boundary regions. The details are also discussed in Chapter 5.

2.4.3 Depth Construction

3D scanners mainly estimate the distance from the scanner to the point on the surface, and the distance can be directly transformed to the depth. The main research interests are in the reconstruction of depth using noncontact passive 3D scanners. Noncontact passive 3D scanners transform one or a set of 3D videos to 3D depth-image-based representations and thus the techniques are also called 2D to 3D conversion. Generally the algorithms can be categorized as:

1. **two or more images:** two or more images are taken either by multiple cameras or by a single camera with the movement of the camera and objects. The depth cues are called multi-ocular depth cues.
2. **single image:** the image is taken from a single camera by single shot. The depth cues are called monocular depth cues.

2.4.4 Depth-Image-Based Animation

Since the depth-image-based representations improve the image-based representation, they can give the reality of the world to the viewers by directly capturing the real world but they are also limited to generating the plausible and reasonable animation for changing viewpoints. This limitation does not affect their applications to current 3DTV systems. However, providing interactivity in depth-image-based representations is still a hot research topic. Because of the existence of depth maps, the interaction among captured content and adding virtual objects is easily defined and simulated and thus the augmented reality operations generally are designed to process in this representation. However, there is still a long way to go to achieve sufficient interactivity for interactive 3DTV systems.

References

1. P. Heckbert. "Survey of Texture Mapping". *Computer Graphics and Applications, IEEE*, vol. 6, no. 11, pp. 56–67, November 1986.
2. S. Kang. "A Survey of Image-based Rendering Techniques". In: *Proc. SPIE*, pp. 395–302, 1999.
3. M. M. Oliveira, G. Bishop, and D. McAllister. "Relief texture mapping". In: *Proceedings of the 27th annual conference on computer graphics and interactive techniques*, pp. 359–368, 2000.
4. H. Pfister, M. Zwicker, J. van Baar, and M. Gross. "Surfels: surface elements as rendering primitives". In: *Proceedings of the 27th annual conference on computer graphics and interactive techniques*, pp. 335–342, 2000.
5. ISO/IEC14496. "ISO/IEC JTC 1/SC 29/WG 11, Information technology coding of audio-visual objects–part 2: advanced video coding, ISO/IEC 14496–10:2004, May 2004.". 2004.
6. M. Levoy and T. Whitted. "The Use of Points as a Display Primitive". Technical Report 85–022, University of North Carolina at Chapel Hill, 1985.
7. S. Rusinkiewicz and M. Levoy. "QSplat: a multiresolution point rendering system for large meshes". In: *Proceedings of the 27th annual conference on Computer graphics and interactive techniques*, pp. 343–352, 2000.
8. G. Schaufler, J. Dorsey, X. Decoret, and F. Sillion. "Conservative volumetric visibility with occluder fusion". In: *SIGGRAPH '00: Proceedings of the 27th annual conference on computer graphics and interactive techniques*, pp. 229–238, ACM Press/Addison-Wesley Publishing Co., New York, NY, USA, 2000.
9. J. Shade, S. Gortler, L.-w. He, and R. Szeliski. "Layered depth images". In: *Proceedings of the 25th annual conference on computer graphics and interactive techniques*, pp. 231–242, ACM, 1998.
10. R. Parent. *Computer Animation, Second Edition: Algorithms and Techniques*. Morgan Kaufmann Publishers Inc., San Francisco, CA, USA, 2nd Ed., 2007.
11. J. C. Platt and A. H. Barr. "Constraints methods for flexible models". *SIGGRAPH Comput. Graph.*, vol. 22, pp. 279–288, June 1988.
12. A. Witkin and D. Baraff. "Physically-Based Modeling". In: *SIGGRAPH 2001 Course Notes* 2001.
13. A. Witkin and M. Kass. "Spacetime constraints". *SIGGRAPH Comput. Graph.*, vol. 22, pp. 159–168, June 1988.
14. C. Smith. *On Vertex-Vertex Systems and Their Use in Geometric and Biological Modelling*. PhD thesis, University of Calgary, 2006.
15. F. Bernardini and H. Rushmeier. "The 3D Model Acquisition Pipeline". *Computer Graphics Forum*, vol. 21, no. 2, pp. 149–172, 2002.
16. B. Curless. "From range scans to 3D models". *SIGGRAPH Comput. Graph.*, vol. 33, pp. 38–41, November 1999.
17. M. Garland and P. S. Heckbert. "Surface simplification using quadric error metrics". In: *Proceedings of the 24th annual conference on Computer graphics and interactive techniques*, pp. 209–216, 1997.
18. H. Hoppe. "Progressive meshes". In: *Proceedings of the 23rd annual conference on computer graphics and interactive techniques*, pp. 99–108, 1996.

19. H. Hoppe. "View-dependent refinement of progressive meshes". In: *Proceedings of the 24th annual conference on computer graphics and interactive techniques*, pp. 189–198, 1997.
20. J. Popović and H. Hoppe. "Progressive simplicial complexes". In: *Proceedings of the 24th annual conference on computer graphics and interactive techniques*, pp. 217–224, 1997.
21. G. Taubin, A. Guéziec, W. Horn, and F. Lazarus. "Progressive forest split compression". In: *Proceedings of the 25th annual conference on computer graphics and interactive techniques*, pp. 123–132, 1998.
22. A. Guéziec, F. Bossen, G. Taubin, and C. Silva. "Efficient Compression of Non-Manifold Polygonal Meshes". In: *Proceedings of the 10th IEEE Visualization 1999 Conference (VIS '99)*, pp. 73–512, 1999.
23. R. Pajarola, I. C. Society, and J. Rossignac. "Compressed Progressive Meshes". *IEEE Transactions on Visualization and Computer Graphics*, vol. 6, pp. 79–93, 2000.
24. S. Kircher and M. Garland. "Progressive multiresolution meshes for deforming surfaces". In: *Proceedings of the 2005 ACM SIGGRAPH/Eurographics symposium on Computer animation*, pp. 191–200, 2005.
25. B. T. Phong. "Illumination for computer generated pictures". *Commun. ACM*, Vol. 18, pp. 311–317, June 1975.
26. J. T. Kajiya. "The rendering equation". In: *SIGGRAPH '86*, pp. 143–150, 1986.
27. H. Gouraud. "Continuous Shading of Curved Surfaces". *Computers, IEEE Transactions on*, vol. C-20, no. 6, pp. 623–629, June 1971.
28. J. F. Blinn. "Models of light reflection for computer synthesized pictures". *SIGGRAPH Comput. Graph.*, vol. 11, pp. 192–198, July 1977.
29. N. Greene. "Environment Mapping and Other Applications of World Projections". *Computer Graphics and Applications, IEEE*, vol. 6, no. 11, pp. 21–29, 1986.
30. M. Kilgard. "A Practical and Robust Bump-mapping Technique for Today's GPUs". In: *Game Developers Conference*, pp. 143–150, 2000.
31. C. M. Goral, K. E. Torrance, D. P. Greenberg, and B. Battaile. "Modeling the interaction of light between diffuse surfaces". In: *SIGGRAPH '84: Proceedings of the 11th Annual Conference on Computer Graphics and Interactive Techniques*, pp. 213–222, 1984.
32. A. S. Glassner. *An Introduction to Ray Tracing*. Academic Press, 1989.
33. T. Whitted. "An improved illumination model for shaded display". *Commun. ACM*, Vol. 23, No. 6, pp. 343–349, 1980.
34. E. P. Lafortune and Y. D. Willems. "Bi-Directional Path Tracing". In: *Proceedings of third international conference on computational graphics and visualization techniques (Computer Graphics Proceeding '93)*, pp. 145–153, 1993.
35. E. Veach and L. J. Guibas. "Metropolis Light Transport". In: *SIGGRAPH '97*, pp. 65–76, 1997.
36. H. W. Jensen. *Realistic Image Synthesis Using Photon Mapping*. AK Peters, 2001.
37. T. Akenine-Möller, E. Haines, and N. Hoffman. *Real-Time Rendering 3rd Edition*. A. K. Peters, Ltd, Natick, MA, USA, 2008.
38. M. Pharr and G. Humphreys. *Physically-Based Rendering from Theory to Implementation*. Morgan Kaufmann, 2nd Ed., 2004.
39. L. Piegl and W. Tiller. *The NURBS Book (Monographs in Visual Communication)*. Springer-Verlag, New York, 1997.
40. P. J. Schneider. "NURBS curves: A guide for the uninitiated". Tech. Rep. 25, Apple Tech., 1996.
41. M. Eck and H. Hoppe. "Automatic reconstruction of B-spline surfaces of arbitrary topological type". In: *Proceedings of the 23rd annual conference on computer graphics and interactive techniques*, pp. 325–334, 1996.
42. V. Krishnamurthy and M. Levoy. "Fitting smooth surfaces to dense polygon meshes". In: *Proceedings of the 23rd annual conference on computer graphics and interactive techniques*, pp. 313–324, 1996.
43. D. R. Forsey and R. H. Bartels. "Surface fitting with hierarchical splines". *ACM Trans. Graph.*, vol. 14, pp. 134–161, April 1995.
44. F. J. M. Schmitt, B. A. Barsky, and W.-h. Du. "An adaptive subdivision method for surface-fitting from sampled data". *SIGGRAPH Comput. Graph.*, vol. 20, pp. 179–188, August 1986.
45. J. Stam. "Exact evaluation of Catmull-Clark subdivision surfaces at arbitrary parameter values". In: *Proceedings of the 25th annual conference on computer graphics and interactive techniques*, pp. 395–404, 1998.
46. E. E. Catmull. *A subdivision algorithm for computer display of curved surfaces*. PhD thesis, The University of Utah, 1974. AAI7504786.

47. D. Zorin, P. Schröder, and W. Sweldens. "Interpolating Subdivision for meshes with arbitrary topology". In: *Proceedings of the 23rd annual conference on computer graphics and interactive techniques*, pp. 189–192, 1996.
48. D. Doo and M. Sabin. *Behaviour of recursive division surfaces near extraordinary points*, pp. 177–181. ACM, 1998.
49. C. Loop. *Smooth Subdivision Surfaces Based on Triangles*. Master's thesis, Univ. of Utah, 1987.
50. L. Kobbelt. "Interpolatory Subdivision on Open Quadrilateral Nets with Arbitrary Topology". In: *Computer Graphics Forum*, pp. 409–420, 1996.
51. U. Reif. "A unified approach to subdivision algorithms near extraordinary vertices". *Computer Aided Geometric Design*, vol. 10, pp. 153–174, March 1995.
52. D. Zorin, P. Schröder, and W. Sweldens. "Interactive multiresolution mesh editing". In: *Proceedings of the 24th annual conference on computer graphics and interactive techniques*, pp. 259–268, 1997.
53. A. Lee, H. Moreton, and H. Hoppe. "Displaced subdivision surfaces". In: *Proceedings of the 27th annual conference on computer graphics and interactive techniques*, pp. 85–94, 2000.
54. A. Khodakovsky, P. Schröder, and W. Sweldens. "Progressive geometry compression". In: *Proceedings of the 27th annual conference on computer graphics and interactive techniques*, pp. 271–278, 2000.
55. M. Lounsbery, T. D. DeRose, and J. Warren. "Multiresolution analysis for surfaces of arbitrary topological type". *ACM Trans. Graph.*, Vol. 16, pp. 34–73, January 1997.
56. J. P. Grossman and W. J. Dally. "Point Sample Rendering". In: *In Rendering Techniques 98*, pp. 181–192, Springer, 1998.
57. R. Szeliski and D. Tonnesen. "Surface modeling with oriented particle systems". *SIGGRAPH Comput. Graph.*, vol. 26, pp. 185–194, July 1992.
58. Y. Yemez and F. Schmitt. "Multilevel representation and transmission of real objects with progressive octree particles". *Visualization and Computer Graphics, IEEE Transactions on*, vol. 9, no. 4, pp. 551–569, October–December 2003.
59. Y. Yemez and F. Schmitt. "Progressive multilevel meshes from octree particles". In: *Proc. Int. Conf. 3-D Digital Imaging and Modeling*, pp. 290–299, 1999.
60. S. Fleishman, D. Cohen-Or, M. Alexa, and C. T. Silva. "Progressive point set surfaces". *ACM Trans. Graph.*, vol. 22, pp. 997–1011, October 2003.
61. S. Rusinkiewicz and M. Levoy. "Streaming QSplat: a viewer for networked visualization of large, dense models". In: *Proceedings of the 2001 symposium on interactive 3D graphics*, pp. 63–68, 2001.
62. M. Botsch, A. Wiratanaya, and L. Kobbelt. "Efficient high quality rendering of point sampled geometry". In: *Proceedings of the 13th Eurographics workshop on Rendering*, pp. 53–64, ubEurographics Association, Aire-la-Ville, Switzerland, Switzerland, 2002.
63. M. Zwicker, H. Pfister, J. van Baar, and M. Gross. "Surface splatting". In: *Proceedings of the 28th annual conference on computer graphics and interactive techniques*, pp. 371–378, 2001.
64. M. Zwicker, J. Räsänen, M. Botsch, C. Dachsbacher, and M. Pauly. "Perspective accurate splatting". In: *Proceedings of Graphics Interface 2004*, pp. 247–254, 2004.
65. R. Pajarola, M. Sainz, and P. Guidotti. "Confetti: Object-space point blending and splatting". *IEEE Transactions on Visualization and Computer Graphics*, vol. 10, pp. 598–608, 2004.
66. M. W. Jones and R. Satherley. "Voxelisation: Modelling for volume graphics". *In: Vision, Modeling, and Visualisation 2000*, pp. 319–326, 2000.
67. J. Foley, A. van Dam, S. Feiner, and J. Hughes. *Computer Graphics: Principles and Practice, second edition*. Addison-Wesley Professional, 1990.
68. M. G. Brian, B. Curless, and S. M. Seitz. "Multi-View Stereo Revisited". In: *In CVPR*, pp. 2402–2409, 2006.
69. B. Curless and M. Levoy. "A volumetric method for building complex models from range images". In: *Proceedings of the 23rd annual conference on computer graphics and interactive techniques*, pp. 303–312, 1996.
70. X. Zabulis and K. Daniilidis. "Multi-camera reconstruction based on surface normal estimation and best viewpoint selection". In: *2nd International Symposium on 3D Data Processing, Visualization and Transmission, 2004. 3DPVT 2004. Proceedings*. pp. 733–740, September 2004.
71. K. N. Kutulakos and S. M. Seitz. "A Theory of Shape by Space Carving". *Int. J. Comput. Vision*, vol. 38, pp. 199–218, July 2000.
72. W. B. Culbertson, T. Malzbender, and G. G. Slabaugh. "Generalized Voxel Coloring". In: *Proceedings of the International Workshop on Vision Algorithms: Theory and Practice*, pp. 100–115, 2000.

73. G. Kamberov and G. Kamberova. "Topology and geometry of unorganized point clouds". In: *2nd International Symposium on 3D Data Processing, Visualization and Transmission, 2004. 3DPVT 2004. Proceedings*. pp. 743–750, September 2004.

74. A. Kaufman and E. Shimony. "3D scan-conversion algorithms for voxel-based graphics". In: *Proceedings of the 1986 Workshop on Interactive 3D Graphics*, pp. 45–75, ACM, New York, NY, USA, 1987.

75. J. Huang, R. Yagel, V. Filippov, and Y. Kurzion. "An accurate method for voxelizing polygon meshes". In: *Proceedings of the 1998 IEEE symposium on volume visualization*, pp. 119–126, ACM, New York, NY, USA, 1998.

76. F. D. Ix and A. Kaufman. "*Incremental Triangle Voxelization*". In: *Proc. Graphics Interface*, 2000.

77. N. Stolte. "Robust Voxelization of Surfaces". Tech. Rep., State University of New York at Stony Brook, 1997.

78. E. Eisemann and X. Décoret. "Single-pass GPU Solid Voxelization and Applications". In: *GI '08: Proceedings of Graphics Interface 2008*, pp. 73–80, Canadian Information Processing Society, 2008.

79. D. Haumont and N. Warze. "Complete Polygonal Scene Voxelization". *Journal of Graphics, GPU, and Game Tools*, vol. 7, no. 3, pp. 27–41, 2002.

80. M. Sramek and A. Kaufman. "Alias-free voxelization of geometric objects". *Visualization and Computer Graphics, IEEE Transactions on*, vol. 5, no. 3, pp. 251–267, July 1999.

81. Z. Dong, W. Chen, H. Bao, H. Zhang, and Q. Peng. "Real-time Voxelization for Complex Polygonal Models". In: *PG '04: Proceedings of the Computer Graphics and Applications, 12th Pacific Conference*, pp. 43–50, IEEE Computer Society, Washington, DC, USA, 2004.

82. E. Eisemann and X. Décoret. "Fast Scene Voxelization and Applications". In: *ACM SIGGRAPH Symposium on Interactive 3D Graphics and Games*, pp. 71–78, ACM SIGGRAPH, 2006.

83. S. Fang and H. Chen. "Hardware Accelerated Voxelization". *Computers and Graphics*, Vol. 24, pp. 433–442, 2000.

84. B. Heidelberger, M. Teschner, and M. Gross. "Real-time Volumetric Intersections of Deforming Objects". *In: Proceedings of Vision, Modeling, and Visualization 2003*, pp. 461–468, 2003.

85. C. Sigg, R. Peikert, and M. Gross. "Signed Distance Transform Using Graphics Hardware". *Visualization Conference, IEEE*, pp. 83–90, 2003.

86. G. Varadhan, S. Krishnan, Y. J. Kim, S. Diggavi, and D. Manocha. "Efficient max-norm distance computation and reliable voxelization". In: *SGP '03: Proceedings of the 2003 Eurographics/ACM SIGGRAPH symposium on geometry processing*, pp. 116–126, Eurographics Association, Aire-la-Ville, Switzerland, Switzerland, 2003.

87. S. W. Wang and A. E. Kaufman. "Volume sampled voxelization of geometric primitives". In: *VIS '93: Proceedings of the 4th conference on Visualization '93*, pp. 78–84, IEEE Computer Society, Washington, DC, USA, 1993.

88. H. Chen and S. Fang. "Fast voxelization of three-dimensional synthetic objects". *J. Graph. Tools*, vol. 3, no. 4, pp. 33–45, 1998.

89. S.-H. Chang, Y.-C. Lai, Y. Niu, F. Liu, and K.-L. Hua. "Real-time Realistic Voxel-based Rendering". In: *Pacific Conference on Computer Graphics and Applications*, pp. 1–6, 2011.

90. V. Forest, L. Barthe, and M. Paulin. "Real-Time Hierarchical Binary-Scene Voxelization". *Journal of Graphics Tools*, vol. 29, no. 2, pp. 21–34, 2009.

91. E.-A. Karabassi, G. Papaioannou, and T. Theoharis. "A Fast Depth-Buffer-Based Voxelization Algorithm". *Journal of Graphics, GPU, and Game Tools*, vol. 4, no. 4, pp. 5–10, 1999.

92. I. Llamas. "Real-time voxelization of triangle meshes on the GPU". In: *ACM SIGGRAPH 2007 sketches*, p. 18–, 2007.

93. M. Gervautz and W. Purgathofer. "A Simple Method for Color Quantization: Octree Quantization". In: *New Trends in Computer Graphics*, Springer Verlag, Berlin, 1988.

94. I. Garnagntini. "Linear octree for fast processing of three-dimensional objects". *Computer Graph. Image Process*, vol. 20, pp. 365–374, 1982.

95. I. Carlbom, I. Chakravarty, and D. Vanderschel. "A Hierarchical Data Structure for Representing the Spatial Decomposition of 3-D Objects". *IEEE Comput. Graph. Appl.*, vol. 5, pp. 24–31, April 1985.

96. J. L. Bentley. "Multidimensional binary search trees used for associative searching". *Commun. ACM*, vol. 18, pp. 509–517, September 1975.

97. M. de Berg, M. van Krevald, M. Overmars, and O. Schwarzkopf. *Computer Geometry*. Springer-Verlag, Inc., New York, NY, USA, 2000.

98. W. E. Lorensen and H. E. Cline. "Marching cubes: A high resolution 3D surface construction algorithm". *SIGGRAPH Comput. Graph.*, Vol. 21, pp. 163–169, August 1987.

99. E. H. Adelson and J. R. Bergen. "The Plenoptic Function and the Elements of Early Vision". In: *Computational Models of Visual Processing*, pp. 3–20, MIT Press, 1991.

100. G. Z. Hendrik, H. P. A. Lensch, N. Ahmed, M. Magnor, and H. Peter Seidel. "Multi-Video Compression in Texture Space". In: *Proc. IEEE International Conference on Image Processing (ICIP04)*, pp. 2467–2470, 2004.

101. M. Brown and D. G. Lowe. "Recognising Panoramas". In: *ICCV '03: Proceedings of the Ninth IEEE International Conference on Computer Vision*, p. 1218–, 2003.

102. M. Brown, R. Szeliski, and S. Winder. "Multi-image matching using multi-scale oriented patches". In: *IEEE Computer Society Conference on Computer Vision and Pattern Recognition, 2005*, pp. 510–517 vol. 1, 2005.

103. D. Milgram. "Computer Methods for Creating Photomosaics". *IEEE Transactions on Computers*, vol. C-24, no. 11, pp. 1113–1119, 1975.

104. R. Szeliski. "Image alignment and stitching: a tutorial". *Found. Trends. Comput. Graph. Vis.*, vol. 2, pp. 1–104, January 2006.

105. S. E. Chen. "QuickTime VR: an image-based approach to virtual environment navigation". In: *Proceedings of the 22nd annual conference on computer graphics and interactive techniques*, pp. 29–38, 1995.

106. M. D. I. Pro. "http://www.microsoft.com/products/imaging.". 2012.

107. Realviz. "http://www.realviz.com.". 2012.

108. A. Smolic, K. Mueller, P. Merkle, T. Rein, M. Kautzner, P. Eisert, and T. Wieg. *"Free viewpoint video extraction, representation, coding and rendering"*. In: *Proc. IEEE International Conference on Image Processing*, 2004.

109. M. Levoy and P. Hanrahan. "Light field rendering". In: *Proceedings of the 23rd annual conference on computer graphics and interactive techniques*, pp. 31–42, 1996.

110. S. J. Gortler, R. Grzeszczuk, R. Szeliski, and M. F. Cohen. "The lumigraph". In: *Proceedings of the 23rd annual conference on computer graphics and interactive techniques*, pp. 43–54, 1996.

111. B. Wilburn, M. Smulski, K. Lee, and M. A. Horowitz. "The light field video camera". *In: Media Processors 2002*, pp. 29–36, 2002.

112. J. C. Yang, M. Everett, C. Buehler, and L. McMillan. "A real-time distributed light field camera". In: *Proceedings of the 13th Eurographics workshop on rendering*, pp. 77–86, 2002.

113. R. Azuma. "A Survey of Augmented Reality". *Presence*, vol. 6, pp. 355–385, 1997.

114. S.-U. Yoon, E.-K. Lee, S.-Y. Kim, and Y.-S. Ho. "A Framework for Representation and Processing of Multi-view Video Using the Concept of Layered Depth Image". *J. VLSI Signal Process. Syst.*, vol. 46, no. 2–3, pp. 87–102, 2007.

115. A. Smolic and D. McCutchen. "3DAV exploration of video-based rendering technology in MPEG". *Circuits and Systems for Video Technology, IEEE Transactions on*, vol. 14, no. 3, pp. 348–356, March 2004.

116. D. Scharstein. *"Learning conditional random fields for stereo"*. In: *In IEEE CVPR*, 2007.

117. M. Cowan and L. Nielsen. *"3D – how do they do it?"*. Presentation at Holywood Post Alliance Summar School, LosAngeles, 2007.

118. C. Fehn, P. Kauff, M. O. D. Beeck, F. Ernst, W. IJsselsteijn, M. Pollefeys, L. V. Gool, E. Ofek, and I. Sexton. "An Evolutionary and Optimised Approach on 3D-TV". In: *In Proceedings of International Broadcast Conference*, pp. 357–365, 2002.

119. C. Fehn. "Depth-image-based rendering (DIBR), compression, and transmission for a new approach on 3D-TV". In: A. J. Woods, J. O. Merritt, S. A. Benton, & M. T. Bolas, Ed., *Society of Photo-Optical Instrumentation Engineers (SPIE) Conference Series*, pp. 93–104, May 2004.

120. "ISO/IEC JTC 1/SC 29/WG 11, Information technology-generic coding of moving pictures and audio:video, ISO/IEC 13818–2:1996, April 1996", 1996.

121. Digital video broadcast project (Online), 2006. Available at: http://www.dvb.org.

122. W. Mark. "Post-Rendering 3D Image Warping: Visibility, Reconstruction, and Performance for Depth-Image Warping". Tech. Rep., University of North Carolina at Chapel Hill, 1999.

123. L. McMillan, Jr.,, and R. S. Pizer. "An Image-Based Approach To Three-Dimensional Computer Graphics". Tech. Rep., Univeristy of North Carolina at Chapel Hill, 1997.

124. Y. Bayakovski, L. Levkovich-Maslyuk, A. Ignatenko, A. Konushin, D. Timasov, A. Zhirkov, M. Han, and I. K. Park. "Depth image-based representations for static and animated 3D objects". In: *Image Processing*. 2002. Proceedings. 2002 *International Conference on*, pp. III-25–III-28 vol. 3, 2002.

125. S.-C. Chan, Z.-F. Gan, K.-T. Ng, K.-L. Ho, and H.-Y. Shum. "An object-based approach to image/video-based synthesis and processing for 3-D and multiview televisions". *IEEETrans. Cir. and Sys. for Video Technol.*, vol. 19, no. 6, pp. 821–831, 2009.

126. S.-U. Yoon, E.-K. Lee, S.-Y. Kim, Y.-S. Ho, K. Yun, S. Cho, and N. Hur. "Inter-camera coding of multi-view video using layered depth image representation". In: *Proceedings of the 7th Pacific Rim Conference on Advances in Multimedia Information Processing*, pp. 432–441, 2006.

127. C. L. Zitnick, S. B. Kang, M. Uyttendaele, S. Winder, and R. Szeliski. "High-quality video view interpolation using a layered representation". *ACM Trans. Graph.*, vol. 123, pp. 600–608, August 2004.

3

3D Display Systems

3.1 Depth Cues and Applications to 3D Display

To perceive a 3D scene by a human visual system (HVS), the display system should be designed to present sufficient depth information for each object such that the HVS can reconstruct each object's 3D positions. The HVS recognizes an objects' depth in the real 3D world through depth cues, so the success of a 3D display depends on how well the depth cues are provided such that the HVS can observe a 3D scene. In general, depending on how many viewpoints are provided, the depth cues can be classified into two main categories: monocular and binocular.

3.1.1 Monocular Depth Cues

The category of monocular depth cue consists of depth cues observed from only one sequence of 2D images captured from one viewpoint. Depending on the availability of temporal information, it can be further classified into two subcategories: spatial monocular depth cue and spatial-temporal monocular depth cue. We list three major spatial monocular depth cues in [1]:

- Focus/defocus cues: The HVS associates the focus with a known depth plane, which is often refered to as accommodation. For an image captured by an aperture camera, the objects associated with the focusing plane of the optics are sharper than the other objects located away from this focusing plane. HVS can perceive an object's depth by differentiating the sharper objects from the blurred objects through accommodation.
- Geometric cues: Geometric cues include linear perspective, known size, relative size, texture gradient, and height in picture. The depth cue from linear perspective comes from the real-life knowledge that parallel lines intersect at infinite distance in a 3D world, but distances between parallel lines vary according to the related depth when they are shown in a 2D image. Similarly, the size information also reveals depth cues. When there are multiple objects with the same physical size shown in a 2D image, the closer object will look bigger. The gradient of a texture also exhibits the same

3D Visual Communications, First Edition. Guan-Ming Su, Yu-Chi Lai, Andres Kwasinski and Haohong Wang.
© 2013 John Wiley & Sons, Ltd. Published 2013 by John Wiley & Sons, Ltd.

depth cue: the gradient of an observed texture is more spread out when it is closer to the observer. The height in picture refers to our general experience that the objects shown at the bottom of an image is often closer than the objects shown nearer the top.

- Color and intensity cues: The color and light perceived by the eyes may vary according to the distance between object and eye. This category includes atmospheric scattering, light and shadow distribution, figure-ground perception, and local contrast. When light rays are scattered by the atmosphere, further objects have a bluish tint and with less contrast than the closer objects. HVS can utilize this real-world color experience of atmospheric scattering depth cue to tell the depth. The shadow cast by the sun or other light sources will vary according to the depth of the object in a 3D scene. The figure-ground perception refers to the perceived depth from edges and regions. When two regions are separated by an edge, one region at this edge has a definite shape (called the figure) and the other region appears shapeless (called the ground). The depth cue is perceived as the figure looking closer than the ground.

Spatial-temporal monocular depth cues include occlusions and motion parallax. This kind of depth cue is obtained when the viewer watches a sequence of 2D images along the time domain. The occlusion depth cue comes from the observations that background objects are covered by foreground objects, and the covered areas may increase or decrease when objects have movement. Motion parallax refers to the observations that when viewers move, the movement of further static objects is slower than the movement of the closer ones.

3.1.2 Binocular Depth Cues

When a viewer can perceive two images from two different viewpoints, the binocular depth cues may be observed. The binocular depth cues mainly include angular disparity and horizontal disparity [2]:

- Angular disparity: The angular disparity is the angle between two lines representing the viewing directions from that left and right eyes to the targeted object. It is also referred to as vergence angle.
- Horizontal disparity: When a particular point in a 3D world is captured on two images from two horizontally separated viewpoints, the projected points on the left image plane and the right image plane may not have the same horizontal position in each image's coordinates. The distance between these two projected points is called the horizontal disparity.

When the angular disparity or the horizontal disparity is zero, the viewer cannot observe the depth.

From the above discussions, a 3D display system should contain sufficient depth cues such that the viewers can observe the depth. The most effective approach for 3D display systems is to explore the binocular depth cues by showing the captured left image to the left eye and right image to the right eye. Based on this principle, there are different 3D display technologies that have been developed. Depending on how a stereo image pair is multiplexed from and/or de-multiplexed to left image and right image, the 3D display can be categorized as a stereoscopic display or an autostereoscopic display.

3.2   Stereoscopic Display

The general framework of stereoscopic display consists of two components: a multiplexing process to encode the stereo image pair at the display side, and a de-multiplexing process to retrieve the left and right view at the viewer side. To conduct the de-multiplexing, the viewers are required to wear special glasses. In the following, we discuss different multiplexing methods used in the stereoscopic display.

3.2.1   Wavelength Division (Color) Multiplexing

The color reproduction mechanism described in classic color theory provides a method to deliver the left and right image by separating the visible spectrum (370–730 nm) into two different wavelength bands. The most common approach for wavelength division multiplexing is to multiplex the higher spectral band (red) of the left image and the lower spectral band (blue/cyan) of the right image in the display side; and the viewers can de-multiplex the signal by wearing anaglyph glasses whose left and right glass can filter different spectral information such that each eye perceives its corresponding color. Anaglyph is the least costly method of displaying 3D images wherever the device can comprise primary colors, that is paper, film, CRT/LCD. A common and simple way to generate an anaglyph image is to take the linear combination of color information from left and right image: Let the red, green, and blue information (codeword stored in image file) of one given pixel located at coordinate (x,y) in the left image as $\mathbf{s}^L = \begin{bmatrix} s_0^L & s_1^L & s_2^L \end{bmatrix}^T$ and one pixel located at the same coordinate (x,y) in the right image as $\mathbf{s}^R = \begin{bmatrix} s_0^R & s_1^R & s_2^R \end{bmatrix}^T$, the pixel in the anaglyph image $\mathbf{s}^a = \begin{bmatrix} s_0^a & s_1^a & s_2^a \end{bmatrix}^T$ can be constructed through a linear combination process with one 3×6 matrix $\mathbf{M}$:

$$\mathbf{s}^a = \mathbf{M} \begin{bmatrix} \mathbf{s}^L \\ \mathbf{s}^R \end{bmatrix} \tag{3.1}$$

One example of the matrix is

$$\mathbf{M} = \begin{bmatrix} 1 & 0 & 0 & 0 & 0 & 0 \\ 0 & 0 & 0 & 0 & 1 & 0 \\ 0 & 0 & 0 & 0 & 0 & 1 \end{bmatrix}. \tag{3.2}$$

With this simple implementation, the red component of pixel $\mathbf{s}^a$ has a value from the red component of the left image; and the green and blue color information for pixel $\mathbf{s}^a$ are from the green and blue color channel in the right image, respectively.

The optimal solution for $\mathbf{M}$ by addressing the unique characteristics of a primary color system adopted in different displays and spectral response of different filter chosen in anaglyph glasses can be derived via orthogonal projection [3]. Let the display gamma function as $g(\cdot)$ and the gamma corrected value $\bar{s}_i^L = g(s_i^L)$ and $\bar{s}_i^R = g(s_i^R)$ for $i = 0$, 1, and 2. To facilitate our discussion, we denote the three color components of one pixel located at the same position (x,y) from left and right image as vector forms $\bar{\mathbf{s}}^L = \begin{bmatrix} \bar{s}_0^L & \bar{s}_1^L & \bar{s}_2^L \end{bmatrix}^T$ and $\bar{\mathbf{s}}^R = \begin{bmatrix} \bar{s}_0^R & \bar{s}_1^R & \bar{s}_2^R \end{bmatrix}^T$, respectively. Denote $d_i(\lambda)$, $i = 0$, 1, and 2, as the spectral density functions of the RGB display phosphors, and $p_j(\lambda)$, $j = 0$, 1, and 2, as the color matching functions for the selected primary colors. The spectral density for the left image and right image at wavelength λ from three color channels can be expressed as

$$W^L(\lambda) = \sum_{i=0}^{2} \tilde{s}_i^L d_i(\lambda) \quad \text{and} \quad W^R(\lambda) = \sum_{i=0}^{2} \tilde{s}_i^R d_i(\lambda). \tag{3.3}$$

When the display only shows the left image or the right image, the perceived pixel value at the jth primary is

$$\tilde{s}_j^L = \int p_j(\lambda) W^L(\lambda) d\lambda \quad \text{and} \quad \tilde{s}_j^R = \int p_j(\lambda) W^R(\lambda) d\lambda. \tag{3.4}$$

The above equations can be expressed in the matrix form by first denoting

$$c_{ji} = \int p_j(\lambda) d_i(\lambda) d\lambda. \tag{3.5}$$

then, bringing in (3.5) and (3.3) to (3.4), the perceived pixel value can be expressed as a linear combination of the gamma corrected pixel value as follows:

$$\tilde{s}_j^L = \sum_{i=0}^{2} c_{ji} \tilde{s}_i^L \quad \text{and} \quad \tilde{s}_j^R = \sum_{i=0}^{2} c_{ji} \tilde{s}_i^R. \tag{3.6}$$

Denote $\tilde{\mathbf{s}}^L = \begin{bmatrix} \tilde{s}_0^L & \tilde{s}_1^L & \tilde{s}_2^L \end{bmatrix}^T$ and $\tilde{\mathbf{s}}^R = \begin{bmatrix} \tilde{s}_0^R & \tilde{s}_1^R & \tilde{s}_2^R \end{bmatrix}^T$. We can arrive at the following matrix form for a "six primary" color system,

$$\tilde{\mathbf{s}} = \begin{bmatrix} \tilde{\mathbf{s}}^L \\ \tilde{\mathbf{s}}^R \end{bmatrix} = \begin{bmatrix} \mathbf{C} & \mathbf{0} \\ \mathbf{0} & \mathbf{C} \end{bmatrix} \begin{bmatrix} \tilde{\mathbf{s}}^L \\ \tilde{\mathbf{s}}^R \end{bmatrix} = \mathbf{C}' \begin{bmatrix} \tilde{\mathbf{s}}^L \\ \tilde{\mathbf{s}}^R \end{bmatrix}, \tag{3.7}$$

where $[\mathbf{C}]_{ji} = c_{ji}$.

Since the display only has three primary colors, we need to generate the anaglyph pixel $\mathbf{s}^a$ and the corresponding gamma corrected value $\tilde{s}_i^a = g(s_i^a)$ for $i = 0, 1,$ and 2. Denote the three color channels as a vector, $\tilde{\mathbf{s}}^a = \begin{bmatrix} \tilde{s}_0^a & \tilde{s}_1^a & \tilde{s}_2^a \end{bmatrix}^T$. The spectral density for the anaglyph pixel $\mathbf{s}^a$ at wavelength λ from three color channels can be expressed as:

$$W^a(\lambda) = \sum_{i=0}^{2} \tilde{s}_i^a d_i(\lambda). \tag{3.8}$$

Let the spectral absorption function of the anaglyph glasses filter at left view and right view be $f^L(\lambda)$ and $f^R(\lambda)$. When the display shows the anaglyph pixel $\mathbf{s}^a$, the perceived pixel value at the jth primary through the left filter and right filter are

$$\tilde{s}_j^{a,L} = \int p_j(\lambda) W^a(\lambda) f^L(\lambda) d\lambda \tag{3.9a}$$

and

$$\tilde{s}_j^{a,R} = \int p_j(\lambda) W^a(\lambda) f^R(\lambda) d\lambda \tag{3.9b}$$

respectively.

To simplify the discussion, we define two constants as follows:

$$a_{ji}^L = \int p_j(\lambda)d_i(\lambda)f^L(\lambda)d\lambda \tag{3.10a}$$

$$a_{ji}^R = \int p_j(\lambda)d_i(\lambda)f^R(\lambda)d\lambda \tag{3.10b}$$

Substituting (3.8) and (3.10a) into (3.9a), the perceived left pixel value can be expressed as a linear combination of the gamma corrected pixel value as follows:

$$\tilde{s}_j^{a,L} = \sum_{i=0}^2 a_{ji}^L \cdot \bar{s}_i^a \tag{3.11a}$$

Similarly, the perceived right pixel value can be derived by substituting (3.8) and (3.10b) into (3.9b) and expressed as

$$\tilde{s}_j^{a,R} = \sum_{i=0}^2 a_{ji}^R \cdot \bar{s}_i^a. \tag{3.11b}$$

Denote $\tilde{\mathbf{s}}^{a,L} = \begin{bmatrix} \tilde{s}_0^{a,L} & \tilde{s}_1^{a,L} & \tilde{s}_2^{a,L} \end{bmatrix}^T$ and $\tilde{\mathbf{s}}^{a,R} = \begin{bmatrix} \tilde{s}_0^{a,R} & \tilde{s}_1^{a,R} & \tilde{s}_2^{a,R} \end{bmatrix}^T$. The perceived anaglyph image through glasses filter can be expressed in the following matrix form:

$$\tilde{\mathbf{s}}^a = \begin{bmatrix} \tilde{\mathbf{s}}^{a,L} \\ \tilde{\mathbf{s}}^{a,R} \end{bmatrix} = \begin{bmatrix} \mathbf{A}_L \\ \mathbf{A}_R \end{bmatrix} \bar{\mathbf{s}}^a = \mathbf{A}\bar{\mathbf{s}}^a, \tag{3.12}$$

where $[\mathbf{A}_L]_{ji} = a_{ji}^L$ and $[\mathbf{A}_R]_{ji} = a_{ji}^R$. Denote the cth column of $\mathbf{A}$ as $\mathbf{a}_c$.

We can formulate this anaglyph system as an optimization problem to find the optimal anaglyph image ($\mathbf{s}^a$) by minimizing the norm of the difference between the individually perceived image ($\tilde{\mathbf{s}}$) from the display excited by the original stereo image pair and the perceived image ($\tilde{\mathbf{s}}^a$) from the anaglyph image through the glasses:

$$\min_{\mathbf{s}^a} \left\| \tilde{\mathbf{s}}^a - \tilde{\mathbf{s}} \right\| \tag{3.13}$$

In [3], an orthogonal projection method is proposed to resolve the above optimization problem. Define the general inner product for two vectors $\mathbf{x}$ and $\mathbf{y}$ as

$$\langle \mathbf{x}, \mathbf{y} \rangle = \mathbf{x}^T \mathbf{W}\mathbf{y}, \tag{3.14}$$

where $\mathbf{W}$ is a positive-definite matrix representing the required weighting factors for different color channels.

The projection can be constructed by first forming the following 3×3 Grammian matrix

$$\mathbf{\Phi} = \begin{bmatrix} \langle \mathbf{a}_0, \mathbf{a}_0 \rangle & \langle \mathbf{a}_1, \mathbf{a}_0 \rangle & \langle \mathbf{a}_2, \mathbf{a}_0 \rangle \\ \langle \mathbf{a}_0, \mathbf{a}_1 \rangle & \langle \mathbf{a}_1, \mathbf{a}_1 \rangle & \langle \mathbf{a}_2, \mathbf{a}_1 \rangle \\ \langle \mathbf{a}_0, \mathbf{a}_2 \rangle & \langle \mathbf{a}_1, \mathbf{a}_2 \rangle & \langle \mathbf{a}_2, \mathbf{a}_2 \rangle \end{bmatrix}, \tag{3.15}$$

and a 3×1 matrix

$$\mathbf{B} = \begin{bmatrix} \langle \mathbf{a}_0, \tilde{\mathbf{s}} \rangle \\ \langle \mathbf{a}_1, \tilde{\mathbf{s}} \rangle \\ \langle \mathbf{a}_2, \tilde{\mathbf{s}} \rangle \end{bmatrix}. \tag{3.16}$$

Note that $\mathbf{\Phi} = \mathbf{A}^T \mathbf{WA}$ and $\mathbf{B} = \mathbf{A}^T \mathbf{W\tilde{s}}$.

The projection can be expressed as:

$$\hat{\mathbf{s}}^a = \mathbf{\Phi}^{-1} \mathbf{B}$$

$$= (\mathbf{A}^T \mathbf{WA})^{-1} \mathbf{A}^T \mathbf{W\tilde{s}}$$

$$= (\mathbf{A}^T \mathbf{WA})^{-1} \mathbf{A}^T \mathbf{WC}' \begin{bmatrix} \bar{\mathbf{s}}^L \\ \bar{\mathbf{s}}^R \end{bmatrix} \tag{3.17}$$

Since $(\mathbf{A}^T \mathbf{WA})^{-1} \mathbf{A}^T \mathbf{WC}'$ is a fixed matrix describing the characteristics of display and glasses filter, it can be precalculated after the viewing condition is settled. The optimal anaglyph image can be calculated through a simple linear algebra from the original stereo image pair.

On the other hand, the simple anaglyph approach, which allows the left eye to watch lower wavelength band and the right eye the higher wavelength band, suffers loss of color information in both eyes and causes visual discomfort known as color rivalry. In addition, the overlapped spectrum provided by three different primary colors in the display and by imperfect spectral separation filter in the glasses filter result in crosstalk between left and right channels. To alleviate these issues, one could adopt a multiple interleaved spectral band approach by dividing the spectrum into six different bands from lower wavelength to higher wavelength as $[B_L\ B_R\ G_L\ G_R\ R_L\ R_R]$ and assigning band $[B_L\ G_L\ R_L]$ to the left eye and band $[B_R\ G_R\ R_R]$ to the right eye [4]. Each view image will be filtered by one set of multi-band filters to preserve spectral information in either $[B_L\ G_L\ R_L]$ or $[B_R\ G_R\ R_R]$ before multiplexing together in the display. The viewers' glasses should also be able to separate the different sets of multi-band information to the corresponding eye. Theoretically, having assigned complementary RGB information can improve the full color perception in left and right eyes. In practice, the quality of the perceived images depends on (a) how the spectrum is divided into multiple intervals such that each eye has its own color gamut to reduce color rivalry, and (b) how accurately designed the color filter in the display and glasses are to reduce the crosstalk. With a known spectral absorption function of the multi-band filter, it is also feasible to combine the aforementioned orthogonal projection method to construct the optimal anaglyph image.

The further improvement over the aforementioned multi-band method is proposed in [5]. The spectrum is partitioned into nine difference bands from lower wavelength to higher wavelength as $[B_{1L}\ B_{2R}\ B_{3L}\ G_{1L}\ G_{2R}\ G_{3L}\ R_{1L}\ R_{2R}\ R_{3L}]$. Bands $[B_{1L}\ B_{3L}\ G_{1L}\ G_{3L}\ R_{1L}\ R_{3L}]$ are assigned to the left eye and bands $[B_{2R}\ G_{2R}\ R_{2R}]$ are assigned to the right eye. We can merge bands B_{3L} and G_{1L} together as one band, and G_{3L} and R_{1L} as one band, which results in four different bands in the left eye. This 3–4 band filter design has the advantage of increasing the luminous efficiency and requiring no or less color correction. Note that the spectrum can be further partitioned into more bands with narrow intervals, but the simulation results show only 3–4 band filter designs achieve the optimal luminous efficiency. The main reason that using more bands won't bring better gain is that when we increase the number of bands, the number of gaps between bands also increases. Each gap will contribute to a loss of efficiency and thus the overall efficiency cannot be improved.

3.2.2 Polarization Multiplexing

Unpolarized light comprises mutually orthogonal orientations of oscillations and can be decomposed into different polarizations through differently polarized filters. Polarization multiplexing multiplexes a 3D image pair by polarizing each view with different polarized filters in the display/projector, and the viewers can de-multiplex the left and right image by wearing a glasses with correspondingly polarized filters. When the polarization projector is used, a special nondepolarizing screen is needed to maintain the state of polarization from each view during the projection.

There are two polarization methods commonly deployed, linear polarization and circular polarization. When linear polarization multiplexing is adopted, one view will be polarized horizontally and the other view will be polarized vertically. When the circular polarization multiplexing is selected, one view will be polarized in a right-hand circular (RHC) state and the other view image in left-hand circular (LHC) state. The main drawback of linear polarization is that crosstalk will increase when the difference of orientation between the viewers' glasses and the display increases, which greatly limits the freedom of viewers' head movement and rotation. Besides, when the viewers turn their heads away from the screen, the viewers will observe the brightness of the image becoming darker and darker until finally the viewers can't see anything. This problem can be significantly alleviated by choosing the circular polarization method. However, the manufacturing cost of circular polarization filters is higher than for linear polarization.

To deploy the circular polarization method in the consumer LCD TV market, the patterned retarder (PR) technology has been introduced. This adds a patterned retarder sheet over the 2D LCD panel by employing a lamination process. This patterned retarder consists of rows of retarders that are aligned with the rows of the LCD panel. The odd rows are polarized in one state and retarded to a RHC polarized state. The even rows are polarized in the direction orthogonal to the odd row and retarded to a LHC polarized state. The patterned retarder technology was developed using glasses in the earlier years with higher manufacturing cost. The cost is reduced by using film material as film-type patterned retarder (FPR) recently. The input to the screen interleaves the left view and right view vertically such that the odd rows show the left image and the even rows show the right image. The viewers can observe left view and right view simultaneously with passive polarized glasses. One noticeable disadvantage of deploying PR via interleaving views is the reduction of vertical resolution.

Since polarization does not band-limit the color spectrum, polarization multiplexing based method can provide full color reproduction. However, the polarization filter will block a large amount of light such that the viewers can observe the lightness is significantly darker when they wear the polarization glasses. To overcome this problem, the polarization display needs to increase its brightness to compensate this brightness difference and potentially the 3D content may need brightness adjustment during the mastering process to match the brightness of the corresponding 2D version.

3.2.3 Time Multiplexing

The time multiplexing approach is to display the left view and right view image interleaved along the time domain at the display side. At the viewer side, the users need to wear shutter glasses (such as liquid crystal shutter (LCS) glasses) which can switch on and off to let the corresponding image pass through. Suppose the display has frame refresh rate F frames per second (fps); and equivalently the display can show F different images in one second. The left view and the right view image belonging to one stereo image pair can be displayed alternately. Synchronization signals indicating the time instances are needed to pass to the shutter glasses [6]. With those timing signals, the left eye of the shutter glasses will let the light pass through when the display shows the left image and block the light when the display shows the right image. The right eye of the shutter glasses will perform the opposite operation by blocking the light when the display shows the left image and letting the light pass through when the display shows the right image. Ideally, time multiplexing approach can provide the full spatial resolution and full display color gamut.

The normal film frame rate is 24 fps. We can divide one second into 24 time slots. In each time slot t, we display one stereo image pair with left view image $L(t)$ and right view $R(t)$. The minimum frame refresh rate for time-multiplexing 3D display should be at least 48 fps to display both views properly. Intuitively, one could display the stereo video with the order $L(0)$, $R(0)$, $L(1)$, $R(1)$, $L(2)$, $R(2)$, ..., $L(23)$, $R(23)$ sequentially at 48 fps. However, it has been observed that this displaying order can cause motion confusion. This is because the left eye and the right eye need to be able to see the motion appearing at the same time. The time-multiplexing method offsets the motion timing and the parallax changes. The motion confusion problem can be alleviated by flashing the stereo image pair several times in each time slot (i.e., 1/24 second) with a display capable of much higher frame refresh rate. For example, the "double flash" system will show the stereo image picture in the order of $L(0)$, $R(0)$, $L(0)$, $R(0)$, $L(1)$, $R(1)$, $L(1)$, $R(1)$, $L(2)$, $R(2)$, $L(2)$, $R(2)$, ..., $L(23)$, $R(23)$, $L(23)$, $R(23)$ sequentially at 96 fps; and the "triple flash" system will show the stereo image picture in the order of $\{L(t), R(t), L(t), R(t), L(t), R(t),$ for $t = 0, 1, ..., 23\}$, sequentially at 144 fps. Field testing has shown that triple flash surpasses the fusion threshold for much smoother motion and can provide smaller phase difference between the left and right images.

Note that the active shutter glasses needs a battery set to perform the switching mechanism and a wireless interface to synchronize it with the display, which often results in a bigger and heavier glasses frame and causes more inconvenience during viewing. In addition, halving time to let light pass through the shutter glasses reduces the perceived brightness, which needs brightness correction on either the 3D display side or the post-production of the 3D content creation stage. Supporting higher frame rate (≥ 120 fps) to reduce flickering and motion confusion is often required, but this requirement often poses a higher design and manufacturing cost in both the display and shutter glasses hardware. Since the response time of the liquid crystal has sample-and-hold characteristics, it is important to select liquid crystal material with fast response time and to design the switching and synchronization mechanism in the shutter glasses to alleviate the potential crosstalk caused by partially on/off during the on-off transition period [7]. Other design constraints on the shutter glasses, such as low voltage, low power consumption, and low cost, also affect the deployment of time-multiplexing based display.

For the projection applications, the wavelength division multiplexing and polarization multiplexing method normally need two projectors, which often consume more energy than a single projector and suffer pixel alignment problems from two different physical locations of the projector. One can build a hybrid system by bringing the additional time multiplexing method into the wavelength division multiplexing and polarization multiplexing system. The hybrid system can use only one projector with a switching mechanism in front of the projector to alter the desired filter used by the left and right view at different time instances.

Stereoscopic projectors enable the deployment of immersive virtual reality environments, which provides an interactive environment for users to experience a virtual 3D world. Cave automatic virtual environment (CAVE) is one of the systems providing virtual reality [8]. The system is set up inside a room, and several 3D projectors project 3D images to several walls around the room. With the detection of the user's position and viewing angle, the 3D projectors can be made to display the required content, and the perceived content can be de-multiplexed by head-mounted 3D glasses worn by the user.

3.3   Autostereoscopic Display

Instead of splitting left and right view image with the aided glasses at the viewer side for a stereoscopic display, the autostereoscopic display adopts the spatial multiplexing method to direct light emitted by pixels belonging to different views to the corresponding eyes. According to how the light-directing mechanism and optical effect are adopted, in general, we can categorize the autostereoscopic display into two major approaches: occlusion-based and refraction-based.

3.3.1   Occlusion-Based Approach

The occlusion-based approach exploits the parallax effects from the human visual system by utilizing the straight line direction characteristics of light. Imagining watching a scene through a small pinhole with the left eye only or the right eye only, each eye will observe a different image owing to the viewing angle and the occlusion caused by the opaque areas around the pinhole. By carefully applying this principle, one can build a parallax barrier display with a two-layer design as shown in Figure 3.1. The back layer consists of a pixelated emissive display panel, such as LCD, which interleaves the pixels from the left image and the right image such that the odd column pixels show the image for one eye and the even column pixels for the other eye. The front layer consists of an opaque layer with narrow regularly spaced vertical slits to allow light pass only to the desired viewing eye.

Since the light emitted from the left and right pixels is directed/blocked by the parallax barrier, the viewers need to watch the stereo image pair from the designed position, or so called viewing zone or sweet spot defined by the display. We use Figure 3.2 to illustrate the fundamental design principle for the parallax barrier. Denote the viewing distance between the viewers and the LCD panel as Z_e, the distance between the parallax barrier and the emissive display panel as Z_b, the viewing distance between viewers and parallax barrier as Z_{eb} ($Z_{eb} = Z_e - Z_b$), the emissive display pixel pitch as P_d, the parallax barrier slit pitch as P_b, and the distance between the left eye and the right eye as P_e. By applying similar triangular geometry, we have the following equation:

$$\frac{Z_{eb}}{Z_e} = \frac{P_b}{2P_d} \tag{3.18}$$

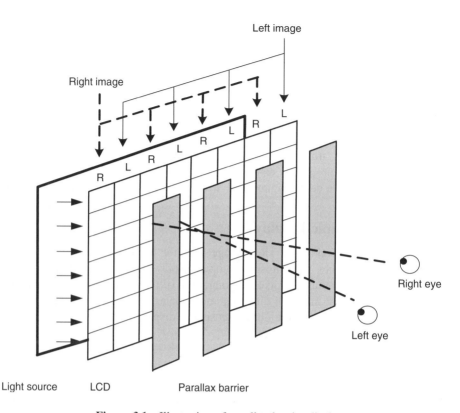

Figure 3.1 Illustration of parallax barrier display.

Bringing $Z_{eb} = Z_e - Z_b$ to (3.18), the viewing distance Z_e for best viewing quality can be expressed as

$$Z_e = \frac{2P_d Z_b}{2P_d - P_b}.$$ (3.19)

The other triangular geometry equation can be formed as:

$$\frac{P_b/2}{P_e} = \frac{Z_b}{Z_e}.$$ (3.20)

Then, the pitch of the parallax barrier P_b can be expressed as:

$$P_b = \frac{2P_e Z_b}{Z_e}.$$ (3.21)

Substituting (3.19) to (3.21), we obtain:

$$P_b = 2P_d \frac{P_e}{P_d + P_e}.$$ (3.22)

The above equation indicates that the design of the barrier pitch should be less than twice the display pixel pitch.

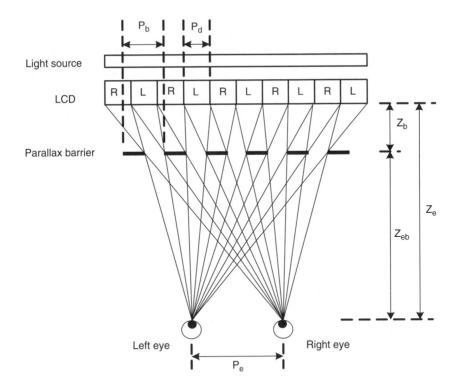

Figure 3.2 Design principle of parallax barrier display.

Multiple viewing zones are formed in terms of the viewing distance and the viewing angle. As illustrated in Figure 3.3, as the viewer moves horizontally in front of the parallax barrier display and watches the display from different angles, he/she will leave one viewing zone and enter the next one. When a viewer watches a 3D video from the defined viewing zone, light from partial pixels belonging to different view may enter the opposite eye and cause crosstalk artifacts. When a viewer straddles between two different viewing zones, the viewer will experience pseudoscopic (reversed stereo) image where the left eye perceives the image representing the right view and the right eye observes the image representing the left view.

The crosstalk caused by the imperfect separation of the left and right images can be alleviated by reducing the pitch of the opaque slit aperture. However, reducing the pitch of slit aperture blocks more light from the emissive pixels and causes more loss of light. The other way to alleviate the crosstalk is to place the parallax barrier between the backlight and the LCD. The drawback brought by this kind of design is that the intensity needs more control for uniformity. Therefore, the tradeoff between crosstalk and the light efficiency is the major problem in the occlusion-based approach.

Besides the hardware solution, the crosstalk can be reduced by software solutions, such as precorrecting the video signals before displaying the left and right image [9]. Denote the intensity value of the j th row for each column at the left image and right image as $I_L(j)$ and $I_R(j)$, respectively; and denote the perceived intensity value at the j th row for

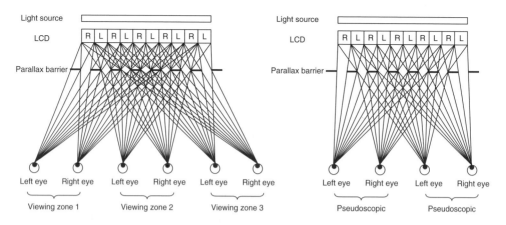

Figure 3.3 Viewing zone and pseudoscopic image.

each column at the left image and right image as $B_L(j)$ and $B_R(j)$ respectively. Assume the leakage from the other view to one view as p. Then, the perceived value for the pixel pair (affected by the crosstalk) can be expressed as a linear combination of the original left and right image:

$$\begin{bmatrix} B_L(j) \\ B_R(j) \end{bmatrix} = \begin{bmatrix} 1 & p \\ p & 1 \end{bmatrix} \begin{bmatrix} I_L(j) \\ I_R(j) \end{bmatrix} \tag{3.23}$$

If the original pixel value is precorrected to $P_L(j)$ and $P_R(j)$, similar to (3.23), the perceived signal of the precorrected pixel pair (affected by crosstalk) can be represented as

$$\begin{bmatrix} P_L'(j) \\ P_R'(j) \end{bmatrix} = \begin{bmatrix} 1 & p \\ p & 1 \end{bmatrix} \begin{bmatrix} P_L(j) \\ P_R(j) \end{bmatrix}. \tag{3.24}$$

The goal for this precorrection process is to make the perceived signal of the precorrected value as close to the original pixel value as possible, namely:

$$P_L'(j) = I_L(j) \quad \text{and} \quad P_R'(j) = I_R(j). \tag{3.25}$$

Substituting (3.25) to (3.24), the optimal precorrected pixel pair can be calculated as follows:

$$\begin{bmatrix} P_L(j) \\ P_R(j) \end{bmatrix} = \begin{bmatrix} 1 & p \\ p & 1 \end{bmatrix}^{-1} \begin{bmatrix} I_L(j) \\ I_R(j) \end{bmatrix}$$

$$= \frac{1}{1 - p^2} \begin{bmatrix} 1 & -p \\ -p & 1 \end{bmatrix} \begin{bmatrix} I_L(j) \\ I_R(j) \end{bmatrix} \tag{3.26}$$

Besides the direct-view display shown above, the occlusion-based approach can be implemented through projectors by using two parallax barriers [10]. The parallax barrier projector consists of four layers: multiple 2D projectors at the lowest layer, the first layer of parallax barrier, a projection screen, and the second layer of parallax barrier on the top. The first parallax barrier controls the output of the projectors such that the size of image pixels on the projection screen matches the width of slit aperture. The functionality of the image pixel on the projection screen is similar to the pixelated emissive display panel used in the direct-view parallax barrier display. The second parallax barrier is placed in front of the projection screen and its functionality is the same as the parallax barrier used in direct-view display.

3.3.2 Refraction-Based Approach

Light changes its direction when it passes through mediums with different refractive index. We could take the advantage of this refraction property to direct the light through optical systems to our desired direction. For the 3D direct-view display application, lenticular technology places a vertically cylindrical microlens in front of the pixelated emissive display panel, as shown in Figure 3.4. Each vertical microlens is placed in front of two corresponding columns of pixels and the light from each pixel belonging to either left or right images will be directed to its targeted direction. One could further extend the refraction methodology to have a display equipped with both horizontal and vertical parallax, which is normally called an integral image display. Instead of using cylindrical microlenses, the integral image display uses a large number of small convex lenslets to pass light to its intended direction. These convex lenslets are arranged as a regular 2D

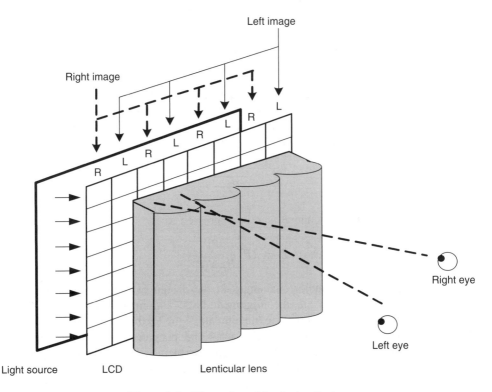

Figure 3.4 Illustration of lenticular display.

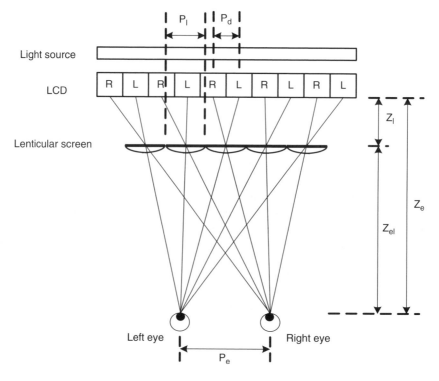

Figure 3.5   Design principles of lenticular display.

array, or fly's eye, in the integral imaging display. Each microlens directs light to the targeted horizontal and vertical directions to generate the required parallax.

Similar to the parallax barrier display, the viewing distance Z_e for the best viewing quality can be found via similar triangles in Figure 3.5 as:

$$Z_e = \frac{2P_d Z_l}{2P_d - P_l}.$$ (3.27)

Then, the pitch of the lenticular P_l can be expressed as:

$$P_l = 2P_d \frac{P_e}{P_d + P_e}.$$ (3.28)

There are several common major challenges in the design of refraction-based 3D display. The top two concerns are the alignment issue and intensity variation. As the refraction-based system is designed to manipulate light to the targeted direction, any slight misalignment between the lenticular array and pixelated emissive display panel will cause distortion for the perceived image. This problem will become worse when the required image dimension increases. The second issue arises when the viewer walks along the viewing zone: he/she will observe the brightness changes. Additional challenges based on the lenticular optics manufacturing are the additional coating needed on the surface of lenticular lens to alleviate the reflection from the viewer side and handling the light scatting inside the lenticular lens.

Besides the direct-view system, one could also apply the refraction-based approach to 3D projector design [11]. Similar to the occlusion-based 3D projector, the lenticular projector also consists of four layers: 2D projectors at the lowest layer, the first layer of lenticular screen, one projection screen, and the second layer of lenticular screen on the top.

To display a stereo color image, each pixel with square ratio consists of three subpixels alternating horizontally as shown in Figure 3.6a. Each subpixel has vertical rectangle ratio to represent different primary colors, namely, red, green, and blue. Each color subpixel has its own viewing zone and the overall observed combined color depends on the viewing angle as illustrated in Figure 3.6b. In some viewing zones, the viewer may encounter the color separation (or color dispersion) problem that the observed color is distorted.

Since the occlusion-based and refraction-based approach adopt the spatial multiplexing method, subject to the limited number of pixels in the horizontal resolution, the left image and the right image pixels are column interleaved to represent the stereo image. The simplest way is to put the odd column of the left view image at the odd column LCD pixels and the even column of the right view image at the even column LCD pixels. By doing so, the pixel perceived in each eye is only half resolution along the horizontal direction for a two-view system. Approaches with low-pass filtering with half decimation should be adopted to alleviate the aliasing during the half-resolution image generation process [12]. Note that the interleaving can be further implemented at the subpixel level, as seen in Figure 3.6a, where the odd and even subpixel columns display the image from left and right view, respectively.

The pixel subsampling problem will be relieved with the newly introduced higher resolution 4K (3840×2160) display. Since the number of pixels in the 4K display in the horizontal direction is twice the resolution of HD 2K (1920×1080) video, the 4K display should be able to display the full resolution of the original 2K content in two views.

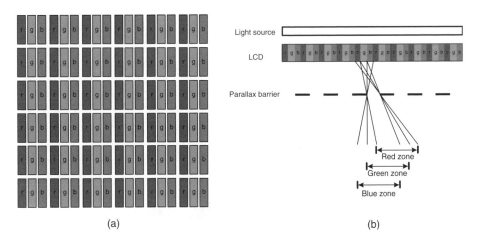

(a)   (b)

Figure 3.6 Illustration of subpixels in autostereoscopic display. The rectangle box with label "r", "g", and "b" represent the red, green, and blue subpixel, respectively. (a) RGB subpixel layout. (b) Viewing zone for each color component.

Rather than applying spatial multiplexing on one single LCD panel, a full-resolution, full color, and high intensity system for each view can be realized by using dual LCD panels, each of which is perpendicular to the other. The back layer of each LCD panel is equipped with a field len to direct light from light source through LCD. A half mirror is placed 45° between two LCD panels to further direct each view to its corresponding eye [13]. This system is shown in Figure 3.7. Note that as the position of the light source changes, the viewing window changes, too. We can take this property to design a 3D display to support multiple viewers and provide greater freedom to change viewing angles. To support multiple viewers, we can install additional light sources, and each light source will direct light to a different viewing zone. With a head-tracking system and a steerable light source, the light will be directed to the viewer's eyes.

3.4 Multi-View System

As the autostereoscopic display provides one more successful step toward real 3D scene reconstruction, the viewers may further expect to observe motion parallax (i.e., observing

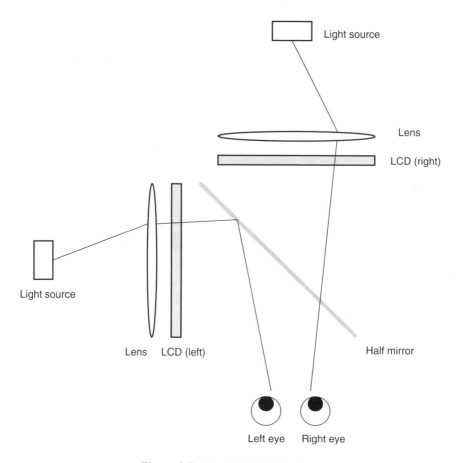

Figure 3.7 Dual-LCD 3D display.

scenes from different angles by changing the viewing angle). Subject to the autostereo-scopic display design, the viewers will feel confused about the objects' shapes since objects are always perceived from the same angle. To realize a 3D scene reconstruction with full motion parallax support, a 3D display providing multiple views is desired. Several multi-view technologies have been developed to meet such a requirement. One realization of a multi-view system is to install a head tracking system to monitor the viewer's position and render the corresponding view on the two-view 3D display. The other realization is to develop a 3D display to show multiple views simultaneously so the viewers can watch the desired view from different viewing angles.

3.4.1 Head Tracking Enabled Multi-View Display

The head tracking system can provide the viewers with geometric information related to the 3D display, such as positions and orientation, in real time. There exist many head tracking technologies, such as electromechanical, electromagnetic, acoustic tracking, inertial tracking, and optical tracking. Passive markers and active emitters/receivers are often deployed together to improve the tracking accuracy. For the applications related to 3D display, the fundamental requirement for such a tracking system is to track the center line of the face such that the display can prepare and respond to the requirements of the two eyes, one either side of the center line. Another important requirement for a 3D head tracking system is the need for a fast tracking result such that the display can have up-to-date information responding to the movement of viewers.

Having a head tracking system installed in a stereo 3D display, the 3D system is equipped with the capability to provide multi-view/look-around features. As the viewer moves around, the related position and viewing angle are calculated and the images from the corresponding view are rendered. Note that recent advanced head tracking systems can already track multiple viewers and it is feasible to provide a multi-view experience to multiple viewers simultaneously. Temporally multiplexed method with aided glasses seems to provide a straightforward way to display full-resolution pictures for each view observed by each viewer. However, to support N different views ($N > 2$), the hardware in both the display and glasses requires high speed operation and high video data bandwidth for N times the stereo frame refresh rate, which is often constrained by the state-of-the-art hardware technology. Therefore, the head tracking enabled multi-view 3D display is not scalable at this moment.

3.4.2 Automultiscopic

The alternative for supporting multiple users watching 3D scenes from multiple views is to extend the design principle of autostereoscopic display to the multi-view system (called automultiscopic). The practical design for the current automultiscopic display is based on the occlusion-based approach or the refraction-based approach. A four-view system is illustrated in Figure 3.8. For the parallax barrier approach, the optimal viewing distance for a N-view system is:

$$Z_e = \frac{N P_d Z_b}{N P_d - P_b}. \tag{3.29}$$

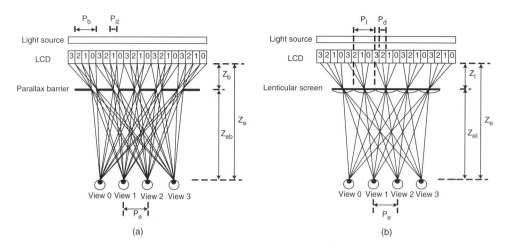

Figure 3.8 (a) Design principle of occlusion-based automultiscopic. (b) Design principle of refraction-based automultiscopic.

and the pitch of slit can be expressed as:

$$P_b = N P_d \frac{P_e}{P_d + P_e}.$$ (3.30)

For the lenticular approach, the optimal viewing distance for a N-view system is:

$$Z_e = \frac{N P_d Z_l}{N P_d - P_l}.$$ (3.31)

And the pitch of slit can be expressed as:

$$P_l = N P_d \frac{P_e}{P_d + P_e}.$$ (3.32)

Similar to the discussion for autostereoscopic display, to support N views in the automultiscopic display, each view will be downsampled N times in the horizontal direction such that those N views can be presented at the existing LCD plane simultaneously. As the number of views increases, the horizontal resolution is significantly reduced. On the other hand, there is no dimension reduction along the vertical direction and thus the resolutions in horizontal and vertical directions are not balanced. Another disadvantage of this simple extension is that the black mask between LCD pixels will be viewed as black lines when viewers change their viewpoints and pseudoscopic images are observed during the viewpoint transition.

Slanted multi-view 3D display [14] is one of the technologies to resolve this unbalance issue by slightly slanting the parallax barrier or the lenticular microlens by a small degree deviated from the vertical axis of the LCD pixel panel, as shown in Figure 3.9. The subpixels belonging to each view are indicated by the region bounded by the neighboring two dashed lines shown in the figure. Having the slanted structure, the distribution of pixels in the horizontal and vertical directions will be more uniform. Besides, this new

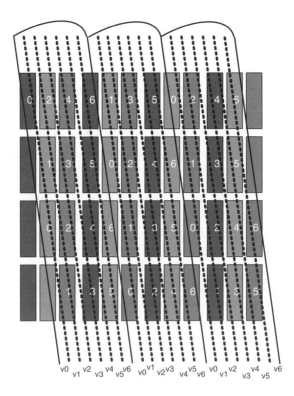

Figure 3.9   Slanted lenticular multi-view system (seven-view).

layout can alleviate the pseudoscopic problem and make the black mask less visible. In a similar way to slanting the lenticular screen, the LCD pixels can be arranged in a slanted structure to achieve the balance of horizontal and vertical resolution, though it involves significant changes during the LCD manufacturing process and makes it less practical for mass production.

Since the automultiscopic display needs to conduct spatial subsampling to prepare the displayed pixel for each view, the display suffers from aliasing artifacts from the high frequency replica, owing to the decimation. Consequently, the high frequency component in the viewing image may be distorted. For the spatially regular subsampled layout, the anti-aliasing filter should be carefully applied after deploying the decimation so that the aliasing from the other spectrum replica can be eliminated. However, for slanted structure automultiscopic display, the pixels in each view do not form a regular 2D lattice, which causes the difficulty of applying the traditional digital filter design. Several approaches to address the irregularly spatial subsampling have been proposed to alleviate the aliasing issue. One solution is to approximate the irregular subsampling layout by a regular grid in the spatial domain and then design an anti-aliasing filter based on the regular grid structure [15]. An approximation to a regular grid can be produced by using either an orthogonal lattice, a nonorthogonal lattice, or a union-of-cosets. The selection depends on the desired tradeoff between accuracy and computation complexity. A frequency domain based solution to designing an anti-aliasing filter is proposed in [16].

As well as the aliasing artifacts resulting from the subsampling process, automultiscopic displays also suffer from crosstalk with neighboring views. As each lenticular microlens cannot fully cover each LCD subpixel owing to the device's physical constraints, the viewer will observe light from some subpixels belonging to other views when watching one particular view. The leakage of neighboring view information will make the viewers uncomfortable, even giving them a headache. Mathematically, the crosstalk can be expressed as follows. Denote the intensity value at the jth row for each subpixel column as $I(j)$ and the subpixel column as $\mathbf{I} = [I(0)\ I(1)\ I(2)\ \ldots\ I(h-1)]^T$, where h is the number of rows in a subpixel column. As illustrated in Figure 3.9, assuming a two nearest neighbors intensity leakage model, the perceived light around subpixel location j comes from three different subpixels which are located at row $j-1$ (right neighboring view), j (current view), and $j+1$ (left neighboring view) within the same color channel (subpixel column). Let the proportions of the received light from the current view v, right neighboring view $v+1$, and left neighboring view $v-1$ as p_v, p_{v+1}, and p_{v-1}. And $p_v + p_{v+1} + p_{v-1} = 1$. The perceived value, $I_B(j)$, can be expressed as follows:

$$I_B(j) = p_{v-1}I(j+1) + p_v I(j) + p_{v+1}I(j-1) \tag{3.33}$$

To facilitate our discussion, we define the perceived subpixel column as $\mathbf{I}_B = [I_B(0)\ I_B(1)\ I_B(2)\ \ldots\ I_B(h-1)]^T$. Several hardware solutions – such as adding a pixel mask on the lenticular microlens display or lowering aperture ratio in parallax barrier 3D display – have been proposed to reduce crosstalk. The crosstalk can be also reduced by a software based solution, namely, a pixel value correction process, before those values are sent to the display. In [17], the value for each subpixel is corrected by taking the portion of intensity leakage from the two neighboring views into account. Let the corrected value at the jth row as $I_C(j)$ and the corrected subpixel column as $\mathbf{I}_C = [I_C(0)\ I_C(1)\ I_C(2)\ \ldots\ I_C(h-1)]^T$. The perceived subpixel column becomes:

$$\mathbf{I}_B = \begin{bmatrix} p_v & p_{v-1} & 0 & \cdots & 0 \\ p_{v+1} & p_v & p_{v-1} & \cdots & 0 \\ 0 & p_{v+1} & p_v & \cdots & 0 \\ \vdots & \vdots & \vdots & \vdots & \vdots \\ 0 & 0 & 0 & p_{v+1} & p_v \end{bmatrix} \mathbf{I}_C = \mathbf{P}\mathbf{I}_C. \tag{3.34}$$

To reduce the crosstalk, we can formulate the system to find the optimal corrected intensity value for each subpixel column $\mathbf{I}_C$ such that $\mathbf{I}_B$ is as close to $\mathbf{I}$ as possible. A simple solution is to formulate the problem as an unconstrained optimization problem to find the optimal corrected intensity value as follows:

$$\tilde{\mathbf{I}}_C = \arg\min_{\mathbf{I}_C} \left\| \mathbf{I}_B - \mathbf{I} \right\|^2 = \arg\min_{\mathbf{I}_C} \left\| \mathbf{P}\mathbf{I}_C - \mathbf{I} \right\|^2 \tag{3.35}$$

We can find the optimal subpixel column $\tilde{\mathbf{I}}_C$ via the least squared solution:

$$\tilde{\mathbf{I}}_C = (\mathbf{P}^T\mathbf{P})^{-1}\mathbf{P}^T\mathbf{I} \tag{3.36}$$

However, given a finite bit depth for each subpixel, the numerical value for each corrected intensity value is constrained. For example, pixels with 8-bit precision should be

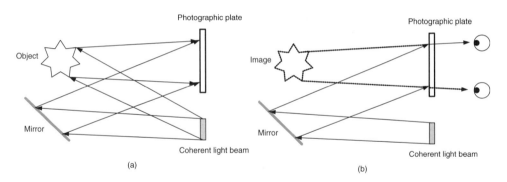

Figure 3.10   (a) Hologram recording. (b) Hologram reconstruction.

constrained as an integer with range [0 255]. Thus, the rounding and clipping operation following the least squared solver is needed to keep the pixel value inside the valid numerical range. Therefore, the obtained solution only approximates to the optimal solution within a certain level.

3.5   Recent Advances in Hologram System Study

Holographic 3D display is a type of display device to reconstruct the optical wave field such that the reconstructed 3D light beam can be seen as the physical presentation of the original object. The difference between conventional photography and holography is that photography can only record the amplitude information for an object but holography attempts to record both amplitude and phase information. Knowing that current image recording systems can only record the amplitude information, holography needs a way to transform the phase information such that it can be recorded in an amplitude-based recoding system.

Figure 3.10(a) illustrates the principle of hologram recording, which uses a coherent light beam. The light is reflected by a mirror as a reference beam and scattered from the object as the object beam. The interference between the reference beam and the object beam is recorded on the photographic plate as a hologram. When the hologram is illuminated by the original reference beam as shown in Figure 3.10b, the reference beam will be diffracted by the hologram to create a light field which closely approximates to the scattered beam from the object in phase, direction, and intensity. In other words, the light field is reconstructed from the observer's point of view, even the original object does not physically appear in its original place. The holography indeed provides a true 3D image reconstruction.

For digital holography, the photographic plate is replaced by the pixelated liquid crystal spatial light modulator (SLM). Several types of SLM exist by either modulating the amplitude or the phase of the incident beam for each pixel [18]. The required size and resolution for SLM are the major technique parameters to provide a satisfactory viewing experience. However, the information stored in the analog photographic plate is extremely large, which becomes a storage problem during the digitization process and a computation problem during the reproduction process for digital holography. The problems will become worse when we want a holographic video, which requires frame refresh in a small time interval. 3D digital video holography requires more research to resolve the above-mentioned challenges and make it commercially available.

References

1. L. Zhang, C. Vázquez, and S. Knorr, "3D-TV Content Creation: Automatic 2D-to-3D Video Conversion", *IEEE Trans. on Broadcasting*, vol. 57, no. 2, June 2011, pp. 372–383.
2. L. Hill and A. Jacobs, "3-D liquid crystal displays and their applications", *Proceedings of the IEEE*, vol. 94, no. 3, March 2006, pp. 575–590.
3. E. Dubois, "A projection method to generate anaglyph stereo images", *Proc. IEEE International Conference on Acoustics Speech Signal Processing*, vol. 3, May 2001, pp. 1661–1664.
4. H. Jorke and M. Fritz, *"Infitec – A new stereoscopic visualization tool by wavelength multiplexing imaging"*, in Proc. Electronic Displays, Sept. 2003.
5. H. Jorke and A Simon, "New high efficiency interference filter characteristics for stereoscopic imaging", Proc. SPIE, vol. 8288, no. 1, 2012. 82881D.
6. A. J. Woods and J. Helliwell, "Investigating the cross-compatibility of IR-controlled active shutter glasses", *Proc. SPIE*, vol. 8288, no. 1, 2012. 82881C.
7. A. K. Srivastava, J. L. de B. de la Tocnaye, and L. Dupont, "Liquid crystal active glasses for 3D cinema", *Journal of Display Technology*, vol. 6, no. 10, Oct 2010, pp. 522–530.
8. C. Cruz-Neira, D. J. Sandin, T. A. DeFanti, R. V. Kenyon, and J. C. Hart. "The CAVE: Audio visual experience automatic virtual environment", *Communications of the ACM*, vol. 35, no. 6, 1992, pp. 64–72.
9. J. S. Lipscomb and W. L. Wooten, "Reducing crosstalk between stereoscopic views", *Proc. SPIE*, vol. 2177, pp. 92–96, 1994.
10. Y.-H. Tao, Q.-H. Wang, J. Gu, W.-X. Zhao, and D.-H. Li, "Autostereoscopic three-dimensional projector based on two parallax barriers", *Optics Letters*, vol. 34, no. 20, pp. 3220–3222, 2009.
11. D. Takemori, K. Kanatani, S. Kishimoto, S. Yoshii, and H. Kanayama, "3-D display with large double lenticular lens screens", SID Digest, 1995, pp. 55–58.
12. A.V. Oppenheim and R.W. Schafer, "Discrete-Time Signal Processing", 3rd ed. Prentice Hall, 2009.
13. D. Ezra, G. J. Woodgate, B. A. Omar, N. S. Holliman, J. Harrold, and L. S. Shapiro, "New autostereoscopic display system", *Proc. SPIE*, vol. 2409, no. 1, pp. 31–40, 1995.
14. C. van Berkel, "Image preparation for 3D LCD", *Proc. SPIE*, vol. 3639, no. 1, pp. 84–91, 1999.
15. J. Konrad and P. Angiel, "Subsampling models and anti-alias filters for 3-D automultiscopic displays", *IEEE Trans. Image Processing*, vol. 15, no. 1, pp. 128–140, Jan. 2006.
16. A. Jain and J. Konrad, "Crosstalk in automultiscopic 3-D displays: Blessing in disguise?" in Proc. *SPIE*, vol. 6490, pp. 12.1–12.12, January 2007.
17. X.-F. Li, Q.-H. Wang, D.-H. Li, and A. H. Wang, "Image processing to eliminate crosstalk between neighboring view images in three-dimensional lenticular display", *Journal of Display Technology*, vol. 7, no. 8, August 2011, pp. 443–447.
18. L. Onural, F. Yaras, and H. Kang, "Digital holographic three-dimensional video displays", *Proc. of the IEEE*, vol. 99, no. 4, April 2011. pp. 576–589.

4

3D Content Creation

With the wide deployment of 3DTVs at home but the severe lack of 3D content on the market, 3D content creation techniques have attracted more and more attentions recently. In this chapter, we demonstrate the whole process of 3D content creation, from modeling and representation, capturing, 2D-to-3D conversation, to 3D multi-view generation. We showcase three practical examples that are adopted in the industrial 3D creation process to provide a clear picture of how things work together in a real 3D creation system.

4.1 3D Scene Modeling and Creation

In general, 3D scene modeling and representation approaches can be classified into three categories: geometry-based modeling, image-based modeling, and hybrid modeling which combines the geometry-based and image-based modeling in some way to represent a 3D scene at better storage cost or with better precision. Geometry-based modeling represents the scene using pure 3D computer graphics components, for example, 3D meshes or other means to represent 3D surfaces, texture maps, object material properties such as opacity, reflectance, and so on, and environment properties, such as lighting models, with the purpose of enhancing the realism of the models. Image-based modeling goes to the other extreme, using no 3D geometry, but rather using a set of images captured by a number of cameras with predesigned positions and settings. This approach tends to generate high quality virtual view synthesis without the effort of 3D scene reconstruction, and typically the synthesis quality increases with the availability of more views. The challenge for this approach is that a tremendous amount of image data needs to be stored, transferred, and processed in order to achieve a good quality synthesized view, otherwise interpolation and occlusion artifacts will appear in the synthesized image due to lack of source data. The hybrid approach can leverage these two representation methods to find a compromise between the two extremes according to given constraints; for example, using multiple images and corresponding depth maps to represent 3D scene is a popular method in which the depth maps are the geometric modeling component, but this hybrid representation can reduce the storage and processing of many extra images to achieve the same high-quality synthesized view as the image-based approach.

3D Visual Communications, First Edition. Guan-Ming Su, Yu-Chi Lai, Andres Kwasinski and Haohong Wang.
© 2013 John Wiley & Sons, Ltd. Published 2013 by John Wiley & Sons, Ltd.

In industry, many such 3D modeling tools have been adopted for 3D content creation. For example, NewSight provides 3D content creation tools to do 3D modeling, animation, and rendering, and the results are displayed at its autostereoscopic 3D displays. InTru3D is a brand from Intel that allows content created through the Intel's animation technology to be viewed in stereoscopic 3D. Along with InTru3D and ColorCode 3-D, the DreamWorks and PepsiCo's SoBe Lifewater have made Super Bowl XLIII a 3D event. ColorCode 3-D is a 3D stereo system with a novel left/right view encoding algorithm so that the composed image appears essentially as an ordinary color image with slightly increased contrast and with distant or sharp-edge objects surrounded by faint holes of golden and bluish tints, and the ColorCodeViewer has amber and blue filter with complex spectral curves to separate the left/right views at the end. The ColorCode 3-D image works on all display types ranging from computers and TV displays and digital projects to analogue films.

4.1.1 Geometry-Based Modeling

Geometry-based modeling automatically generates 3D scenes by computer; although the current graphics card with modern GPUs are very powerful in rendering and computation, the efforts of 3D scene reconstruction are still complex and time consuming. Typically the camera geometry estimation, depth map generation and 3D shape generation are fundamental components of scene reconstruction efforts. The introduced errors during the estimation process may cause noticeable visual artifacts; sometimes user interactions and assistance are used in order to generate high-quality production of geometry models.

The Shape-from-Silhouette approach is one of the prominent methods in geometry reconstruction. A silhouette of an object representing the contour separates the object from the background. With multiple view images of the 3D scene, the retrieved silhouettes from these views are back projected to a common 3D space with projection centers equal to the camera locations, and a cone-like volume is generated for each projection. By intersection all the cones, a visual hull of the target 3D object is generated. After that, a texturing process is applied to assign colors to the voxels on the surfaces of the visual hull and the realistic rendering process makes the reconstructed 3D object in good visual quality.

4.1.2 Image-Based Modeling

As mentioned earlier, the advantage of image-based modeling is to avoid the complicated 3D scene reconstruction process, as a potential high quality virtual view can be synthesized from the other views obtained during the capturing process by cameras in different locations and at different angles. However, the benefit is paid for by dense sampling of the real world with sufficient number of cameras in various positions, which will produce large volumes of data for further processing.

The plenoptic function [1] plays a very important role in image-based modeling, as the modeling process is indeed a sampling process for capturing the complete flow of light in a region of the environment, thus the well-known 7D data, which includes viewing position (3D), viewing direction (2D), time and wavelength, are popular for describing the visual information. In order to reduce the data size while keeping the rendering quality, researchers have tried different approaches. For example, [2] introduces a 5D function that ignores the wavelength and time dimensions; and light fields [3] and Lumigraph [4] reduced the data to 4D by ignoring the wavelength and time dimensions and assuming that radiance does not change along a line in free space, thus light rays are recorded by their intersections with two planes with two sets of 2D coordinates. Furthermore, [5] reduces the dimensions of the plenoptic function to 3D by restricting both the cameras and the viewers to the same plane.

4.1.3 Hybrid Approaches

It is important to introduce the concept of disparity here. Disparity is typically interpreted as the inverse distances to the observed objects. In order to obtain disparity between two views, a stereo correspondence (or stereo matching) algorithm is called, which compares the correlation of local windows or features and matches these features one by one. Clearly some constraints such as occlusion can make the matching process very challenging. It is worth mentioning that Scharstein and Szeliski [6] created a website, Middlebury stereo vision page, to investigate the performance of around 40 stereo matching algorithms running on a pair of rectified images.

Depth or disparity maps representing the depth information for each sample of an image are often used along with the 2D image to form a 2.5D representation of the 3D scene. Layered depth images are a natural extension where the ordered depth layers are used to store pixel intensities. The current popular multi-view video plus depth representation for 3D scenes is another extension that uses multiple depth maps according to the multiple images to get a more precise scene reconstruction.

4.2   3D Content Capturing

With different types of cameras, the 3D content capturing process is completely different. The stereo camera or depth camera simultaneously captures video and associated per-pixel depth or disparity information; multi-view cameras capture multiple images simultaneously from various angles, then a multi-view matching (or correspondence) process is required to generate the disparity map for each pair of cameras, and then the 3D structure can be estimated from these disparity maps. The most challenging scenario is to capture 3D content from a normal 2D (or monoscopic) camera, which lacks disparity or depth information. In this chapter, we showcase a real-time 3D capturing system with a monoscopic mobile phone in Section 4.2.4.

4.2.1 Stereo Camera

Basically, a typical stereo camera uses two cameras mounted side by side for the recording, although some variants may build them into one with two lenses. We list below a few examples:

- Fusion camera system: the concept was first developed by James Cameron and Vince Pace many years ago. The Sony Fusion 3D Camera System was presented at NAB 2007 using two Sony HDCF950 HD cameras, which are presumably variants of the Sony CineAlta range.

- TDVision provides TDVCam, a true stereoscopic high definition digital video camera that records 3D video in MPEG4 format.
- Silicon Imaging unveiled the very first integrated 3D cinema camera and stereo visualization system, based on two SI-2K camera heads, and a single control, processing, and recording platform to encode the raw images obtained from two synchronized cameras directly to a single stereo CineForm RAW file.
- Panasonic produced a professional 3D full HD production system, which consists of a twin-lens P2 professional camera recorder and a 3D-compatible high-definition plasma display. The concept model was exhibited at NAB 2009.
- Iconix provides end-to-end stereoscopic 3D workflow solutions with 3D head rigged with two Iconix RH1 cameras recording to capture close-up stereoscopic footage.

There are also companies that develop and rent specialized stereoscopic (3D) image capture equipment for the motion picture entertainment industry, for example, a company called the 3D Camera Company. On the other hand, 3ality recently began making its state-of-the-art 3flex™ camera rigs. They claim that when used with 3ality Digital's rig software controller (SPC) and Stereo Image Processing Systems (SIPS), the 3flex rigs will allow operators to capture nearly pixel-perfect live-action 3D footage.

4.2.2 Depth Camera

Depth camera refers to a class of cameras that have sensors that are able to measure the depth for each of the captured pixels using a principle called time-of-flight. It gets 3D information "by emitting pulses of infrared light to all objects in the scene and sensing the reflected light from the surface of each object." The objects in the scene are then ordered in layers in the z-axis, which gives you a grayscale depth map that a game or any software application can use.

When talk about depth camera, it would be unfair if not mentioning Kinect, the Guinness World Record holder of being the "fastest selling consumer electronics device", which holds a record of selling a total of 8 million units in its first 60 days. Kinect uses a range camera technology by Israeli developer PrimeSense, which developed a system that can interpret specific gestures, making completely hands-free control of electronic devices possible by using an infrared projector and camera and a special microchip to track the movement of objects and individuals in three dimension. The depth sensor consists of an infrared laser projector combined with a monochrome CMOS sensor, which captures video data in 3D under any ambient light conditions. Kinect is capable of automatically calibrating the depth sensor based on gameplay and the player's physical environment, accommodating for the presence of furniture or other obstacles.

4.2.3 Multi-View Camera

Commercial multi-view camera systems are rare in the market, although Honda Motor announced in September 2008 that it had developed a prototype multi-view camera system which displays views from multiple wide-angle CCD cameras on the vehicle's navigation screen to reduce blind spots, support smooth parallel or garage parking, and support comfortable and safe driving at a three-way intersection where there is limited visibility or on narrow roads. There are many multi-view cameras (or camera arrays) set up in labs for research efforts, where the synchronization among these cameras is conducted by gunlock devices.

4.2.4 3D Capturing with Monoscopic Camera

The major difference between a stereo image and a mono image is that the former provides the feel of the third dimension and the distance to objects in the scene. Human vision by nature is stereoscopic due to the binocular views seen by our left and right eyes in different perspective viewpoints. It is our brains that are capable of synthesizing an image with stereoscopic depth. In general, a stereoscopic camera with two sensors is required for producing a stereoscopic image or video. However, most of the current multimedia devices deployed are implemented within the monoscopic infrastructure. In this section, we showcase a new concept for obtaining real-time stereo images and videos by using a monoscopic mobile camera phone.

In the past decade, stereoscopic image generation has been actively studied. In [7], the video sequence is analyzed and the 3D scene structure is estimated from the 2D geometry and motion activities (which is also called structure from motion, or SfM). This class of approaches enables the conversion of recorded 2D video clips to 3D; however, its computational complexity is rather high so that it is not feasible to use it for real-time stereo image generation. On the other hand, since SfM is a mathematically ill-posed problem, the result might contain artifacts and cause visual discomfort. Some other approaches first estimate depth information from a single-view image and then generate the stereoscopic views after that. In [8], a method for extracting relative depth information from monoscopic cues, for example retinal sizes of objects, is proposed, which is useful for the auxiliary depth map generation. In [9], a facial-feature-based parametric depth map generation scheme is proposed to convert 2D head-and-shoulders images to 3D. In [10], an unsupervised method for depth-map generation is proposed, but some steps in the approach, for example the image classification in preprocessing, are not trivial and may be very complicated to implement, which undermines the practicality of the proposed algorithm. In [11], a real-time 2D-to-3D image conversion algorithm is proposed using motion detection and region segmentation; however, artifacts are unavoidable due to the inaccuracy of object segmentation and object depth estimation.

Clearly, all the methods mentioned above consider only the captured monoscopic images. Some other approaches use auxiliary sources to help generate the stereo views. In [12], a low-cost auxiliary monochrome or low-resolution camera is used to capture the additional view, and it then uses a disparity estimation model to generate the depth map of the pixels. In [13], a monoscopic high resolution color camera is used to capture the luminosity and chromaticity of a scene, and an inexpensive flanking 3D-stereoscopic pair of low resolution monochrome "outrigger" cameras are used to augment luminosity and chromaticity with depth. The disparity maps generated from the obtained three views are used to synthesis the stereoscopic pairs. In [14], a mixed set of automatic and manual techniques are used to extract the depth map (sometimes the automatic method is not reliable), and then a simple smoothing filter is used to reduce the visible artifacts of the result image.

In the following text, we introduce the new concept of using the auto-focus function of the monoscopic camera sensor to estimate depth map information [15], which avoids not only using auxiliary equipment or human interaction as mentioned above, but also the introduced computational complexity of SfM or depth analysis. The whole system design is novel, and is generic for both stereo image and video capture and generation. The additional but optional motion estimation module can help to improve the accuracy of the depth map detection for stereo video generation. The approach is feasible for low-power devices due to its two-stage depth map estimation design. That is, in the first stage, a block-level depth map is detected, and an approximated image depth map is generated by using bilinear filtering in the second stage. By contrast, the proposed approach uses statistics from motion estimation, auto-focus processing, and the history data plus some heuristic rules for estimating the depth map.

In Figure 4.1, the proposed system architecture that supports both stereo image and video data capturing, processing, and display is shown. In the system, an image is first captured by a monoscopic camera sensor in the video front end (VFE), and then it goes through the auto-focus process, which helps to generate a corresponding approximated depth map. The depth map is further processed either using bilinear filtering for still-image or taking into account the motion information from the video coding process for video. After that, a depth-based image pair generation algorithm is used to generate stereo views. Clearly the 3D effect can be accomplished by choosing different display technologies such as holographic, stereoscopic, volumetric, and so on. In this prototype work, we present the results using red-blue anaglyph.

In Figure 4.2, the system architecture for still images is shown, which is simpler than the generic architecture in Figure 4.1.

In this work, we take advantage of the autofocus process of the camera sensor for automatic depth map detection. For capturing still images and video, we use different approaches due to the different focus length search algorithm employed in these scenarios.

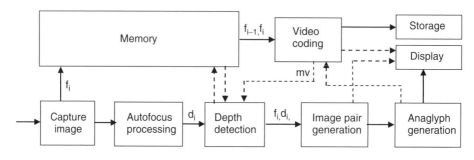

Figure 4.1 System architecture.

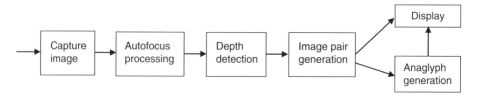

Figure 4.2 System architecture for still images.

4.2.4.1 Depth Estimation by Autofocus Processing

In digital cameras, most focusing systems choose the best focus position by evaluating image contrast on the imager plane. Focus value (FV) is a score measured via a focus metric over a specific region of interest, and the autofocusing process of the camera normally chooses the position corresponding to the highest focus value as the best focus position of the lens. In some cameras, the high frequency content of an image is used as the focus value, for example, the high pass filter (HPF):

$$HPF = \begin{bmatrix} -1 & 0 & 0 & 0 & -1 \\ 0 & 0 & 4 & 0 & 0 \\ -1 & 0 & 0 & 0 & -1 \end{bmatrix}, \tag{4.1}$$

can be used to capture the high frequency components for determining the focus value.

It is important to know that there is a relationship between the lens position from the focal point and the target distance from the camera (as shown in Figure 4.3), and the relationship is fixed for a specific camera sensor. Various camera sensors may have different statistics of such relationships. It means that once the autofocus process locates the best focus position of lens, based on the knowledge of the camera sensor's property, we are able to estimate the actual distance between the target object and the camera, which is also the depth of the object in the scene. Therefore, the proposed depth map detection relies on a sensor-dependent autofocus processing.

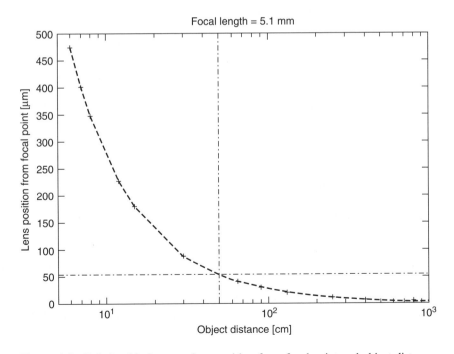

Figure 4.3 Relationship between lens position from focal point and object distance.

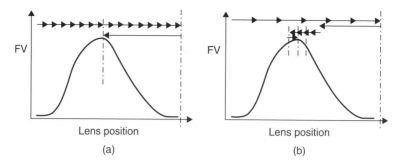

Figure 4.4 Examples of exhaustive search algorithm. (a) Global search. (b) Coarse-to-fine search.

4.2.4.2   Depth Map Generation for Still Images

For still-image capturing, most digital camera sensors choose an exhaustive search algorithm (as shown in Figure 4.4), which determines the best focus position by moving its lens through the entire focusing range and selecting the focus position with the maximum focus value. A typical example of an exhaustive search algorithm is global search shown in Figure 4.4a, which scans the whole focus range with the smallest motor step. Figure 4.4b shows another popular solution, coarse to fine search, which searches the whole focus range using a bigger step first, then search around the peak position using a smaller step.

Clearly, the accuracy of the depth map generated for a still image is purely dependent on the sizes of the spot focus windows selected for the image. In general, we split the image into N×N sub-blocks, which are also called spot focus windows, and calculate the focus values for each focus window during the autofocus process. After exhaustive search, the best focus position of the lens is obtained for each focus window, and thus the depth of the object corresponding to each window can be estimated. Clearly, the smaller the focus window size, the better accuracy of the depth map, and the higher the computational complexity. In this work, we define two types of depth maps: image depth map (IDM) and block depth map (BDM). For an image depth map, the depth value of every pixel is stored; for a block depth map, the depth value of each focus window is stored. In Figure 4.5b, the image depth map corresponding to the still-image shown in Figure 4.5a is obtained by setting the focus window size as 1×1 and thus the map is in pixel-level accuracy, where pixels with higher intensity correspond to objects closer to the viewpoint. However, this setting is normally infeasible for most applications due to the excessive computational complexity for autofocusing. An example of block depth map is shown in Figure 4.5c where N is set to 11, and it is a more practical setting for cameras with normal computational capability.

In general, the block depth map needs to be further processed to obtain an approximate image depth map; otherwise, some artifacts may appear. An example of a synthesized 3D anaglyph view using the block depth map shown in Figure 4.5c is shown in Figure 4.5d, where artifacts appear due to the fact that the sharp depth gap between neighboring focus windows at the edges does not correspond to the actual object shape boundaries in the image. The artifacts can be reduced after we have processed the depth map with a bilinear filter, and the filtered depth map is shown in Figure 4.5e.

Figure 4.5 Examples of image depth map and block depth map. (a) Original image. (b) Image depth map. (c) Block depth map. (d) Synthesized 3D anaglyph view using the block depth map. (e) Approximated image depth map.

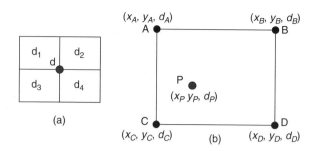

Figure 4.6 Example of pixel depth approximation.

The artifact reduction process consists of two steps. In the first step, we find the depth value of the corner points of each block in Figure 4.5c, and the depth value would be the average value of its neighboring blocks as shown in Figure 4.6a where the depth of the middle point $d = \dfrac{d_1 + d_2 + d_3 + d_4}{4}$, and where d_1, d_2, d_3, and d_4 are depth value of the neighboring blocks. After the depth values of all corner points are obtained, we use a bilinear filtering approach to obtain the depth value of the pixels inside the windows. As shown in the example in Figure 4.6b, the position and depth values for the corners points A, B, C, and D of the window are available as (x_A, y_A, d_A), (x_B, y_B, d_B), (x_C, y_C, d_C), (x_D, y_D, d_D), so the depth value of all the pixels within the window can be calculated. For example for point P (x_P, y_P, d_P), the depth can be obtained by:

$$
\begin{aligned}
d_P = {} & \frac{(x_P - x_A)^4 + (y_P - y_A)^4}{\begin{array}{c}(x_P - x_A)^4 + (y_P - y_A)^4 + (x_P - x_B)^4 + (y_P - y_B)^4 \\ + (x_P - x_C)^4 + (y_P - y_C)^4 + (x_P - x_D)^4 + (y_P - y_D)^4\end{array}} d_A \\[2mm]
& + \frac{(x_P - x_B)^4 + (y_P - y_B)^4}{\begin{array}{c}(x_P - x_A)^4 + (y_P - y_A)^4 + (x_P - x_B)^4 + (y_P - y_B)^4 \\ +(x_P - x_C)^4 + (y_P - y_C)^4 + (x_P - x_D)^4 + (y_P - y_D)^4\end{array}} d_B \\[2mm]
& + \frac{(x_P - x_C)^4 + (y_P - y_C)^4}{\begin{array}{c}(x_P - x_A)^4 + (y_P - y_A)^4 + (x_P - x_B)^4 + (y_P - y_B)^4 \\ + (x_P - x_C)^4 + (y_P - y_C)^4 + (x_P - x_D)^4 + (y_P - y_D)^4\end{array}} d_C \\[2mm]
& + \frac{(x_P - x_D)^4 + (y_P - y_D)^4}{\begin{array}{c}(x_P - x_A)^4 + (y_P - y_A)^4 + (x_P - x_B)^4 + (y_P - y_B)^4 \\ + (x_P - x_C)^4 + (y_P - y_C)^4 + (x_P - x_D)^4 + (y_P - y_D)^4\end{array}} d_D.
\end{aligned}
\tag{4.2}
$$

4.2.4.3 Depth Map Generation for Video

For video cameras, the exhaustive search algorithm is not feasible due to the excessive delay caused in determining the best focus. Hill-climbing focusing is more popular because of its faster search speed. It searches the best focus position like climbing a hill. When the camera starts to record, an exhaustive search algorithm is used to find the best focus position as an initial position, but after the initial lens position is located, the camera needs to determine in real time the direction that the focus lens has to move and by how much in order to get to the top of the hill.

Clearly, to get accurate depth maps for videos during autofocus processing is much more difficult than than for still images. The reason is that hill-climbing focusing only obtains the correct depth for the area in focus, while not guaranteeing the correctness of depth for other blocks. In addition, the exhaustive search, which guarantees the correctness of depth for all blocks, is only called at the starting point of the recording, so it is impossible to correct the depths of all the blocks during the video recording period.

In this work, we propose a novel depth map detection algorithm for video capturing as shown in Figure 4.7. Let us denote by n the current frame index, $\{D_n(i, j)\}$ and $\{F_n(i, j)\}$ ($i = 1, 2, \ldots N$, $j = 1, 2, \ldots N$) the final determined BDM and FV map of the current frame, $\{M_n(i, j)\}$ and $\{V_n(i, j)\}$ the internal BDM and FV map obtained by auto-focusing, and $\{P_n(i, j)\}$ and $\{T_n(i, j)\}$ the internal BDM and FV map obtained by motion prediction. During the process, the focus position of current frame is first determined by hill-climbing focusing and the corresponding block depth map $\{M_n(i, j)\}$ and FV map $\{V_n(i, j)\}$ is obtained. Then, the motion information (if available) is analyzed and the global motion vector (GMV) is obtained. If the global motion (i.e., the GVD is

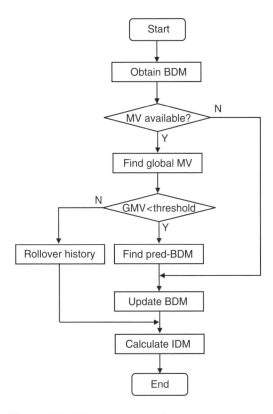

Figure 4.7   Flowchart of the depth map generation.

greater than a threshold) is detected, this means that the camera lens is moving to other scenes, then the tasks of maintaining an accurate scene depth history and estimating the object movement directions become different. For this case we set $D_n(i, j) = M_n(i, j)$ and $F_n(i, j) = V_n(i, j)$, and we clean up the stored BDM and FV map history of previous frames.

In general systems, the motion information sometimes might be unavailable for all kinds of reasons: for example, the video is not coded, or the motion estimation module of the coding algorithm has been turned off. In these cases, we assume that the motion vectors are zeros for all blocks. On the other hand, if the motion information is available, we are able to predict the BDM and FV map of current frame $P_n(i, j)$ and $T_n(i, j)$ from those of the previous frame by using

$$P_n(i, j) = \begin{cases} D_{n-1}(a, b) & if\,|V_n(i, j) - F_{n-1}(a, b)| < FV\_TH \\ D_{n-1}(i, j) & otherwise \end{cases} \tag{4.3}$$

and

$$T_n(i, j) = \begin{cases} F_{n-1}(a, b) & if\,|V_n(i, j) - F_{n-1}(a, b)| < FV\_TH \\ F_{n-1}(i, j) & otherwise \end{cases}, \tag{4.4}$$

where block (a,b) in $(n-1)$th frame is the prediction of block (i, j) in the nth frame, and FV_TH is a threshold for FV difference.

In this work, we assume that the better focus conveys more accurate depth estimation. Therefore, we treat the focal lens position corresponding to the largest FV as the best choice. Based on such logic, the final BDM and FV map is determined by

$$D_n(i, j) = \begin{cases} D_{n-1}(i, j) & if\ F_{n-1}(i, j) \geq V_n(i, j)\&F_{n-1}(i, j) \geq T_n(i, j) \\ M_n(i, j) & if\ V_n(i, j) \geq F_{n-1}(i, j)\&V_n(i, j) \geq T_n(i, j) \\ P_n(i, j) & if\ T_n(i, j) \geq F_{n-1}(i, j)\&T_n(i, j) \geq V_n(i, j) \end{cases} \tag{4.5}$$

and

$$F_n(i, j) = \max[F_{n-1}(i, j), V_n(i, j), T_n(i, j)]. \tag{4.6}$$

As expected, (4.5) and (4.6) are not accurate for all cases. They would fail for some difficult scenarios such as when occlusion/exposure occurs. In general, it is reasonable if we assume that the video frames are captured at a speed of 15–30 frames per second, and the object in the frames is moving at reasonable speed, so that an object would not move too far away in neighbor frame.

After the BDM is obtained, the IDM is calculated from the BDM results based on the approach mentioned in the earlier section.

An example for demonstrating the proposed algorithm is shown in Figure 4.8, where 4.8a and 4.8b show the image of the first frame and the corresponding BDM, 4.8c and 4.8d show the 30th frame of the video and its corresponding BDM, and 4.8e and 4.8f show the 60th frame of the video and its corresponding BDM. In the video, a plastic bottle rolls toward the camera from the far distance. It can be seen from these figures that the proposed algorithm is capable of catching the movements of the objects in the scene and reflecting these activities in the obtained depth maps.

In Figure 4.9, the IDMs generated from the BDMs show in Figures 4.8b, 4.8d and 4.8f are shown, which are obtained by using the approach mentioned earlier.

Figure 4.8 Examples of video frames and their corresponding BDMs.

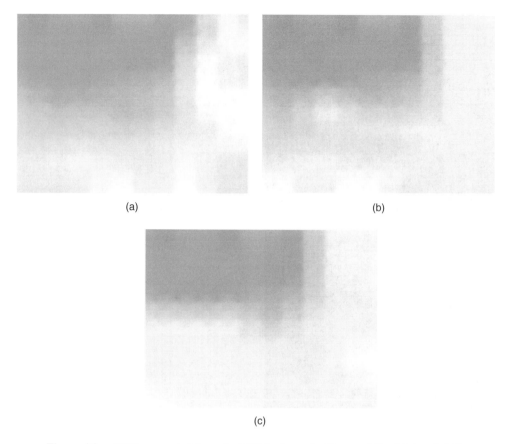

(a)   (b)

(c)

Figure 4.9   IDMs generated from the BDMs shown in Figures 4.8b, 4.8d, and 4.8f.

4.2.4.4   Stereo Image Pair Generation

So far, we have captured an image and obtained its corresponding depth map. In this section, we propose a novel stereo image pair generation algorithm by using Z-buffer-based 3D surface recovery. The algorithm flowchart is shown in Figure 4.10. We assume that the obtained image is the left view of the stereoscopic system; then, based on the depth map, we are able to calculate the disparity map (the distance in pixels between the image points in both views) for the image. Then a Z-buffer-based 3D interpolation process is called to construct a 3D visible surface for the scene from the right eye. Finally, the right view can be obtained by projecting the 3D surface onto the projection plane.

4.2.4.5   Disparity Map Generation

In Figure 4.11, the geometry model of binocular vision is shown, where F is the focal length, $L(xL, yL, 0)$ is the left eye, $R(xR, yR, 0)$ is the right eye, $T(x_T, y_T, z)$ is a 3D point in the scene, and $P(x_P, y_P, F)$ and $Q(x_Q, y_Q, F)$ are the projection points of the T onto the left and right projection planes. Clearly, the horizontal position of

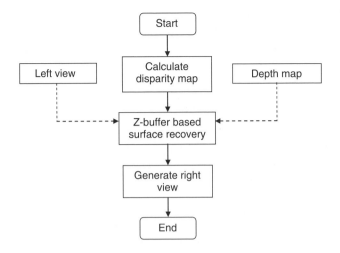

Figure 4.10 Flowchart of the stereo image pair generation.

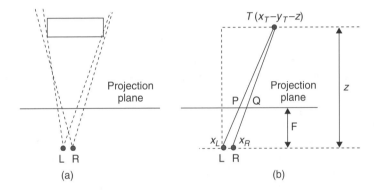

Figure 4.11 Geometry model for binocular vision.

P and Q on the projection planes are $(x_P - x_L)$ and $(x_Q - x_R)$, and thus the disparity is $d = [(x_Q - x_R) - (x_P - x_L)]$.

As shown in Figure 4.11,

$$\frac{F}{z} = \frac{x_P - x_L}{x_T - x_L} = \frac{x_Q - x_R}{x_T - x_R}, \tag{4.7}$$

so

$$x_P - x_L = \frac{F}{z}(x_T - x_L), \tag{4.8}$$

$$x_Q - x_R = \frac{F}{z}(x_T - x_R), \tag{4.9}$$

and thus the disparity can be obtained as:

$$d = \frac{F}{z}(x_L - x_R). \tag{4.10}$$

Therefore, for every pixel in the left view, its counterpart in the right view is shifted to the left or right side by a distance of the disparity value obtained in (4.10). However, the mapping from left-view to right-view is not 1-to-1 mapping due to possible occlusions, therefore further process is needed to obtain the right-view image.

4.2.4.6 Z-Buffer-Based 3D Surface Recovering

We propose a Z-buffer-based 3D surface recovering algorithm for right-view generation. Since the distance between two eyes compared to the distance from eyes to the objects (as shown in Figure 4.11) is very small, we can approximately think that the distance from object to the left eye is equal to the distance from itself to the right eye, which would greatly simplify the calculation.

In this method, we maintain a depth map $Z(x, y)$ for the right view where x, y are pixel positions in the view. Here the purpose is to reconstruct the 3D visible surface for the right view. At the beginning, the depth map is initialized as infinity. Then, for every pixel (x_0, y_0) in the left view with depth z_0 and disparity value d_0, we update the depth map for its corresponding pixel in the right view as:

$$Z(x_0 + d_0, y_0) = \min[Z(x_0 + d_0, y_0), z_0]. \tag{4.11}$$

After all the pixels in the left view are processed, we check the reconstructed depth map and search for the pixels with values equal to infinity (the pixels without a valid map on the left view). For such pixels, we first calculate its depth by 2D interpolation based on its neighbor pixels with available depth value. After that, we find the disparity value following the computing using (4.10) and then inversely find its corresponding pixel in the left view. If the corresponding pixel is available, then the corresponding intensity value can be used on the right-view pixel; otherwise, we use interpolation to calculate the intensity value based on its neighbor pixels in the right view with available intensity values. It is important to point out that the benefit of using the proposed algorithm over the direct intensity interpolation method is that it considers the 3D continuity of the object shape which results in better realism for the stereo effect.

Clearly, the problem of recovering the invisible area of the left view is an ill-posed problem. In the solution of [16], the depth of the missing pixel is recovered by using its neighbor pixel in the horizontal direction corresponding to a further surface with an assumption that there are no other visible surfaces behind in the scene. For some cases, the assumption might be invalid. To consider more possible cases, in the proposed solution, the surface recovering considers depths of all the neighbor pixels in all directions, which will reduce the chances of invalid assumption and will result in better 3D continuity of the recovered surface.

4.2.4.7 Experimental Results

In these experiments, we used an inexpensive red-blue anaglyph to demonstrate the resulting 3D effect, although the generated stereo views can be displayed by other mechanisms such as holographic and stereoscopic devices. In the first experiment, we calculate the stereo image pairs using different kinds of image depth map and generate the corresponding anaglyph images. As shown in Figure 4.12a, this is generated by using the

(a)   (b)

Figure 4.12 Examples of the resulting anaglyph image. (a) Anaglyph generated by using the depth map in Figure 4.5e. (b) Anaglyph generated by using the depth map in Figure 4.5b.

approximated image depth map shown in Figure 4.5e, and Figure 4.12b is generated by using the accurate image depth map shown in Figure 4.5b. Clearly, the results indicate that the approximated image depth map result in a similar image quality as using the accurate depth map, which proves the good performance of the proposed algorithm.

In the second experiment, the generated anaglyph video frames corresponding to the frames and their IDMs shown in Figures 4.8 and 4.9 are demonstrated in Figure 4.13. Clearly, the resultant video clip has a significant 3D effect as can be observed by the selected frames.

4.3 2D-to-3D Video Conversion

In Section 4.2.4, we demonstrated a practical automatic 2D-to-3D video conversion module in a low-power mobile phone system. In this section, we cover the wider scope of 2D-to-3D conversion technology. In general, 2D-to-3D conversion is to convert the current 2D video content in DVD/Blu-ray or other formats into a 3D format with depth sensation. The efforts can be classified into two categories:

- Real-time solution: it is typically connected to the back-end display, and the conversion is done before the output is rendered. Currently, almost all major TV companies have built real-time 2D-to-3D conversion systems in their 3DTVs, some are using their own proprietary technology, and others are using rdthird party vendors, for example, DDD with a technology called TriDef, and Sensio's technology.
- Off-line solution: it handles the conversion in a much finer way with user interaction. The following companies are well known in this area:
  - In-Three plans to re-release the converted 3D version of *Star Wars*.
  - IMAX has converted a few footages, such as *Superman Returns*.
  - 3DFusion has an off-line 2D-to-3D conversion solution (built on top of Philip's solution) for membership based services.

- DDD claimed to have its proprietary offline conversion solutions.
- Akira provides 2D-to-3D conversion and 3D content creations services for its customers.
- Legend films, a San Diego based startup company, provides services for converting 2D films into stereoscopic 3D.

In general, the key component of this conversion technology lies in the generation of a depth map for the 2D image; the depth map is a 2D function that provides the depth value for each object point as a function of the image coordinates. If there is only one 2D image, also called the monocular case, then the depth map has to be derived from various depth cues, such as the linear perspective property of 3D scenes, the relationship between object surface structure and the rendered image brightness according to specific shading models, occlusion of objections, and so on. Otherwise, binocular or multi-ocular cases with two or more images are used to reconstruct the 3D scene. Typically these images are captured from slightly different viewpoints, thus the disparity can be utilized to recover the 3D object depth. Other depth cues also include the disparity over time due to motion,

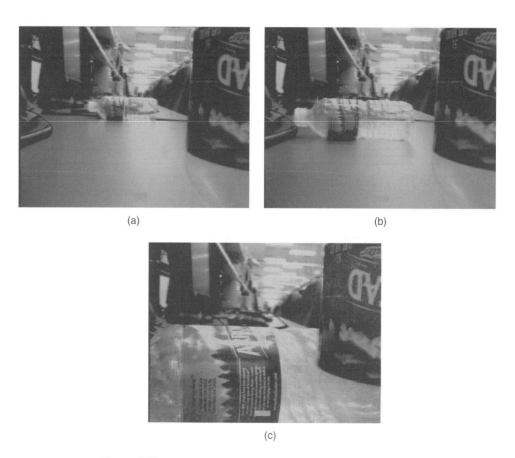

(a)   (b)

(c)

Figure 4.13   Examples of the resulting anaglyph video frames.

the degree of blurring or focus, and so on. In this section, we focus on the monocular cases, and will discuss the binocular or multi-ocular cases in Section 4.4.

4.3.1 Automatic 2D-to-3D Conversion

In this section, we discuss methods in the field of automatic 2D-to-3D conversion. In other words, the human interaction is not considered in this scope and the images are captured in monocular devices. As mentioned above, the depth cues derivation is the focus of this conversion, and the source data has major impact on the approach to choose, for example, the derivation depth from a single image is the most challenging task due to the lack of information; if we have two or more images captured from the same camera (like a video clip), more useful information, like object motion, can be used in obtaining the depth map.

4.3.1.1 Depth Derivation from a Single Image

Depth from Geometric Cues
From a geometric point of view, many objects with long parallel edges, such as railroad tracks, share the same linear perspective property that the edges are converging with distance and eventually reach a vanishing point, which is typically the farthest position away from the camera. In [10] and [17], a gradient plane assignment approach was proposed to detect these edges and find interaction points, among which the interaction point with most edges passing through is determined as the vanishing point. The major lines close to the vanishing points are determined as the vanishing lines, and the lines form a few gradient planes which can map into certain structural models, for example, up case, down case, inside case, and so on. In the depth map generation process, the vanishing points are labeled with largest depth value, and the other points are labeled with depth interpolation according to the gradient structural model.

Depth from Planar Model
This approach assumes that all the 3D scenes are composed of planes or curved surfaces and thus can be approximated by simple models to reconstruct the 3D structure. For example, open sky can be modeled with a spherical surface; a scene consisted of a long-range view and flat ground of water can be represented by a model with a plane and a cylindrical surface, and so on. Once the planar model is determined, the relative depth map can be generated accordingly. As an example, a planar model can be used on indoor environment reconstruction, in which the indoor background is modeled with a few horizontal (floor or ceiling) and vertical (walls and doors) planes. To detect and extract the planes from the image, the wall borders and corners are first extracted with a Harris corner detector in the gradient map of the input image, then a filter-and-merge process is used to keep all meaningful segments which delimit the relevant planes of the scene.

Depth from Focus and Defocus
This approach relies on the blurriness of different regions in the image, that is, the objects in-focus are typically not blurred while the blurriness will be observed on the objects out-of-focus. In this way, the objects are distinguished as foreground objects and

background objects, which also gives an indication of the depth level of the objects. In [18], a relationship between the depth and blurriness is proposed as:

$$u = \begin{cases} \frac{fs}{s-f-kf\sigma} & if \ u > v \\ \frac{fs}{s-f+kf\sigma} & if \ u < v \end{cases} , \tag{4.12}$$

where u is the depth, v is the distance between the lens and the position of the perfect focus, σ is the blur radius, s, f, and k are camera parameters, in which s is the distance between the lens and the image plane, f is the focal length of the lens, and k is a constant determined by the camera lens configuration. Clearly, the depth can be obtained once the blur radius is determined, as the camera parameters s, f, and k can be obtained from camera calibration.

As mentioned in Section 4.1.4, a depth from focus approach is proposed for a low-power mobile device [15]. In the proposal, the autofocusing process of the device positions the lens through an entire focusing range and selects the focus position with a maximum focus value. Thus the device can create a block depth map automatically using statistics from the autofocusing step and in a second-stage generating an image depth map.

Depth from Shading

This approach uses the relationship between scene object surface geometry and the brightness of the image pixels. Clearly the scene object surfaces can be described as a set of 3D points $(x, y, Z(x, y))$, and thus the surface slopes at this point are $[1, 0, \frac{\partial Z}{\partial x}]^T$ and $[0, 1, \frac{\partial Z}{\partial y}]^T$. By assuming a known light source with orthographic projection mode, and a known reflectance model (for example Lambertian), the relationship between the estimated reflectance map and the surface slopes can be formalized. By adding smoothness constraint, the problem can be converted into a minimum energy function and thus eventually can derive the depth map. In [19], a shape from shading approach is proposed by using finite-element theory.

4.3.1.2 Depth Derivation from an Image Sequence

Depth from Motion

This is also called structure from motion (SfM), because the purpose is to extract the 3D structure and the camera movement from an image sequence; typically we assume that the objects in the scene do not deform and the movements are linear. The 2D velocity vectors of each image points, due to the relative motion between the viewing camera and the observed scene are referred to as the motion field, which can be calculated via the object's translational velocity vector, the camera's angular velocity, and perspective projection transformation to map the 3D space to 2D. Once the motion field can be reconstructed from the image sequence, the 3D structure reconstruction can be done in the similar way as the binocular case (which will be discussed in Section 4.4). The motion field becomes almost equivalent to a stereo disparity map if the spatial and temporal variances between the consecutive images are sufficiently small.

The motion field estimation is typically done via optical flow based approach or feature based approach. The key point of optical flow is assuming that the apparent brightness of a 3D object is constant, thus the spatial and temporal derivatives of image brightness for a small piece on the same object are calculated to maintain the image brightness constancy equation:

$$(\partial E)^T_{xy} v + (\partial E)_t = 0, \tag{4.13}$$

where the image brightness is represented as a function of image coordinates and the time, and the partial differentiation of E with respect to the spatial (also called gradient) and time are used to represent the motion velocity of the image point in space and time.

Feature based motion field estimation generates sparse depth maps by tracking separate features in the image sequence. A typical approach in this category is the Kalman filter, which is a recursive algorithm that estimates the position and uncertainty of moving feature points in the subsequent frames.

Hybrid Approach

Hybrid approach means to use a combination of depth cues to detect the depth map, for example, considering combined cues of motion based and focus cues; the motion based cue is used to detect the depth ordinals of the regions in each frame, and a focusing algorithm is applied to estimate the depth value for each pixel in the region. In [20], three different cues were used to obtain the final depth map. Firstly, a blur estimation stage is applied to generate a blur map for the whole frame to find foreground (unblurred region) and background (blurred region); then an optical flow algorithm is used to detect the occlusion in each consecutive frames; after that, a depth ordinal method is adopted to detect the spatial relation according to occlusion information; finally a disparity map is constructed using the blur map and the depth ordinal information.

4.3.1.3 Complexity Adaptive 3D Conversion Algorithm

In this section, we demonstrate a complexity adaptive algorithm for automatic 2D-to-3D image and video conversion. First of all, a novel image classification approach is proposed that can classify an image into flat or non-flat type, which reduces the computational complexity for processing flat image, and helps to reduce possible outliers in the image depth map generation. Then a novel complexity adaptive algorithm was proposed for image depth map estimation, which is a rule based approach that uses object segmentation to help adjust the depth of pixels belonging to the same object, and use temporal depth smoothing to avoid the visual discomfort caused by segmentation errors. The complexity is adaptive in the sense that the procedure can be simplified to trade estimation accuracy with processing speed.

The focus of this work is to convert a 2D image sequence into a 3D image sequence, while the other issues such as the bit stream format of the input images (i.e., compressed or raw data) and the display methods for the output video are not within the scope. Without loss of generality, we assume that the images for processing are in the YUV or RGB format, and the outputs are left and right views.

We propose a complexity adaptive depth-based image conversion algorithm, and its system architecture is shown in Figure 4.14. When an image is coming in, a color-based image analysis approach is used to detect if the image represents a flat scene. If so, then both views would be identical and thus the original image can be used for the view. Otherwise, a rule based image pixel depth estimation method is used to assign

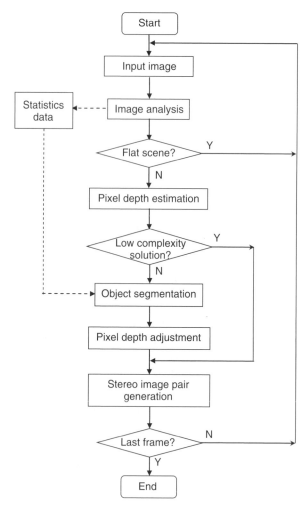

Figure 4.14 System architecture of the complexity adaptive depth-based image conversion algorithm.

approximated depth for each pixel. If there are no low-complexity constraints, the depths are adjusted by using object segmentation so that the pixels representing the same object can have similar depth values. Otherwise, this step is skipped or partially skipped to trade accuracy with speed. The generated depth map is processed by an algorithm to automatically generate the stereo image pairs representing the left and right views.

In the following text, we demonstrate a novel approach to estimate depth for each pixel in the image. It is evident that the stereo views can be generated by a monoscopic image and its associated depth map. Generally, our approach is based on a set of rules obtained from observations. As an example, for outdoor images the upper side has a good chance of representing the sky, and the ground is normally positioned at the bottom of the image. This matches the observations that there is a tendency that the center and bottom parts of the image are nearer than the upper sides in general images.

Figure 4.15 Examples of zoomed images.

Figure 4.16 Examples of view-from-above with a 90° camera elevation angle.

We first classify the images into flat image and non-flat image. The former class contains almost no depth information and thus no depth estimation is needed. We observe that there are two kinds of images that are potentially flat images: (1) zoomed images as shown in Figure 4.15, where the pixel depth differences in the image are visually negligible due to the zooming effect; (2) images corresponding to view-from-above (or below) with a 90° camera elevation angle as shown in Figure 4.16.

In addition, we observe that views with elevation angles less than 90°, as shown in Figures 4.17 and 4.18, contain sufficient depth information. Moreover, the depth information from these views is easier to extract than from the views with a 0° elevation angle because the view angle increases the depth perception.

In this work, we assume that the videos for processing are carefully produced, thus the visual discomfort has been limited to a low probability. Therefore, it would be valid to assume that the occurrences of upside down images, and view-from-above (or below) with a 90° camera elevation angle, in the video are negligible. We assume that the camera orientation is normally aligned with our normal perception.

Since zoom-in and zoom-out are commonly used camera operations in video capture, in order to detect the flat images, we need to be able to automatically detect the zoomed frames. Ideally for zoom in frames, the "blow out" motion pattern would happen in motion estimation. In other words, the motion vectors of the macroblocks will point

Figure 4.17   Examples of view-from-above.

(a)   (b)   (c)

Figure 4.18   Examples of view-from-below.

outward from the center of the zoom operation with vector length proportional to the distance from the center of the zoom operation. However, the noise in the frames might cause inaccurate motion estimation and thus false detection, plus motion estimation is quite computationally intensive for low-complexity applications. In this work, we propose a color-based zoomed image detection algorithm.

We observe that in most video sequences the camera zoom operation follows the sequence of zoom-in → stay → zoom-out, or zoom-in → stay → scene change, so that the zoomed image can be detected by color-histogram change. Let us denote by n the index of the current frame f_n, T_n the zooming type of the current image ($T_n = 1$ represents the zoomed image, otherwise $T_n = 0$), V_n the variance of the current image, $H_n(C_{n,m})$ the 32-bin color histogram and $C_{n,m}$ the color with sorted histogram (i.e., $C_{n,0}$ the color with the highest histogram), and $S(f_{n-1}, f_n)$ the scene similarity between two frames f_{n-1} and f_n ($S(f_{n-1}, f_n) = 1$ means there is a scene change). $S(f_{n-1}, f_n)$ is defined as follows:

$$S(f_{n-1}, f_n) = \begin{cases} 1 & if \quad Sim[H_{n-1}(\vec{C}_{n-1}), H_n(\vec{C}_n)] > Th \\ 0 & otherwise \end{cases}, \qquad (4.14)$$

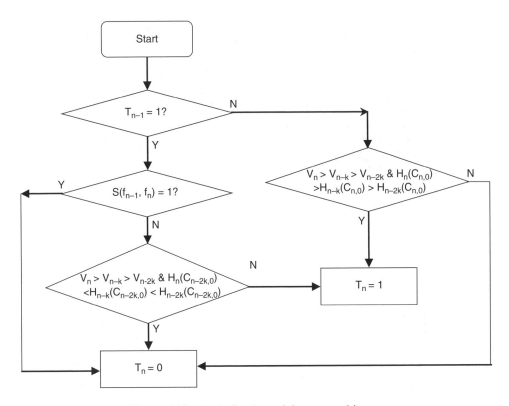

Figure 4.19 Logic for determining zoomed image.

where

$$Sim(\vec{x}, \vec{y}) = \frac{\vec{x} \cdot \vec{y}}{||\vec{x}|| \cdot ||\vec{y}||}, \qquad (4.15)$$

and *Th* is a threshold to detect the image similarity.

The zoomed image can be detected by the logic shown in Figure 4.19. Clearly, if the previous frame is a zoomed image and the current frame is not a scene change, we need to detect if the camera is zooming out. The zooming out scenario can be determined by the gradual increasing of image variation and the gradual deceasing of the percentage of certain colors (primary color components of the previous frame) in the recent frames. Similarly, if the previous frame is not a zoomed image, we need to detect if the camera is zooming in. In Figure 4.19, the value k is a constant that determined by the frame-rate and normal zooming speed. For a 30-frame second per video clip, $k = 10$ could be a reasonable setting for the proposed algorithm.

Then we handle the non-flat images. It is important to realize that in this application, our purpose is not to recover the actual depth of the image pixels, but to generate or estimate an image depth map to enhance the 3D effect of the original image. Our approach is based on two fundamental assumptions: First, the scene is composed of a number of objects, and the pixels corresponding to the same object have closer depth values, and their differences can be negligible. Second, for most non-flat images, the depth of the objects decreases from

(a)   (b)

Figure 4.20 Example of indoor images. (a) Case that is contrary to the assumption. (b) Case that agrees with the assumption.

the top to the bottom. There are some counter-examples, such as indoor scenes as shown in Figure 4.20a, and cases when occlusion occurs, but to detect such scenes is extremely difficult and time-consuming and there are so far no low-complexity solutions available. In general, we observe that the assumptions are valid for most video clips, and the counter-examples do not have significant impact on the visual effect of the generated 3D images.

Initially, we assign each pixel a depth value which is proportional to its vertical coordinate value. After that, we adjust the depth map based on the results of the object segmentation. As shown in Figure 4.21, to reduce the computational complexity we could select only a portion of the image for segmentation when it is necessary. Since the center and bottom regions normally correspond to closer objects that are more visually sensitive, we choose these regions as the aea for segmentation. In this work, we use a complexity adaptive scheme, that is, when a higher complexity solution is acceptable, we apply motion estimation to get motion information and use both color and motion information for object segmentation. When a medium complexity solution is expected, we only use color information for segmentation. For real-time applications or when a low complexity solution is expected, we skip the segmentation operations to avoid heavy computation. We assume that there is a feedback channel from the system controller to inform this application of

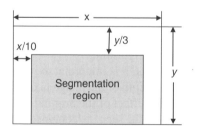

Figure 4.21 The selected segmentation region.

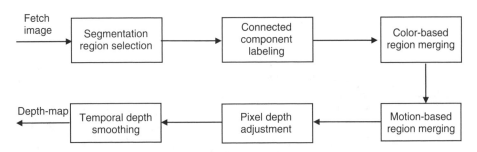

Figure 4.22 Primary flow of image depth map adjustment.

the current status of the system, for example resource allocation and CPU usage, so that our proposed system can choose the solution adaptively, based on the image complexity.

In Figure 4.22, more details of the depth map adjustment are shown. After the segmentation region is selected, we use a connected component labeling approach to divide the image into a number of small connected regions where the pixels inside the same region have similar color intensity. Then a color-based region merging algorithm is used to merge these small regions into bigger regions if any neighboring subregions have close mean color intensity. Motion information (if available) is used further to merge regions moving in the similar direction into bigger objects. After the segmentation steps are completed, we adjust the pixel depth for each object, and assign the depth of each pixel inside an object to be the minimum depth of the pixels in the object. Finally, a temporal depth smoothing process is needed to avoid sharp depth change between adjacent frames. The motivation behind this is that in general the frame rate of video clips is high enough so that the objects in the scene does not move very fast in depth except for some occlusion cases. Let us denote by $d_{n-1}(i, j)$ and $d_n(i, j)$ the depth of pixel (i, j) in the $(n-1)$th and nth frame, so the $d_n(i, j)$ is adjusted as follows:

$$d_n(i, j) = \begin{cases} d_n(i, j) & if \ 0.7 < \frac{d_n(i,j)}{d_{n-1}(i,j)} < 1.5 \\ \frac{2d_n(i,j)+d_{n-1}(i,j)}{3} & otherwise \end{cases}. \qquad (4.16)$$

An example of the generated depth map is shown in Figure 4.23, where b is the estimated depth map corresponding to the original image shown in Figure 4.23a. In the map, the lighter area corresponds to the further objects, and the darker area corresponds to the closer objects. Clearly, the results indicate that the proposed algorithm is capable of approximately distinguishing further objects from closer ones, although some misclassified objects exist due to the lack of semantic information for better segmentation.

4.3.2 Interactive 2D-to-3D Conversion

The interactive 2D-to-3D conversion is also called offline conversion, as human interaction is required in certain stages of the process flow, which could be in terms of object segmentation, object selection, object shape or depth adjustment, object occlusion order specification, and so on. In the next section, we showcase a real scenario that demonstrates many interactive components in a 3D conversion system.

 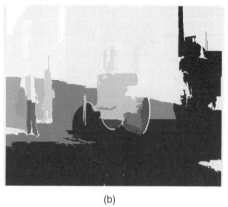

(a)   (b)

Figure 4.23 Example of the generated depth map. (a) Original image. (b) Estimated depth map (the darker the smaller depth).

4.3.3 Showcase of 3D Conversion System Design

In this section, we showcase an example 2D-to-3D conversion system, which is a novel hybrid design that contains both a real-time and an offline conversation system; in other words, the framework uses an interactive 2D-to-3D conversion environment (i3DV) to train an automatic 2D-to-3D conversion solution (a3DC); the interactive environment provides built-in intelligent processing toolkits and friendly user-interfaces to reduce the user interaction and supervision to a minimum, and at the same time it enhances a knowledge base to support the training of the a3DC. The automatic solution, a3DC, starts with a very simple gravity-based depth generation algorithm, with the new rules generated and adjusted by the knowledge base, then the a3DC is able to incorporate the rules and consequent execution procedures into the system to enhance the accuracy of the generated 3D views. To the best of our knowledge, this is the first framework that has been proposed in literature to use a training system for the automatic creation of 3D video content.

Clearly, this framework is very useful for media service providers, where the content for broadcast or delivery are controlled. The media server can start the services of the 3D movie (converted from a 2D content) by creating content using the i3DV; then with more and more titles being generated and the i3DV knowledge base expanding to a mature degree, the a3DC would become more accurate and eventually could significantly reduce the workload and user interactions of i3DV. For similar reasons, the framework would be useful for the content creator and even for TV vendors who have portal services.

As you can imagine, to implement such a framework is not a trivial task. We list below the major challenges and difficulties to consider:

For i3DTV, we need:

- an intuitive, efficient and powerful user interface to support segmented object boundary correction, object selection, scene/object depth specification and adjustment, 3D effect preview, etc.,
- a built-in video shot segmentation algorithm to simplify the video editing and frame/ object management tasks,

- a built-in temporal object tracking/management algorithm to guarantee the temporal coherence in 3D depth and to reduce user interaction,
- a built-in scene geometric structure detection algorithm to help the user to determine depth hierarchy of the scene (including the vanish point/lines) with few interactions,
- a built-in interactive (or semiautomatic) object segmentation algorithm to speed up user interactivity,
- (advanced/optional) a built-in scene/object classification model/database and training system (with hand-labeling) to enhance the built-in knowledge base for semantic scene/object recognition (with various poses and even in deformed shapes),
- a depth-based image rendering algorithm to generate left/right views from a depth+2D image input,
- a built-in objective 3D perceptual visual quality measurement mechanism to provide feedback to the end user for the derived 3D content.

For a3DC, we need:

- a user interface to specify the computational complexity expectation and customize the adopted algorithms and processing modules,
- a plug-in interface to download hinting information from the i3DV knowledge base to enhance the system accuracy,
- a built-in automatic object segmentation algorithm,
- a built-in rule based scene/object depth hierarchy estimation scheme,
- a depth based image rendering algorithm to generate left/right views from a depth+2D image input.

As an interactive system, the i3DV's architecture design (shown in Figure 4.24) follows the model-view-controller (MVC) architectural pattern, in which the system consists of three major components that may run at different platform (or machines):

- Model: the information reflects the application's operations. As shown in Figure 4.24, it is the i3DV internal data.
- View: the rendered format for user interaction. As shown in Figure 4.24, it is the 2D or 3D video preview window for the user's further interaction.
- Controller: the agent to process user interactions and change the model accordingly. In this system, the event handler plays this role.

In i3DV, to speed up the user interactivities, a set of built-in toolkits are supported for processing the model; these include automatic key frame selection and scene geometry structure detection. As shown in Figure 4.24, there are six parallel threads running simultaneously:

- Video structure management: the automatic key frame selection module initially analyzes the original video to detect the scene change, frames with geometry structure change, or new objects appearing, and thus break the video frames into a few chunks starting with key frames. The user can review the break points and adjust the locations or increase/decrease key frames. In principle, a significant portion of the user interactions are allocated for processing these key frames.

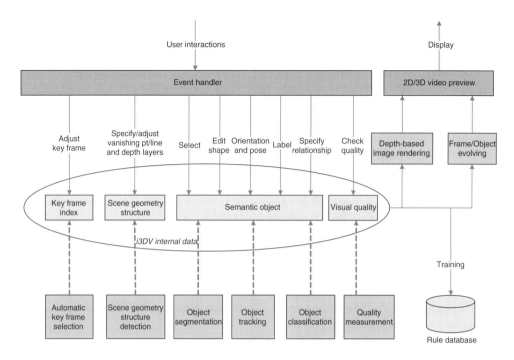

Figure 4.24 The system architecture of i3DV.

Figure 4.25 An example of scene geometry structure shown in [10]. Source: S. Battiato, S. Curti, M. L. Cascia, M. Tortora, and E. Scordato (2004) "*Depth Map Generation by Image Classification*", in Proc. SPIE, Vol. 5302, pp. 95–104. Reproduced with permission from the author.

- Scene geometry structure management: the scene geometry structure detection module detects the orientation of the scene considering geometry factors, such as vanishing point and the vanishing line as shown in Figure 4.25. The orientation helps to expand the 2D image into 3D with depth direction. With user interaction, the scene geometry structure can be refined or adjusted to reflect natural perceptual feelings.

Figure 4.26 An example of object classification shown in [21]. Source: J. Shotton, J. Winn, C. Rother, and A. Criminisi (2009) "TextonBoost for Image Understanding: Multi-class Object Recognition and Segmentation by Jointly Modeling Texture, Layout, and Context", International Journal of Computer Vision, Vol. 81, No. 1.

- Semantic object management: the interactive object segmentation and tracking modules cut a set of foreground objects out of the image, and a few operations on the object can be conducted to refine the object boundary and to specify the depth information and the orientation of the object. Other than that, the object recognition and classification module would classify the object into a known class, for example, sky, water, or tiger (an example is shown in Figure 4.26), and the user can add labels to the object as well.
- Final or internal results preview: once the depth layer of the scene is specified or detected, the depth-based image rendering module can be called to generate the left/right view to be rendered in the 3D display. Also, the internal results – such as an object evolving along the time sequence or the chain of selected key frames – can be displayed as a sanity check.
- Visual quality control: a non-reference 3D quality evaluation module is deployed to generate a score to rate the perceptual quality of the converted 3D scene from the 2D image. The feedback is shown to the user so that they can refine the results.
- Semantic rules collection: a training system is available to learn the intelligence in scene orientation detection, object segmentation and object classification, and to refine a knowledge base for future usage in automatic 2D-to-3D conversion and other applications.

In the following text, we will focus on the visual data management and semantic rules collection parts, as others will be covered in other chapters of this book.

4.3.3.1 Visual Data Management

In i3DV, there are three threads of visual data management at different levels: video sequence level (video structure and key frame management), frame level (scene geometric structure management), and object level (object management). The management tasks include detecting or recognizing a component, adding/removing a component, selecting a component for editing and manipulation, and analyzing the component from user input and interaction.

Video Structure Management

Video structure analysis is important for i3DV as it differentiates the video frame into various hierarchical levels so that many frames that have significant similarity to their neighbors can use less user interaction for the depth map refinement work. Many video clips, such as newscast and sports video, exhibit characteristic content structure. There are lots of studies on the understanding of newscast video which take advantage of the spatial and temporal structure embedded in the clip. The spatial structure information includes the standardized scene layout of the anchor person, the separators between various sections, and so on, while the temporal structure information refers to the periodic appearances of the anchor person in the scene, which normally indicates the starting point of a piece of news. Similarly, sports video has well-defined temporal content structure, in which a long game is divided into smaller pieces, such as games, sets, or quarters, and there are fixed hierarchical structures for such sports. Also, there are certain conventions for camera work for each sports; for example, when a service is made in a tennis game, the scene is usually commutated with an overview of the field. In [22], tennis videos are analyzed with a hidden Markov model (HMM). The work first segments the player using dominant color and shape description features, and then uses the HMMs to identify the strokes in the video. In [23] and [24], soccer video structure is analyzed by using HMMs to model the two basic states of the game, "play" and "break", so that the whole game is treated as switching between these two states. The color, motion and camera view features are used in their works; for example, the close-ups normally relate to break state while global views are classified for play. In [25], the stylistic elements, such as montages and *mises en scène*, of a movie are considered as messengers for video structure understanding. Typically, montage refers to the special effect in video editing that comprises different shots (a shot is the basic element in videos that represents the continuous frames recorded from the moment the camera is on to the moment it is off) to form the movie scenes, and it conveys temporal structure information, while the *mise en scène* relates to the spatial structure. In their work, statistical models are built for shot duration and activity, and a movie feature space consists of these two factors formed so that it is possible to classify the movies into different categories.

Key frame extraction (or video summary) is the technique of using a few key frames to represent the fundamental structure of a video story. Clustering techniques [26] are widely used in this area. In [27] an unsupervised clustering was proposed to group the frames into clusters based on the color histogram features in the HSV color space. The frames closest to the cluster centroids are chosen as the key frames. In [28] cluster validity analysis was applied to select the optimal number of clusters, and [29] uses graph modeling and optimization approaches to map the original problem into a graph theory problem, where a spatial–temporal dissimilarity function between key frames is defined, and thus by maximizing the total dissimilarity of the key frames a good content coverage of the video summary can be achieved.

Clearly, most of the works mentioned above are concentrated from the semantic point of view, while none of them considers 3D scenarios or the depth structure concept. In i3DV, a novel key frame extraction scheme is proposed that uses the 3D scene depth structure change as the major concern for shot boundary detection. This way, the classified non-key frames do not cause significant change in the scene depth structure, so that the depth map automatically generated from these frames (or derived from its preceding neighboring frame) needs less user interaction for refinement.

Scene Geometric Structure Estimation

Although quite a luxury to achieve, reconstructing scene geometric structure can significantly improve the accuracy of the depth map estimation. In [10] the linear perspective property is used for scene structure estimation, that is, in perspective viewing mode the parallel lines converge at a vanishing point, thus by detecting the vanishing points and lines, the projected far-to-near direction of the image can be obtained and thus the geometric structure can be derived. Then [30] proposes a stereoscopic image editing tool using the linear perspective property that was adopted in [10] for scene depth map estimation; the tool manually segments the objects into various layers and maps the depth to these objects before the 3D rendering process.

In i3DV, a novel scene geometric structure estimation approach is used based on semantic object classification and orientation analysis. The general image patterns are modeled thus the potential topological relationship between objects can be derived and thus the scene structure with the maximum probability is obtained.

Semantic Object Management

It is observed in [31] the semantic objects are the basic units for image understanding by our eyes and brains; in other words, these objects provide meaningful cues for finding the scene content. Furthermore, the interactions among semantic objects and the changes of their relative positions often produce strong depth sensation and stereo feelings for viewers. In this section, we discuss the following issues relating to object management in i3DV:

- how to cut an object out from its surrounding environment,
- how to describe the orientation and depth-directional thickness of an object,
- how to maintain a reasonable evolving path of an object crossing the time domain in a video sequence,
- how to describe the relative distances among objects,
- how to provide semantic meaning to an object.

Object Segmentation

Object segmentation [32], as a useful tool to separate the scene content into its constituent parts, has been widely studied in image/video processing, pattern recognition, and computer vision for the past several decades; however, so far there is no unified method that can detect all semantic objects [31] due to the fact that each object may have certain prior knowledge base for spatial/temporal pixel classification and processing, while different objects may have different characteristics. In recent years, much effort has been focused on interactive image segmentation; [33, 34], provide much better performance compared to the automatic algorithms.

In Figure 4.27, the user interaction as well as the results achieved by using various methods are compared and demonstrated. In the magic wand method [35], shown in 4.27a, the user specifies a few points inside the object region thus a region of connected pixels that covers these points based on color statistics would be segmented out. In the intelligent

Magic wand Intelligent scissors Bayes matte   Knockout 2   Graph cut   Grab cut

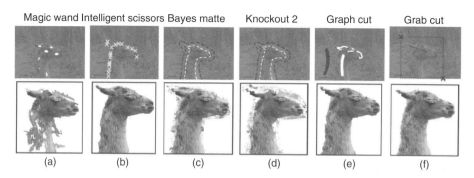

   (a)   (b)   (c)   (d)   (e)   (f)

Figure 4.27 Comparision of various segmentation tools in [35]. Source: C. Rother, V. Kolmogorov, and A. Blake (2004) "GrabCut – interactive foreground extraction using iterated graph cuts," in Proc. SIGGRAPH 2004, pp. 309–314.

scissors method [36], the user traces the object boundary with the mouse, and in the meantime selects the minimum cost path from the current mouse position to the last clicked point when moving the mouse. In the Bayes matte [37] and knockout 2 [38] methods, the user specifies the masks (white mask for foreground and red mask for background) for a trimap which includes background, uncertain areas, and foreground. For the graph cut method [39], the user has a red brush to paint on the background region and a white brush to paint on the foreground region, then an energy minimization formulation based optimization process is trigged to conduct the segmentation. GrabCut [34] greatly simplifies the user interactions by only requiring the user to drag a rectangle loosely around an object and then the object would be extracted automatically. It extends the graph cut algorithm by iteratively optimizing the intermediate steps, which allows increased versatility of user interaction. For the cases that the initial user labeling is not sufficient to allow the entire segmentation to be completed automatically, the GrabCut would use the same user editing approach used in graph cut for further refinement. Figure 4.28 shows

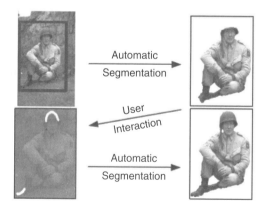

Figure 4.28 Further user editing process in GrabCut [35]. Source: C. Rother, V. Kolmogorov, and A. Blake (2004) "GrabCut – interactive foreground extraction using iterated graph cuts," in Proc. SIGGRAPH 2004, pp. 309–314.

an example of such scenarios. The authors of [40] extend the framework to the video segmentation and make the user interactions in 3D video cube space instead of 2D image space. In [41], a new segmentation algorithm based on cellular automation is proposed, which provides an alternative direction to graph theory based methods.

In i3DV, we extend the GrabCut method to 3D video space, and with motion estimation a 3D bounding pipe for an object can be derived from the 2D bounding box specified by the user, and with modest user interactions the object moving path in the 3D space can be extracted. The temporal cues in the 3D pipe make the 3D-GrabCut algorithm more accurate than the original GrabCut in 2D spaces.

Object Orientation and Thickness Specification

Once the object is segmented out, we need to estimate the depth of the object in the scene, thus the orientation and thickness of the object matters. In i3DV, the objects are classified into three categories:

- very far objects, for which the depths can be set as a default large value and the thickness can be considered as zero; the tree and sky in Figure 4.26 are good examples for such objects,
- objects with significant thickness, for example, the grass and road in Figure 4.26,
- flat objects for which the thicknesses are negligible, for example, the body object in Figure 4.26.

Clearly the object orientation only matters for the objects with significant thickness, as shown in Figure 4.29, the user can specify the object orientation by linking the most far point of the object with the nearest point of the object (see the red dash arrow lines in Figure 4.29 to specify the orientations for grass and road objects), this way the orientation of the object is determined. This approach works with an assumption that the pixels in the same object aligned in the same horizontal line are in the same depth in the scene.

However, this assumption does not work for all scenarios; in which case, the far surface and the nearest surface of the object need to be specified. Figure 4.29 shows an example of such a scenario, where both near and far surfaces are specified with boundaries and a number of orientation directions in dashed lines are specified so that the remaining directions can be interpolated from the specified major ones.

Clearly with the specification of object orientation and thickness, the relative depths of all the pixels on the object can be easily derived.

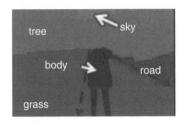

Figure 4.29   An example of object orientation specification.

Figure 4.30   An example of object orientation specification.

Tracing Objects in the Time Domain

For many video clips, object tracing in the time domain is trivial if the object movement and transformation activities are not heavy and the camera viewpoint remains the same all the time. However, there are tough scenarios (see for example Figures 4.30 and 4.31) where the camera is in zoom in/out mode, which makes overall depth range of the scene change all the time as well as the sizes and positions of objects in the scene. For such cases, certain user interactions have to be made to ensure correct object tracing thus making the object depths/thicknesses consistent along the time domain.

Topological Relationship among Objects

In i3DV, a scene registration and object management scheme is adopted to maintain the consistency of the topological relationship among objects and between the object and the scene. For example, in Figure 4.29, the depth of the body object is the same as the nearest surface of the grass object, and the body feet are on the same horizontal line as the nearest boundary edge of the grass object. However, the same rule cannot be applied in Figure 4.30, where the depth of the wall (which is a flat object) should be larger than that of the most distant surface of the speaker object, although at the bottom of the image, their edges are on the same horizontal line. By assigning depth value to the object surfaces, the topological relationship among objects can be uniquely determined.

Object Classification and Labeling

In i3DV, the purposes of object classification are as follows:

- The scene geometric structure can be derived from the labeled object categories, thus the topological relationship among objects can be investigated from a semantic point of view.
- The scene composition pattern can be used for video structure analysis and frame management.
- Automatic object classification speeds up the user interaction for labeling.
- The user interactions for correcting the object classification can help in building and refining the backend object database for future applications.

Figure 4.31 An example of tough scenarios for object tracing.

So far there are many efforts in literature on object classification [21–42]. In [43], a limited number of datasets are trained to categorize small number of object classes, such as building, grass, tree, cow, sky, face, car, bicycle, and so on. Most methods are based on the textons or texton histograms; that is, the training images are convolved with a filter-bank to generate a set of filter responses, and these responses are clustered over the whole training set to result in high-dimensional space feature vectors, also called textons. Both [44, 45] aim to collect a much larger dataset of annotated images with web-based resources. First [44] pairs two random online users who view the same target image and try to make them read each other's mind and agree on an appropriate name for the target image as quickly as possible. This effort was very successful and it has collected over 10 million image captions with images randomly drawn from the web. Then [45] provides a web-based annotation tool called LabelMe (see Figure 4.32 for an example of its user interface), in which the user can annotate any object by clicking along its boundary and then indicating its identity. After sufficient annotations of a specific object class are obtained, a detector can be trained again and again from coarse to fine [46], and it can support the labeling process to become semi-automatic.

Figure 4.32 An example of LabelMe snapshot user interface. Source: B. C. Russell, A. Torralba, K. P. Murphy, W. T. Freeman (2008) "LabelMe: a database and web-based tool for image annotation", International Journal of Computer Vision, pp.157–173, Volume 77, Numbers 1–3.

In i3DV, a quite similar approach is used for object classification and labeling: during the user interactions for object labeling, the object dataset is enlarged gradually and the algorithm training process is going on to refine the features to eventually reduce the user interaction frequency and thus make the object classification task more automatic.

4.3.3.2 Semantic Rules Collection

In this section, we demonstrate how i3DV helps in building the a3DC with all the semantic knowledge obtained from machine learning. Typically depending on the applications, the relationship between i3DV and a3DC follows either of the two models below:

- Loose connection model: in which the a3DC is a well-established system that takes inputs (rules, heuristics, etc.) from i3DV's rule database. In this model, the a3DC can accelerate certain modules with hardware accelerators, while the rules provided by i3DV can improve its intelligence but is not an imperative condition, which gives more flexibility for a3DC implementation. Figure 4.33a shows the diagram of this model.
- Tight connection model: as shown in Figure 4.33b, in this model the a3DC systems are generated from i3DV according to the application scenarios, so the flexibility of a3DC implementation is reduced. Typically a3DC systems are automatically derived software solutions, as the i3DV is evolving with more and more video clips are processed and more user interactions are feed into the system. Consequently the performance of the a3DC system improves as the i3DV gets more mature.

In i3DV, a machine learning system is deployed to extract semantic rules for increasing automation of the system. Ideally the i3DV can achieve the following items of video understanding with the support of user interaction:

- objects are segmented from each other;
- objects are labeling with their category;

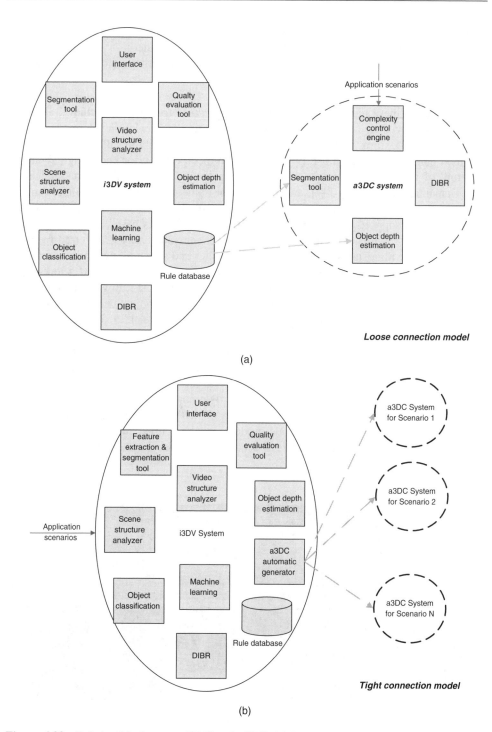

Figure 4.33 Relationship between i3DV and a3DC. (a) Loose connection model for i3DV and a3DC. (b) Tight connection model for i3DV and a3DC.

- object orientation and thickness are labeled;
- object evolving procedures along the time domain are specified;
- scene constitution and semantic meanings are obtained with topological relationship among objects.

Theoretically these high-level semantic items are goals for a3DC to achieve, although they are not trivial at all. A practical approach is to use the low-level features, such as color, edge, texture, and so on, which are achievable in both a3DC and i3DV, as common platforms, and then use Bayes models to incorporate prior knowledge about the structure of the video content, to bridge the gap between low-level features and high-level semantics. Also, [25], [47], and [48] use the same concept in video understanding work. Typically the semantic scenes and events are modeled with a predefined statistical framework that supports an inference of unobservable concepts based on their relevance to the observable evidence. This way the high-level semantics may be inferred from the input evidence with a statistical model based classifier and semantic networks. As shown in Figure 4.34, [49] considers five typical semantics in baseball games, and it links these high-level semantics with mid-level semantics (fast panning, fast tilting, regular panning, regular tilting, zoom, etc.) and low-level features (object size, object number, background color, etc.) with a statistical network for training (see Figure 4.35 for the conceptual framework).

In i3DV, a semantic network modeling framework is used to bridge the high-level semantics with lower level features. To the best of our knowledge, this is the first effort that uses a machine learning approach to generate an automatic 2D-to-3D conversion algorithm completely from an off-line system (if tight connection models are considered). The significant advantage is that the single effort of i3DV development produces a side-product with extra effort, but this side-product can be refined more and more during i3DV usage, and can eventually achieve acceptable accuracy without the need for user supervision.

Figure 4.34 An example of typical semantics for baseball games (overview, runner, defending, pitching, batter) [49]. Source: H. Shih, and C. Huang (2003) "A Semantic Network Modeling for Understanding Baseball Video", in Proc. ICASSP.

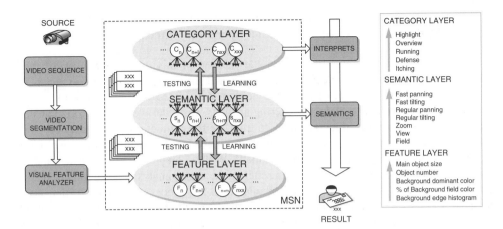

Figure 4.35 Video understanding framework proposed in [49]. Source: H. Shih, and C. Huang (2005) "MSN: Statistical Understanding of Broadcasted Baseball Video Using Multi-level Semantic Network", IEEE Trans. Broadcasting.

4.4 3D Multi-View Generation

In this section, we discuss the topic of how to derive a multi-view 3D content from a stereo image pair, as the future glass-free displays require multi-view content. So far, no automatic multi-view generation algorithm can claim to reach a satisfactory visual quality, so some human editing or tuning is necessary during the processing. A few fundamental automatic modules are required in the process:

- Depth extraction from stereo content: stereo matching is a typical approach to estimate disparity from a given stereo image pair. In [6], a large number of efforts in this field have been evaluated.
- New view synthesis: 3D warping is a key approach in depth-based view synthesis, in which the pixels in a reference image are back-projected to 3D spaces, and then reprojected onto the target viewpoint. In this approach, visual errors, such as black-contours appearing, and holes around boundaries, need to be fixed using filtering or in-painting techniques.

In this process, the major challenges can be summarized as follows:

- Missing information due to occlusion will produce noticeable errors in the newly generated views.
- Flickering artifacts around object boundaries and disoccluded regions in the new views will cause degradation in viewing experiences.
- The viewing condition related aspects, such as display size, light condition, specific autostereoscopic display characteristics and constraints, and so on, should be taken into account in the process.
- The user preference aspects, such as depth range and viewing distance, should also be taken into account.

- Effective user interaction into a multi-view environment is hard to design.
- Pixel-based view representation makes the editing very difficult.

So far there are very few solutions in the market on this topic. In almost all these efforts, the processing is conducted in a view-based mode, thus objects evolving in the time domain across the video frames are seldom considered in the framework, which undermines its capability to reduce flickering artifacts. However, very few efforts consider user interaction as an effective assistance to improve the content quality. It may be worth considering a new concept which is aligned with the human intuition of object-based access and manipulation in the 3D environment. With a patented 3D data format and the associated data derivation and generation scheme, the stereo analysis, object manipulation, and final 3D view rendering are fully decoupled in the process. The data format needs to have a good extensibility that can be converted to and from other multi-view 3DTV formats, such as MVD (multi-view video plus depth). A set of computer vision algorithms need to be deployed to reduce human intervention during the process to the minimum, but this approach needs to have the extensibility to be optimized for various autostereoscopic displays.

References

1. E. H. Adelson and J. R. Bergen, *"The plenoptic function and the elements of early vision"* in *Computational Models of Visual Processing, Landy, and Movshon*, Eds. MIT Press, Cambridge, 1991.
2. L. McMillan, and G. Bishop, "Plenoptic modeling: an image-based rendering system" in *Proc. SIGGRAPH* 1995.
3. M. Levoy and P. Hanrahan, "Light field rendering" in *Proc. SIGGRAPH* 1996.
4. S. J. Gortler, R. Grzeszczuk, R. Szeliski, and M. F. Cohen, "The Lumigraph" in *Proc. SIGGRAPH* 1996.
5. H. Y. Shum and L. W. He, "Rending with concentric mosaics" in *Proc. SIGGRAPH* 1999.
6. D. Scharstein and R. Szeliski, *Middlebury Stereo Vision Page*, www.middlebury.edu/steoreo, 2005.
7. T. Jebara, A. Azarbayejani, and A. Pentland, "3D structure from 2D motion", *IEEE Signal Processing Magazine*, vol. 16, no. 3, pp. 66–83, May 1999.
8. S. B. Xu, "Qualitative depth from monoscopic cues" in *Proc. Int. Conf. on Image Processing and its Applications*, pp. 437–440, 1992.
9. C. Weerasinghe, P. Ogunbona, and W. Li, "2D to pseudo-3D conversion of head and shoulder images using feature based parametric disparity maps" in *Proc. International Conference on Image Processing*, pp. 963–966, 2001.
10. S. Battiato, S. Curti, M. L. Cascia, M. Tortora, and E. Scordato, "Depth Map Generation by Image Classification" in *Proc. SPIE*, vol. 5302, pp. 95–104, April 2004.
11. C. Choi, B. Kwon, and M.Choi, "A real-time field-sequential stereoscopic image converter", *IEEE Trans. Consumer Electronics*, vol. 50, no. 3, pp. 903–910, August 2004.
12. S. Sethuraman and M. W. Siegel, "The video Z-buffer: a concept for facilitating monoscopic image compression by exploiting the 3D stereoscopic depth map" in *Proc. SMPTE International Workshop on HDTV'96*, pp. 8–9, Los Angeles, 1996.
13. K. Kim, M. Siegel, and J. Y. Son, "Synthesis of a high-resolution 3D-stereoscopic image pair from a high-resolution monoscopic image and a low-resolution depth map" in *Proc. SPIE/IS&T Conference*, vol. 3295A, pp. 76–86, January, 1998.
14. H. Wang, H. Li, and S. Manjunath, *"Real-time Capturing and Generating Stereo Images and Videos with a Monoscopic Low Power Mobile Device"*, US Patent, 2012.
15. S. Curti, D. Sirtori, and F. Vella, *"3D effect generation from monocular view"* in *Proc. First International Symposium on 3D Data Processing Visualization and Transmission (3DPVT 2002)*, 2002.
16. P. Kozankiewicz, "Fast algorithm for creating image-based stereo images" in *Proc. 10th International Conference in Central Europe on Computer Graphics, Visualization and Computer Vision*, Plzen-Bory, Czech Republic, 2002.

17. S. Battiato, A. Capra, S. Curti, and M. L. Cascia, "3D stereoscopic image pairs by depth-map generation" in *Proc. 2nd International Sysmposium on 3D Data Processing, Visualization and Transmission*, pp. 124–131, 2004.

18. A. P. Pentland, "Depth of Scene from Depth of Field", *IEEE Trans. Pattern Analysis and Machine Intelligence*, vol. 9, no. 4, pp. 523–531.

19. G. Kang, C. Gan, and W. Ren, "Shape from Shading based on Finite-Element" in *Proc. International Conference on Machine Learing and Cybernetics*, vol. 8, pp. 5165–5169.

20. Y. Feng, J. Jayaseelan, and J. Jiang, "Cue Based Disparity Estimation for Possible 2D-to-3D Video Conversion" in *Proc. VIE'06*, 2006.

21. J. Shotton, J. Winn, C. Rother, and A. Criminisi, "Texton Boost for Image Understanding: Multi-class Object Recognition and Segmentation by Jointly Modeling Texture, Layout, and Context", *International Journal of Computer Vision*, vol. 81, no. 1, January 2009.

22. M. Petkovic, W. Jonker, Z. Zivkovic, "Recognizing strokes in tennis videos using hidden Markov models", in *Proc. IASTED International Conference on Visualization, Imaging and Image Processing*, Marbella, Spain, 2001.

23. L. Xie, S-F. Chang, A. Divakaran, and H. Sun, "Structure analysis of soccer video with hidden Markov models", In *Proc. International Conference on Acoustic, Speech, and Signal Processing (ICASSP)*, 2002.

24. P. Xu, L. Xie, S-F. Chang, A. Divakaran, A. Vetro, and H. Sun, "Algorithms and system for segmentation and structure analysis in soccer video", In *Proc. International Conference on Multimedia and Exposition (ICME)*, Tokyo, August 2001.

25. N. Vasconcelos and A. Lippman, "Statistical models of video structure for content analysis and characterization", *IEEE Trans. Image Processing*, vol. 9, no. 1, January 2000.

26. S. Lee and M. H. Hayes, "A fast clustering algorithm for video abstraction" in *Proc. International Conference on Image Processing*, vol. II, pp. 563–566, Sept. 2003.

27. Y. Zhuang, Y. Rui, T. S. Huang, and S. Mehrotra, "Adaptive key frame extraction using unsupervised clustering" in *Proc. International Conference on Image Processing*, Chicago, pp. 866–870, October 1998.

28. A. Hanjalic and H. Zhang, "An integrated scheme for automatic video abstraction based on unsupervised cluster-validity analysis", *IEEE Trans. Circuits and Systems for Video Technology*, vol. 9, December 1999.

29. S. Lu, I. King, and M. R. Lyu, "Video summarization by video structure analysis and graph optimization" in *Proc. IEEE International Conference on Multimedia and Expo*, Taipei, Taiwan, June 2004.

30. C. O. Yun, S. H. Han, T. S. Yun, and D. H. Lee, "Development of Stereoscopic Image Editing Tool using Image-based Modeling" in *Proc. CGVR'06*, Las Vegas, 2006.

31. K. N. Ngan and H. Li, "Semantic Object Segmentation", *IEEE MMTC E-Letter*, vol. 4, no. 6, July 2009.

32. H. Li and K. N. Ngan, "Automatic video segmentation and tracking for content-based applications", *IEEE Communications Magazine*, vol. 45, no. 1, pp. 27–33, 2007.

33. Y. Li, J. Sun, C.-K. Tang, and H.-Y. Shum, "Lazy snapping" in *Proc. SIGGRAPH* 2004, pp. 303–308, 2004.

34. C. Rother, V. Kolmogorov, and A. Blake, "GrabCut – interactive foreground extraction using iterated graph cuts" in *Proc. SIGGRAPH* 2004, pp. 309–314, 2004.

35. Adobe Systems Inc. *Adobe Photoshop User Guide*, 2002.

36. E. Mortensen, and W. Barrett, "Intelligent Scissors for Image Composition" in *Proc. ACM SIGGRAPH* 1995, pp. 191–198, 1995.

37. Y.-Y. Chuang, B. Curless, D. Salesin, and R. Szeliski, "A Bayesian approach to digital matting" in *Proc. IEEE Conf. Computer Vision and Pattern Recog.*, 2001.

38. Corel Corp., *Knockout User Guide*, 2002.

39. Y. Boykov, and M. –P. Jolly, "Interactive graph cuts for optimal boundary and region segmentation of objects in N-D images" in *Proc. IEEE Int. Conf. on Computer Vision*, 2001.

40. J. Wang, P. Bhat, R. A. Colburn, M. Agrawala, and M. F. Cohen, "Interactive video cutout" in *Proc. SIGGRAPH* 2005, pp. 585–594, 2005.

41. V. Vezhnevets and V. Konouchine, "GrowCut – Interactive Multi-Label N-D Image Segmentation by Cellular Automata" in *Proc. Graphicon* 2005, pp. 150–156, 2005.

42. L. Fei-Fei, R. Fergus, and P. Perona, "One-shot learning of object categories", *IEEE Trans. Pattern Recognition and Machine Intelligence*, vol. 28, no. 4, pp. 594–611, April 2006.

43. J. Winn, A. Criminisi, and T. Minka, "Object categorization by learned universal visual dictionary" in *Proc IEEE Intl. Conf. on Computer Vision*, 2005.

44. L. von Ahn and L. Dabbish, "Labeling images with a computer game" in *Proc. SIGCHI conference on Human factors in Computing Systems*, 2004.

45. B. C. Russell, A. Torralba, K. P. Murphy, and W. T. Freeman, "LabelMe: a database and web-based tool for image annotation", *International Journal of Computer Vision*, pp. 157–173, Volume 77, Numbers 1–3, May 2008.

46. Y. Abramson and Y. Freund, "Semi-automatic Visual Learning (Seville): a Tutorial on Active Learning for Visual Object Recognition" in *Proc. Intl. Conf. Computer Vision and Pattern Recognition*, San Diego, 2005.

47. I. Kozintsev, M. Naphade, T. S. Huang, "Factor graph framework for semantic video indexing", *IEEE Trans. Circuits and Systems for Video Technology*, vol. 12, no. 1, pp. 40–52, 2002.

48. H. Shih and C. Huang, "MSN: Statistical Understanding of Broadcasted Baseball Video Using Multi-level Semantic Network", *IEEE Trans. Broadcasting*, 2005.

49. H. Shih, and C. Huang, "A Semantic Network Modeling for Understanding Baseball Video" in *Proc. ICASSP*, 2003.

5

3D Video Coding and Standards

5.1 Fundamentals of Video Coding

With the advancement of 2D video compression technology, end users can experience better visual quality at much lower bit rate. To take advantage of the successful development from existing 2D video coding tools and their fast deployment in the marketplace, the 3D video codecs are often built based on the popular 2D video codecs, especially with consideration of the availability of hardware platforms. The mature state-of-the-art video codec, H.264 (MPEG-4 Part 10, Advanced Video Coding (AVC)) [1], has often been selected as a fundamental building block and code base to construct advanced 3D video codecs. Before we introduce the 3D video codecs, we first overview the fundamentals of 2D video coding and the important components adopted in H.264. A short overview of the next generation video codec, high efficiency video coding (HEVC), will be presented at the end of this section.

The modern consumer video codecs often deploy lossy compression methods to achieve higher compression efficiency, so the reconstructed pixels in each frame may not be bit-to-bit accurate when compared to the original video data. The degradation of the perceived video quality is related to the encoded bit rate: a stream with higher bit rate can provide better visual quality and vice versa. The key methodologies adopted in lossy video compression are prediction, transform, quantization, and entropy coding technologies. The concept of a prediction process consists of two coding paths: the reconstruction path and the prediction path. The reconstruction path will decode the already encoded elements and reconstruct the elements to serve as the prediction base. The prediction path is: predict a raw unencoded element from prediction bases, which are normally already encoded elements from the reconstruction path; compute the difference between the predicted value and the raw unencoded value as the prediction error (residual); and encode the prediction error. Note that including the reconstruction path in the prediction process can reduce the overhead for transmitting the initial prediction base. A better prediction can result in smaller prediction error (residual) and thus a potentially smaller number of bits to encode the prediction error. The reconstruction path is presented in both the encoder and the decoder; and the prediction path only appears at the encoder. The transform process

3D Visual Communications, First Edition. Guan-Ming Su, Yu-Chi Lai, Andres Kwasinski and Haohong Wang.
© 2013 John Wiley & Sons, Ltd. Published 2013 by John Wiley & Sons, Ltd.

is to convert data from one domain to another. It is often observed that the energy in the pixel domain is widely spread among most pixels, which leads to the need to encode almost all pixels into the compressed bit stream. The main purpose of transform is to compact the energy from the original pixel domain to the new domain such that we have as few significant coefficients as possible. Having the transform process, we only need to encode those important coefficients to reduce the required number of bits. The quantization process can be deployed during the encoding process to further reduce the required bits since it can reduce the size of the codeword. However, the quantization process loses information and introduces quantization distortion. The quantization step size has the role of trading off between bit rate and video quality. Entropy coding is a process for compressing data as much as possible in a lossless way. The goal of this lossless compression is to approach the entropy of the coding elements as closely as possible.

Note that modern codecs often adopt block based coding methodology by partitioning one image into multiple nonoverlapped small blocks. The block based processing can help the coding tools to explore the local characteristics of the video data. For color video compression, the video codec often converts the common capture/display three-primary-color space RGB, which represent the red, green, and blue in each color channel, to coding color space YCbCr. The Y component in YCbCr color space represents the luminance information and Cb/Cr represents the chrominance information. As human eyes are more sensitive to the luminance than the chrominance, the Cb and Cr components can be further spatially downsampled to reduce the bit rate.

To be more specific, we show the encoder architecture and the decoder architecture for H.264 in Figure 5.1a, and Figure 5.1b, respectively. As revealed from the figure, the functionality of the encoder is a superset of the decoder. The decoder only consists of the reconstruction path to obtain the decoded signal. The encoder consists of both the prediction path and the reconstruction path. The fundamental coding tools adopted in H.264 consist of (1) intra-frame prediction, (2) inter-frame prediction, (3) de-correlation transform coding, (4) quantization, (5) entropy coding, and (6) deblocking filter.

The intra-prediction process is to explore the spatial redundancy in each individual video frame. It is often observed that neighboring blocks exhibit similar content. For example, an edge may go across multiple blocks; and neighboring blocks may have similar edge direction and/or analogous texture on both sides, separated by the edge. Instead of directly encoding each block, one could deploy the spatial prediction from already decoded pixels in the neighboring blocks to predict the pixels in the current block. Depending on the color component, namely, luma or chroma, there are different block sizes supported in the H.264 standard such that the optimal block size can be chosen adaptively according to local characteristics. The block size for luma intra-prediction defined in H.264 has three different width and height dimensions: 4×4, 8×8, or 16×16. Since an edge in an image may point in a variety of directions, or blocks may contain directional texture, the spatial prediction accuracy depends on the direction of the edges and/or texture. Multiple prediction directions for different block sizes are defined in H.264. As an example, for a 4×4 block there are nine different prediction methods that we can choose, namely, vertical prediction, horizontal prediction, DC prediction, diagonal down-left prediction, diagonal down-right prediction, vertical-right prediction, horizontal down prediction, vertical-left prediction, and horizontal-up prediction. The intra-prediction process is illustrated in Figure 5.2. Each rectangle box represents one pixel and the white

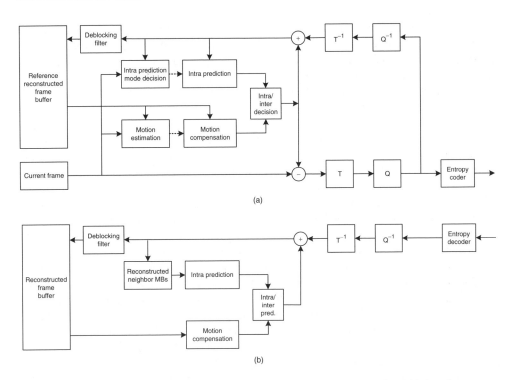

(a)

(b)

Figure 5.1 (a) Architecture of H.264 encoder. (b) Architecture of H.264 decoder.

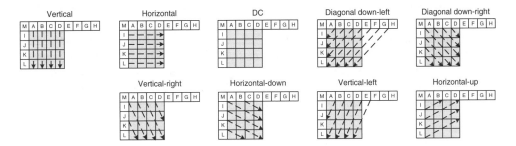

Figure 5.2 Nine different prediction methods for 4×4 block in H.264.

and gray boxes represent the reconstructed (after encoding and decoding) pixels in the neighboring blocks and the current to-be-encoded pixels in the current block, respectively. Pixels A, B, C, D, E, F, G, H are from top neighbor (TN) blocks; pixel I, J, K, L are from left neighbor (LN) block; and pixel M is from top-left neighbor block (TLN). The dotted line with arrow represents the prediction direction indicating that the pixels along the dotted line in the current block are predicted from the neighbor block's pixel(s) associated with the dotted line. For example, in the vertical prediction, the first column of the pixel in the current block is predicted using pixel A. When the horizontal prediction method is used, the first row of the block is predicted from pixel I. Depending on the location and coding mode surrounding the current block, some neighbor blocks may not be available. The actual prediction process needs to be dynamically readjusted to address the different availability of neighbor blocks. Note that this adaptive prediction is conducted in both the encoder and the decoder through the reconstruction path to ensure the correct usage of neighboring information to avoid wrong operations. For the luma intra 8×8, there are also nine different prediction methods similar to the 4×4 block size defined in H.264 spec. Besides the block size, the major difference between intra 8×8 and intra 4×4 is that the pixels in the neighbor blocks are low-pass filtered first and then served as the predictor for intra 8×8 case. This low-pass filtering process can help to alleviate the high frequency noise and improve the prediction accuracy and thus overall encoding performance. For the luma intra-prediction based on 16×16 block, there are four different prediction methods: vertical prediction, horizontal prediction, DC prediction, and plane prediction. The block size for chroma intra-prediction defined in H.264 only supports dimension with 8×8. There are four prediction modes for chroma intra-prediction and the prediction modes are the same as luma intra 16×16 modes.

With the rich set of multiple prediction sizes and directions, the encoder has more freedom to decide which prediction block size and prediction direction to apply with the consideration of rate and distortion. After having the predicted pixels for each block, we will take the difference between the original pixels and the predicted pixels to output the residual. The residual will be sent to the next stage known as the transform process.

Besides the spatial intra-prediction, it is often observed that consecutive video frames have similar content, and each object has a certain level of displacement from frame to frame. This kind of temporal redundancy can be explored by finding the object movement between neighboring frames along the time domain. More precisely, the modern video codec will partition the current video frame into multiple fixed-size blocks, and try to find the best matched block from the existing decoded frames (as reference frame) via a motion estimation process. We show the motion estimation process in Figure 5.3. In this example, for the rectangular block with line pattern in the current video frame, one can find a "best matched" block with the same dimension in the reference. The relative displacement between the original block and the best matched block is called the motion vector.

The criteria for "best matched" block depend on the optimization objectives defined in the encoder. A commonly adopted measurement is the mean of absolute difference

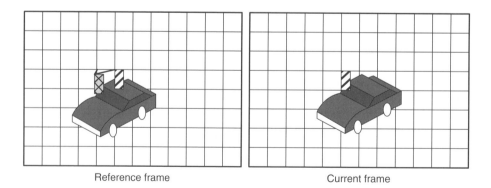

Reference frame   Current frame

Figure 5.3   Illustration of motion estimation.

(MAD) among all pixels between the current block in current frame, denoted as B_c, and the candidate block in the reference frame, denoted as B_r.

$$MAD(m_x, m_y) = \sum_{(x,y)\in A} |B_c(x, y) - B_r(x - m_x, y - m_y)| \qquad (5.1)$$

where A is the set of coordinates in the current block, (m_x, m_y) is the motion vector with magnitude m_x in the horizontal direction and m_y in the vertical direction. By searching all possible motion vectors, one can choose the optimal motion vector to minimize the MAD. Note that the encoding motion vector also requires a certain number of bits. Besides, the MAD measurement only presents the energy of prediction error and does not indicate the required number of bits to encode the prediction error. A more advanced method from rate-distortion optimization perspective will be discussed in Chapter 10.

After finding the motion vectors, for each to-be-encoded block, we will perform motion compensation with the aid of motion vectors. The best-matched block from the reference frame will be placed at the current block to serve as the predictor. After calculating the difference between the current undistorted block and the motion compensated predictor, we send this residual to the next stage for transform coding. Note that there are several advanced methods to improve the performance of motion estimation; such as:

- subpixel motion estimation: due to the fixed sampling grid on the camera sensors, the actual movement of an object may not appear exactly on the integer grid. Instead, the true motion vectors may be located in the fractional pixel. In this case, interpolation from existing reconstructed pixels are needed to obtain the upsampled reference pixels,
- multiple reference frames: an object may appear in multiple reference frames. Since the movement and lighting condition may change from frame to frame, best motion vectors may be found by allowing search among several decoded reference frames,
- variable block size: having fixed the size of block in the motion estimation/motion compensation process we may not be able to address the different characteristics locally. Allowing different block size can facilitate minimizing the residual for different size of object,
- weighted prediction: multiple motion predicted values from multiple matched blocks can be fused via weighted prediction to achieve better prediction.

The residual that is generated either from the spatial intra-prediction or the temporal inter-prediction will be transformed via block based 2D discrete cosine transform (DCT) to de-correlate the correlation exhibited in the pixel domain. As the coding gain via the DCT transform has been shown as the closest one to the theoretical upper bound, KLT, among all other transforms, under the assumption with first order Markov process in the pixel domain. After 2D DCT, the pixels in each block are represented by DCT coefficients, in which each 2D DCT coefficient indicates the magnitude of the corresponding spatial frequency in both horizontal and vertical directions. For most nature images, there is a larger amount of energy shown in the low spatial frequency, such as smooth areas, and less at high spatial frequency, such as sharper edges. By applying DCT, the energy of each block in the DCT domain will be compacted into a few low frequency DCT coefficients. This process will facilitate the encoding tradeoff between rate and distortion, that is, we may want to preserve more low frequency coefficient information than high frequency ones when the bit budget is limited. The 2D-DCT transform for an input $N \times N$ block $f(x, y)$ in the pixel domain to output $F(u, v)$ in the DCT domain can be performed as follows:

$$F(u, v) = \frac{2}{N} C(u) C(v) \sum_{x=0}^{N-1} \sum_{y=0}^{N-1} f(x, y) \cos \frac{(2x+1)u\pi}{2N} \cos \frac{(2y+1)v\pi}{2N}, \quad (5.2)$$

with u, v, x, and y being 0,1, 2, $\ldots$, $N - 1$ and $C(u)$ and $C(v)$ defined as:

$$C(u), C(v) = \begin{cases} \frac{1}{\sqrt{2}} & \text{for } u, v = 0 \\ 1 & \text{otherwise} \end{cases}$$

In the older standards, such as MPEG-2, the DCT transform is conducted in the floating point fashion, which might result in slightly different output at the decoder since different platforms and hardware have different implementations for floating point calculation. To achieve bit-to-bit accuracy among all decoders, H.264 adopts an integer DCT transform. Two different DCT transform block sizes, 4×4 and 8×8, are standardized in the H.264 spec, which provides freedom for the encoder to select according to the content complexity. For intra 4×4 coding, a Hardamard transform is again applied on top of all the collected 16 DC DCT coefficients from a 16×16 block for further bit rate reduction.

The quantization process will take place after the DCT transform to quantize each of the DCT coefficients. The concept of quantization is to use a smaller set of codewords to approximately represent a larger set of codewords. Consequently, the de-quantized signal is a coarser representation of the original signal. A general form for quantizing a signal x with quantization step size, QS, is performed as follows:

$$\tilde{x} = floor \left(\frac{x + \theta}{QS} \right), \quad (5.3)$$

where θ is the rounding offset. The de-quantization process to obtain the reconstructed value, $\hat{x}$, is conducted as follows:

$$\hat{x} = \tilde{x} \cdot QS. \quad (5.4)$$

Note that the quantization process is the only component to lose information in the whole video encoding process. Quantization also plays an important role in controlling the bit rate and the quality. With a larger quantization step size, the quantized coefficients have smaller magnitude, thus the encoder can use fewer bits encoding the quantized values. On the other hand, with smaller quantization step size, the coefficients have larger magnitude, resulting in a higher bit rate. To allow a fine granularity of quantization step size for better visual quality and bit rate control, the H.264 standard defines a lookup table to map the quantization parameter (QP) specified from the bit stream syntax to the actual quantization step size.

In H.264, the DCT transform and the quantization are merged into the one process to reduce the computational complexity. It is observed that the magnitude of quantized DCT coefficients in both high horizontal and/or high vertical frequency is smaller than the low frequency coefficients, or close to zero. Instead of directly encoding those quantized coefficients in a raster scan order, having those coefficients reordered according to the magnitude in a descending way can further improve the coding efficiency in the

Table 5.1 Exp-Golomb code

Symbol	Codeword
0	1
1	010
2	011
3	00100
4	00101
5	00110
6	00111
7	0001000
8	0001001

next encoding stage. After this joint process, the encoding order of the quantized DCT coefficients will be reordered in a zigzag way such that the low frequency DCT coefficients are scanned and encoded first and high frequency coefficients are processed later.

The final stage of the codec is the entropy coding. The main purpose of entropy coding is to explore the statistical redundancy among the coding symbols constructed from the quantized DCT coefficients. The principle of entropy coding is to assign fewer codewords to the symbols appeared more frequently and longer codewords for symbols occurred less frequently. In this way, we can achieve statistical gain. There are three different entropy coding approaches adopted in H.264 codec: Exp-Golomb coding, context adaptive variable length coding (CAVLC), and context adaptive binary arithmetic coding (CABAC) [2]:

- Exp-Golomb coding: The Exp-Golomb code is designed to optimize the statistical gain when the symbols have geometric distribution. A group of video coding symbols are first mapped to a list of code numbers via a table. Note that different type of coding elements may have different mapping tables and symbols with sign (+/−) can also be encoded by Exp-Golomb code through mapping. The mapping process should ensure that the most frequently occurring symbols are assigned with the smallest value of code numbers; and the least frequently occurring symbols are assigned with the largest code numbers. The Exp-Golomb coding will encode each code number to construct the encoded bit stream with the following structure:

$$[n \text{ bits of } 0] \, [1] \, [n \text{ bits of INFO}]$$

where

$$n = floor(\log_2(\text{code number} + 1))$$
$$\text{INFO} = \text{code number} + 1 - 2^n$$

We show one example in Table 5.1.

The Exp-Golomb code is used universally for almost all symbols in H.264 except for the transform coefficients.

- CAVLC: CAVLC is based on Huffman coding to explore the symbols' distribution, especially when the distribution is not the geometric distribution used in Exp-Golomb code. The Huffman coding is to build a coding/decoding Huffman code tree which best approximates the entropy via an integer number of bits representation. The construction of a Huffman code tree is illustrated in Figure 5.4. Assume that we have four coding symbols, s0, s1, s2, and s3 and the occurrence of each symbol has probability 0.25, 0.55, 0.15, and 0.05, respectively. The tree building process is to merge two nodes with the lowest probability together to form a new parent node and assign the probability of this new node as the sum of the probability from these two child nodes. This process is repeated until we reach the root. Taking Figure 5.4 as an example, in the first step, node s2 and s3 have the lowest probability and we will merge them as node A and assign its probability as 0.2. In the next step, node s0 and node A have the lowest probability, 0.25 and 0.2, respectively. We will merge s0 and A to form node B with a new merged probability 0.45. The last stage is to merge node s1 and B to construct node C. The codeword for each symbol is assigned by tracking back the Huffman tree from the root to the leaf. Note that Huffman coding can be improved by grouping several different symbols together as vector Huffman coding to achieve finer probability representation so as to improve the coding efficiency. In addition, H.264 adopts the context adaptive approach to choose a different Huffman table with different probability distribution with consideration of the neighbor's context.

- CABAC: The major disadvantage of Huffman coding is that it cannot closely approach the entropy bound since each symbol needs at least one integer bit. The arithmetic coding solution is to modify the concept of the vector Huffman coding method but to convert a variable number of symbols into a variable length codeword. The real implementation of arithmetic coding is to represent a sequence of symbols by an interval in the number line from zero to one. Note that the basic form of arithmetic coding uses floating point operation to construct the interval in the number line and needs multiplication operations. Fast binary arithmetic coding with probability update via lookup table can enable multiplication-free calculation to reduce the computation complexity. To utilize the fast binary arithmetic coding, an encoding symbol needs to be binarized through a binarization process such that a symbol is represented by multiple binary bins according to the local context. The binary arithmetic coding operates on those binary bins to output the compressed bit streams.

As those codewords have variable length, any bit error introduced into the stream may lead to different symbols during the decoding process, as no synchronization signal is present to help.

As the quantization is conducted on the DCT coefficients, the reconstructed video often shows blocky artifacts along the boundaries of blocks. For video codecs developed earlier than H.264, those artifacts are often alleviated by video post-processing, which is not mandatory in the codec design. In H.264, the deblocking process is included as an in-loop process to equip the codec with the ability to reduce the blocky artifacts through FIR filtering across block boundaries. Note that the deblocking process can improve the subjective visual quality, but often shows little gain in the objective metric. To avoid deblocking a true edge and apply different strengths of deblocking filtering adaptively, there are multiple criteria and filtering rules defined in the spec. Since those operations involves lots of "if-else" conditions, which are difficult to implement through parallel computing, the computation complexity of the deblocking process takes around at least 30% of overall decoding computation even in a highly optimized software [3].

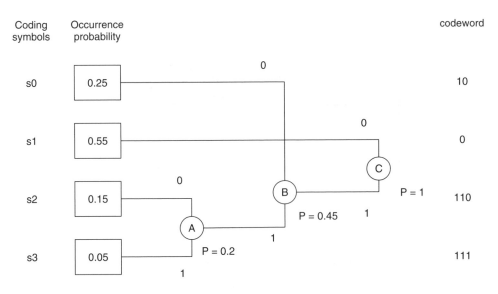

Coding   Occurrence   codeword
symbols   probability

Figure 5.4   Construction of Huffman code tree.

In Figure 5.5, we show the coding hierarchy of H.264 codec. The basic coding unit (CU) in the video codec is called the macroblock (MB), which has dimension 16×16 (the chroma has different dimension depending on the chroma sampling format). Each MB is further partitioned into smaller blocks. The dimension of those smaller blocks can be 16×16, 16×8, 8×16, or 8×8. For an 8×8 block, we can further partition it into sub-blocks of size 8×8, 4×8, 8×4, and 4×4. For each block or sub-block, we can choose a different prediction method to achieve our targeted R-D performance. The upper hierarchy on top of the MB is the slice, which defines a global attribute, such as allowing intra-prediction only (I-slice), or adding one more temporal prediction (P-slice), or having intra, single, and bi-prediction (B-slice). A slice can be independently decoded without information from any other slices. This self-contained property makes the bit stream more robust to bit error during the transmission. Each video frame can contain multiple slices, which increases the robustness of the bit stream and enables the possibility of parallel decoding for real-time playback. A frame can be an I (intra-) frame if it contains only I-slice(s), P-frame if it contains both I and P slices, and B-frame if it contains I, P, and B slices, as shown in Figure 5.5. All pictures between two I-frames are grouped together and called a group of pictures (GOP). Note that in H.264, a predictive frame can have multiple reference frames which are stored in the reference picture buffer, and possibly the reference frames' time stamp can be before intra-coded frames. To allow random access to a particular scene, an instantaneous decoder refresh (IDR) coded picture is defined in H.264 to clear the data stored in the reference picture buffer. With IDR, all following received slices can be decoded without reference to any frames decoded prior to the IDR picture.

In the older video standards, a B-frame can only use I and P-frames as reference frames to find the best matched blocks. H.264 allows B-frames to serve as reference frames. This increased freedom enables the encoder to find better matched blocks in the finer scale time domain for more bit rate saving. In addition, this new freedom can construct hierarchical

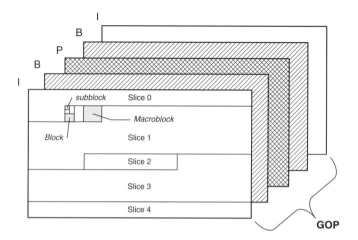

Figure 5.5   Syntax and coding hierarchy.

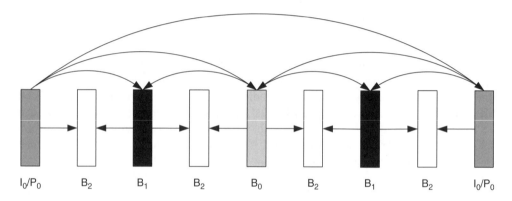

Figure 5.6   Coding structure for hierarchical B-frame.

prediction [4]. As shown in Figure 5.6, the first level of hierarchical B-frame, denoted as B_0, is bi-predicted from two nearby I_0/P_0 frames. After obtaining the reconstructed B_0, we can further use the first level B-frames for motion references. The second level of the hierarchical B-frames, denoted as B_1, is bi-predicted from two nearby I_0/P_0 frames and the first level hierarchical B-frames. The third level of hierarchical B-frames can be constructed in a similar way. The advantages of using hierarchical B-frames include better coding efficiency and temporal scalability support. The penalty brought by this method is the longer decoding delay and larger memory buffer.

For the video streaming applications, owing to the varying bandwidth in the transmission channel, it is often desired to have an adaptive streaming design so that the bit rate of the encoded video streams can fit into the allocated bandwidth dynamically. For the on-line encoded applications with feedback from the receiver, real-time encoding can adjust the coding parameters to change the bit rate. However, for the off-line encoded stored video, the transmitter side needs to prepare multiple versions of the same content and each one is encoded at a different target bit rate. According to the allocated bandwidth, the transmitter will switch to the version with the highest possible bit rate through the current channel such that the end users will experience smooth playback with less viewing disturbance. Owing to the motion compensation across video frames, the switch points are only allowed at the IDR pictures to avoid drifting artifacts. Since the time interval between two nearby IDR pictures is often long, to reduce the coding penalty brought by intra coding, the stream switch time is long and the application cannot respond to the fast varying bandwidth in a timely manner. On this regard, switching P (SP) and switching I (SI) slices are introduced into the H.264 spec [5].

The usage of SP-frame in the bit stream switching from stream 0 to stream 1 is illustrated in Figure 5.7. There are two types of SP-frame: primary and the secondary. The primary SP-frame is encoded in each bit stream and serves as a switching point. Denote the frame index of the desired switching point as n. Frame $SP_{0,n}$ and $SP_{1,n}$ are the primary SP-frames. The secondary SP-frame, denoted as $SP_{01,n}$ in Figure 5.7, is only transmitted when the switching request is issued for the desired switching point n. The SP-frame is designed to ensure that the reconstructed values for $SP_{1,n}$ and $SP_{01,n}$ are identical, which allows frame $P_{1,n+1}$ to perform motion compensation without any drifting. The SI-frame has similar functionality but without any prediction from original viewed stream.

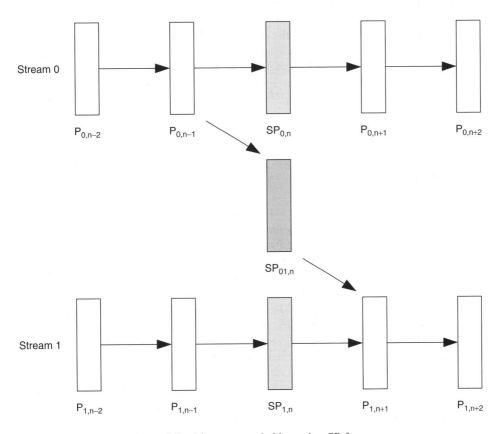

Figure 5.7 Bit stream switching using SP-frame.

We have seen the encoded bit stream in H.264 exhibiting strong decoding dependency owing to the advanced prediction and entropy coding, and so any bit error during the streaming process will cause error propagation until the next independent coding block. There are several coding tools developed in H.264 to address the issues for transmitting streams over error prone channels.

- Redundant slice: A slice can have another redundant representation in addition to its original version. In the error-free decoding process, the decoder will ignore the redundant slice. When a slice is found with errors, the decoder will find the associated redundant slice to replace this damaged slice. The penalty of the additional robustness brought by the redundant slices is the need of extra bandwidth to carry those redundant slices.
- Arbitrary slice order (ASO): H.264 defines a flexible syntax, *first_mb_in_slice*, to specify the position of the first macroblock in the current slice. Although the slice index always starts from 0 and grows monotonically, specifying *first_mb_in_slice* to a different value can physically change the slide order. For example, let's assume there are four slices in a video frame with resolution 1920×1088 and each slice has an equal number of MBs: $(1920 \times 1088)/(16 \times 16)/4 = 2040$ MBs. In other words, the aforementioned setting partitions a picture into four quarters. One can specify *first_mb_in_slice* in slice 0, 1, 2, and 3 as 2040, 6120, 0, and 4080. Slice 0, 1, 2, and 3 represent the second, fourth, first, and third quarters of the picture. With ASO, the codec is equipped with data interleaving ability to improve error resilience and to facilitate error concealment.
- Slide groups/flexible macroblock order (FSO): The macroblocks in a video frame can be grouped into several slices via a mapping table. In other words, the neighboring macroblocks can belong to different slices. Besides the traditional raster scan, six different map types of slice group are supported: interleaved/dispersed, explicit, foreground/background, box-out, and wipe. The slice group provides additional error resilience and a better base for error concealment. When a slice group is corrupted, the missing macroblocks in that slice group can be estimated from the other correctly received slice groups.

Recently, there has been a significant effort to standardize a new video codec, high efficiency video coding (HEVC) [6], which is based on the existing H.264 codec with lots of improved coding efficiency tools and software/hardware deployment consideration. The Joint Collaborative Team on Video Coding (JCT-VC) is a group of video coding experts from the ITU-T Study Group 16 (VCEG) and ISO/IEC JTC 1/SC 29/WG 11 (MPEG) to develop HEVC with a target of reducing by 50% the data rate needed for high quality video coding, as compared to the H.264/AVC standard. Although many coding tools are being added or improved, the overall decoder complexity is expected to be about twice that of H.264. There is no single encoding tool to boost the whole encoding efficiency, rather the encoding performance improvement is obtained by combining several coding tools.

- Coding hierarchy: The coding hierarchy of HEVC has major differences compared to H.264. A picture in HEVC consists of several nonoverlapped coding treeblocks, referred to as the largest coding unit (LCU). Each LCU can be further split into four sub-blocks via recursive quad-tree representation. If a sub-block has no further splitting, we call this sub-block a coding block, and a coding block can have size from 8×8 to 64×64. HEVC decouples the usage of blocks adopted in the prediction and transform processes. In other words, a block used in the transform process can cross the block boundary used in the prediction process. Prediction unit (PU) is defined in each CU and can have size from 4×4 to 64×64. Transform unit (TU) is defined in each CU and has block size from 4×4 to 32×32. The basic coding unit (CU) consists of PUs and TUs and associated coding data. In addition to the above coding hierarchy changes, to reduce the coding performance loss due to partitioning caused by slicing and to enable parallel processing, HEVC introduces the tile structure. Tiles are constructed by partitioning a picture horizontally and vertically into columns and rows. The partition boundary can be specified individually or uniformly spaced, and each tile is always rectangular with an integer number of LCUs.

- Intra-prediction: When a scene is captured by two different spatial resolution cameras, the object in the higher resolution image will include more pixels, and consequently there are more distinguished edge directions. As HEVC aims at supporting higher resolution images, the INTRA mode used in H.264 is not sufficient to cope with the larger image resolutions and bigger block size in CU. Advanced INTRA modes, including angular intra-prediction (33 different prediction directions), planar prediction, luma-based chroma prediction, mode dependent intra smoothing (MDIS), are added to improve the prediction performance.

- Inter-prediction: A similar problem is encountered in the inter-prediction for high spatial resolution content, as the small prediction unit used in H.264 cannot provide better compression performance. To achieve better prediction accuracy, a flexible partition size is introduced by including further partitioning of a CU to multiple PUs and asymmetric motion partition (AMP), which partitions a CU into unequal block size (for example, one PU with size 64×16 and one PU with size 64×48 inside one 64×64 CU). Other advanced coding tools, such as CU (PU) merging, advanced MV prediction (AMVP) via motion vector competition, 2D separable DCT-based interpolation filters (DCT-IF) for subpixel motion estimation/compensation, improved skip mode, and increased bit depth precision (14 bits) at the filter output, are included to enhance the compression performance.

- Transform: For higher resolution content, most image patterns in a block represent a small part of objects which can be described as homogeneous texture patterns with little variation. To take advantage of this, the residual quad-tree (RQT) is introduced by segmenting a CU into multiple transform blocks to fit into different size of homogeneous texture areas. Furthermore, the non-square quad-tree transform (NSQT) is included to tackle the scenario when a CU is split into non-square PUs (via AMP) or the scenario when the implicit TU splitting into four non-square TUs. The in-loop filtering used in HEVC is also refined by the three-step process: (1) deblocking, (2) sample adaptive offset (SAO), and (3) adaptive loop filtering (ALF).

- Entropy coding: In HEVC, the entropy coding component removes the CAVLC method and only adopts the CABAC method. The coefficients scanning (re-ordering) method adopted in HEVC CABAC is via a diagonal scan instead of the zigzag scan used in most video codec standards.

- Parallel processing: To enable parallel processing, the concept of wavefront process-ing is introduced. Wavefront parallel processing lets each LCU row run in its own decoding thread and each decoding thread proceeds to the next LCU immediately once its corresponding decoding dependency is resolved (such as the nearby top LCU being decoded).

5.2 Two-View Stereo Video Coding

In this section, we discuss the early development of 3D video coding technologies based on existing single-view video codecs. There are two basic coding methodologies: individual view coding and inter-view coding.

5.2.1 Individual View Coding

Two-view stereo video coding considers the simplest scenario which consists of two videos representing the left and right views from two slightly different viewpoints. These two viewpoints are separated by a distance similar to the distance between a human's two eyes. A straightforward approach to realizing two-view stereo video coding is to apply an existing 2D video coding scheme to each view independently with some extra design consideration at the application level. First, the synchronization for playback between the two views should be maintained to make sure that both views show the correct frames at the targeted display time. Second, if the random access and/or trick plays (such as fast/slow forward/backward) capability are needed, the IDRs or I-frames should be inserted in both views at the targeted access points. The advantage of the individual view coding is the low computation complexity needed in the viewer device side since the device just needs two instances of video decoders to decode these two bit streams and render them directly without any extra computation. Besides, the error propagation is limited inside each view since there is no prediction across different views, which provides a good error resilience mechanism. The main disadvantage of this approach is doubling the required bandwidth to transmit two 2D streams compared to only one 2D bit stream.

To further reduce the required bit rate in the individual view coding system, we can deploy the asymmetric stereo video coding methodology to take the advantage of the human visual system. The asymmetric stereo video coding is to adopt different coding methods in each view such that the required bit rates in both views are different. Although the view with lower bit rate has lower reconstructed 2D video quality, the perceived binocular visual quality is still similar to the symmetric stereo video coding. The asymmetric stereo video coding method can be categorized as spatial asymmetry, temporal asymmetry, or signal-to-noise ratio (SNR) asymmetry [7].

To exploit the spatial asymmetry in stereo video coding, one could resort to the study of binocular suppression theory [8], which shows that: (1) when both views have different level of sharpness, the subjective stereoscopic experience of the overall binocular experience is close to the sharper view; (2) when the two views have different levels of blocking artifacts, the overall subjective stereoscopic rating is close to the mean quality of both views. In other words, by given an existing good quality stream for one view (dominant view) and a smaller fixed bandwidth to deliver the other view (non-dominant view), fitting the non-dominant view into the bandwidth through spatial resolution reduction/downsampling-upsampling (more blur but fewer blocking artifacts) can provide better subjective viewing experience than the one through higher QP in video compression (less blur but more blocking artifacts) [9]. Since the former approach mixes two different resolutions in the 3D bit stream, we often call it mixed resolution stereo video coding. Mixed resolution stereo coding is more appropriate in the mobile environment which consists of a low bit rate channel and low computation/power resources. Although mixed-resolution coding provides one possibility for 3D video deployment, the asymmetrical spatial resolution may bring viewing fatigue with a longer viewing period. Besides, different end users may have different dominant eye positions [10]. Switching dominant view between left and right when a scene cut appears could be a solution to remedy this problem.

The temporal asymmetry can also be conducted in stereo video coding. The principle of the temporal asymmetry is to reduce the number of frames encoded in the non-dominant view so the bit rate is reduced in the corresponding bit stream. This is equivalent to performing downsampling/decimation along the time domain. The real implementation in the codec can be achieved by either encoding with lower frame refresh rate or inserting a skip mode for each macroblock in the intended dropping frames. The unequal frame rate method is shown as an effective solution for slow motion video sequences [11]. The spatial asymmetry and temporal asymmetry can be deployed together and the downsampling ratio along each domain can be adaptively selected according to the video characteristics and feedback from subjective testing.

SNR asymmetry coding is the easiest approach to implement of the three asymmetric coding approaches. The main reasons for easy deployment of SNR asymmetry coding include: no modification in the existing video codec; less computation complexity since other asymmetry coding methods need to perform upsampling along spatial and/or temporal domains; and more granularity to control the level of degradation via the quantization parameter. The principle of SNR asymmetry is to increase the quantization parameter in the non-dominant view so that the bit rate is reduced in the corresponding bit stream. Simulations in [7] suggest that when the peak signal-to-noise ratio (PSNR) in the non-dominant view is reduced but above a just-noticeable threshold (JNT) level in terms of PSNR threshold, the perceived binocular quality is dominated by the higher quality in the dominant view. The study also shows that the JNT level is not only content dependent, but also 3D display technology dependent, namely, polarized projector or parallax barrier. When both views are coded above the JNT level, the SNR asymmetric coding method provides better perceived visual quality when compared to symmetric coding method. On the other hand, if at least one of the views is coded below the JNT level, then symmetric coding achieves better perceived visual quality.

5.2.2 Inter-View Prediction Stereo Video Coding

Since two nearby views have similar content, compression efficiency can be improved by adopting both the traditional intra-view prediction along the time domain in each view and performing inter-view prediction between two adjacent views. An early attempt to achieve this goal is defined in H.262/MPEG-2 multi-view profile as shown in Figure 5.8. The algorithm encodes the left view independently using MPEG-2 codec, and encodes the right view via inter-view and intra-view prediction by generalizing the concept of predictive (P), or bipredictive (B) frames widely adopted in the H.26x/MPEG-x series. The prediction direction is illustrated as the arrows shown in Figure 5.8.

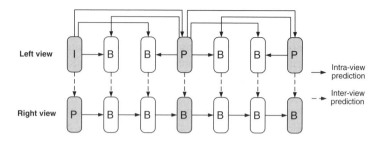

Figure 5.8   Illustration of H.262/MPEG-2 multi-view profile.

The improvement of compression efficiency provided by the H.262/MPEG-2 multi-view profile is limited compared to the results from individual coding of each view. The main bit rate saving factor comes from the replacement of intra-coded frames in the right view by inter-view prediction from the left view, since the inter-view redundancy can be exploited. However, other frames in the right view benefit less from inter-view prediction since the motion estimation and motion compensation mechanism usually find a better match (thus less residual) among intra-view frames than the inter-view frames.

The asymmetric coding methodology mentioned earlier can also be applied to the stereo coding technology with inter-view prediction. Inter-view prediction is predicted from the dominant view to construct the predicted signal. By subtracting the predicted signal from the original non-dominant view, we have the prediction error as a residual signal. Then, the spatial downsampling method is applied on the residual to generate the downsampled residual [12]. The downsampled residual signal is transformed to the DCT domain, and the DCT coefficients are quantized and encoded by the entropy coding. Note that the spatial downsampling is an in-loop process. To reconstruct frames to serve as prediction references for motion estimation and compensation used in other P and B-frames, the quantized DCT coefficients are de-quantized, converted from DCT domain back to pixel domain, and then upsampled to the same resolution as the original dimension.

5.3   Frame-Compatible Stereo Coding

To deploy the two-view stereo video over the existing content delivery infrastructure, which normally supports one 2D video stream, the stereo video should be processed such that it is frame- and format-compatible during the transmission phase. There are two different types of frame-compatible stereo coding according to the picture resolution and discussed separately in the following two sections.

5.3.1   Half-Resolution Frame-Compatible Stereo Coding

In order to deploy stereo video through current broadcasting infrastructure originally designed for 2D video coding and transmission, almost all current 3D broadcasting solutions are based on multiplexing the stereo video into a single coded frame via spatial subsampling, that is, the original left and right views are subsampled into half resolution and then merged into a single video frame for compression and transmission over the infrastructure widely used for 2D video programs. At the decoder side, the de-multiplexing and interpolation are conducted to reconstruct the dual views [13]. By doing so, the frame merged from left and right view is frame compatible to existing video codec.

The half-resolution frame-compatible encoder consists of three components: (a) spatial resampling, (b) resampled pixel repacking, and (c) compression of packed frames. For the spatial resampling component, there are three common methods: (a) side-by-side format, which downsamples the original full-resolution video frame in each view with a factor of two horizontally, (b) over/under format, which downsamples the original full-resolution video frame in each view with a factor of two vertically, and (c) checkerboard format, which downsamples the original full-resolution video frame in each view in the quincunx grid manner. It has been demonstrated that the side-by-side format and over/under format have very similar compression performance, and the checkerboard format has the worst compression performance. The generic codec structure is depicted in Figure 5.9. The downsampling process should be applied to both luma and chroma components. The

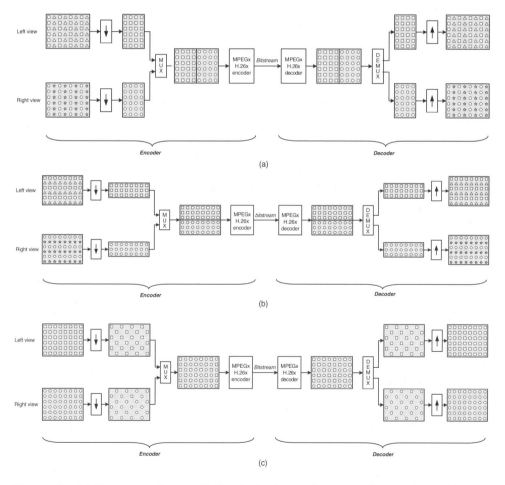

Figure 5.9 (a) Side-by-side format. (b) Over/under format. (c) Checkerboard (quincunx) format.

decimation can be performed by taking the same position of pixels from each view (e.g., odd columns from left view and odd columns from right view for side-by-side format); or a different position from each view (e.g., odd columns from left view and even columns from right view for side-by-side format). The former method is referred to as the common decimation method and the latter one is often called complementary decimation. And it may also involve filtering procedures to reduce the aliasing for better quality. After the downsampling, the downsampled pixels will be packed/multiplexed to fit them into the one full-resolution video frame. By doing so, the packed frame can be compressed by any video codec, such as MPEG-x or H.26x. At the decoder side, a corresponding video decoder is deployed first to decode the packaged video frame. The re-multiplexing module will unpack the pixels and put them back to the original sampling coordinates and the associated views. An upsampling procedure is followed to interpolate the missing pixels so that the dimension of each frame is restored to its original size.

The temporal multiplexing approach, by interleaving left and right view into one video sequence, can also be adopted in frame-compatible video coding. However, this approach will double the required bandwidth to deliver the two-times frame refresh rate. Subject to the channel bandwidth in the existing infrastructure, the temporal multiplexing scheme should be carried out in a half-frame-rate fashion in each view, which often cannot provide satisfactory visual quality.

5.3.2   Full-Resolution Frame-Compatible Layer Approach

Although half-resolution frame-compatible stereo video coding provides a convenient way to meet today's infrastructure requirement, the end user's viewing quality still suffers from the reduced spatial resolution. Based on the existing half-resolution frame-compatible stereo video coding, one could apply the layered video coding technology to send additional information in the enhancement layers to improve the final reconstructed full-resolution frame [14].

One straightforward method is to apply the spatial scalability coding tools [15] provided by the scalable video coding (SVC) extension of H.264/AVC [16]. An example using side-by-side format is illustrated in Figure 5.10. The base layer of the spatial scalability codec works as the legacy half-resolution frame-compatible video codec. To utilize the tools provided by SVC, the encoder will also construct the reference frames in a side-by-side format but with dimension $2W \times H$. The base layer will be first upsampled to the same dimension, $2W \times H$, and the encoder will perform inter-layer prediction from the upsampled base layer to generate the residual for encoding. When the decoder receives the enhancement layer, the decoder performs the same upsampling operations and adds the enhancement layer information back to improve the overall video quality.

Another approach based on SVC is to utilize both spatial and temporal scalability, which is shown in Figure 5.11. The enhancement layer of the left view is carried through the region-of-interest spatial scalability layer by upsampling the left view portion of the reconstructed base layer, and the enhancement layer of right view will be encoded through the temporal scalability from the enhanced left view.

There are other layered full-resolution frame-compatible approaches based on the multi-view video coding (MVC) extension of H.264/AVC [17], which will be discussed later. One realization is shown in Figure 5.12. Note that although MVC provides a way to

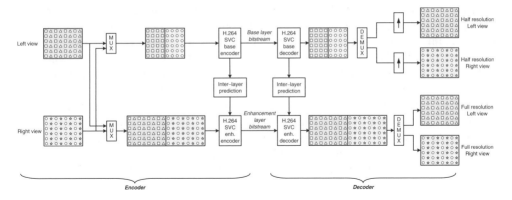

Figure 5.10   Full-resolution frame compatible format based on SVC spatial scalability.

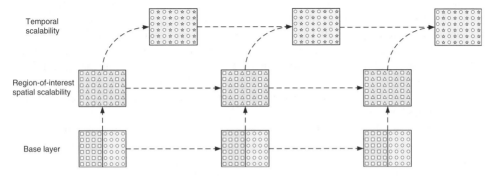

Figure 5.11   Full-resolution frame-compatible format based on SVC spatial plus temporal scalability.

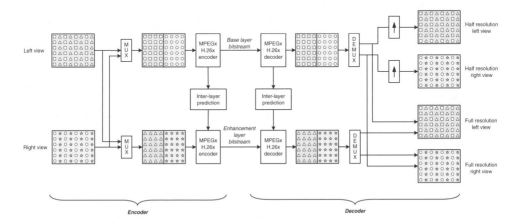

Figure 5.12   Full-resolution frame compatible format based on MVC.

compress multiple views in a single stream, it does not provide the capability to support the full-resolution frame-compatible format. On the other hand, MVC provides a container to deliver multiple video sequences in the bit stream. Similar to the SVC-based solution, the base layer of MVC-based codec operates as the required half-resolution frame-compatible video codec to generate the base view. The pixels that are not included in the sampling grid in the half-resolution base view will be filtered and encoded in the enhancement view. Note that the resampling in the base view and enhanced view should be performed properly to alleviate the aliasing artifact. The alternative to reduce the resampling artifact is proposed through the usage of three-view MVC [18], which has the base layer to provide the half-resolution frame-compatible sequence and other two views to contain the full resolution sequence for the left view and the right view individually.

5.4   Video Plus Depth Coding

We have reviewed many different approaches to compress stereo video sequences. We notice that the main principles of all the discussed approaches so far only take the information directly from the pixels captured by stereo cameras and try to utilize the existing video coding framework to deliver the video with the highest possible fidelity. Potentially, the video coding performance can be further improved during the stereo video codec design phase by addressing both the geometric location of the camera arrays and the 3D scene to video camera. One potential solution is through the depth-image-based rendering (DIBR) approach [19, 20].

The inputs of the DIBR process consist of one color image frame, which represents the color information, and one depth map, which represents the depth information for each corresponding pixel in the image. The 3D coordinate for each pixel from the input image frame can be calculated with the aid of the depth information. Then, the DIBR process sets up two virtual cameras in a parallel configuration, which represent left view and right view, and projects those pixels in the 3D coordinate back to each virtual 2D image plane belonging to each virtual camera.

Figure 5.13 illustrates the details of the DIBR process. Let C_C represent the viewpoint of the original captured camera, C_L the viewpoint of the virtual left camera, and C_R the viewpoint of the virtual right camera. Denote f as the focal length of the camera C_C, and d as the distance from each virtual camera to the central camera. For each pixel X_C with location (x_c, y) in C_C camera coordinate, we have its corresponding depth information $z(x_c, y)$ and can construct its 3D position as $p(x_c, y)$, as shown in the figure. The horizontal distance between p and C_C is $|x_c| \cdot z(x_c, y)/f$ and the horizontal distance between p and C_L is $d + x_c \cdot z(x_c, y)/f$. The projection of pixel p on the left virtual camera image plane has the coordinate (x_l, y), where

$$x_l = x_c + d\frac{f}{z(x_c, y)} \tag{5.5}$$

Similarly, the projection of pixel p on the right virtual camera image plane has coordinate (x_r, y), where

$$x_r = x_c - d\frac{f}{z(x_c, y)} \tag{5.6}$$

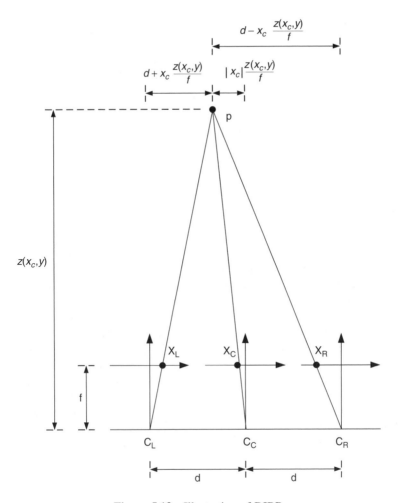

Figure 5.13 Illustration of DIBR.

The rendering process will take place for all pixels to generate the required two views. With a fixed camera configuration d and f, the DIBR rendering process will simply be a horizontal offset and can be implemented via a lookup table approach regarding to the depth.

To successfully compress the 3D video using DIBR technology, the depth map should also be compressed to achieve the required compression efficiency. It has been observed that the characteristics of depth map show that: (1) the dynamic range of depth information is scene-dependent and can be very large or very small with different granularity; and (2) the human perceptual system is more sensitive to the depth changes in nearby objects than farther objects. To satisfy the aforementioned requirements and potentially to reuse the existing video coding tools for depth information compression, one promising solution is to quantize the depth map into eight bits, supported in most existing coding tools, according to the inverted real-world depth as follows [21]:

$$
QZ(x_c, y) = \left\lfloor 255 \frac{\left(\dfrac{1}{z(x_c, y)} - \dfrac{1}{z_{max}} \right)}{\left(\dfrac{1}{z_{min}} - \dfrac{1}{z_{max}} \right)} + 0.5 \right\rfloor
\tag{5.7}
$$

where Z_{max} and Z_{min} are the maximum depth and minimum depth in one image. The inverse quantization to decode the depth information is:

$$
\hat{z}(x_c, y) = \frac{1}{\dfrac{QZ(x_c, y)}{255} \left(\dfrac{1}{z_{min}} - \dfrac{1}{z_{max}} \right) + \dfrac{1}{z_{max}}}
\tag{5.8}
$$

Having all real-world depth information converted to quantized inverted real-world depth, QZ, we observe that QZ is smooth or near constant across one object and has sharp transitions between foreground and background. The eight-bit depth map QZ can be treated as a monochromatic, luminance-only image, taking values between 0 and 255, and can be efficiently compressed via existing video codecs (e.g., the MPEG-x codec). As defined in MPEG-C Part 3 [22], the depth information can be treated as auxiliary pixel data to facilitate the backward compatibility with original MPEG codecs.

Bringing in DIBR technology, the left view and right view video can be synthesized via one video sequence and one depth video sequence, as shown in Figure 5.14 [23, 24]. The general video compression algorithm can be applied to the color video and depth video independently. After compression, both bit streams are sent to the receiver, and new views can be synthesized with color and depth information in the display. In general, the required bit rate to encode the depth information is around 10–20% of the compressed color video bit stream such that the decoder has sufficient precision to generate proper stereoscopic images [25].

Although video plus depth coding provides a promising solution, it still has several challenges to overcome. The first major problem is the newly exposed areas (also known as holes) appearing in the synthesized views, as shown in Figure 5.15. Those holes often appear along the object boundaries whose depth values change significantly. The main cause of those holes is that those areas are covered by the foreground objects in the original view but become visible to the new viewpoints. Since those covered pixels are not encoded in the color video sequences, we cannot fill in the color information for those missing pixels in the synthesized views.

Several solutions have been proposed to fill in the missing values for those holes and can be categorized into (1) post-processing techniques and (2) preprocessing techniques [26]. For post-processing solutions, an intuitive method is to horizontally interpolate the holes from its neighbors, regardless of whether neighboring pixels belong to the foreground or the background. However, the interpolated areas will blend the foreground and background objects together and blur the edges. The hole-filling algorithms can be improved by referring to depth information to determine whether a pixel in the boundary belongs to foreground or background and extrapolating those pixels according to the area to which it belongs [27, 28]. The resulting images are shown in Figure 5.16. The extrapolation process can preserve the object boundaries but the filled areas still look unnatural owing

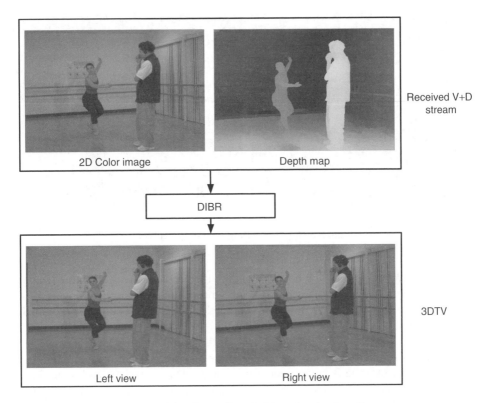

Figure 5.14   Illustration of video plus depth coding.

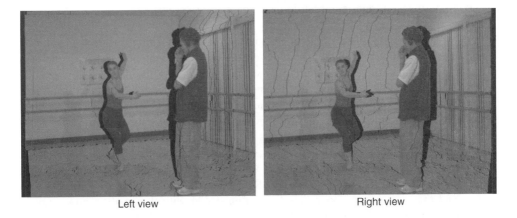

Figure 5.15   Hole artifacts in left view and right view after the DIBR process.

Left view   Right view

Figure 5.16   Hole filling by extrapolation.

to the use of extrapolation. Filling holes by finding the occluded areas along the temporal domain also helps to reduce the artifacts, since those hidden areas may appear in the past or future video frames [29]. For the preprocessing methods, one can try to smooth the depth map along the boundary to alleviate the sharp transition between foreground and background, which reduces the appearance of the occluded areas [30]. However, this approach brings geometrical distortion owing to the smoothed depth map.

Another important issue is how to encode the depth map to achieve both high fidelity and high compression ratio. The current video plus depth coding approach adopts the existing state-of-the-art video compression technology used for the texture component to compress the depth map. However, the traditional video codecs are optimized to compress nature images. The depth map shows significantly different characteristics from nature images in both spatial and temporal domains.

- In the spatial domain, there are homogeneous or smooth transitions inside scene objects and sharp transitions along the boundaries between different objects. A depth map explicitly captures the 3D structure of a scene by recording the distance between 3D objects and the camera. Because the distance between the camera and object's surfaces generally changes gradually, large portions of typical depth images depicting object surfaces change smoothly. In contrast, the object boundaries, especially the ones separating foreground and background objects of the depth map exhibit abrupt changes as sharp edges. To address these unique characteristics of the depth map, with deployment of H.264 codec it is often observed that the homogeneous regions are encoded with the simplest and largest modes, such as SKIP, Inter 16×16 or Intra 16×16. It is also observed that the objects' boundaries are often coded with the smallest and simplest prediction mode, such as Intra 4×4.
- In the temporal domain, the depth map shows lower consistency than the texture image, namely, the depth value for a static object may vary a lot for consecutive frames. The inconsistency is mainly due to the noise and/or insufficient precision in the depth capture device, or the depth estimation used in stereo matching does not effectively take temporal consistency into consideration. The penalty of inconsistency along the time

domain is to have a large amount of residual after motion estimation and to degrade the encoding performance for the P and B-frame type when we compress the depth video using the H.264 codec.

It is important to notice that the depth map is not directly used for viewing. It functions like a predictor during the virtual view synthesis, which is similar to the motion vector used in motion compensation. The encoding artifacts brought by lossy hybrid video codec, such as blocking artifacts along the coding block boundaries and ringing artifacts along the edges, will degrade the depth maps and affect the final quality of the synthesized virtual view, especially on the important edges.

To overcome the rendering artifacts caused by the lossy video codec, techniques adopted to alleviate common compression artifacts can be used to improve the decoded depth map. Introducing in-loop filters specific to depth information improvement in the existing video codec is shown to be a good candidate to suppress the artifacts [31, 32]. Bilateral filter is known as an edge-preserving process in which each pixel is a weighted average from its neighbors within a window and the weighting factor for each neighboring pixel is contributed with consideration of both distance to the central pixel and pixel value difference [33]. Denoting I_p as the pixel value at position p in the depth map, given an $N \times N$ window S centered at pixel p, the filtered pixel value can be expressed as follows:

$$I'_p = \frac{1}{W_p} \sum_{q \in S} G(\|p - q\|, \sigma_s) \cdot G(|I_p - I_q|, \sigma_d) \cdot I_q, \qquad (5.9)$$

where the $G(x, \sigma)$ is the Gaussian kernel and has the following formula:

$$G(x, \sigma) = \frac{1}{\sigma\sqrt{2\pi}} \exp\left(-\frac{x^2}{2\sigma^2}\right) \qquad (5.10)$$

The terms σ_s and σ_d are the filter parameters needing to be tuned for best performance and transmitted as metadata for the decoder to conduct the filtering. The first Gaussian kernel weights the distance between pixel p and q, and the second Gaussian kernel weights the pixel value difference between pixel p and q. To maintain a constant DC value before and after the filtering process, the filtered value needs a normalization factor W_p:

$$W_p = \sum_{q \in S} G(\|p - q\|, \sigma_s) \cdot G(|I_p - I_q|, \sigma_d). \qquad (5.11)$$

The bilateral filter is applied after the depth map is reconstructed from the bit stream. When the bilateral filter is used as an in-loop filter, the filtered reconstructed depth map will be served as reference frames for motion estimation and compensation. The advantage of the in-loop filter is to provide better reference frames to improve the depth map quality. However, the computation load for bilateral filtering on each pixel is high. Introducing the in-loop filter into the codec indicates that the encoder and the decoder need to perform the same operations, which brings more computation complexity into the decoder.

When the window crosses an edge, pixels having similar pixel value can contribute more to the final filtered output, thus preventing the leakage of value from different objects. Owing to the high similarity of structure between the depth map and the color image, one could extend the bilateral filter to a trilateral filter by further considering the pixel value change in the color video information part to reduce depth map coding artifacts while preserving the sharpness of edges and higher spatial coherence [34]. Let C_p be the pixel value at position p in the luminance component of the color video sequence. The trilateral filter can be expressed as:

$$I'_p = \frac{1}{W_p} \sum_{q \in S} G(\|p - q\|, \sigma_s) \cdot G(|I_p - I_q|, \sigma_d) \cdot G(|C_p - C_q|, \sigma_c) \cdot I_q. \qquad (5.12)$$

The normalization factor needs to address the new Gaussian kernel for pixel value difference in the color image:

$$W_p = \sum_{q \in S} G(\|p - q\|, \sigma_s) \cdot G(|I_p - I_q|, \sigma_d) \cdot G(|C_p - C_q|, \sigma_c). \qquad (5.13)$$

The processing can be further improved by considering the available information along the time domain, which is commonly used in video processing technologies, such as spatial-temporal noise reduction. One can further build a quad-lateral filter extended from the trilateral filter by further considering temporal variation to improve both the accuracy of the depth map and the temporal consistency [35].

Dedicated approaches, which are not built on top of existing video codecs, are also proposed to handle the unique characteristics of the depth map. To capture the unique characteristics of the depth image, namely, that large parts depicting surfaces contain smoothly changing gray levels and the objects' boundaries exhibit abrupt changes, one could use a piecewise smooth (platelet-based) functions to model a depth image [36]. Two different classes of functions are used to model different areas. The first class is the piecewise-constant function which models the regions with constant depth such as flat unslanted surfaces and contains the following two modes:

- single constant function: approximate each pixel in the whole block by a constant value. This mode requires only one parameter to represent this constant value.
- piecewise constant function (wedgelet function): divide the whole block into two partitions and each pixel in each partition has a constant value. This mode requires three different parameters: one to describe the line to separate a block into two partitions, one to represent the constant value in the first partition, and the third paramter is another a constant value for the second partition.

The second class is the piecewise-linear function which models regions with gradually changing gray level such as ground plane and walls. This class contains the following two modes:

- single linear function: approximate each pixel (x, y) in the whole block by a linear function with three parameters:

$$I(x, y) = a_0 + a_1 x + a_2 y. \qquad (5.14)$$

- piecewise linear function (platelet-based): divide the whole block into two partitions and each partition has its linear function as (5.14).

The coefficients in each function can be obtained via data fitting to minimize the approximation distortion. For the piecewise constant function and piecewise linear function, we need to determine the partitioning lines and surface parameters. A full search method can be deployed by testing all possible lines and the corresponding optimal parameters. To provide finer granularity for modeling different size of objects and backgrounds to the required level of fidelity, a quad-tree decomposition to hierarchically divide the image into blocks is adopted. The quad-tree decomposition is conducted recursively until the R-D performance cannot be further improved. In each iteration, for each parent block, we can calculate the optimal parameters for each function and choose the function which achieves the best R-D performance. Then, we can further divide this block into four child blocks. For each child block, we can conduct the same procedure to select the best function. If the overall R-D performance from these four child blocks is better than that of the parent block, the parent block will be decomposed into four child blocks. The aforementioned quad-tree decomposition procedure will be conducted recursively for each child block. Otherwise, the decomposition for this parent block is terminated. Although the R-D performance of the depth map coding using platelet-based method is worse than H.264 based depth map coding, the R-D performance of the synthesized view using the platelet-based method is better than H.264 based depth map coding owing to the sharp edge preservation.

In [37], the R-D performance of the depth video can be further improved via adaptive geometry based intra-prediction. The performance gain is contributed to by the following factors:

- The accuracy of the partitioning curves plays an important role in preserving the sharpness of the boundary. To improve the partitioning accuracy using linear line, edge detection followed by Hough transform technology is introduced.
- The object's boundary in one block is often a higher order curve. Partitioning a block by a linear line may not be sufficient to represent two regions separated by the boundary. To have a better approximation, further sub-block partitioning is needed to make the approximation close to the original boundary. On the other hand, further partitioning means more compression overhead to transmit the side information. The R-D performance can be improved by deploying a higher order curve (such as an arc) to partition a block.
- As commonly used in H.264, intra-prediction can bring coding gain owing to the higher spatial correlation among neighboring blocks. After the partitioning is done for each block, each sub-block can be predicted from its available neighboring reconstructed blocks. By doing so, the residual in each block is reduced and thus bit rate can be reduced.

To resolve the issue of depth variation in the depth map along the time domain, namely inconsistent depth values for static objects for consecutive depth frames which causes low coding efficiency for inter-prediction, an object-adaptive depth compensated inter-prediction method is proposed in [38]. It is observed that the depth value of each object in the reference frame has a roughly constant depth offset compared to the corresponding object in the current frame. The inter-prediction error can be significantly reduced when both the object partitions/boundaries are precisely found in the time domain and the depth offsets are compensated for each object. Two key components are introduced to address these unique characteristics:

- A threshold-based algorithm to separate foreground and background is conducted via a bi-section search within each block. An initial threshold is selected by taking the average of the maximum and minimum depth value in one block. The foreground and background are chosen by selecting the pixels whose depth value is no less than and less than this threshold, respectively. The new threshold is constructed by taking the average of the mean depth value of the foreground and the mean depth value of the background. If the new threshold is different from the old threshold, we will partition the foreground and the background again according to this new threshold. This process is repeated until there is no change between the new and old threshold. The foreground and background partitioning algorithm will be deployed for both the reference block (in the reference frame) and the current block (in the current frame). The depth offset are calculated by taking the difference between the mean of depth values in the partition of the reference block and the mean of depth values in the corresponding partition of the current block. Note that the depth offset should be conducted for both foreground and background.
- The tradition motion estimation methods often fail to find the true motion vectors when the mean depth values are shifted between reference and current block. One possible improved motion estimation method is to conduct the motion vector search based on the mean-removal distortion measurement. In other words, the MAD measurement used in (5.1) is modified as follows:

$$MRMAD(m_x, m_y) = \sum_{(x,y) \in A} |(B_c(x, y) - \bar{B}_c) - (B_r(x - m_x, y - m_y) - \bar{B}_r)| \quad (5.15)$$

where $\bar{B}_c$ and $\bar{B}_r$ are the mean depth pixel value in the current and reference block, respectively. The alternative to address the depth map motion estimation is to conduct the motion estimation based on the edge map obtained from the depth map. This is because the edge map already contains the information of the object's boundaries (as edges) and also removes the mean depth values.

5.5 Multiple View Coding

Multi-view video provides a new immersive visual experience where end users can watch a scene from different angles by moving the users' viewing position or other advanced interactive approaches. As illustrated in Figure 5.17, a multi-view autostereoscopic capable device can render several images from different views simultaneously. Therefore, each user can watch one stereo pair from any given viewpoint and multiple users can watch their desired views from different viewpoints at the same time.

To deliver the multi-view video to end users, the required bandwidth is significantly larger than that needed in stereo video. The straightforward methods, including using multiple single view or multiple stereo view compression technology, still encounter the bandwidth problem imposed by current content delivery infrastructure. To address the need of efficiently compressing multiple views, H.264 multiple view coding (MVC) [39–41] extends two-view stereo video coding discussed above into a more general scheme.

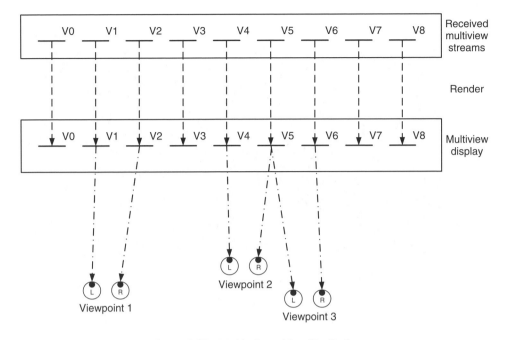

Figure 5.17   Multi-view video 3D display.

There are several fundamental requirements during the standardization procedure of MVC codec besides the coding efficiency. First, MVC should ensure backward compatibility; namely, passing H.264 MVC bit stream into an existing non-MVC H.264 decoder should not affect the whole syntax parsing process and should successfully output one base view. Backward compatibility is important for deployment of 3D video to users with 3D-capable and 2D-only displays. To ensure this requirement, some high level syntax of the stream header should be modified to ensure that both MVC and non-MVC syntax parsers can recognize the base view and other enhancement views. Second, temporal random access is fundamental as it allows users to fast forward and backward a video clip to a target scene. View-switching random access is also important to enable users to switch to a desired target viewpoint. Third, as the huge amount of data in multi-view video streams and all viewpoints should be decoded and displayed in designed display timeline, defining a MVC bit stream with parallel-processing-friendly syntax can significantly reduce the hardware implementation costs.

To achieve higher compression efficiency for multi-view video, we notice that all views are taken from different viewpoints of a 3D scene at each time instance, as illustrated in Figure 5.18 [23, 24]. Denote the frame captured by the Vth camera at the Tth time instance as $f(V,T)$. Although we have higher volume of captured data to compress, each view has highly similar context as the rest of the views. Besides exploring the temporal redundancy through motion compensation inside each individual view used in the traditional single view video codec, that is taking reference frames from $f(V,T')$ with $T' \neq T$ inside view V, multi-view video codec can further explore the inter-view redundancy via disparity compensation to improve the coding performance, namely, taking reference frames from

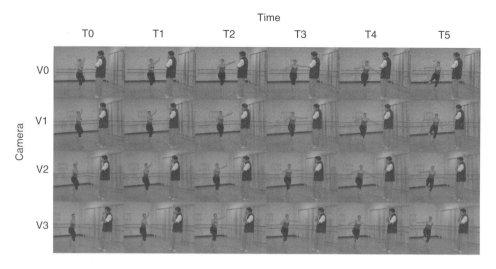

Figure 5.18 Input multiple view video sequences.

$f(V',T)$ with $V' \neq V$ at time T. Note that one can expect to obtain even higher coding gain by taking joint temporal/inter-view prediction from other views at different time instance, namely, predicting a macroblock at $f(V,T)$ from $f(V',T')$ where $V' \neq V$ and $T' \neq T$. The study in [42] shows that mixed temporal/inter-view prediction does not provide significant coding gain but introduces lots of additional computation complexity and a complicated buffer management problem. Therefore, the mixed temporal/inter-view prediction is not included in H.264 MVC.

There are some other fundamental issues existing in the whole multi-view video compression pipeline. The most noticeable is that different views' video sequences are captured by different cameras from different viewpoints. Since the cameras cannot be calibrated perfectly due to the mechanical precision and the lighting/environment in the real world along each camera capturing direction is different, the illumination, color, and focus of captured objects may vary from camera to camera, which causes performance degradation of inter-view prediction. Tools to compensate those illumination/color/focus mismatches among multiple cameras inside the video codec are proposed in [43–45]. The advantage of having mismatch compensation tools inside the video codec is to make the codec more robust and self-contained. The disadvantage is to bring much higher computation complexity on both the encoder and the decoder side. However, those mismatches can be compensated as a preprocess before feeding the uncompressed video data into the multi-view video codec, for example, by setting higher quality video cameras with careful calibration and performing preprocessing procedures to alleviate those mismatches in the studio mastering process. Shifting the mismatch compensation to the beginning of the whole 3D video ecosystem significantly reduces the cost of decoders on the consumer side, which results in the exclusion of those advanced tools in the MVC spec at the current stage.

According to the aforementioned discussion, the H.264 MVC codec uses only the inter-view and intra-view prediction from neighboring cameras and consecutive frames to reduce the inter-view and intra-view redundancies to enhance the compression efficiency.

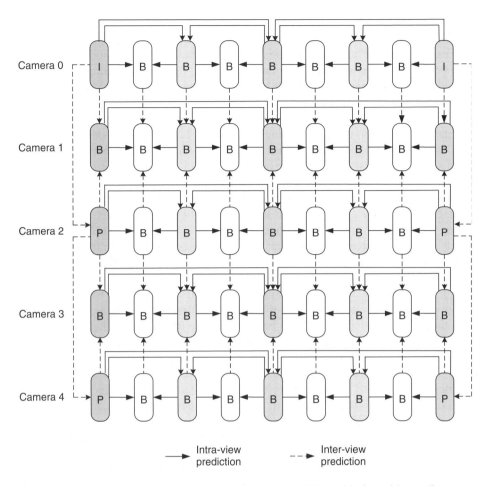

Figure 5.19 Illustration of prediction structure in H.264 multi-view video coding.

The prediction structure of H.264 MVC codec is depicted in Figure 5.19. The solid arrows and dashed arrows indicate the intra-view and inter-view prediction direction, respectively. Camera 0 is encoded as the base view without referring to any other views. Camera 2 uses one-direction inter-view prediction from camera 0. Camera 1 can explore the view information redundancy from both camera 0 and camera 2. The coding efficiency can be further improved with the usage of hierarchical B-frames, in which B-frames are arranged in a temporally hierarchical fashion and are predicted by using the two nearest pictures of the next lower temporal level as references.

The coding performance for MVC has been reported in some references and has shown different ranges of gain depending on the scenarios and the prediction structures used [13]. For the scenario with up to eight views, an average of 20% overall bit rate reduction to achieve the same video quality was reported with comparison to individual view encoding. For the two-view stereo scenario, 20–30% average bit rate reduction and 43% peak rate reduction were achieved.

Given that MVC codec explores one more dimension of redundancy among the views, the MVC encoder has more freedom to choose the coding parameters such that rate-distortion performance can be optimized. However, the high dimensional search space also imposes high computational requirements to reach the optimal setting. Similar to the real implementation issues encountered in the H.264 encoder, a fast algorithm which can save computation by trading in a small amount of perceived quality is often acceptable and preferred.

Similar to the motion estimation using intra-view prediction, each coding block in the inter-view prediction (also called disparity estimation) finds a best matched block in other views to achieve the optimal R-D performance. However, the computation requirement for the disparity estimation is as heavy as the motion estimation. It would be beneficial if both disparity estimation and motion estimation operated in a reduced search space. Although there already exist many fast motion estimation algorithms, it is observed that applying fast motion estimation techniques to disparity estimation may be inefficient since disparity exhibits different characteristics from the motion model. With the knowledge of camera geometry, one could reduce the search space for disparity estimation to speed up the search [46].

Besides the disparity and motion estimation, each MB in MVC also has the possibility of choosing the encoding modes from the rich, but different, inter/intra-prediction methods. Although the optimal solution can be found via the full search method that calculates the RD cost for each mode, the search process is very time-consuming and computationally intensive. A fast mode decision algorithm is desired to reduce the encoding time. The generic methodology for fast mode decision methods is to associate content characteristics/statistics with the probability of the optimized chosen modes from a massive simulation. In other words, one needs to find good content features or statistics measurements which exhibit high correlation to the frequency of the chosen modes found in the full-search simulation. Owing to similar content in neighboring views, it is observed that the selected coding modes in neighboring views have similar distribution under the consideration of R-D cost [47]. In addition, a two-view video sequence simulation to compare the mode distribution between individual video coding and MVC coding shows that when the current MB contains objects with fast motion or occlusions, the intra mode selected in the individual coding is often replaced by the disparity prediction in the MVC. Once the encoder completes the mode decision in one view, the encoder can use the afore-mentioned observations to have a fast search guideline for the mode decision in other views. Early skip mode decision and early termination for mode decision also improves the search speed since the search stops after the searching criteria are satisfied [48]. The stopping criteria are also obtained by addressing the statistics of encoded content. Similar principles can be applied to determining the block size decision for disparity estimation and motion estimation [49].

5.6 Multi-View Video Plus Depth (MVD) Video

Although MVC can provide 20% bit rate reduction on average when we compare MVC with the simulcast scenario, the experimental results show that the coding gain is not scalable enough as the number of views grows. In fact, there is a linear relationship between the number of views and the total bit rate, that is the required bandwidth to transmit M-view video using MVC is $0.8M$ times the bit rate summed from all M views using individual single-view coding [42]. When M goes to a large number, the required bandwidth exceeds the capacity of existing communication and storage infrastructure, which makes the deployment of multi-view video content delivery infeasible.

One possible solution is to utilize the DIBR concept mentioned in the video plus depth coding. On the encoder side, we transmit the 2D video of the central view and its corresponding depth information. The decoder will simply render all other viewpoints using DIBR technology. As discussed in video plus depth coding, the hole artifacts and hole filling solutions remain major concerns for occluded regions. In addition, it is observed that the exploration artifacts introduced in the DIBR process increase when the number of viewpoints increases, which makes extending video plus depth coding technology from stereo to multi-view impractical. Thus, though single video plus depth stream provides great flexibility for the view synthesis to alleviate this problem, the solution is not scalable enough to resolve the large changes in view condition.

This problem can be alleviated by sending multi-view video plus depth (MVD) streams, as shown in Figure 5.20. For an M-view 3D system, the encoder will select N ($N < M$) views and encode each view's color and depth information into video plus depth format. At the receiver side, the MVD decoder parses and decodes N video plus depth streams.

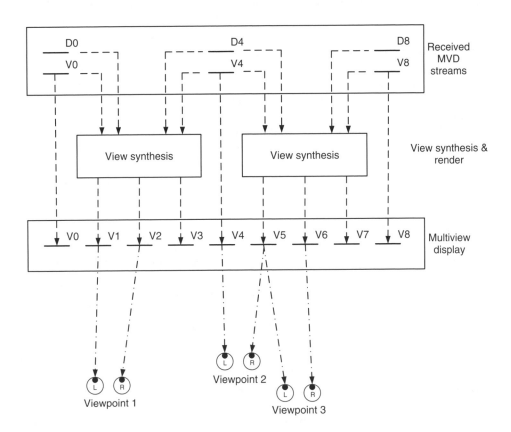

Figure 5.20   Decoding and rendering process in multi-view video plus depth video coding.

With N 2D color image frames and corresponding N depth maps, the decoder performs the view synthesis process to generate all the other M-N intermediate views. The viewers may see the view either from the original 2D images or synthesized images, depending on the viewing position. An an example shown in Figure 5.20, the decoder receives 2D color video images and depth map from view 0, 4, and 8. Views 1, 2, 3, 5, 6, and 7 need to be synthesized. Users in viewpoint 2 will watch real image with the left eye, but receive the synthesized image at the right eye. At viewpoints 1 and 3, viewers will receive synthesized images for both eyes. Possible dissocclusions in M displays can be minimized by selecting the viewpoints and the number of video-plus-depth streams.

Note that instead of encoding N video-plus-depth streams individually, one feasible format of MVD for further bit rate reduction is to separate color sequences and depth sequences into two different multi-view sequence groups and encode each group with the H.264 MVC codec [50]. In other words, the MVD format can be delivered by two MVC streams. It has been reported that the PSNR for the luma component can show up to 0.5dB improvement, and the depth and chroma components can have up to 0.3dB performance gain. Since the color video sequence and the depth map show the same object in different representations, the object displacement and movement should be highly consistent in both groups of sequences. The motion vectors and selected coding mode used in the color video compressed bit stream and the depth map bit stream should have high correlation. Therefore, the mode decision and the motion vectors chosen in the color video sequence can be referenced during the depth map coding to reduce the encoder computation complexity. Moreover, it is proposed not to send the bits for motion vectors in the depth map bit stream to further reduce the bit rate. At the decoder, the decoding process of the depth map stream ignores the slack motion vectors stored in the depth map stream and performs motion compensation by taking motion vectors from the color video bit stream [51].

The success of MVD relies on the way the intermediate view is synthesized via view synthesis prediction (VSP). There have been several proposals to create a better synthesized view [52, 53]. The basic procedure for view synthesis consists of the following three steps: First, the view synthesis process will be invoked by projecting all the pixels in the two neighboring original views to the targeted virtual image planes. A collection process will follow to select the representative color information from each view. Finally, a fusion process is conducted to merge the color information from two nearby views.

If the cameras are calibrated with known parameters during the video capture stage, the projection can be conducted as follows. Denote the central camera as C_1, the left side view camera as C_0, and the right side view camera C_2. Let $\mathbf{M}_{i,0}$, $\mathbf{M}_{i,1}$, $\mathbf{M}_{i,2}$ be the intrinsic matrices representing the intrinsic parameters, including the focal length, mapping between camera coordinate and image coordinate system, and geometric distortions, for left, central, and right cameras, respectively. Similarly, for each camera, let $\mathbf{M}_{e,0}$, $\mathbf{M}_{e,1}$, $\mathbf{M}_{e,2}$ be the extrinsic matrices representing the necessary geometric information to coordinate transform from the external coordinate system to the camera coordinate system. The extrinsic matrix, $\mathbf{M}_{e,k}$, has dimension 4×3 and consists of one 3×3 rotation matrix $\mathbf{R}_e$ and one 3×1 translation matrix $\mathbf{t}_e$ (i.e., $\mathbf{M}_{e,k} = [\mathbf{R}_{e,k} \ \mathbf{t}_{e,k}]$). Projection matrices $\mathbf{M}_0$, $\mathbf{M}_1$, $\mathbf{M}_2$, which are defined as multiplication of intrinsic matrix and extrinsic matrix (i.e., $\mathbf{M}_k = \mathbf{M}_{i,k} \ \mathbf{M}_{e,k}$), are used to project the 3D world points into the targeted image planes. To project a pixel in one original view to the new image plane, we first need to inverse project the pixel back to the world coordinate by taking the inverse projection matrix, $\mathbf{M}_k^{-1}$, and then project it onto the targeted plane using an interpolated projection matrix $\bar{\mathbf{M}}_k$. As suggested in [54], the rotation matrix is interpolated via spherical linear interpolation to ensure the orthonormality of matrix, but the rest of parameters in the interpolated project matrix are linearly interpolated with weighting factor according to the distance to two neighboring cameras.

For each pixel with coordinate $\mathbf{v}_k = [x_k \; y_k \; z_k]^T$ in its own camera coordinate for view k, we can have its corresponding position in the new virtual image plane as $\bar{\mathbf{M}}_k \mathbf{M}_k^{-1} \mathbf{v}_k$. Note that the projection won't create a one-to-one mapping to fill in both color and depth information for every pixel in the new image plane. Each pixel position may consist of n projected pixels, where $n \geq 0$. A selection process is needed for depth and color information for the $n > 0$ case. The selection based on nearest estimated depth should be a good candidate since it represents the foreground object and may cover other backgrounds. Thus, a projected pixel with the nearest distance to the camera will be selected. The new depth information will be the new estimated depth, and the new color information will take the values from its corresponding pixel in the original view. At the end of this process, we will have two synthesized images for a targeted intermediate view: one is synthesized from the left-neighboring view and the other is synthesized from the right-neighboring view. The last stage is to linearly combine the two aforementioned synthesized images with a weighting factor according to the distance to the two neighboring cameras.

When the camera parameters are not available, one can resort to disparity estimation to calculate the disparity map between two neighboring views. The intermediate view will be synthesized by using the disparity information [55]. Similar to the video plus depth coding, the boundary artifact in the reconstructed depth map can be improved by the filtering process described in Section 5.4.

5.7 Layered Depth Video (LDV)

Although MVD can synthesize any infinitely dense intermediate views with high fidelity from a limited number of sparse views transmitted through the network, the overall required bandwidth to convey all the color and depth information of the N views (including central and side views) is still comparatively large, even bringing in the MVC coding for color and depth information. To further reduce the bit rate, one could deploy conventional video coding on the central view only; apply view synthesis technologies on the decoded and reconstructed central view to generate other $N - 1$ side views; and take the difference between the projection and the neighboring camera result as residual information. The residual consists of disoccluded information and is therefore mainly concentrated along depth discontinuities of foreground objects as well as image boundary data in both side views. The overall bit stream consists of three major components: (1) complete color and depth information from the central view; (2) parameters for view synthesis, such as geometry parameters for camera and real-world depth range; and (3) residual of color and depth information in the side views. At the decoder side, as shown in Figure 5.21, the decoder will first reconstruct the central view once having received the bit stream. Then, the decoder projects the central camera view into the other neighboring views using the view synthesis parameters to synthesize side views. The residual is added back to the

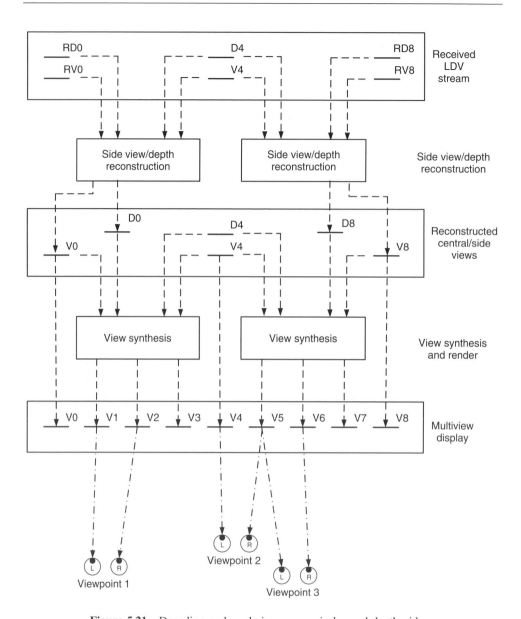

Figure 5.21 Decoding and rendering process in layered depth video.

synthesized side views to reconstruct all N views. Having those N views available, the rest of the intermediate views can be synthesized via techniques used in MVD.

It has been observed that the aforementioned straightforward method could introduce corona artifacts in the intermediate synthesized views. To remedy this problem, layered depth video (LDV) [56] is proposed. The basic idea of LDV is to identify the reliability of each depth pixel, especially the ones along the object boundaries, since those boundary pixels are often mixed with foreground and background, degraded by lossy compression artifacts, and may contain potential errors from imperfect depth estimation. The unreliable depth pixels are detected via the Canny edge detector, marked by a seven-pixel-wide area along depth discontinuities, and classified as the background boundary layer. A layer extraction procedure is conducted to preserve reliable pixels and to remove pixels in the background boundary layer. Then, the layer projection is performed during view synthesis by synthesizing pixels in the extracted layer to ensure the reliability of projected view. The projected side view will be further filtered to remove invalid disoccluded areas to reduce the synthesis error. The residual information will be taken from the original side view and the filtered projected side view.

5.8   MPEG-4 BIFS and AFX

Standardization of representation formats can facilitate content exchange and encourage the popularity of consumer advanced display devices. An early attempt to standardize 3D representation is conducted by MPEG-4 via binary format for scenes (BIFS) [57]. BIFS is specified as an extension of virtual reality model language (VRML) and inherits all features from VRML. VRML is a text format and defines a set of elements to transmit 3D graphics, including the geometric primitives, 3D meshes, textures, and appearance. The VRML data can be rendered by a VRML player. The interactivity between users and the virtual world, including light sources and collision, is supported. BIFS enriches VRML by providing a better representation, delivery, and rendering for interactive and streamable rich-media services, including 2D and 3D graphics, images, text, and audiovisual material. In place of the text format and the download-and-play of VRML, BIFS adopts binary representation and has a streaming format already adopted in MPEG-4 design. MPEG-4 BIFS extends VRML to include the following new features. First, MPEG-4 BIFS supports integration and management of different audio and video objects seamlessly in a scene. Besides, graphical constructs for 2D and 3D graphics, authoring of complex face and body animation, tools for 3D mesh encoding, and representation of 2D and 3D natural and synthetic sound models are also provided in MPEG-4 BIFS. BIFS enables interactivity between the client-side scene and remote servers by defining input elements such as keyboard and mouse. MPEG-4 scenes equip two types of scripted behavior: a Java API can control and manipulate the scene graph and the built-in ECMA script (JavaScript) support that can be used to create complex behaviors, animations, and interactivity. The BIFS also provides streamable scene description to detail the spatial and temporal graphics in a BIFS-Command stream. With commands, a stream can edit the scene graph to replace, delete, and insert elements in the scene graph. With MPEG-4 system layer, the audio and visual content can be tightly synchronized with other A/V content.

However, BIFS cannot fulfill the emerging requirements of the interactivity and navigability of 3D worlds. An extension to MPEG-4, animation framework extension (AFX) [57], is proposed to equip with the better ability to handle computer games and animation. The AFX defines six components in a hierarchical way to accomplish the designed goal. The first component is the geometric component which describes the appearance and the form of an object. An extension of the geometric models with additional linear or non-linear deformations is included in the modeling component to allow transformation. The third component is the physical component describing the objects' physics in the virtual world, such as motion and gravity. Based on the physical component, a biomechanical component is defined to describe the muscles on animals. There are two other higher level components, namely, behavior component and cognitive component, which define objects' reactive behavior and learning ability.

Four different categories of tools are included in AFX:

1. Shape: NURBS, subdivision surfaces, MeshGrid, particle systems, solid representation.
2. Texturing: procedural texture, depth image based rendering, light-field mapping.
3. Deformation: nonlinear deformer, freeform deformer.
4. Animation: skeleton/muscle/skin-based animator.

We have noticed that MPEG has defined many audiovisual standards, a vendor may want to choose different 3D/visual coding tool with different audio capability from one of the MPEG-x family to meet its unique market. To facilitate this great flexibility, MPEG-A [58] specifies multimedia application formats (MAFs) to assemble the existing MPEG audio/video coding tools to achieve the targeted immersive 3D applications.

5.9   Free-View Point Video

A free viewpoint 3D video system allows end users to arbitrarily change the viewing position and angle to enrich viewers' immersive experiences. The key bridging technology between content generation, transmission, and display stages of a 3D video system is the 3D scene representation. As discussed in Chapter 2, there are two fundamental approaches to defining 3D scenes: image-based and geometry-based representation [59].

Image-based representation uses a set of camera views arranged in a 1D/2D array to represent the 3D world, which can be represented as a set of sparse sampling of the plenoptic function [60]. There have been several similar requirements and operations in video processing applications, such as spatial upsampling or frame rate upconversion, where new pixels are generated by utilizing the information from the existing pixels. For the free viewpoint 3D application, a new view can be synthesized from this sparse set of samples of the plenoptic function. The main advantage is the high quality of virtual view synthesis and an avoidance of 3D scene reconstruction. The computation complexity via image-based representation is proportional to the number of pixels in the reference and output images, but in general not to the geometric complexity such as triangle counts. However, the synthesis ability provided by image-based representation is limited by the viewing angle covered by all the existing views. Besides, the quality of the synthesized views depends on the scene depth variation, the resolution of each view, and the number of views.

The geometry-based representation uses a set of tranglar meshes with a texture to represent the 3D world. The main advantage is that, once geometry information is available, the 3D scene can be rendered from any viewpoint and view direction without any limitation, which meets the requirement for a free viewpoint 3D video system. The main disadvantage is in the computational cost of rendering and storage, which depends on the scene complexity, that is the total number of triangles used to describe the 3D world. In addition, geometry-based representation is generally an approximation to the 3D world. Although there are offline photorealistic rendering algorithms to generate views matching our perception of the real world, the existing algorithms using a graphics pipeline still cannot produce realistic views on the fly.

The recent development of 3D scene representation attempts to bring these two different technologies together to make the technology spectrum broader. By adding geometric information into image-based representation, the disocclusion and resolution problem can be relieved. Similarly, adding image information captured from the real world into geometry-based representation can reduce the rendering cost and storage. Thus, the combination of geometry-based and image-based representation is proposed to render the 3D scene for free viewpoint TV [61].

Depending on how to distribute the computation load in the server side and the client side, and the bandwidth budget, there are three major architectures to enable an end-to-end free viewpoint video system [62]. The first approach is a light client side solution where the encoder performs most of the computation resources in the server side, including 3D scene representation, depth estimation, new view synthesis, and encoding the bit stream for two views intended for each eye via the aforementioned two-view stereo video coding method or MVC. The client side will simply decode the streams and display the two views. Note that the required bandwidth for this method is also smallest as it also contains two-view content. A real-time feedback to track the required viewing angle for the end users is needed so that the server side can synthesize and encode the desired views. The second approach allocates most of the computation load in the client side. The server side encodes via the MVC codec and transmits all captured views through the channel to the receiver. The receiver is responsible for decoding the compressed multi-view streams and estimating the depth from the decompressed images, and synthesizing the required views. The required bandwidth is much higher than the first approach. The third method is to move the depth estimation component to the server side to reduce a certain level of computation load in the client side. However, the estimated depth information needs to be compressed and transmitted through the channel, too. The required codec to deliver both texture and depth image will be the MVD codec.

A standardization activity for free viewpoint TV in MPEG, denoted as MPEG-FTV, was started since April 2007. The effort was based on the aforementioned third architecture, that is MVD codec, to decouple the capture and display component in the whole ecosystem. A Call for Proposals was issued by MPEG for 3D video coding technology (3DVC) March 2011 [63] and tried to provide a solution for efficient compression and high quality view reconstruction of an arbitrary number of dense views.

References

1. T. Wiegand, G. J. Sullivan, G. Bjøntegaard, and A. Luthra, "Overview of the H.264/AVC Video Coding Standard", *IEEE Trans. on Circuits and Systems for Video Technology*, vol. 13, no. 7, July 2003, pp. 560–576.
2. D. Marpe, H. Schwarz, and T. Wiegand, "Context-based adaptive binary arithmetic coding in the H.264/AVC video compression standard", *IEEE Transactions on Circuits and Systems for Video Technology*, vol. 13, no. 7, July, 2003, pp. 620–636.
3. V. Lappalainen, A. Hallapuro, and T.D. Hämäläinen, "Complexity of optimized H.26L video decoder implementation", *IEEE Transactions on Circuits and Systems for Video Technology*, vol. 13, no. 7, July, 2003, pp. 717–725,
4. H. Schwarz, D. Marpe and T. Wiegand, "Analysis of Hierarchical B Pictures and MCTF", *IEEE International Conference on Multimedia and Expo*, 2006, pp. 1929–1932.
5. M. Karczewicz and R. Kurceren, "The SP- and SI-frames design for H.264/AVC", *IEEE Trans. on Circuits and Systems for Video Technology*, vol. 13, no. 7, pp. 637–644, Jul. 2003.

6. JCTVC-H1003 High Efficiency Video Coding (HEVC) text specification Working Draft 6 (B. Bross, W.-J. Han, G. J. Sullivan, J.-R. Ohm,T. Wiegand) (CD).

7. G. Saygili, C. G. Gurler, and A. M. Tekalp, "Evaluation of asymmetric stereo video coding and rate scaling for adaptive 3D video streaming", *IEEE Trans. on Broadcasting*, vol. 57, no. 2, June 2011, pp. 593–601.

8. L. Stelmach, W. J. Tam, D. Meegan, and A. Vincent. "Stereo image quality: effects of mixed spatio-temporal resolution". *IEEE Trans. on Circuits and Systems for Video Technology*, vol. 10, no. 2 , Feb 2000, pp. 188–193.

9. H. Brust, A. Smolic, K. Mueller, G. Tech, and T. Wiegand. "Mixed resolution coding of stereoscopic video for Mobile devices". *IEEE 3DTV Conference*, 2009.

10. W. J. Tam, "Image and depth quality of asymmetrically coded stereoscopic video for 3D-TV", *JVT-W094*, San Jose, CA, April 2007.

11. A. Aksay, C. Bilen, E. Kurutepe, T. Ozcelebi, G. B. Akar, R. Civanlar, and A. M. Tekalp, *"Temporal and spatial scaling for stereoscopic video compression" in Proc*. EUSIPCO, Florence, Italy, 2006, pp. 4–8.

12. H. Lee, S. Cho, K. Yun, N. Hur, and J. Kim., "A backward-compatible, mobile, personalized 3DTV broadcasting system based on T-DMB" in *Three-Dimensional Television Capture, Transmission, Display*. New York: Springer, 2008.

13. A. Vetro, T. Wiegand, and G. J. Sullivan, "Overview of the stereo and multiview video coding extensions of the H.264/MPEG-4 AVC standard", *Proceedings of the IEEE*, vol. 99, no. 4, April 2011. pp. 626–642.

14. A. Vetro, A. M. Tourapis, K. Muller, and T. Chen, "3D-TV content storage and transmission", *IEEE Trans. on Broadcasting*, vol. 57, no. 2, June 2011, pp. 384–394.

15. C.A. Segall and G.J. Sullivan, "Spatial scalability within the H.264/AVC scalable video coding extension", *IEEE Trans. on Circuits and Systems for Video Technology*, vol. 17, no. 9, Sept. 2007, pp. 1121–1135.

16. H. Schwarz, D. Marpe, and T. Wiegand, "Overview of the scalable video coding extension of the H.264/AVC standard", *IEEE Trans. on Circuits and Systems for Video Technology*, vol. 17, no. 9, September 2007, pp. 1103–1120.

17. A. Tourapis, et. al., "A frame compatible system for 3D delivery", *m17925, ISO/IEC JTCl/SC29/WGll*, Geneva, Switzerland, July 2010.

18. Y. Chen, R. Zhang, and M. Karczewicz, "MVC based scalable codec enhancing frame-compatible stereoscopic video", *IEEE International Conference on Multimedia and Expo*, 2011.

19. C. Fehn, P. Kauff, M. O. d. Beeck, F. Ernst, W. IJsselsteijn, M. Pollefeys, L. Van Gool, E. Ofek, and I. Sexton. "An evolutionary and optimized approach on 3D-TV", *Proc. Int. Broadcast Conf., Amsterdam*, The Netherlands, September 2002, pp. 357–365.

20. Fehn C. *"3D-TV using depth-image-based rendering (DIBR)"*, Proc. Picture Coding Symp., San Francisco, CA, USA, December 2004.

21. K. Müller, P. Merkle, and T. Wiegand, "3D Video Representation Using Depth Maps", *Proceedings of the IEEE*, vol. 99, no. 4, April 2011, pp. 643–656.

22. A. Bourge, J. Gobert, and F. Bruls. "MPEG-C part 3: Enabling the introduction of video plus depth contents", *Proc. of IEEE Workshop on Content Generation and Coding for 3D Television*, 2006.

23. MSR 3D Video Download, available at http://research.microsoft.com/en-us/um/people/sbkang /3dvideodownload/.

24. C. L. Zitnick, S. B. Kang, M. Uyttendaele, S. Winder, and R. Szeliski, "High-quality video view interpolation using a layered representation", *ACM SIGGRAPH and ACM Trans. on Graphics*, Los Angeles, CA, Aug. 2004, pp. 600–608.

25. A. Smolic K. Mueller, N. Stefanoski, J. Ostermann, A. Gotchev, G. B. Akar, G. Triantafyllidis, and A. Koz, "Coding algorithms for 3DTV – A Survey.", *IEEE Trans. on Circuits and Systems for Video Technology*, 2007; 17(11):1606–1621.

26. L. Zhang, C. Vázquez, and S. Knorr, "3D-TV Content Creation: Automatic 2D-to-3D Video Conversion", *IEEE Trans. on Broadcasting*, vol. 57, no. 2, June 2011, pp. 372–383.

27. C. Fehn, "Depth-image-based rendering (DIBR), compression and transmission for a new approach on 3D-TV", *SPIE Conf. Stereoscopic Displays Virtual Reality System XI. CA*, Jan 2004, vol. 5291, pp. 93–104.

28. C. Vazquez, W. J. Tam, and F. Speranza, "Stereoscopic imaging: filling disoccluded areas in depth image-based rendering", *SPIE Conf. 3DTV, Video, Display V* , 2006, vol. 6392, 63920D.

29. R. Klein Gunnewiek, R.-P. M. Berretty, B. Barenbrug, and J. P. Magalhães, "Coherent spatial and temporal occlusion generation" in *Proc. SPIE* 7237, 2009, p. 723713.

30. W. J. Tam, G. Alain, L. Zhang, T. Martin, and R. Renaud, "Smoothing depth maps for improved stereoscopic image quality" in *SPIE Conf*. 3–D TV, Video, Display III, Philadelphia, PA, Oct. 2004, vol. 5599, pp. 162–172.

31. P. Lai, A. Ortega, C. C. Dorea, P. Yin, and C. Gomila, "Improving view rendering quality and coding efficiency by suppressing compression artifacts in depth-image coding", *Proc. SPIE VCIP*, San Jose, CA, Jan. 2009.

32. K.-J. Oh, A. Vetro, and Y.-S. Ho,, "Depth coding using a boundary reconstruction filter for 3D video systems", *IEEE Trans. on Circuits and Systems for Video Technology*, vol. 21, no. 3, March 2011, pp. 350–359.

33. S. Paris, P. Kornprobst, J. Tumblin, and F. Durand, "Bilateral Filtering: Theory and Applications", *Foundations and Trends in Computer Graphics and Vision*, vol. 4, no. 1 2008, pp. 1–73.

34. S. Liu, P. Lai, D. Tina, and C. W. Chen, "New depth coding techniques with utilization of corresponding video", *IEEE Trans. on Broadcasting*, vol. 57, no. 2, June 2011, pp. 551–561.

35. C.-M. Cheng, S.-J. Lin, and S.-H. Lai, "Spatio-temporally consistent novel view synthesis algorithm from video-plus-depth sequences for autostereoscopic displays", *IEEE Trans. on Broadcasting*, vol. 57, no. 2, June 2011, pp. 523–532.

36. P. Merkle, Y. Morvan, A. Smolic, D. Farin, K. Muller, P.H.N. deWith, and T. Wiegand, "The effects of multiview depth video compression on multiview Rendering", *Signal Processing: Image Communication*, vol. 24, no. 1, 2009, pp. 73–88.

37. M.-K. Kang, Y.-S. Ho, "Depth video coding using adaptive geometry based intra-prediction for 3D video system", *IEEE Transactions on Multimedia*, vol. 14, no. 1, February 2012.

38. M.-K. Kang, J. Lee, I. Lim, Y.-S. Ho, "Object-adaptive depth compensated interprediction for depth video coding in 3D video system,", *IS&T/SPIE Electronic Imaging*, pp. 1–12, Jan. 2011.

39. A. Smolic, K. Mueller, N. Stefanoski, J. Ostermann, A. Gotchev, G. B. Akar, G. Triantafyllidis, and A. Koz, "Coding algorithms for 3DTV – A Survey", *IEEE Trans. on Circuits and Systems for Video Technology*, vol. 17, no. 11, Nov. 2007, pp. 1606–1621.

40. M. Flierl and B. Girod, "Multi-view video compression", *IEEE Signal Processing Magazine*, vol. 24, no. 6, December 2007, pp. 66–76.

41. K. Muller, P. Merkle, and T. Wiegand, "Compressing time-varying visual content", *IEEE Signal Processing Magazine*, vol. 24, no. 6, December 2007, pp. 58–65.

42. P. Kerkle, A. Smolic, K. Mueller, and T. Wiegand, "Efficient prediction structures for multi-view video", *IEEE Trans. on Circuits and Systems for Video Technology*, vol. 17, no. 11, Nov. 2007, pp. 1461–1473.

43. J.-H. Hur, S. Cho, and Y.-L. Lee, "Adaptive local illumination change compensation method for H.264/AVC-based multiview video", *IEEE Trans. on Circuits and Systems for Video Technology*, vol. 17, no. 11, November 2007, pp. 1496–1505.

44. K. Yamamoto, M. Kitahara, H. Kimata, T. Yendo, T. Fujii, M. Tanimoto, S. Shimizu, K. Kamikura, and Y. Yashima, "Multiview video coding using view interpolation and color correction", *IEEE Trans. on Circuits and Systems for Video Technology*, vol. 17, no. 11, Nov. 2007, pp. 1436–1449.

45. J. H. Kim, P. Lai, J. Lopez, A. Ortega, Y. Su, P. Yin, and C. Gomila, "New coding tools for illumination and focus mismatch compensation in multiview video coding", *IEEE Trans. on Circuits and Systems for Video Technology*, vol. 17, no. 11, November 2007, pp. 1519–1535.

46. J. Lu, H. Cai, J.-G. Lou, and J. Li, "An epipolar geometry-based fast disparity estimation algorithm for multiview image and video coding", *IEEE Transactions on Circuits and Systems for Video Technology*, vol. 17, no. 6, 2007, pp. 737–750.

47. L. Ding, P.-K. Tsung, S.-Y. Chien, W.-Y. Chen, and L.-G. Chen, "Content-aware prediction algorithm with inter-view mode decision for multiview video coding", *IEEE Transactions on Multimedia*, vol. 10, no. 8, pp. 1553–1563, December 2008.

48. L. Shen; Z. Liu, P. An, R. Ma, and Z. Zhang, "Low-complexity mode decision for MVC", *IEEE Transactions on Circuits and Systems for Video Technology*, vol. 21, no. 6, 2011, pp. 837–843.

49. L. Shen, Z. Liu, S. Liu, Z. Zhang, and P. An, "Selective disparity estimation and variable size motion estimation based on motion homogeneity for multi-view coding", *IEEE Transactions on Broadcast*, vol. 55, no. 4, pp. 761–766, December 2009.

50. P. Merkle, A. Smolic, K. Muller, and T. Wiegand, "Multi-view video plus depth representation and coding", *Proc. IEEE ICIP*, vol. I, 2007, pp. 201–205.

51. H. Oh and Y.-S. Ho, "H.264-based depth map coding using motion information of corresponding texture video", *Adv. Image Video Technology*, vol. 4319, 2006.

52. P. Kauff, N. Atzpadin, C. Fehn, C. Muller, O. Schreer, A. Smolic, and R. Tanger, "Depth map creation and image-based rendering for advanced 3DTV services providing interoperability and scalability", *Signal Processing: Image Communication*, vol. 22, no. 2, 2007, pp. 217–234.

53. S. Yea and A. Vetro, "View synthesis prediction for multiview video coding", *Signal Processing: Image Communication*, vol. 24, no. 1, 2009, pp. 89–100.

54. K. Muller, A. Smolic, K. Dix, P. Merkle, P. Kauff, and T. Wiegand, "View synthesis for advanced 3D video systems", *EURASIP Journal on Image and Video Processing*, vol. 2008, article ID 438148, 2008.

55. X. Xiu, D. Pang, and J. Liang, "Rectification-based view interpolation and extrapolation for multi-view video coding", *IEEE Trans. on Circuits and Systems for Video Technology*, vol. 21, no. 6, June 2011, pp. 693–707.

56. K. Muller K, A. Smolic, K. Dix, P. Kauff, and T. Wiegand, "Reliability-based generation and view synthesis in layered depth video", *IEEE Workshop on Multimedia Signal Processing*, 2008, pp. 34–39.

57. M. Bourges-Sevenier and E. S. Jang, "An introduction to the MPEG-4 animation framework eXtension", *IEEE Transactions on Circuits and Systems for Video Technology*, vol.14, no. 7, July 2004, pp. 928–936.

58. K. Diepold, F. Pereira, and W. Chang, "MPEG-A: multimedia application formats", *IEEE Multimedia*, vol. 12, no. 4, Oct/Dec 2005, pp. 34–41.

59. A. Smolic and P. Kauff, "Interactive 3D Video Representation and Coding Technologies", *Proceedings of the IEEE*, vol. 93, no. 1, January 2005, pp. 98–110.

60. E. Adelson and J. Bergen, "The plenoptic function and the elements of early vision", *Computational Models of Visual Processing*. Cambridge, MA: MIT Press, 1991, pp. 3–20.

61. A. A. Alatan, Y. Yemez, U. Gudukbay, X. Zabulis, K. Muller, C. E. Erdem, C. Weigel, and A. Smolic, "Scene Representation Technologies for 3DTV – A Survey", *IEEE Trans. on Circuits and Systems for Video Technology*, vol. 17, no. 11, Nov. 2007, pp. 1587–1605.

62. M. Tanimoto, M. P. Tehrani, T. Fujii, and T. Yendo "FTV for 3D spatial communication", *Proceedings of the IEEE*, vol. 100, no. 4, April 2012, pp. 905–917.

63. Call for Proposals on 3D Video Coding Technology, ISO/IEC JTC1/SC29/WG11 MPEG, N12036, March 2011.

6

Communication Networks

Technological advances during the past hundred years have led to the pervasive deployment of networking technologies that allow for the delivery of a wide array of services. Video services, and in particular 3D video, can be transmitted through all the main types of networks currently in existence. In this chapter we highlight some of the most important network technologies by providing an introduction to the main concepts that will be used and expanded in the following chapters. We will first discuss IP technology as it supports networking services for all types of networks, both wired and wireless. After this, the rest of the chapter will cover different wireless communication technology, leading to and concluding with an introduction to 4G wireless standards.

6.1 IP Networks

The backbone of today's widespread networking is the Internet technology that can be better characterized as a packet-switched, store-and-forward, communication network running the Internet family of protocols at the network and transport layers. This single-sentence description entails several key concepts that will be described in the following subsections. More detailed information on these topics can be found on the many very good current textbooks on networking, such as [1], [2] and [3].

6.1.1 Packet Networks

With the development of communication networks came the need to develop switching techniques so as to connect one network node to another network node through the communication process. In early networks, the adopted techniques followed a paradigm known as "circuit switching". This paradigm is based on establishing at the beginning of a call, a connection between the communicating nodes that is maintained for the duration of the call. In this way, the resources needed for a communication session are exclusively reserved for that session for as long as it lasts. Probably the best example of a circuit switched system is the plain old telephone system (POTS), where the connection is established during dialing, and its resources are reserved until the call ends. An important property to note for circuit switching networks is that the reservation of resources for

3D Visual Communications, First Edition. Guan-Ming Su, Yu-Chi Lai, Andres Kwasinski and Haohong Wang.
© 2013 John Wiley & Sons, Ltd. Published 2013 by John Wiley & Sons, Ltd.

a connection effectively establishes a state within the network. Connection setup and tear-down procedures manage these states within the network.

After several decades of circuit switching dominance, network switching saw the emergence of a new paradigm, called "packet switching" or "store-and-forward" networks. In this paradigm, the information to be communicated is separated into blocks, usually called the "data payload". Before transmission of any of the blocks, they are appended to a "header". The header is a block of metadata, this is, information about the data in the payload. The combined payload data along with its associated metadata in the header is called a "packet".

The purpose of the information contained in the packet header is to ensure that the payload could be communicated from the sending node to the destination node. As such, a critical element of the metadata contained in the header is the identification of the destination node. While the payload data is, of course, important for the destination node, the metadata is used to control the protocols running in the network nodes involved in the communication process. Importantly, the information contained in the header should be sufficient to ensure that a packet can be treated and processed as an independent element in all network nodes. To see this important point, let's suppose that a communication process sends a packet from a source node to a destination node, visiting in between a number of other intermediate nodes, which will simply help route the packet through the network, toward the destination node. At any of the intermediate nodes, the metadata in the header allows the node to find out what is the node destination and, based on this information, forward the node to another node in the direction of the destination. The information in the header also allows a packet to be temporarily stored in the memory of a node until it can be processed for routing.

6.1.2 Layered Network Protocols Architecture

A network can be seen as an infrastructure that supports the distributed execution of software. The software can be the application itself, which in this book consists of a 3D video playback system. As such, at the transmitter side, the software performs operations such as source and channel encoding, buffering, and data framing. At the receiver side, it is common to also find buffering operations and the decoding operations to match the encoding at the transmitter. The two main components in the network infrastructure are the nodes, which generate, forward, or receive data, and the links that interconnect the nodes.

Another key component needed to form a network is the *protocols*. Protocols are a set of coordinating rules that establish the format and structure by which two separate ends of distributed software interact. For example, in a routing algorithm the transmitter side needs to specify what the address of the destination is, in a format that is understood by the intermediate nodes executing an algorithm to route the data packet.

The network protocols are divided into *"layers"*, where each layer is specialized on a set of functions. The layers are organized into a stack, with the layers piled up one on top of the other. Viewed at the transmitter side, the functions of a layer provide services to the layers immediately above in the stack. Therefore, the lower the layer is in the stack, the more basic are the communication functions that are provided by the associated protocol. The aggregated result from all stacked protocols at different layers is the complete set of functions required by the networking process.

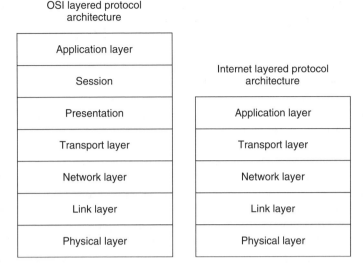

OSI layered protocol
architecture

| Application layer |
| Session |
| Presentation |
| Transport layer |
| Network layer |
| Link layer |
| Physical layer |

Internet layered protocol
architecture

| Application layer |
| Transport layer |
| Network layer |
| Link layer |
| Physical layer |

Figure 6.1   OSI and Internet layered protocol architectures.

The idea for a network protocols architecture where they are divided into stacked layers was introduced in 1980 by the International Organization for Standardization (ISO) through the "Open Systems Interconnection" (OSI) reference model [4]. As shown in Figure 6.1, this model introduced an architecture with seven layers. Today's modern networks, included wireless networks, are based on an architecture based on the Internet protocol stack. As seen in Figure 6.1, this architecture has five layers: the physical layer (also called Layer 1, or the PHY layer), the data link layer (also called Layer 2), the network layer (or Layer 3), the transport layer (or Layer 4) and the application layer (or Layer 5). The function of these layers is as follows:

- *Physical layer*: This provides to the upper layer those services related to the transmission of unstructured bit streams over a physical medium, by performing a mapping from bits or groups of bits into electrical signals. This layer also provides, at times, forward error control (FEC) services.
- *Data link layer*: This is one of the most complex layers in terms of the breadth of services provided to upper layers. Because of this, it is frequently divided into sublayers. One common such sublayer is the *logical link control* (LLC) sublayer, which provides node-to-node flow control, error detection, forward error control (when not implemented at the physical layer or complementing the FEC scheme at the physical layer) and retransmission procedures of link layer frames with errors (ARQ – automatic repeat request). Another very common sublayer is the *medium (or media) access control* (MAC) sublayer, which provides the means for multiple stations to share access to the transmission medium. Regardless of its internal structure, two characteristics differentiate the data link layer. One is that the layer is the lowest in the stack to provide structure into the transmitted bit stream, forming sequences of bits into *frames*. The second important characteristic is that the data link layer, as its name indicates, provides

services exclusively related to links. Here, a link is the direct connection between two nodes, without having any other node in between. Because of this, it is said in summary that the function of the data link layer is to provide reliable transfer of information on a link.

- *Network layer*: This layer is the lowest in the stack providing services that encompass more than just a link and with a network-wide scope. As such, this layer provides the upper layers in the stack with the services needed to switch and route information through the network, enabling a packet to be routed through network nodes from a source to a destination. In the Internet protocol stack, the network layer protocol is the Internet Protocol (IP), today used in the two versions IPv4 and IPv6.
- *Transport layer*: This layer provides reliable transfer of information between end points in a connection. As such, it provides end-to-end congestion and flow control, as well as services for the retransmission of data that is missing or received with errors. At first sight, this layer may seem to provide services very similar to those of the data link layer, but the key difference here is that while the data link layer provides link-oriented services, the transport layer provides services operating on the end-to-end connection established between sender and receiver of data. In terms of Internet technology, while the data link layer can be seen as providing services for a wireless link or the link of an Ethernet local area network, the transport layer would provide services for an end-to-end connection that may include multiple types of links and networks. The best known two examples for Internet transport layer protocols are the Transmission Control Protocol (TCP) and the User Datagram Protocol (UDP).
- *Application layer*: This layer encompasses protocols that enable the distributed execution of an application. As such, there exist many application layer protocols, such as those used for file transfer (e.g., FTP), email (e.g., SMTP, IMAP, POP), hypermedia-based Internet browsing (e.g., HTTP), etc.

6.2   Wireless Communications

The subject matter of this book relates to the transmission of a digital data over a wireless channel. Several stages of processing are needed in order to do this. All these stages, along with the information-generating source and the channel itself, are seen as a *wireless communications system*. Often, an ease of analysis dictates that the system is considered with a simplified structure that includes only the main blocks. These blocks are in the sequential order during transmission and assuming that the source is already in a digital form,

- *In the transmitter*:
  - Source encoder: This block is concerned with the representation of the information from the source, usually appearing as a group of samples organized in a source data block, in digital form (as a sequence of bits). The most important operation that is performed in the source encoder, in what concerns this book, is the representation of the information from the source in a compact and efficient way that usually involves compression of the source data block.
  - Channel encoder: This block protects the sequence of bits from the source encoder against the errors that the wireless channel will unavoidably introduce. This is done

by adding extra redundant bits and a specific structure to the sequence of bits that is presented to the input of the encoder. Because this operation adds redundant bits, the number of bits at the output of the channel encoder is never less than the number of bits at the input. The ratio between the number of bits per unit time at the input of the encoder to the number of bits per unit time at the output to the encoder is called the *channel code rate*. Following its definition, the channel code rate is always less than or equal to one.

- RF (radio frequency) transmit side: In this stage the digital signal to be transmitted is converted into an analog electrical signal able to travel as an electromagnetic wave. Some of the operations included in this block are modulation and power control.

- *Between transmitter and receiver*:

  - Channel: The medium over which the electrical signals are transmitted as electromagnetic waves. The study of the characteristics of the wireless channel will be discussed later on in this chapter.

- *In the receiver*:

  - The blocks in the receiver are the complement of those at the transmitter, in the sense that they perform the reverse operations performed at the transmitter so as to ideally obtain at the output of the receiver the same group of samples as at the input of the transmitter.

Next, we discuss further details about some of these components of a wireless communications system. More detailed information on these topics can be found in the many very good existing textbooks on networking, such as [5], [6] and [7].

6.2.1 Modulation

As summarized in the previous paragraphs, in order to transmit digital data over a wireless channel it is necessary to perform several stages of signal processing before the actual transmission of the information over the wireless channel. While most of these operations are preferably implemented in the digital domain (and over several protocols organized in layers), it is eventually necessary to convert the stream of bits into an analog electrical signal that can travel as electromagnetic radiation over the wireless channel. This operation, performed at the physical layer, is called *modulation*. In order to be able to communicate information, modulation maps the data bits to be transmitted into variations of an electrical signal. These variations, which are referred as the operation of *modulation*, usually take the form of changes in amplitude, phase or frequency in a sinusoidal electrical signal:

$$s(t) = \alpha(t) \cos\left(2\pi f_c t + \phi(t) + \phi_0\right), \quad \text{for } 0 \le t < T_s,$$

where the signal $\phi(t)$ includes both the changes in frequency $f(t)$ and in phase $\theta(t)$ because $\phi(t) = 2\pi f(t)t + \theta(t)$, $\alpha(t)$ is the variation in amplitude, f_c is the carrier frequency, ϕ_0 is an initial phase (which often can be considered equal to zero without loss of generality), and T_s is the duration of the symbol in the equation. Using trigonometric properties, the above data-modulated sinusoid can also be written as:

$$s(t) = \alpha(t) \cos(\phi(t)) \cos\left(2\pi f_c t\right) - \alpha(t) \sin(\phi(t)) \sin\left(2\pi f_c t\right), \text{ for } 0 \le t < T_s,.$$

There are multiple types of modulation scheme, each differing in how the bits are mapped and what sinusoid parameters are actually modulated. Some of the most popular ones are summarized next.

- M-ary phase shift keying (MPSK): in this modulation scheme, blocks of b bits are mapped into different phases. Since there are $M = 2^b$ different blocks with b bits, the modulated signal is:

$$s_i(t) = Ag(t) \cos\left(\frac{2\pi(i-1)}{M}\right) \cos(2\pi f_c t) - Ag(t) \sin\left(\frac{2\pi(i-1)}{M}\right) \sin(2\pi f_c t),$$

where $i = 1, 2, \ldots, M$, is the index assigned to each possible block of input bits, A is a constant to determine the transmit power and $g(t)$ is a non-information-carrying signal used to shape the spectral signature of the modulated signal.
- Binary phase shift keying (BPSK): this is a very important particular case of MPSK, where $b = 1$. Therefore, with $i = 1, 2$, the two possible modulated signals are:

$$s_1(t) = Ag(t) \cos(2\pi f_c t),$$

mapped, for example, to an input bit equal to zero, and:

$$s_2(t) = -Ag(t) \cos(2\pi f_c t),$$

mapped in the example to an input bit equal to one. Note how the two modulated signals differ by a phase of 180°.
- Quaternary phase shift keying (QPSK): this is another important particular case of MPSK where $b = 2$. Therefore, with $i = 1, 2, 3, 4$, the four possible input blocks '00', '01', '10', and '11' are mapped to the modulated signals:

$$s_1(t) = Ag(t) \cos(2\pi f_c t),$$
$$s_2(t) = -Ag(t) \sin(2\pi f_c t),$$
$$s_3(t) = -Ag(t) \cos(2\pi f_c t),$$
$$s_4(t) = Ag(t) \sin(2\pi f_c t).$$

- Quadrature amplitude modulation (QAM): in this modulation scheme the group of input bits is mapped into modulated signals changing both in phase and amplitude. This means that a QAM signal is of the form:

$$s_i(t) = A_i g(t) \cos(\theta_i) \cos(2\pi f_c t) - A_i g(t) \sin(\theta_i) \sin(2\pi f_c t).$$

One common case of QAM is 4QAM, where $b = 2$ and $M = 4$, for which the modulating signals are:

$$s_1(t) = Ag(t) \cos\left(\frac{\pi}{4}\right) \cos(2\pi f_c t) - Ag(t) \sin\left(\frac{\pi}{4}\right) \sin(2\pi f_c t),$$

$$s_2(t) = Ag(t) \cos\left(3\frac{\pi}{4}\right) \cos(2\pi f_c t) - Ag(t) \sin\left(3\frac{\pi}{4}\right) \sin(2\pi f_c t),$$

$$s_3(t) = Ag(t)\cos\left(5\frac{\pi}{4}\right)\cos\left(2\pi f_c t\right) - Ag(t)\sin\left(5\frac{\pi}{4}\right)\sin\left(2\pi f_c t\right),$$

$$s_4(t) = Ag(t)\cos\left(7\frac{\pi}{4}\right)\cos\left(2\pi f_c t\right) - Ag(t)\sin\left(7\frac{\pi}{4}\right)\sin\left(2\pi f_c t\right).$$

Other common cases of QAM are 16QAM, where $b = 4$ and $M = 16$, and 32QAM, where $b = 5$ and $M = 32$.

6.2.2 The Wireless Channel

The communication of information over wireless links presents specially challenging problems due to the nature of the wireless channel itself, which introduce severe impairments to the transmitted signal. Understanding these impairments is of fundamental importance in understanding any wireless communications system. As such, we present in the rest of this section a summary of the main wireless channel characteristics.

The simplest of all impairments are those that *add* a random noise to the transmitted signal. One source for this type of random noise is interference. Additive white Gaussian noise (AWGN) is another very good and important example of this type of additive impairment. Modeling the AWGN as a channel results in the additive white Gaussian noise, where the relation between the output $y(t)$ and the input signal $x(t)$ is given by Figure 6.2,

$$y(t) = \sqrt{\gamma}\, x(t) + n(t)$$

where γ is the loss in power of the transmitted signal, $x(t)$, and $n(t)$ is noise. The additive noise $n(t)$ is a random process where each sample, or realization, is modeled as a random variable with a Gaussian distribution. This noise term is generally used to model background noise in the channel as well as noise introduced at the receiver front end. Also, the AWGN is frequently assumed for simplicity to model some types of interference although, in general, these processes do not strictly follow a Gaussian distribution.

Other wireless channel impairments are classified as either "large-scale propagation effects" or "small-scale propagation effects", where the "scale" in the class names refers to the relative change of distance between transmitter and receiver that is necessary to experience changes in effect magnitude.

Among the large-scale propagation effects, the *path loss* is an important effect that contributes to signal impairment by reducing the propagating signal power as it propagates

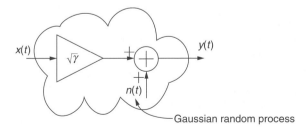

Figure 6.2   Additive white Gaussian noise (AWGN) channel model.

further away from the transmitter to the receiver. The path loss, γ_{dB}, is measured as the value in decibels of the ratio between the received P_R and transmitted signal power P_T:

$$\gamma_{dB} = 10 \log_{10} \frac{P_R}{P_T}$$

The value of the path loss is highly dependent on many factors related to the entire transmission setup. In general, the path loss is characterized by a function of the form:

$$\gamma_{dB} = 10\nu \, \log_{10} \frac{d}{d_0} + c, \qquad (6.1)$$

where d is the distance between transmitter and receiver, ν is the path loss exponent, c is a constant and d_0 is the distance to a power measurement reference point (sometimes embedded within the constant c). In many practical scenarios this expression is not an exact characterization of the path loss, but is still used as a sufficiently good and simple approximation. The constant c includes parameters related to the physical setup of the transmission such as signal wavelength, antenna heights, etc. The path loss exponent ν characterizes the rate of decay of the signal power with the distance. If the path loss, measured in dB, is plotted as a function of the distance on a logarithmic scale, the function in (6.1) is a line with a slope $-\nu$. The path loss exponent takes values in the range of 2 to 6, with 2 being the best case scenario, which corresponds to signal propagation in free space. Typical values for the path loss exponent are 4 for an urban macro cell environment and 3 for an urban micro cell.

Equation (6.1) shows the relation between the path loss and the distance between the transmit and receive antennas, but it does not characterize all the large-scale propagation effects. In practice, the path losses of two receive antennas situated at the same distance from the transmit antenna are not the same. This is, in part, because different objects may be obstructing the transmitted signal as it travels to the receive antenna. Consequently, this type of impairment has been named *shadow loss* or *shadow fading*. Since the nature and location of the obstructions causing shadow loss cannot be known in advance and is inherently random, the path loss introduced by this effect is itself a random variable. Denoting by S the value of the shadow loss, this effect can be incorporated into (6.1) by writing:

$$\gamma_{dB} = 10\nu \, \log_{10} \frac{d}{d_0} + S + c.$$

Through experimental measurements it has been found that S when measured in dB can be characterized as a zero-mean Gaussian distributed random variable. Consequently, the shadow loss magnitude is a random variable that follows a log-normal distribution and its effect is frequently referred as *log-normal fading*.

As discussed earlier, large-scale propagation effects owe the name to the fact that their effects are noticeable over relatively long signal propagation distances. In contrast, for small-scale propagation effects, the effects are noticeable at distances in the order of the signal wavelength. These effects appear as a consequence of multiple copies of the signal arriving at the receiver after each has traveled through different paths. This is because radio signals do not usually arrive at the receiver following a direct line-of-sight propagation path but, instead, arrive after encountering random reflectors, scatterers and attenuators during propagation. Such a channel where a transmitted signal arrives at the receiver with multiple copies is known as a *multipath channel*. Several factors influence the behavior of a multipath channel. In addition to the already mentioned random presence of reflectors, scatterers and attenuators, the speed of the mobile terminal, the speed of surrounding objects and the transmission bandwidth of the signal, are other factors determining the behavior of the channel. Furthermore, the multipath channel is likely to change over time because of the presence of motion at the transmitter, at the receiver, or at the surrounding objects. The multiple copies of the transmitted signal arriving through a different propagation path will each have a different amplitude, phase and delay. The multiple signal copies are added at the receiver creating either constructive or destructive interference with each other. This results in a time varying received signal. Therefore, if denoting the transmitted signal by $x(t)$ and the received signal by $y(t)$, their relation can be written as:

$$y(t) = \sum_{i=1}^{L} h_i(t) x\left(t - \tau_i(t)\right), \tag{6.2}$$

where $h_i(t)$ is the attenuation of the ith path at time t, $\tau_i(t)$ is the corresponding path delay and L is the number of resolvable paths at the receiver. This relation implicitly assumes that the channel is linear, for which $y(t)$ is equal to the convolution of $x(t)$ and the channel impulse response as seen at time t to an impulse sent at time τ, $h(t, \tau)$. From (6.2), this impulse response can be written as:

$$h(t, \tau) = \sum_{i=1}^{L} h_i(t) \delta\left(t - \tau_i(t)\right).$$

Furthermore, in cases when it is safe to assume that the channel does not change over time, there is no need to maintain the functional dependency on time, thus, the received signal can be simplified as:

$$y(t) = \sum_{i=1}^{L} h_i x\left(t - \tau_i\right),$$

and the channel impulse response as:

$$h(t, \tau) = \sum_{i=1}^{L} h_i \delta\left(t - \tau_i\right)$$

When studying the communication of digital information and sources it is convenient to abstract the whole communication system as a complete discrete-time system. The model obtained with this approach is called the discrete-time baseband-equivalent model of the channel, for which the input–output related with the mth discrete time instant can be written as:

$$y[m] = \sum_{k=1}^{L} h_k[m] x[m - k],$$

where $h_k[m]$ are the channel coefficients from the discrete-time channel impulse response. In this relation it is implicit that there is a sampling operation at the receiver and that all signals are considered as in the baseband equivalent model. The conversion to a discrete-time model combines all the paths with arrival time within one sampling period into a single channel response coefficient $h_k[m]$ Also, note that the discrete-time channel model is just a time-varying FIR digital filter. In fact, it is quite common to call the channel model based on the impulse response in the same way as FIR filters are called, as the tapped-delay model. Since the nature of each path, its length and the presence of reflectors, scatterers and attenuators are all random, the channel coefficients $h_k[m]$ of the discrete-time channel model are random processes. If, in addition, it can be assumed that the channel model is not changing over time, then the channel coefficients $h[m]$ of a time-invariant discrete-time channel model are random variables (and note that the redundant time index needs not be specified).

In the discrete-time impulse response model for a wireless channel, each coefficient indicates the attenuation and change of phase for the collection of signals arriving through multiple paths within the same sampling interval. The attenuation of each coefficient is directly related with the power attenuation for each path. The function determined by the average power associated with each path (with a path actually being a collection of paths arriving within the same sample interval) is called the *power delay profile* of the multipath channel. As an illustrative example, Figure 6.3 shows the power delay profile for a typical multipath wireless channel. The example reproduces the wireless channel models specified by the International Telecommunications Union in its standard ITU-R M.1225, [8].

In order to characterize the channel, several parameters are associated with the impulse response but calculated from the power delay profile or its spectral response (Fourier

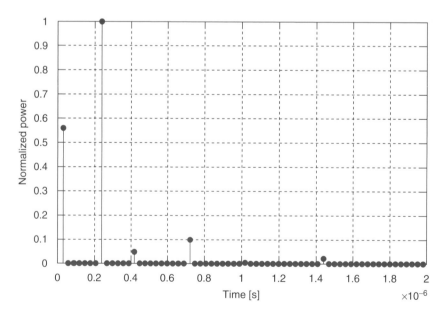

Figure 6.3   The power delay profile for a typical multipath channel. The figure shows the power from each path normalized to the maximum path power.

transform of the power delay profile). These parameters allow the classification of different multipath channels based on how they affect a transmitted signal. The first of these parameters is the *channel delay spread*. The channel delay spread is defined as the time difference between the arrival of the first measured path and the last (there are a few alternative, conceptually similar, definitions but their discussion is irrelevant to this book). Note that, in principle, there may be several signals arriving through very attenuated paths, which may not be measured due to the sensitivity of the receiver. This means that the concept of delay spread is tied to the sensitivity of the receiver.

A second parameter is the *coherence bandwidth*, which is the range of frequencies over which the amplitude of two spectral components of the channel response are correlated (similar to the power delay profile, there are other similar definitions, which will not be discussed here). The coherence bandwidth provides a measurement of the range of frequencies over which the channel shows a flat frequency response, in the sense that all the spectral components have approximately the same amplitude and a linear change of phase. This means that if the transmitted information-carrying signal has a bandwidth that is larger than the channel coherence bandwidth, then different spectral components of the signal will be affected by different attenuations, resulting in a distortion for the spectrum and the signal itself. In this case, the channel is said to be a *frequency-selective channel* or a *broadband channel*. In contrast, when the bandwidth of the information-carrying signal is less than the channel coherence bandwidth, then all the spectral components of the signal will be affected by the same attenuation and by a linear change of phase. In this case, the received signal (i.e., that at the output of the channel) will have practically the same spectrum as the transmitted signal and thus will suffer from little distortion. This type of channel is said to be a *flat-fading channel* or a *narrowband channel*.

Note that while we just described different types of channels, whether a particular channel will appear as being of one type or another (i.e., flat-fading or frequency-selective) does not only depend on the channel, but it also depends on the characteristics of the signal at the input of the channel and how they relate with the characteristics of the channel. To better understand this, Figure 6.4 shows a section of the spectral response of the channel with the power delay profile shown in Figure 6.3. In principle, by looking at Figure 6.4 only, it is not possible to tell whether the channel is a flat fading or a frequency-selective channel. Indeed, the channel frequency response may be seen as roughly flat by a signal with bandwidth equal to a few tens of kHz, but it would be seen as frequency-selective by a signal with a larger bandwidth. To see this, consider that the transmitted signal is a single raised cosine pulse with roll-off factor 0.25 and symbol period 0.05 µs. The pulse is shown on the left of Figure 6.5. The corresponding spectrum can be seen on the right of Figure 6.4. The bandwidth for the transmitted pulse is approximately 2 MHz. As shown in Figure 6.6, the large bandwidth of the transmitted pulse makes the channel behave as a frequency-selective channel, resulting in a distorted transmitted pulse spectrum at the output of the channel.

It is important to understand the distorting effects of a frequency-selective channel in the time domain. Here, the transmitted pulse with a bandwidth that is larger than the channel coherence bandwidth translates into a channel delay spread that is much larger than the duration of the pulse. In this case, and since the channel affects a transmitted pulse by performing a convolution, at the output of the channel there is going to be one delayed and attenuated replica of the transmitted pulse for each of the discernible channel

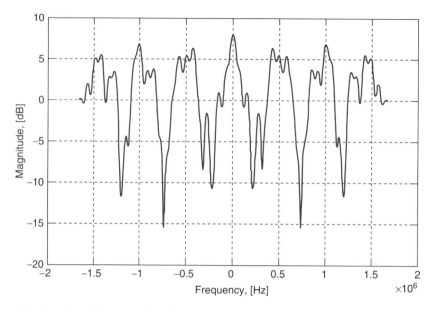

Figure 6.4 Section of the magnitude frequency response for the channel with the power delay profile in Figure 6.3.

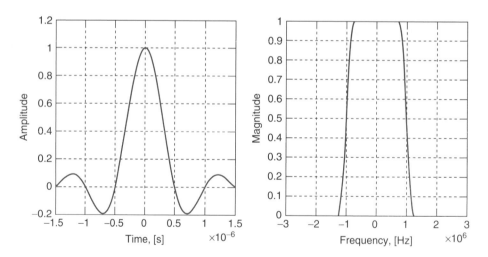

Figure 6.5 The short duration raised cosine pulse sent over the channel in Figure 6.3 – on the left, the time domain signal, on the right, its corresponding magnitude spectrum.

paths. Because of this, the pulse at the output of the channel will see its duration extended to that of the delay spread and its shape severely distorted. This is illustrated in Figure 6.7 where, at the top, it shows the pulse from Figure 6.5 after being transmitted through the channel in Figure 6.3. The figure shows all the pulses arriving through each of the channel paths. The resulting pulse is equal to the addition of the pulses from each of the paths.

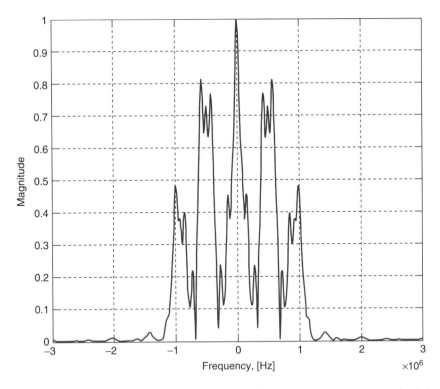

Figure 6.6 The spectrum of the raised cosine pulse in Figure 6.5 after being transmitted through the channel in Figure 6.3.

Figure 6.8 concludes the illustration of a frequency-selective channel by showing the input and output pulses in both the time and frequency domains. It is important to note here how the frequency-selective channel is associated with a large delay spread. The fact that a time domain phenomenon such as instances of a signal arriving with different delays, translates into a frequency domain effect, such as frequency selectivity, can be understood in the following way. When the signals with different delays from the multipath get superimposed at the receive antenna, the different delay translates into different phases. Depending on the phase difference between the spectral components, their superposition may result into destructive or constructive interference. Even more, because the relation between phase and path delay for each spectral component of the arriving signal varies with the frequency of the spectral component, the signal will undergo destructive or constructive interference of different magnitude for each spectral component, resulting in the frequency response of the channel not appearing as a constant amplitude. The extension of the pulse duration has important effects when sending several pulses in succession (as would usually happen when transmitting a bit stream) because the pulses at the output of the channel will overlap with other pulses sent earlier or later. This overlap of transmitted symbols is called *inter-symbol interference* (ISI).

Comparing the effects of frequency-selective channel versus a non-frequency-selective channel, Figures 6.9 through 6.11 shows the time and frequency domains input and output

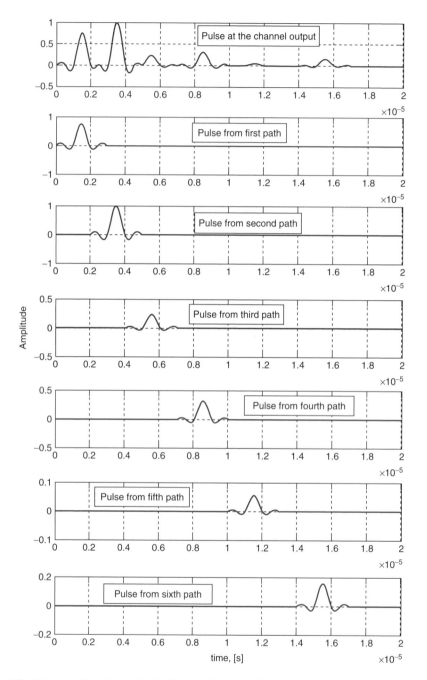

Figure 6.7 The raised cosine pulse in Figure 6.5 after being transmitted through the channel in Figure 6.3 (top). The pulse is the result of adding all the pulses received from each of the channel's paths (in plots below the top one).

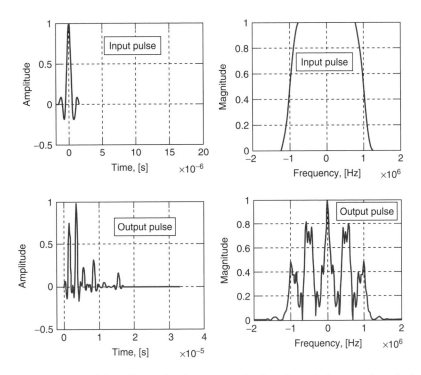

Figure 6.8 Summary of the effects of a frequency-selective channel showing the raised cosine pulse in Figure 6.5 at the input and at the output of the channel, both in time and frequency domain.

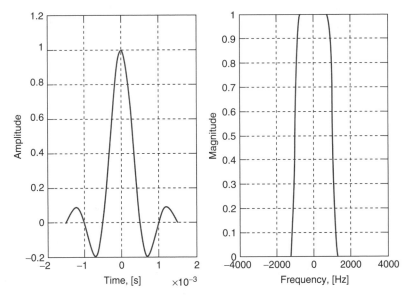

Figure 6.9 The long duration raised cosine pulse sent over the channel in Figure 6.3 – on the left, the time domain signal, on the right, its corresponding magnitude spectrum.

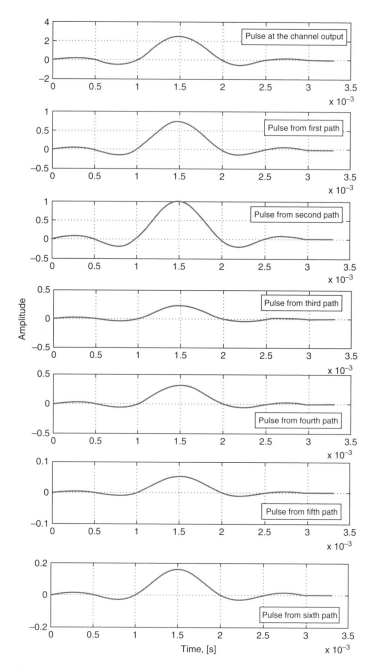

Figure 6.10   The raised cosine pulse in Figure 6.9 after being transmitted through the channel in Figure 6.3 (top). The pulse is the result of adding all the pulses received from each of the channel's paths (in plots below the top one).

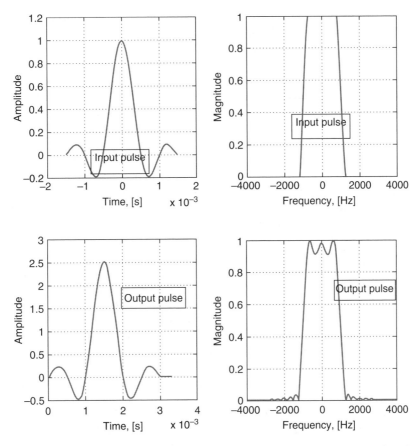

Figure 6.11 Summary of the effects of a non-frequency-selective channel showing the raised cosine pulse in Figure 6.9 at the input and at the output of the channel, both in time and frequency domain.

signals to the channel in Figures 6.3 and 6.4 when the input pulse have a transmission period long enough for the channel to behave as non-frequency-selective. In this case, the input pulse has a bandwidth of approximately 2 kHz, for which the frequency response of the channel appears roughly flat. At the same time, the duration of the input pulse is several times longer than the channel delay spread, which results in little difference relative to the pulse duration in the time each pulse takes to arrive through a different path. In other words, with the longer duration of the pulse, the delays associated with different channel paths can be practically neglected and there is no ISI. Consequently, the transmitted pulse suffers little alterations in both time and frequency domains. While a longer duration pulse avoids the challenges associated with a frequency-selective channel, it also limits the data rate at which information can be sent over the channel.

As mentioned earlier in this section, the motions of the transmitter, the receiver or the signal reflectors along the signal propagation path creates a change in the channel impulse response over time. As such, there are parameters that describe the time-varying characteristics of the wireless channel. The most notable effect introduced by mobility is a shift in frequency due to Doppler shift. To characterize the channel in terms of Doppler shift, the parameters usually considered are the channel *coherence time* and the *Doppler spread*.

As a channel changes over time, the coefficients of the impulse response, and thus the impulse response itself, become a random process, with each realization at different time instants being a random variable. These random variables may or may not be correlated. The channel coherence time is the time difference that makes the correlation between two realizations of the channel impulse response be approximately zero. The Fourier transform of the correlation function between the realizations of a channel coefficient is known as the channel *Doppler power spectrum*, or simply the Doppler spectrum. The Doppler spectrum characterizes in a statistical sense how the channel affects an input signal and widens its spectrum due to Doppler shift. This means that if the transmitter injects into the channel a single-tone sinusoidal signal with frequency, f_c, the Doppler spectrum will show frequency components in the range $f_c - f_d$ to $f_c + f_d$, where f_d is the channel's Doppler shift.

The second parameter usually used to characterize the effects of the channel time variations is the Doppler spread. This is defined as the range of frequencies over which the Doppler power spectrum is nonzero. It can be shown that the Doppler spread is the inverse of the channel coherence time and as such, provides information on how fast the channel changes over time. Similarly to the discussion on frequency selectivity of a channel – a characteristic that depended both on the channel and the input signal – the notion on how fast the channel is changing over time depends also on the input signal. If the channel coherence time is larger than the transmitted signal symbol period, or equivalently, if the Doppler spread is smaller than the signal bandwidth, the channel will be changing over a period of time longer than the input symbol duration. In this case, the channel is said to have *slow fading*. If the reverse is true, the channel is said to have *fast fading*.

We now turn our attention towards the random nature of the channel coefficients and the important related question of what are their statistical properties and what kind of mathematical model can characterize this behavior. There are several models to statistically characterize the channel coefficients; some are analytical, obtained from proposing a simplified representative model, and other models are empirical, having been derived by matching functions to the results of field measurements. One of the most common analytical models for the random channel coefficients is based on an environment known as the "Uniform Scattering Environment". Since this model was introduced by R. H. Clarke and later developed by W. C. Jakes, the model is also known as Clarke's model or Jakes' model. The key assumption in this model is that there is no dominant line-of-sight (LOS) propagation and that a waveform arrives at a receiver through a multipath channel resulting from a very large number of scatterers along the signal path. Furthermore, the scatterers are assumed to be randomly located on a circle centered on the receiver (see Figure 6.12) and that they create a very large number of paths arriving from the scatterers at an angle that is uniformly distributed between 0 and 2π. Furthermore, it is assumed that all the received signals arrive with the same amplitude. This is a reasonable assumption because, given the geometry of the uniform scattering environment, in the absence of a direct LOS path, each signal arriving at the receiver would experience similar attenuations.

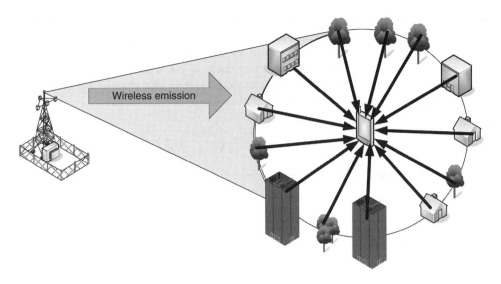

Figure 6.12   The uniform scattering environment.

The theoretical study of the uniform scattering model results in the conclusion that each channel coefficient can be modeled as a circularly symmetric complex Gaussian random variable with zero mean; that is, as a random variable made of two quadrature components, with each component being a zero mean Gaussian random variable with the same variance as the other component σ^2. From this conclusion, it is further possible to derive the probability density function for the magnitude and phase of the complex-valued channel coefficients (i.e., by writing the coefficients in the form $h = re^{j\theta}$). By following straightforward random variables transformation theory, it follows that the magnitude of the channel coefficients is a random variable with a Rayleigh distribution with probability density function (pdf):

$$f_r(x) = \frac{x}{\sigma^2} e^{-x^2/(2\sigma^2)}, x \geq 0,$$

and the phase is a random variable with a uniform distribution in the range $[0, 2\pi]$ and with pdf: $f_\theta(x) = 1/(2\pi)$. Because of the probability distribution for the channel coefficient magnitude, this model is also called the Rayleigh fading model. It is also of interest to calculate the probability density function of the random variable $|h|^2$, the channel coefficient power gain. By applying again random variables transformation theory, it follows that $|h|^2$ is an exponential random variable with probability density function:

$$f_{|h|^2}(x) = \frac{1}{\sigma^2} e^{-x/(2\sigma^2)}, x \geq 0,$$

The Rayleigh fading model is not the only model for the channel coefficients. In fact, in deriving the Rayleigh fading for the uniform scattering environment it was assumed that all the received signals arrive with the same amplitude due to the absence of a direct LOS path and the symmetric geometry of the environment. When there is one LOS path that is received with a dominant power, the assumptions corresponding to the Rayleigh fading model do not hold any more. With the LOS path, the two Cartesian components of the complex-valued channel coefficient are still a Gaussian random variables but now one has a nonzero mean A, which is the peak amplitude of the signal from the line-of-sight path. In this case, it can be shown that the magnitude of the channel coefficient is a Rician-distributed random variable with a probability density function:

$$f_r(z) = \frac{z}{\sigma^2} e^{-\left(\frac{z^2}{2\sigma^2} + K\right)} I_0\left(\frac{2Kx}{A}\right), z \geq 0,$$

where K is a parameter of the Ricean distribution defined as:

$$K = \frac{A^2}{2\sigma^2},$$

and $I_0(x)$ is the modified Bessel function of the first kind and zero order, defined as:

$$I_0(x) = \frac{1}{2\pi} \int_0^{2\pi} e^{x \cos(\theta)} d\theta.$$

Note that in the Rician distribution when $K = 0$, the Rician probability density function becomes equal to the Rayleigh probability density function. This is consistent with the fact that $K = 0$ implies that $A = 0$, that is, there is no LOS path.

As mentioned earlier in this section, another approach to modeling the wireless channel follows an empirical procedure where samples of a practical channel are measured on the field and then the statistics of these samples are matched to a mathematical model. For this it is useful to have a probability density function that can be easily matched to the different possible data sample sets. This function is provided by the Nakagami fading distribution, which has a probability density function given by:

$$f_X(x) = \frac{2m^m x^{2m-1}}{\Gamma(m)\sigma^{2m}} e^{-mx^2/\sigma^2}, m \geq 1/2,$$

where $\Gamma(z)$ is the Gamma function:

$$\Gamma(z) = \int_0^\infty e^{-t} t^{z-1} dt,$$

and m is a parameter used to adjust the pdf of the Nakagami distribution to the data samples. For example, if $m = 1$, then the Nakagami distribution becomes equal to the Rayleigh distribution. One advantage of the Nakagami distribution is that it matches empirical data better than other distributions. In fact, the Nakagami distribution was originally proposed for this very reason.

To summarize the discussion on different random variable distributions for modeling channel fading, Figure 6.13 shows the pdfs presented in this section.

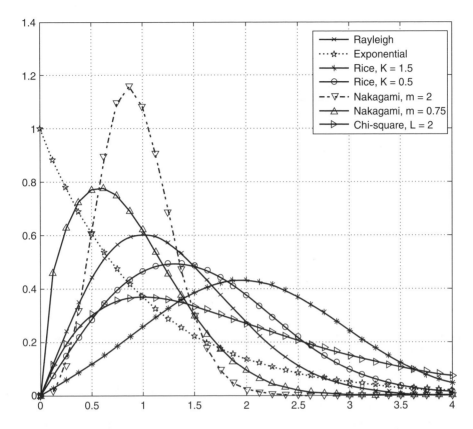

Figure 6.13   Different probability density functions used to model random fading.

6.2.3   Adaptive Modulation and Coding

As should be clear from the discussion so far, the principal characteristic for wireless communications is the need to cope with severe impairments of the channel. For a modulated signal, these impairments will distort the signal to an extent that may result in the receiver misinterpreting the signal for another of the possible modulated signals. When this happens, the demodulator at the receiver will output an erred decision on the transmitted information. The likelihood of this error happening will, of course, depend on the quality of the channel, with worse channels leading to errors with a higher probability. At the same time, and while there are many possible receiver technologies, as a general rule, modulation techniques that achieve a higher bit rate by packing more bits per symbol are also more susceptible to errors. Figure 6.14 illustrates this point by showing the bit error rate as a function of AWGN channel SNR for three MPSK schemes. In the figure it can be seen that if, for example, the channel SNR is 8 dB, then transmission using 16-PSK will have a bit error rate in the order of 10^{-2}, transmission using 8-PSK will have a bit

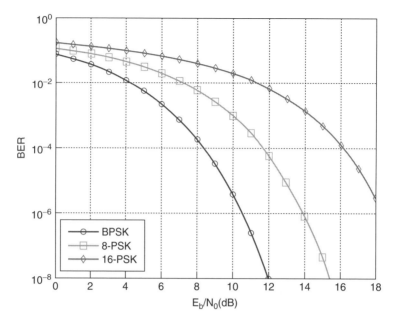

Figure 6.14 Bit error rate as a function of channel signal-to-noise ratio for three cases of MPSK modulation ($M = 2$, $M = 8$ and $M = 16$).

error rate approximately ten times less, and transmission using BPSK will have a bit error rate approximately equal to 10^{-4}.

Figure 6.14 can also be interpreted with a different approach. Assume, as is usually the case, that the traffic being transmitted requires a minimum bit error rate performance during communication. For the sake of this presentation, let us suppose that the requirement is that bit error rate cannot exceed 10^{-4}. In this case, then, Figure 6.14 shows that if the channel SNR is below 8 dB, it will not be possible to meet the service requirement for maximum BER, regardless of the modulation scheme being used. If the channel SNR is between 8 and 12 dB, the transmission will have to use BPSK because it is the only modulation scheme with BER less than 10^{-4}. If the channel SNR is between 12 and 16 dB, there is a choice between BPSK and 8-PSK for transmission because both modulation schemes have BER less than 10^{-4}. Finally, for channel SNRs above 16 dB it would be possible to choose any of the three modulation schemes in Figure 6.14.

When it is possible to choose between different modulation schemes, it is better to choose the one that results in higher transmit bit rate. For the case of Figure 6.14, BPSK sends one bit per modulation symbol, 8-PSK sends three and 16-PSK sends four. Therefore, 16-PSK shows four times the bit rate of BPSK and 8-PSK three times the bit rate of BPSK. Consequently, from the performance shown in Figure 6.14, if the channel SNR is more than 16 dB, the modulation used during transmission would be 16-PSK; if the channel SNR is 12 and 16 dB, the transmission would use 8-PSK; and if channel SNR is between 8 and 12 dB, the transmission would use BPSK. If the channel SNR is less than 8 dB, it would not be possible to meet the maximum BER requirement for modulation choice. Of course, it is usually the case that some type of forward error control (FEC) technique is used during transmission. With FEC, adding extra redundant bits results in a stronger protection against channel errors, allowing meeting the maximum BER requirement at lower channel SNR. At the same time, when using FEC, the extra redundant bits reduce the number of information bits that can be transmitted per unit time when the transmit bit rate is fixed. In other words, the more error protection (equivalently, the more redundant bits) that is added to the transmitted bit stream, the lower the channel SNR that can be used for transmission satisfying BER constraints but, also, the less information bits are transmitted per unit time.

The above discussion highlights that there are two interlinked tradeoffs determining the choice of transmission parameters. One tradeoff is the transmit bit rate versus the channel SNR. The second tradeoff is the amount of FEC redundancy for error protection in a given channel SNR versus the effective transmitted information bit rate. The modulation scheme and the level of FEC redundancy can be chosen at design time after carefully considering these tradeoffs. Nevertheless, modern communication systems allow for a dynamic adaptation of these transmit parameters based on the channel conditions (e.g., channel SNR). This technique is called *adaptive modulation and coding* (AMC). In AMC, the transmitter uses estimates of the channel state to choose a modulation scheme and a level of FEC redundancy that maximizes the transmitted information bit rate for a given channel SNR.

6.3 Wireless Networking

Based on how the nodes are organized there are two types of wireless network architectures. In the first such type, called "infrastructure", all the nodes communicate wirelessly to a central base station, or access point. The network may have several base stations, each covering a different geographical area, and they are typically interconnected through a wired network. In infrastructure-type networks the radio link where the transmitter is a node and the receiver is the access point is called the "uplink". Conversely, the radio link where the transmitter is the access point and the receiver is a node is called the "downlink". With infrastructure networks, the access point is usually connected to the Internet through a high capacity link, that may use fiber optics, and that does not necessarily involves a wireless connection. As such, in infrastructure networks, the wireless link may be only one hop on the transmitter side and a second single link wireless hop to access the destination end of the connection if it is also a wireless device.

The second type of wireless network architectures is the *ad-hoc* network. Here, there is no central base station and all nodes are hierarchically equal. In an ad-hoc network the nodes self-organize to establish the different routes and connections in the network with paths that typically involve multiple wireless hops. Nevertheless, while research into ad-hoc networks has been ongoing for several years, their deployment has been limited, resulting in most of the existing commercial networks being of the infrastructure type.

6.4 4G Standards and Systems

The first mobile telephony systems, based on a cellular network architecture, were deployed during the 1980s. These first systems, called 1G systems as an abbreviation to "first generation", were based on analog FDMA technology, which could only support

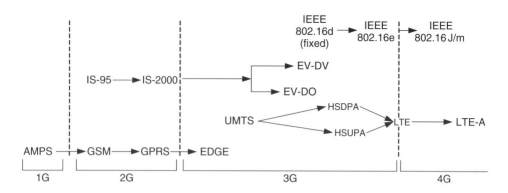

Figure 6.15   The evolution of cellular systems over different generations.

voice services. From there, and roughly every ten years, a new generation has been deployed to provide new and improved services. As such, the 1990s saw the deployment of 2G (second generation) systems, and 3G were deployed during the first decade of the 21st century. At the time of writing, 4G systems are starting to be deployed. Each generation of mobile telephony introduces new technological innovators aimed at improving the spectrum use efficiency, access latency, communication bit rate, reliability, etc. The 2G systems introduced the use of digital wireless technology in the form of time-division multiple access (TDMA) in the GSM standard or code-division multiple access (CDMA) in the IS-95 standard. Third generation systems are best exemplified by the UMTS standard, based on wideband-CDMA technology – see Figure 6.15.

Regardless of the considered technology generation, a recurring and growing source of dissent is to what generation a standard belongs to. This has resulted in increasing lack of clarity, one that may be pointless to achieve from the technological standpoint, with some standards being labeled as "2.5G", "3.5G", or even "3.9G" systems. One important reason for this phenomenon is an eagerness to highlight the advances of a particular standard by classifying it into an advanced generation that the standard may not belong to from a strict technological perspective. In this book, our interest is on how recent technological advances will help communication of 3D video. Therefore, we will not delve into whether a particular standard is strictly 4G or not and we will focus on the technology in standards beyond 3G systems, which we will generically call 4G systems for simplicity. Luckily, we will be aided in this task by the fact that the 4G standards all share many similarities. Because of this, and given that, at the time of writing, LTE/LTE-A is the prevailing 4G standard we will be focusing on these standards for the rest of this chapter. As such, the goal of this section is to provide an overview of the main characteristics of LTE and LTE-A systems. Further details and a quite comprehensive treatment of this topic can be found in [9].

One important characteristic of all 4G systems is that the physical layer design is flexible enough to easily adapt the system to the different bandwidths that may be available with different spectrum allocations in different countries. Because of this, it is more appropriate to talk about the performance of the system in terms of spectral efficiency (measuring the number of bits that can be transmitted per second and per bandwidth measured in MHz), as opposed to simply considering throughput. In this sense, LTE, which is also known by its denomination within the 3rd Generation Partnership Project (3GPP) family of standards as "Release 8", presents an improvement in cell spectral efficiency on the downlink of three to four times compared to the 3GPP Release 6 standard HSDPA, and two to three times improvement in the uplink compared to the 3GPP Release 6 standard HSUPA. This implies peak data rates of up to 100 Mbps on the downlink and up to 50 Mbps on the uplink when the system bandwidth is 20 MHz. Also, LTE is required to support a cell radius of up to 100 km and node mobility for speeds of up to 350 kph (applicable, for example, in the case of travelling in a high speed train).

The LTE standard differentiates between the services and interfaces provided to a user and the services and interfaces used for control messaging within the LTE system. For this, the "U-plane" refers to the interface (implemented through protocols) with users and the "C-plane" refers to the set of protocols implementing the interface for control messages. For access to the wireless channel through the U-plane, the LTE system aims at a latency of no more than 5 ms.

The LTE system architecture was designed with the goal of providing an infrastructure where all the information, be it delay-tolerant data or delay-sensitive interactive multimedia, is communicated as packets, using the Internet protocol (IP). The system infrastructure itself determines what are the main components of the LTE system and their interrelation. As such, the LTE system is divided into two main components:

- The evolved universal terrestrial radio access network (E-UTRAN), which is composed of the eNodeBs (or eNBs, the name given to base stations in the LTE system) and is responsible for the management of radio access and the provision of the U-plane and C-plane services.
- The evolved packet core (EPC) which is the collection of network infrastructure (hardware, protocols, services, etc.) to perform store-and-forward packet networking for mobile nodes.

6.4.1   Evolved Universal Terrestrial Radio Access Network (E-UTRAN)

The E-UTRAN implements the lowest layers of the LTE wireless networking protocol stack. At the base of the stack, it implements a physical layer that is seen from upper layers as providing physical (radio) channels. The physical layer interfaces with the MAC sublayer through "transport channels" (not to be confused with the transport layer in the protocol stack). In LTE, the MAC sublayer manages access to the wireless medium by scheduling data transmission, handling priorities and performing hybrid automatic repeat request (HARQ) functions. The MAC sublayer also manages the access to the wireless medium by mapping the transport channels, interfacing with the physical layer, with the "logical channels". The logical channels interface the MAC sublayer with the radio link control (RLC) sublayer. On the E-UTRAN protocol stack, a packet data convergence protocol (PDCP) sublayer is found immediately above the RLC sublayer. The PDCP sublayer interfaces with the evolved packet core (EPC) component through "radio bearers".

The design goal for the E-UTRAN physical layer was to provide a high performance wireless transmission scheme that could effectively address the many challenges faced with digital communication of information at high bit rate in a mobility scenario. In previous sections we discussed the nature of these challenges. Indeed, transmission at high data bit rate usually requires a signal with a bandwidth that is much larger than the channel coherence bandwidth. In this case, the channel is frequency-selective. Frequency-selective channels, or the dual time-domain effect of multipath channel delay spread, extends the duration of each transmitted pulse. When transmitting several pulses (symbols, bits) in succession, a frequency-selective channel presents the impairments of intersymbol inter- ference, risking the introduction of detection errors at the receiver. This impairment can be addressed with different techniques. One of the most effective techniques, and the one adopted in LTE is *multicarrier modulation*. In multicarrier modulation, instead of trans- mitting a high bandwidth modulated signal, the data bits are transmitted in parallel using multiple mutually orthogonal signals of a bandwidth small enough such that the channel appears as non-frequency-selective. To see this operation, consider that multicarrier mod- ulation is used as an alternative to the transmission of a block of N bits $\{d_k\}_{k=0}^{N-1}$ that are mapped to a high bandwidth modulated signal. The multicarrier modulated symbol is implemented by doing:

$$s(t) = \sum_{k=0}^{N-1} d_k \phi_k(t), \tag{6.3}$$

where $\phi_k(t)$ is the kth subcarrier signal used to transmit the kth data bit (a data symbol, in general). Importantly, the N subcarrier modulating signals have to be orthogonal to each other, which means that for a multicarrier modulated symbol of duration T_s the following has to be true:

$$\langle \phi_k(t), \phi_n(t) \rangle = \frac{1}{T_s} \int_0^{T_s} \phi_k(t) \phi_n^*(t) dt = \begin{cases} 0, & if \ k \neq n, \\ 1, & if \ k = n. \end{cases}$$

This expression assumes a complex baseband interpretation for the transmitted signal that allows for the subcarrier modulating signals to be complex valued, and thus, $\phi_n^*(t)$ denotes the complex conjugate of the function $\phi_n(t)$. Note that different data bits transmit- ted in the multicarrier modulated symbol in (6.3) can be separated at the receiver through a matched filter type of processing, which will lead into the above implementation of integration operations testing whether the subcarrier's modulating signals are orthogonal or not.

There are multiple multicarrier modulation techniques, each using a different choice of orthogonal signals. For the downlink (the transmission from the eNB to the UE) of E-UTRAN, the chosen multicarrier modulation technique was orthogonal frequency division multiplexing (OFDM). This technique is of particular importance beyond LTE because, except for different variations tailored to specific systems, it is the technique that has gained more acceptance as the modulation technique for high data rate wireless networks and 4G mobile broadband standards. In OFDM, the orthogonal signals used for multicarrier modulation are truncated complex exponentials:

$$\phi_k(t) = \begin{cases} e^{j2\pi f_k t}, & for \ 0 \leq t < T_s, \\ 0, & else, \end{cases}$$

where $f_k = f_0 + k\Delta f$, and $\Delta f = T_s$. Because these signals are truncated complex expo- nential, each has a spectrum of the form $\sin(x)/x$, where the argument x includes the shift

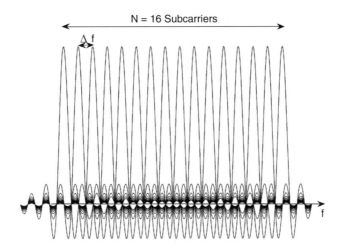

Figure 6.16   The spectrum for 16 OFDM subcarriers.

in frequency $k\Delta f$ with respect to the base frequency f_0. Therefore, the OFDM symbol is:

$$s(t) = \sum_{k=0}^{N-1} d_k e^{j2\pi f_k t}, \quad \text{for } 0 \le t < T_s \tag{6.4}$$

The spectrum of this symbol when $d_k = 1$ for all input bits is shown in Figure 6.16. By setting $d_k = 1$ for all input bits, the figure shows the contribution of each subcarrier to the overall spectrum. This contribution is a frequency-shifted function of the form $\sin(x)/x$. The figure also illustrates how OFDM splits a carrier with large bandwidth into multiple orthogonal subcarriers of much smaller bandwidth. It is also important to note how the orthogonality property between the truncated complex exponentials forming the modulating signals can be seen in the figure, as at the central frequency of any chosen subcarrier (the frequency at which the spectrum for the subcarrier is maximum), the spectrum for all the other subcarriers is zero.

Assume, next, that the OFDM symbol in (6.4) is sampled with a period such that N samples are taken in one symbol, $T_{sa} = T_s/N$. Then, we can write the resulting sampled signal $s[n]$, for the OFDM case, as:

$$s[n] = s(nT_{sa}) = \sum_{k=0}^{N-1} d_k e^{j2\pi f_k nT_s/N}, \tag{6.5}$$

Assuming, without loss of generality, that $f_0 = 0$ we get $f_k = k\Delta f = k/T_s$, leading to (6.5) becoming:

$$s[n] = \sum_{k=0}^{N-1} d_k e^{j2\pi nk/N}. \tag{6.6}$$

This result shows that the OFDM symbol is, in fact, a discrete-time signal $s[n]$ formed from the inverse discrete Fourier transform (IDFT) of the sequence of input data d_k.

This observation will soon be seen to be the basis for one of the main advantages for OFDM because it provides a simple way of generating an OFDM symbol.

In practice, the OFDM symbol as defined in (6.5) is extended with the addition of a *cyclic prefix*. To understand the construction of the prefix, assume a multipath channel with L taps defined through the coefficients $h[0], h[1], \ldots, h[L-1]$. With this in mind, the original discrete-time channel input sequence (6.5) $s[0], s[1], \ldots, s[N-L]$, $s[N-L+1], \ldots, s[N-1]$ will become $s[N-L+1], \ldots, s[N-1], s[0], s[1], \ldots,$ $s[N-L], s[N-L+1], \ldots, s[N-1]$ after adding the cyclic prefix. Note that the prefix is built by just copying the last $L-1$ elements of the original channel input sequence $s[n]$ at the beginning of it. This operation does not affect the OFDM signal or its properties, such as the orthogonality between the multicarrier modulated signals, because it is simply a reaffirmation of the periodicity of the OFDM symbol. This follows from (6.6), because all sequences resulting from the discrete Fourier transform or the inverse discrete Fourier transform of another sequence are periodic with period equal to N. Also note that, following the assumption of a multipath channel with delay spread L, the samples corresponding to the cyclic prefix will be affected by intersymbol interference from the previous OFDM symbol (transmitted over the time lapse $T_s \leq t < 0$). OFDM signals are particularly suitable for communication over multipath, frequency-selective wireless channels because intersymbol interference can be easily combatted by removing the prefix at the receiver without any loss of information in the original sequence and without intersymbol interference affecting the original sequence. Next, we illustrate how adding the cyclic prefix transforms a frequency-selective fading channel into a set of parallel flat fading channels.

Let us call the discrete-time channel input sequence, after adding the cyclic prefix, as s where:

$$s = [s[N-L+1], \ldots, s[N-1], s[0], s[1], \ldots, s[N-L],$$
$$s[N-L+1], \ldots, s[N-1]]$$

The discrete-time output of the channel can be written as the convolution with channel impulse response:

$$y[n] = \sum_{l=0}^{L-1} h[l] x[n-l] + v[n],$$

for $n = 0, 1, 2, \ldots, N+L-1$ and where $v[n]$ is additive white Gaussian noise.

The multipath channel affects through intersymbol interference the first $L-1$ symbols and therefore the receiver ignores these symbols. The received sequence is then given by:

$$y = [y[L], y[L+1], \ldots, y[N+L-1]].$$

Equivalently, the repetition of the last L samples of $s[n]$ as a prefix to this sequence introduces a symmetry into the computation of the convolution that allows us to write the received signal in terms of the original channel input as:

$$y[n] = \sum_{l=0}^{L-1} (h[l] s[n-l-L]) \bmod(N) + v[n],$$

where $(.)\mathrm{mod}(N)$ denotes a modulo-N arithmetic operation. This can be also written in terms of cyclic convolution as:

$$y = h \otimes s + v,$$

where $\otimes$ denotes cyclic convolution. At the receiver, the transmitted data is extracted from the OFDM symbol by, among other operations, removing the cyclic prefix and performing a discrete Fourier transform (DFT), to counter the inverse discrete Fourier transform. The result of these operations is:

$$Y_n = H_n S_n + V_n,$$

where Y_n, H_n, S_n and V_n are the nth point of the N-point DFT of the received signal, channel response, channel input, and noise vector, respectively. The importance of this result is that it implies that at the receiver side, the frequency-selective fading channel has been transformed to a set of parallel flat fading channels.

Figure 6.17 shows a summary of the main operations involved in a communication link using OFDM as a block diagram of a transmitter and a receiver. Highlighting the main operations discussed above, an OFDM symbol is made of a block of N input symbols. At the OFDM transmitter, the N input symbols are converted into an OFDM symbol with N subcarriers through an inverse discrete Fourier transform computation. Before transmission, the OFDM symbol is completed by adding a cyclic prefix to help combat the effects of intersymbol interference introduced by the frequency-selective wireless channel. At the receiver, the originally transmitted data is recovered by performing the reverse operations to those done during transmission. This highlights the benefit when using OFDM as it implements a relatively reduced complexity technique that is effective in combating the effects of a frequency-selective channel.

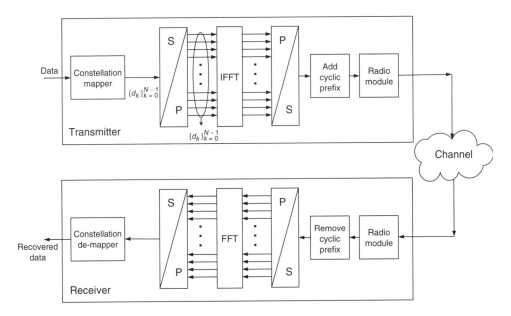

Figure 6.17   OFDM transmitter and receiver block diagram.

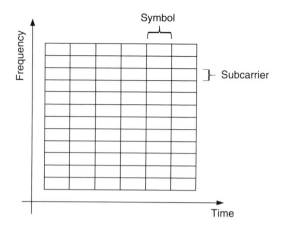

Figure 6.18   Time-frequency structure of an OFDMA frame.

Figure 6.19   LTE downlink processing.

When considering the successive transmission of several OFDM symbols, the data is organized on the channel during transmission following what can be pictured as a grid in a *frequency × time* plane, with a width of N subcarriers (in the frequency dimension) and a depth equal to the number of transmitted OFDM symbols (in the time dimension). This is illustrated in Figure 6.18. Also, Figure 6.19 illustrates the main processing blocks in the downlink of an LTE system.

The processing in the uplink of the LTE physical layer is very similar to the downlink, as shown in Figure 6.19. Perhaps the main difference to note is that the modulation scheme in the uplink is not OFDMA but a related modulated scheme called SC-FDMA (single carrier-frequency division multiple access). Figure 6.20 shows the processing blocks involved in SC-FDMA. By comparing the figure with Figure 6.18, it can be seen that the only difference, on the transmitter side, is the presence of a DFT block before IFFT. The operation in the DFT, essentially a linear precoding step, makes a number of continuous OFDM subcarriers (those chosen by the subcarrier mapper) appear as a single contiguous carrier. When compared to OFDM, this precoding operation results in SC-FDMA operating more on the linear performance region for the power amplifier.

6.4.2   Evolved Packet Core (EPC)

While previous generations of wireless systems necessitated an infrastructure for voice telephony services and another for packet data services, LTE is the first standard to be based on a single infrastructure carrying IP packet data. The component of the LTE infrastructure implementing most of the required functionalities for an all-IP network is

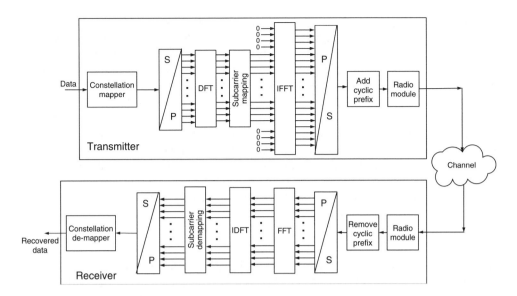

Figure 6.20   SC-FDMA transmitter and receiver block diagram.

the evolved packet core. Doing away with the need for a voice telephony infrastructure results in a simplified architecture for the EPC that allows reduced access latency. In the EPC it is possible to find the main elements necessary to manage IP packets, such as gateways and mobility management modules.

At the EPC there are also the mechanisms necessary to manage nine different quality-of-service (QoS) class identifiers (QCI). As the name indicates, the QCIs identify each data bearer with an identifier that establishes a scheduling priority order, a packet delay budget (with possible values of 50–300 ms) and a target packet error rate loss rate (with possible values of 10^{-2} to 10^{-6}). This function is intended to provide support for the wide variety of traffic types that are with LTE carried using IP packets.

6.4.3   Long Term Evolution-Advance (LTE-A)

The next step of improvements on the LTE system is being incorporated into the long term evolution-advance (LTE-A) standard. Within the family of 3GPP standards, LTE-A corresponds to "Release 10" and "Release 11". Compared with LTE, LTE-A is designed to provide significant improvements in the data communication speed and in the wireless links quality in general. For example, LTE-A aims at providing peak data rates of 1 Gbps on the downlink and 500 Mbps on the uplink and a reduced latency on the U-plane when compared to LTE.

In order to achieve the target performance improvements, LTE-A uses a number of techniques. One of these is the use of advanced network topologies that rely on high-speed, short-range base stations in the form of femtocells and also the introduction of new relay nodes. Also, LTE-A provides for carrier aggregation, where it is now possible to combine several carriers together so as to obtain a larger system bandwidth. Combined with an improved spectral efficiency, carrier aggregation allows for higher data rates. The possible schemes for carrier aggregation are very flexible, even allowing for asymmetric carrier aggregation, with higher capacity allocated to the downlink. For example, it is possible with LTE-A to aggregate, using frequency division duplexing, two 20 MHz bands for the uplink and four 20 MHz bands for the downlink, or aggregate, using time division duplexing, five 20 MHz bands that can subsequently be dynamically allocated between uplink and downlink, using the flexibility provided by the time division duplexing scheme. Also, LTE-A introduces mechanisms that allow various eNBs (base stations in the 3GPP terminology) to collaborate during both transmission and reception of signals. For example, several eNBs can leverage a high speed wireline backhaul connection to implement a distributed beamforming transmission scheme. These techniques have been called "coordinated multipoint" (CoMP) transmission and reception.

6.4.4 IEEE 802.16 – WiMAX

IEEE 802.16 is a family of standards developed under the guidance of IEEE's 802 Standards Committee to provide broadband wireless access capabilities. The standard has been evolving with different variations and updates since the early 2000s and includes variants for both fixed and mobile broadband wireless access. The name "WiMAX", or "worldwide interoperability for microwave access", was introduced by the WiMAX forum, which is an industry alliance created in 2001 to promote 802.16 and certify that products for the standard are compatible.

Because the IEEE 802.16 standard has been evolving for several years and presents variants for mobile and fixed broadband access, different elements of the standards may present some variations. Nevertheless, in a broad view, it can be said that the IEEE 802.16 standard shares numerous common or similar design elements with other 4G cellular systems and, as a matter of fact, pioneer some of them. Specifically, the physical layer for the fixed broadband version, IEEE 802.16d, uses OFDM with a fixed number of 256 subcarriers. In the case of the mobile version, IEEE 802.16e, OFDM is still used but the fixed number of subcarriers was changed to give the possibility of having a variable number. This allows a flexible support of different channel bandwidths from 1.25 MHz to 20 MHz and up to 2048 subcarriers. As with all modern communications standards, WiMAX supports adaptive modulation and coding (AMC) that allows to choose between 64QAM, 16QAM, QPSK, and BPSK as modulation options. The standard also includes provisions for the use of multiple-input, multiple-output (MIMO) antenna technology.

WiMAX also supports different classes of services, which are used to provide the QoS required by different types of applications. Specifically, there are five different classes of services: "unsolicited grant service" which can be used for the transport of real-time fixed-size packets as is done over T1 or E1 digital lines; "extended real-time polling service", which provides the type of QoS needed by real-time variable-sized packets; "real-time polling service", which is applicable to streams generating periodic variable-size packets at periodic intervals; "non-real-time polling service", which, as the name indicates, is for delay-tolerant variable-size data packets that needs to be transmitted at a minimum data rate; and finally a "best effort" type of service. These classes of service are useful for the scheduler to perform subcarrier allocation in an OFDM frame among different requesting services.

It is worth noticing that while the 802.16e standard was designed to provide mobile broadband data access, certain features in the standard, such as the provisions for channel estimation, do not perform as well in a high mobility scenario as those found in standards such as LTE. Consequently, WiMAX has seen a more limited adoption from cellular carriers operators. Finally, the interested reader should note that further details and a quite comprehensive treatment of WiMAX can be found in [10].

More recently, the IEEE 802.16e standard has evolved into the IEEE 802.16m standard, sometimes called the "next-generation mobile WiMAX" or "WiMAX 2", [11]. While the IEEE 802.16e standard is often considered to still be pre-4G (see Figure 6.15), and sometimes is even classified as a "3.9G" standard, the evolved IEEE 802.16m aims at reaching data transfer rates of more than 1 Gbps and support for a wide variety of all-IP services, making it a true 4G standard comparable with LTE-A. At the same time, IEEE 802.16m maintains backward compatibility with previous versions of the WiMAX standard. Some of the improvements incorporated in IEEE 802.16m include explicit protocol design consideration for operation using relay stations, improved MIMO-operation modes and the ability to control and operate over several carriers at the same time by introducing the possibility for a single MAC layer to simultaneously control multiple physical layers. At the same time, backwards compatibility with the previous IEEE 802.16 version leads toward maintaining the use of OFDM and adaptive modulation and coding.

References

1. L. Peterson and B. Davie, *"Computer Networks: A systems approach"*, Morgan Kaufman, 4th edition, 2007.
2. J. F. Kurose and K. W. Ross, *"Computer Networking: A top down approach featuring the Internet"*, Addison Wesley, 4th Edition, 2007.
3. W. Stallings, *"Data and Computer Communications"*, Prentice Hall, 8th Edition, 2007.
4. H. Zimmermann, "OSI Reference Model-The IS0 Model of Architecture for Open Systems Interconnection", *IEEE Transactions on Communications*, vol. 28, no. 4, pp. 425–432, April 1980.
5. A. Goldsmith, *Wireless Communications*, Cambridge University Press, 2005.
6. J. G. Proakis, *Digital Communications*, McGraw-Hill Inc., 2001.
7. T. S. Rappaport, *Wireless Communications, Principles and Practice*, Prentice Hall PTR., 2002.
8. ITU-T. Guidelines for evaluation of radio transmission technologies for IMT-2000. In ITU-R M.1225, 1997.
9. A. Ghosh and R. Ratasuk, *"Essential of LTE and LTE-A"*, Cambridge Wireless Essentials Series, Cambridge University Press, 2011.
10. J.G. Andrews, A. Ghosh, and R. Muhamed, *Fundamentals of WiMAX: Understanding Broadband Wireless Networking*, Prentice Hall Communications Engineering and Emerging Technologies Series, 2007.
11. S. Ahmadi, "An overview of next-generation mobile WiMAX technology", *IEEE Communications Magazine*, 47(6): 84–98, 2009.

7

Quality of Experience

Although 3D video provides a brand new viewing experience, it does not necessarily increase the picture quality [1]. This chapter will first discuss possible 3D video artifacts introduced within the 3D visual communication pipeline. Then we will look at how to measure the quality of experience (QoE) of 3D video from end-users' perspective. Finally, those considering factors for designing QoE oriented systems are discussed.

7.1 3D Artifacts

3D artifacts are the distortions introduced during the whole content production and consumption pipeline [2, 3]. Those artifacts degrade the perception of 3D content and should be removed or alleviated as much as possible at each stage of the 3D pipeline. In this section, the artifacts induced at the stage of coordinate transformations from the real 3D world coordinate to the camera coordinate and from the camera coordinate to the display coordinate are discussed. Thereafter, artifacts induced by the different 3D camera settings and display designs are introduced. Besides, the artifacts induced during the content distribution process, such as compression and transmission, are addressed. At the end, the artifacts generated by the synthesis of new views are introduced when advanced 3D video coding technologies are involved.

7.1.1 Fundamentals of 3D Human Visual System

As discussed in Chapter 3, there are mainly two different categories of depth cues for the human to perceive depth, namely, monocular and binocular. Binocular cues, which require both eyes to perceive, are the fundamental design elements along the whole 3D content consumption pipeline. Figure 7.1 illustrates how the brain constructs binocular vision. The horizontal distance between the left and right eye is known as the interocular distance. By a given observed object, for human visual system (HVS) to perceive the depth, 3D points in the world are projected onto each eye's retina. Note that the projected location of the 3D points on each eye's retina is not necessary the same. The distance between the projected location of the 3D points to the corresponding eye's fovea can

3D Visual Communications, First Edition. Guan-Ming Su, Yu-Chi Lai, Andres Kwasinski and Haohong Wang.
© 2013 John Wiley & Sons, Ltd. Published 2013 by John Wiley & Sons, Ltd.

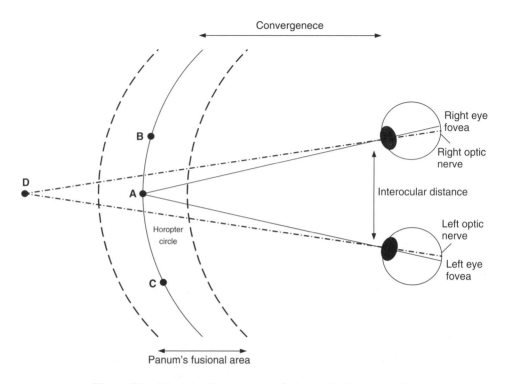

Figure 7.1　Principle of stereoscopic fusion and retinal disparity.

be measured respectively. The difference between the two projection distances is called the retinal disparity, which is the key information for human brains to construct binocular vision. A pair of projected locations is called "corresponding" when they have the same distance, that is they have zero disparity. When HVS looks at an object of interest, for example the *A* point in Figure 7.1, the optical axes of both eyes converge at this object. Those convergence points do not produce any retinal disparities as they are projected to the corresponding location at each eye. A curve connecting all 3D convergence points which are corresponding in the retina is called the Horopter or Vieth-Muller circle. As shown in Figure 7.1, *A*, *B* and *C* are points in the Horopter circle. Points between the Horopter circle and the eyes result in a crossed disparity, and points behind the Horopter circle result in an uncrossed disparity. Points which are far away from the Horopter circle, for example the *D* point, cannot be fused by human brains for binocular vision and cause double images, known as diplopia. The region around the Horopter circle containing points which can be fused by HVS is called Panum's fusional area. [4]

7.1.2　Coordinate Transform for Camera and Display System

To reproduce objects in the 3D world using camera and display systems, the aforementioned HVS principle should be followed. However, there are some differences between the real 3D experience and the capture-store-reproduce system. To understand the difference, the current existing camera and display systems should first be evaluated. There are two common stereoscopic camera configurations regarding how the optical axes are placed between two shooting cameras. As shown in Figure 7.2a, the first type is the toed-in camera configuration where the optical axes of both cameras intersect at C with an angle θ_c. A point of convergence is selected by a joint inward-rotation of the left and right cameras. The image sensors of both cameras are directed toward different image planes, which causes a trapezoidal shape of picture in each view. The second type of the camera configuration, as depicted in Figure 7.2b, is the parallel camera configuration where the optical axes of both cameras are kept parallel. A plane of convergence is constructed by a small sensor. The A point in the 3D world is captured by the left camera at the location S_{Al} and the right camera at the location S_{Ar}. S_{Al} and S_{Ar} are not necessary the same in the coordinate of each camera. Figure 7.3 illustrates the geometrical relation of the reconstructed 3D points in the 3D display system. S_{Al} and S_{Ar} are shown at the point D_{Al} and D_{Ar} respectively in the display coordinate. When the viewing distance is Z_d, the left eye sees D_{Al} and the right eye sees D_{Ar} in order to reproduce the sense of 3D perception of A. Then, A is reconstructed and fused by both eyes to have a depth Z_v. Note that in the real 3D world, eyes focus on the point of interest. In the camera-display pipeline, the point of interest is shown in two different locations in the screen of the display as a pair, and eyes find the convergence points through those pairs and fuse them together to generate the depth perception of the world.

The reconstructed 3D points can be perceived in front of the display when the location belonging to the left view (D_{Al}) is on the right side of the location belonging to the right view (D_{Ar}). This setting is called as negative parallax or crossed parallax. The perceived point can be on the display where both pixels, for example D_{Al} and D_{Ar}, are on the same location. This is known as zero parallax. The perceived points can be in the back of the display when the location to the left view (D_{Al}) is on the left side of the location to the right view (D_{Ar}) This is called positive parallax or uncrossed parallax. When the distance between both locations on the display is larger than the eye separation, there is no convergence point and the divergent parallax is formed. There four different types of parallax are shown in Figure 7.4.

There are several coordinate transformations involved inside the capture-display pipeline as shown in [5]. The first coordinate transformation is to convert a 3D point in the world coordinate to the corresponding point captured by the cameras in the respective camera coordinate. The coordinate transformation varies according to the type of camera configurations. The second coordinate transformation is the conversion from the camera coordinate to the display/screen coordinate, which is normally a magnification/scaling factor when both systems have different pixel resolution. The third coordinate transformation is to convert the display coordinate to the HVS observed coordinate, which depends on several factors including the size of the display, the distance between two eyes and the display, and the distance between two eyes. The coordinate transformations will be discussed in more detail in the following paragraphs.

The transformation from the real world to the camera coordinate is illustrated in Figure 7.2. For a point $A = [X_0, Y_0, Z_0]$ in the 3D world, its captured position $[X_{cl}, Y_{cl}]$ in the left camera coordinate and its captured position $[X_{cr}, Y_{cr}]$ in the right camera coordinate are interesting to know. In Figure 7.2, $2d$ is the distance between two camera centers, f is the camera lens focal length, h is the axial offset from the sensor to the

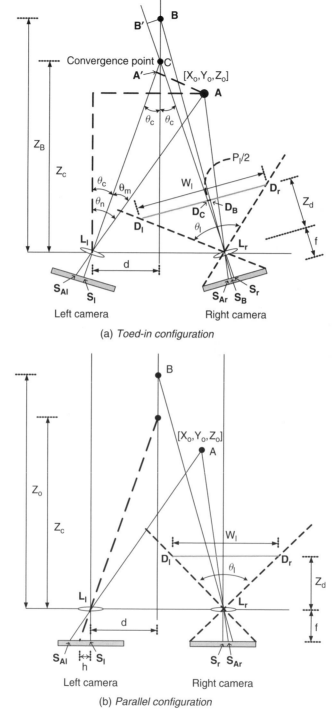

Figure 7.2 (a) Toed-in stereoscopic camera configuration. (b) Parallel stereoscopic camera configuration.

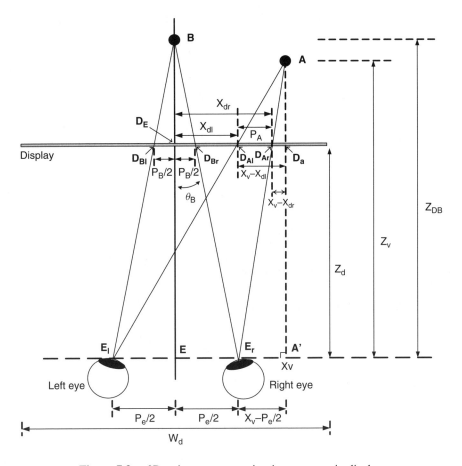

Figure 7.3   3D points reconstruction in stereoscopic display.

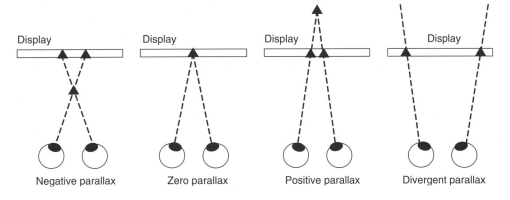

Figure 7.4   Different types of parallax.

camera center which is only for the parallax camera configuration, and θ_c is the camera convergence angle which is for the toed-in camera configuration only. The angle θ_n between the line $\overline{AL_l}$ and the central axis can be computed as:

$$\theta_n = \arctan \frac{d + X_0}{Z_0} \tag{7.1}$$

Then, the angle θ_m between the line $\overline{AL_l}$ and the line $\overline{CL_l}$ is the same as the angle between the line $\overline{S_{Al}L_l}$ whose length is $X_{cl} + h$ and the line $\overline{L_l S_l}$ whose length is f and $\theta_m = \theta_n - \theta_c$. The following triangular equation exists:

$$\frac{X_{cl} + h}{f} = \tan \theta_m = \tan \left(\arctan \left(\frac{d + X_0}{Z_0} \right) - \theta_c \right). \tag{7.2}$$

This can be rearranged to get X_{cl} as:

$$X_{cl} = f \tan \left(\arctan \left(\frac{d + X_0}{Z_0} \right) - \theta_c \right) - h. \tag{7.3}$$

Similarly, for the right camera, X_{cr} can be computed as:

$$X_{cr} = -f \tan \left(\arctan \left(\frac{d - X_0}{Z_0} \right) - \theta_c \right) + h. \tag{7.4}$$

Y_{cl} and Y_{cr} can be expressed as:

$$Y_{cl} = \frac{Y_0 f}{Z_0 \cos \theta_c + (d + X_0) \sin\theta_c},$$

$$Y_{cr} = \frac{Y_0 f}{Z_0 \cos \theta_c + (d - X_0) \sin \theta_c}. \tag{7.5}$$

Denote Z_d as the viewing distance between the eyes and the display, and W_d as the display width. A virtual display, which is back-projected from the camera system to a plane with the viewing distance Z_d, can be constructed as the line $\overline{D_l D_r}$ in Figure 7.2. Let W_l be the width of this virtual display. The coordinate transformation from the camera coordinate $[X_{cl}, Y_{cl}]$ and $[X_{cr}, Y_{cr}]$ to the display coordinate $[X_{dl}, Y_{dl}]$ and $[X_{dr}, Y_{dr}]$ is simply to apply a magnification factor $\frac{W_d}{W_l}$.

The coordinate transformation from the display coordinate $[X_{dl}, Y_{dl}]$ and $[X_{dr}, Y_{dr}]$ to the viewing coordinate $[X_v, Y_v, Z_v]$ can be constructed in the following manner. P_e denotes the distance of eye separation. As illustrated in Figure 7.3, the following triangular equation holds:

$$\frac{\overline{D_{Al} D_a}}{\overline{E_l A'}} = \frac{\overline{D_{Ar} D_a}}{\overline{E_r A'}}. \tag{7.6}$$

Thus,

$$\frac{X_v - X_{dl}}{X_v + P_e/2} = \frac{X_v - X_{dr}}{X_v - P_e/2}. \tag{7.7}$$

This equation can be rearranged as:

$$X_v = \frac{P_e \left(X_{dl} + X_{dr} \right)}{2 \left(P_e + \left(X_{dl} - X_{dr} \right) \right)}. \tag{7.8}$$

Similarly, the following triangular equation can be obtained:

$$\frac{\overline{AD_a}}{\overline{AA'}} = \frac{\overline{D_{Al}D_{Ar}}}{\overline{E_l E_r}}. \tag{7.9}$$

Bringing in the numerical values, (7.9) becomes:

$$\frac{Z_v - Z_d}{Z_v} = \frac{X_{dr} - X_{dl}}{P_e}. \tag{7.10}$$

After rearranging (7.10), the depth in the viewing coordinate is:

$$Z_v = \frac{Z_d P_e}{P_e - \left(X_{dr} - X_{dl} \right)}. \tag{7.11}$$

For Y_v, two points, Y_{vl} and Y_{vr}, can be derived as:

$$Y_{vl} = \frac{Y_{dl} P_e}{P_e - \left(X_{dr} - X_{dl} \right)},$$

$$Y_{vr} = \frac{Y_{dr} P_e}{P_e - \left(X_{dr} - X_{dl} \right)}. \tag{7.12}$$

In the parallel camera configuration, where $\theta_c = 0$, $Y_{cl} = Y_{cr}$ from (7.5). Consequently, $Y_{dl} = Y_{dr}$. Substituting those results into (7.12), these two points Y_{vl} and Y_{vr} become a single point Y_v.

7.1.3 Keystone Distortion

In the toed-in camera configuration, the resulting images have the shape of a trapezoid, and the oppositely oriented trapezoidal shape picture may introduce incorrect vertical and horizontal parallax. As observing (7.12), Y_{vl} is not equal to Y_{vr} when $\theta_c \neq 0$. Both eyes do not see the same point and the brain needs to fuse them together. The difference between these two points creates vertical parallax, which may cause viewing discomfort. Furthermore, Y_{vl} and Y_{vr} are functions of X_0 for a given fixed Z_0. In other words, the vertical offset varies according to the horizontal location. This distortion is the well-known keystone distortion [5, 6], as illustrated by Figure 7.5. For a given picture with a regular grid, the grid on the left side of the left-view image is larger than the other side. The right-view image shows opposite distortion as the left side of the grid is smaller than the other side. The keystone distortion is most noticeable in the image corners. During the shooting process, the degree of the distortion increases when (1) the distance between two cameras increases, (2) the convergence angle increases, and (3) lens focal length decreases.

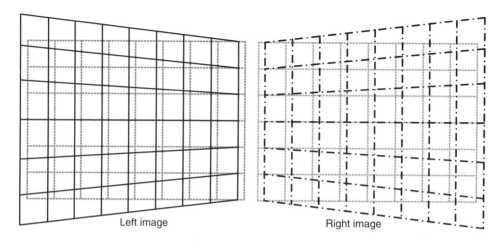

Figure 7.5 Keystone distortion.

7.1.4 Depth-Plane Curvature

As shown in (7.11), for a given fixed Z_0, Z_V is a function of X_0. In other words, an object with a fixed depth in front of the camera can be perceived with different depths according to its relative horizontal location. The corner of the image looks further away from the eyes than the center of the image does. This kind of incorrectly introduced horizontal parallax in the toed-in camera configuration is known as depth plane curvature [5, 6].

7.1.5 Shear Distortion

Besides the aforementioned distortion, [3, 5, 7] have described how the viewers may experience shear distortion when they have sideways movement in front of the display. Assume that the observer moves toward the left-hand side by a distance ΔP, (7.7) can be modified to:

$$\frac{X_v - X_{dr}}{X_v + \Delta P - P_e/2} = \frac{X_v - X_{dl}}{X_v + \Delta P + P_e/2}, \tag{7.13}$$

which can be rearranged as:

$$X_v = \frac{P_e \left(X_{dl} + X_{dr}\right) + 2\Delta P \left(X_{dr} - X_{dl}\right)}{2 \left(P_e + \left(X_{dl} - X_{dr}\right)\right)}. \tag{7.14}$$

The perceived point moves toward the right direction. In other words, if the observer moves his/her viewing position, he/she notices that objects with positive parallax (i.e., the A point) move in the opposite direction from his/her movement. Equations for objects with negative parallax can be derived in a similar fashion and the observer notices that objects with negative parallax have the same direction as the movement. This viewing experience contradicts the experience that users have in their daily life since the objects remain stationary in their daily life. Woods et al. [5] described how shear distortion may result in a wrong perception of relative depth and observers' motion may cause a false sense of the object motion. This problem can be resolved when a head tracking system is deployed to display a correct view when an observer moves.

7.1.6 Puppet-Theater Effect

The puppet-theater effect is a geometric distortion making human characters look small from the perceived video and thus those people look like animated puppets. Although this artifact is not clearly defined, Yamanoue et al. [8] approximately explained it using a simple geometrical calculation. Similar to the analysis done in the previous section, the viewing distance between the cameras and display system is analyzed. In the camera system, the point B is used in Figure 7.2a to explain this effect. Let D_B and D_C be the captured positions in the virtual display represented with the line $\overline{D_l D_r}$ with a viewing distance of Z_d, The distance between D_B and D_C is $P_l/2$. B' is the projected point of B onto the line $\overline{CL_r}$. Z_B and Z_C are the depth of B and C to the camera, respectively. The following triangular equation holds:

$$\frac{\overline{BB'}}{\overline{D_C D_B}} = \frac{\overline{B' L_r}}{\overline{D_C L_r}}. \tag{7.15}$$

Substituting the value of each line into (7.15), the equation becomes:

$$\frac{(Z_B - Z_C) \sin\theta_c}{P_l/2} = \frac{(Z_B - Z_C) \cos\theta_c + \sqrt{Z_C^2 + d^2}}{Z_d}. \tag{7.16}$$

This can be rearranged to get the value of P_l as:

$$P_l = \frac{2Z_d (Z_B - Z_C) \sin\theta_c}{(Z_B - Z_C) \cos\theta_c + \sqrt{Z_C^2 + d^2}}. \tag{7.17}$$

In the normal shooting condition, d is much smaller than Z_C, and θ_c is very small, so the following approximations can be applied:

$$\sin\theta_c \cong \frac{d}{Z_C},$$

$$\cos\theta_c \cong 1,$$

$$\sqrt{Z_C^2 + d^2} \cong Z_C, \tag{7.18}$$

and P_l can be approximated as:

$$P_l = \frac{2Z_d (Z_B - Z_C) d}{Z_B Z_C}. \tag{7.19}$$

The reconstructed point B is considered in the display system (Figure 7.3). Let E_l, E_r, and E be the position of the left eye, the right eye, and the mid point between the eyes, respectively. The lines $\overline{BE_r}$ and $\overline{BE}$ intersect the display plane at D_{Br} and D_E. The length of the line $\overline{D_{Br}D_E}$ is $P_B/2$. The depth from B to the eyes is Z_{DB}. The following triangular equation holds:

$$\frac{\overline{D_{Br}D_E}}{\overline{BD_E}} = \frac{\overline{E_r E}}{\overline{BE}}. \tag{7.20}$$

Bringing in the length of each line, this becomes:

$$\frac{P_B/2}{Z_{DB} - Z_d} = \frac{P_e/2}{Z_{DB}}. \tag{7.21}$$

The perceived depth of the reconstructed point B is:

$$Z_{DB} = \frac{P_e Z_d}{P_e - P_B}. \tag{7.22}$$

The camera-display reproduction magnification factor can be expressed as:

$$\frac{P_B/2 - h}{P_l/2} = \frac{W_l}{W_d}. \tag{7.23}$$

Thus,

$$P_B = \frac{W_l}{W_d} P_l + 2h. \tag{7.24}$$

Bringing in Eqns (7.24) and (7.19), (7.22) becomes:

$$Z_{DB} = \frac{P_e Z_d}{P_e - \dfrac{W_l}{W_d} P_l - 2h}$$

$$= \frac{P_e Z_d}{P_e - \dfrac{W_l}{W_d} \dfrac{2Z_d \left(Z_B - Z_C\right) d}{Z_B Z_C} - 2h}$$

$$= \frac{1}{\dfrac{1}{Z_d} - \dfrac{W_l d}{W_d P_e} \dfrac{2}{Z_C} + \dfrac{W_l d}{W_d P_e} \dfrac{2}{Z_B} - \dfrac{2h}{Z_d P_e}}. \tag{7.25}$$

For a toed-in camera configuration, where $h = 0$, the depth can be expressed as:

$$Z_{DB} = \frac{1}{\dfrac{1}{Z_d} - \dfrac{W_l d}{W_d P_e} \dfrac{2}{Z_C} + \dfrac{W_l d}{W_d P_e} \dfrac{2}{Z_B}}. \tag{7.26}$$

For a parallax camera configuration, Z_C is infinite. Assuming $h = P_e/2$, the equation can be further approximated as:

$$Z_{DB} = \frac{W_l d}{2W_d P_e} Z_B. \tag{7.27}$$

Denote W_o as the real size of an object around B, W_p as the object size projected on the virtual display, W_s as the size shown on the display, and W_v as the size perceived by the eyes. From Figures 7.2 and 7.3, the size in different coordinate can be transformed as follows:

$$W_p = \frac{Z_d}{Z_B} W_o,$$

$$W_s = \frac{W_d}{W_l} W_p,$$

$$W_v = \frac{Z_{DB}}{Z_d} W_s. \tag{7.28}$$

Thus,

$$W_v = \frac{Z_{DB}}{Z_B} \frac{W_d}{W_l} W_o. \tag{7.29}$$

This magnification factor between W_v and W_o can be further defined as:

$$M_W = \frac{W_v}{W_o} = \frac{Z_{DB}}{Z_B} \frac{W_d}{W_l}. \tag{7.30}$$

For the parallel camera configuration, the magnification factor can be simplified by bringing in (7.27) to (7.30) as follows:

$$M_W = \frac{d}{2P_e}. \tag{7.31}$$

The perceived object size is a function of the camera separation and the eye separation.

For the toed-in camera configuration, the magnification factor can be simplified by bringing in (7.26) to (7.30) as follows:

$$M_W = \frac{1}{Z_B} \frac{W_d}{W_l} \frac{1}{\frac{1}{Z_d} - \frac{W_l d}{W_d P_e} \frac{2}{Z_C} + \frac{W_l d}{W_d P_e} \frac{2}{Z_B}}. \tag{7.32}$$

Yamanoue et al. [8] conducted subjective testing to confirm the size magnification factor in puppet-theater effect for both camera configurations.

7.1.7 Cardboard Effect

Shimono and Yamanoue et al. [8, 9] described the cardboard effect as an artifact that the objects look flattened, without different depth shown on the surface. The cardboard effect makes objects look like standing cardboard cutouts placed at different depths. The effect generally happens when the shooting target is far away and the convergence point is set at the shooting target. This effect is also not clearly known yet, but can be approximately explained by some geometrical calculations.

Let ΔZ_0 be the changes in the real depth of an object around B, and ΔZ_V be the changes in the depth perceived by the eyes. The reproduction magnification factor in the depth changes can be defined as:

$$M_Z = \frac{\Delta Z_v}{\Delta Z_0}. \tag{7.33}$$

The depth changes can be observed through an object with finite length. Thus, the gradient magnification can be defined as:

$$M_C = \frac{M_Z}{M_W}. \tag{7.34}$$

For the parallel camera configuration, M_Z and M_C can be calculated from (7.27) as:

$$M_Z = \frac{\partial Z_{DB}}{\partial Z_B} = \frac{W_l d}{2 W_d P_e}, \tag{7.35}$$

$$M_C = \frac{M_Z}{M_W} = \frac{W_l}{W_d}. \tag{7.36}$$

In this case, the cardboard effect is related to the ratio between the viewing angle and camera len's field of angle.

For the toed-in camera configuration, M_Z and M_C can be calculated using (7.26) as:

$$
M_Z = \frac{\partial Z_{DB}}{\partial Z_B}
$$

$$
= \left(\frac{1}{\frac{1}{Z_d} - \frac{W_l d}{W_d P_e} \frac{2}{Z_C} + \frac{W_l d}{W_d P_e} \frac{2}{Z_B}} \right)^2 \frac{2 W_d P_e}{W_l d} \left(\frac{1}{Z_B} \right)^2, \tag{7.37}
$$

$$
M_C = \frac{M_Z}{M_W}
$$

$$
= \left(\frac{1}{\frac{1}{Z_d} - \frac{W_l d}{W_d P_e} \frac{2}{Z_C} + \frac{W_l d}{W_d P_e} \frac{2}{Z_B}} \right) \frac{2 P_e}{d} \frac{1}{Z_B}. \tag{7.38}
$$

We further assume that the shooting target is near the convergence point, namely, $Z_B = Z_C$. Then, M_C can be approximated as:

$$M_C = \frac{M_Z}{M_W} = \frac{2 P_e}{d} \frac{Z_d}{Z_B}. \tag{7.39}$$

With the aforementioned assumption, the cardboard effect in the toed-in camera configuration is related to the distance between the two eyes, the distance between the stereo cameras, and the viewing distance between the eyes and the display. Yamanoue et al. [8] conducted a subjective testing to confirm the size magnification factor in the cardboard effect.

7.1.8 Asymmetries in Stereo Camera Rig

Due to the finite mechanical accuracy of manufacturing stereo cameras, the stereo image pair may not be aligned precisely as the originally designed configuration, that is, the toed-in or parallel configuration. The focal length may differ between the cameras after manufacturing and they may not synchronize with each other when the focuses of the two cameras are readjusted during shooting, which causes different depth perception. Lenses in the cameras also suffer radial distortions and chromatic aberration. The main cause of chromatic aberration is the refraction index of the lenses and is a function of the wavelength. Different wavelengths of light have different focal points, which causes color fringes around object edges. Synchronization of shooting is also important, to make sure that the scene is captured at the same time. Asymmetries in the stereo cameras generally result in additional geometrical distortion, such as vertical parallax, and causes visual fatigue. To alleviate the geometrical distortion from internal stereo camera manufacturing factors, a calibration process is needed to make sure that the left and right cameras perform as closely as possible.

Smolic et al. [10] described how the asymmetries of color, luminance, and contrast in the cameras also bring binocular rivalry. Pastoor et al. [11] discussed how eye strain and visual fatigue are often the consequence for significant colorimetric asymmetry. Asymmetries on luminance and contrast cause time delay in the obscured eye, resulting in unwanted parallaxes along the movement direction of the cameras or subjects, and this affects the 3D perception. In addition, Mendiburu et al. [12] showed that those asymmetries degrade stereo video compression efficiency. Zilly et al. [13] proposed that those asymmetries should be corrected and alleviated as much as possible during the post-production stage via primary and secondary color correction.

7.1.9 Crosstalk

As discussed in Chapter 3, crosstalk is a major concern in 3D display. Crosstalk is caused by imperfect separation of the left and right view images such that each eye not only perceives its corresponding view but also the other view. Daly et al. [14] discussed how crosstalk can be perceived in several forms of artifacts according to the magnitude of leakage, disparities, contrast, and the affected areas of the image. For mildest crosstalk distortion, the observers can see a hardly visible halo associated with edges. When the disparities of the objects between the left and right image increase, the severity of the crosstalk becomes worse and even possibly induces double edges. With higher amplitude of leakage and higher disparities, the crosstalk may induce a ghost effect in the perception, which distracts the stereoscopic fusion and changes the perceived depth of objects. The extreme case of crosstalk is the pseudoscopic (reversed stereo) image where the left eye sees the image representing the right view and the right eye sees the image representing the left view. From a viewing experience point of view, crosstalk may make observers feel annoyed or uncomfortable, and they may experience stereoscopic depth breakdown.

7.1.10 Picket-Fence Effect and Lattice Artifacts

Autostereoscopic displays based on the parallax barrier technique (see Chapter 3) use a black mask between columns of pixels in the LCD display to control the light emitted to each eye. From some viewing angles, the observer may notice interleaved brighter and darker stripes (as vertical banding) caused by the black mask [15]. For a slanted multi-view system (see Chapter 3), the visible subpixels in each view are not in a regular orthogonal grid and each view may be perceived at different subpixels located in different positions. The observer may feel different brightness across neighboring subpixels and feel that they are perceiving objects through a lattice.

7.1.11 Hybrid DCT Lossy Compression Artifact

The lossy 3D video codec also introduces coding artifacts that affect the final perceived video quality. Before entering the whole video encoding process, each image in RGB color space is first converted to YCbCr color space to de-correlate color redundancy and then the chroma part (Cb and Cr) is further downsampled from $4:4:4$ format to either $4:2:2$ (half resolution in horizontal direction only) or $4:2:0$ (half resolution in both horizontal and vertical direction) format. Part of the chroma information will be lost during this downsampling process, and missing values will be regenerated via upsampling in the decoder side. New colors may be generated via the interpolation from the decoded chroma samples and may cause noticeable unwanted colors.

As discussed in Chapter 5, most state-of-the-art 3D video compression codecs depend on the hybrid block-based motion-compensated DCT technology. In the ideal video encoding process, the procedure which loses information and introduces distortion is the quantization process of the DCT coefficients, which represent the magnitude of spatial frequency. Yuen et al. [16] described how the quantized DCT coefficients may introduce several coding artifacts.

1. As the DC DCT coefficients represent the average value for each block, different reconstructed DC values among neighboring blocks have brightness discontinuity along the block boundaries and may bring tiling/blocking artifacts.
2. When the bit rate of the compressed bit stream is constrained by the limited communication bandwidth or storage size, high frequency DCT coefficients are often quantized by larger quantization step sizes and thus the reconstructed values are often zero or with higher distortion. Under this scenario, ringing artifacts are often observed around sharp edges in the reconstructed images.
3. The quantization on low frequency DCT coefficients also introduces some level of detail loss and causes blurring artifacts. The blurring artifact in the chrominance component will be observed as smearing of the color between areas of different color, which is well known as the color bleeding artifact. False edge artifact can be introduced for inter-frame coding because the highly quantized DCT coefficients cannot compensate for the block boundary discontinuities in the reference frame. The loss of details from quantizing DCT coefficients may also make a smooth area look like partitioning the whole area into multiple bands with contours along the band boundaries, which is well known as the false contouring/banding artifact. Owing to the design of 2D DCT basis images, which are often horizontally or vertically oriented, staircase artifact is also observed along the diagonal edges and features [17].

Motion estimation and motion compensation is one of the key factors to significantly improve the video coding efficiency. However, the true motion vector related to one block in the current frame may not be found in the reference frames. The corresponding block will have high prediction residual and the coding efficiency is degraded. The consequence of this failure may introduce visible distortion as padding the mismatched block from the reference frame to the current block location, which is often known as motion compensation mismatch. The ringing and motion compensation mismatch together bring mosquito noise, which is often observed as fluctuations of different color components in the highly contrasting edges or moving objects. In addition, stationary area temporal fluctuation is observed in the smooth area owing to different selected coding modes/parameters in the same area along the temporal domain. With a scene containing high motion, motion judder artifacts may be observed, owing to the temporal aliasing without sufficient sampling rate along the time domain. Advanced displays with high frame rate motion compensated methods could alleviate this artifact.

7.1.12 Depth Map Bleeding and Depth Ringing

When the depth map is compressed using the hybrid block-based motion-compensated DCT codec, the depth map suffers the same artifact as the 2D color images. Furthermore, those 2D artifacts may affect the final perceived depth after the DIBR rendering process. The blurred reconstructed depth map may bring depth bleeding between foreground and background. The ringing artifact in the depth map causes depth ringing in the perceived image.

7.1.13 Artifacts Introduced by Unreliable Communication Networks

Owing to the unreliable nature of the communication networks, the compressed 3D video streams may suffer packet loss or bit corruption, as discussed in Chapter 6. Because the state-of-the-art 3D video codecs explore the view-spatial-temporal redundancy, the encoded streams exhibit strong dependency on the previous decoded syntaxes and reconstructed contexts (see Chapter 5). Therefore, having corruption of some bits or losing packets results in the following successful received packets/bit streams being undecodable and degrading the final reconstructed 3D video. For real-time playback, packet delays may cause display jitter along the time domain when they miss the targeted display time. The details of the aforementioned issues will be discussed in Chapter 8.

7.1.14 Artifacts from New View Synthesis

As discussed in Chapter 5, advanced 3D video codecs adopt a view synthesis method to generate the required views. For the scenarios using the DIBR technology, the major problem is the newly exposed areas appearing in the synthesized views. Hole-filling algorithms are needed to assign values for those areas. Several techniques, including preprocessing and post-processing discussed in Chapter 5, are still imperfect and may suffer artifacts such as false depth distortion and nonmatching textures between eyes in those newly filled regions, which cause binocular rivalry [14].

For a free viewpoint 3D video system, because a new view is synthesized from other views without extra information, it is expected that the free viewpoint system will exhibit some other unique artifacts. According to the capturing environment, the artifacts can be categorized as constrained on unconstrained artifacts [18]. When camera parameters can be calibrated precisely in a highly constrained environment such as a camera studio, visual artifacts in view synthesis arise principally from an inexact geometric representation of the scene. The artifacts can be further categorized into global errors and local errors. The global errors take place in the gross shape including phantom volume, phantom protrusion, and hole. The local errors are shown in the exact surface, position including sunken or raised surfaces, and blurring. Ambiguity in shape caused by occlusion may produce phantom volume or phantom protrusion. Areas incorrectly marked as background induce holes on the visual hull. The undetermined surface coming from ambiguity in the stereo analysis for a region due to lack of structure or repeating patterns results in a sunken or raised surface. Limitation in surface placement precision and image resolution may blur the final result when blending multiple images.

For the scenario where the lighting conditions and background are not constrained, such as a football stadium, the videos may have different resolution and levels of motion blur. The camera parameters need estimation or correction from the captured video sequences. The ambiguity in the input data and the inaccuracies during calibration and matting cause significant differences between the reconstructed view and the original true view. In the unconstrained scenario, the errors can be further classified as errors in shape and errors in appearance. Errors in shape appear in the areas where a synthesized image misses a foreground element or contains an extraneous foreground element when compared to the ground-truth image. Errors in appearance occur when a region in the synthesized image contains different pixel values to a region in the ground-truth image. This can happen through the rendering of the incorrect surface or due to incorrect sampling of the input image.

7.1.15 Summary of 3D Artifacts

Before creating the objective quality estimation metric for 3DTV, the first step is to identify the unique 3D artifacts, which could arise in various usage scenarios involving stereoscopic content. In the previous sections, the common artifacts are discussed. Additionally, Boev et al. [2] provide a summary of possible artifacts in each stage of the 3DTV processing pipeline including content creation, compression, delivery, and consumption. Table 7.1 presents the summary of the artifacts for each stage. The noise can be categorized as structure, color, motion, and binocular. Structure represents those artifacts that will affect human perception of image structure such as contours and texture. The color and motion rows represent artifacts that affect the color and motion vision, accordingly. The binocular row represents those artifacts that affect the stereoscopic perception of 3D world.

7.2 QoE Measurement

The 3D artifacts produced from the current 3D technology pipeline have been introduced in the previous section. Ultimately, a human observer is the final quality determiner and it is important to conduct 3D video quality assessment to measure and ensure the quality of experience (QoE). Therefore, it is of interest to evaluate the perception of 3D videos in the process of acquisition, communication, and processing. Quality assessment (QA) is the term used for techniques that attempt to quantify the quality of a 3D signal as seen by

Table 7.1 Summary of the artifacts for the 3D artifacts [2]. In addition to the stereoscopic artifact, the autostereoscopic display may have unique artifacts, crosstalk, showing up in display [19]. Crosstalk is caused by imperfect separation of the left and right view images and is perceived as ghosting artifacts. The magnitude of crosstalk is affected by two factors: position of the observer and quality of the optical filter. The extreme of crosstalk is the pseudoscopic (reversed stereo) image when the left eye sees the image representing the right view and the right eye sees the image representing the left view

	Capture	Representation /conversion	Coding	Transmission /error resilience	Visualization
Structure	Barrel distortion Pincushion distortion Interlacing Temporal and spectral aliasing Down sampling and noise introduction	Temporal and spatial aliasing Line replication	Blocking artifacts Mosaic patterns Staircase effect Ringing	Data loss Data distortion Jitter	Flickering Resolution limitation Aspect ratio distortion Geometry distortion Spatial aliasing by sub-sampling on nonrectangular grid
Color	Chromatic aberration Vignetting – decreasing intensity	Temporal and spatial aliasing	Cross-color artifacts Color bleeding	Color bleeding	Contrast range Color representation Baking and long-term use Viewing angle dependent color representation Rainbow artifacts
Motion	Motion blur Temporal mismatch		Motion compensation artifacts Mosquito noise Judder	Loss/distortion in motion Jitter	Smearing Blurring Judder
Binocular	Depth plane curvature Keystone distortion Cardboard effect	Ghosting by disocclusion Perspective binocular rivalry (WOW artifact)	Cross distortion Cardboard effect Depth 'bleeding'/ depth 'ringing'	Data loss, one channel Data loss, propagating	Shear distortion Ghosting by crosstalk Angle dependent binocular aliasing Accommodation convergence rivalry Lattice artifacts Puppet theater effect Image flipping (pseudoscopic image)

a human observer. Generally, quality assessment plays a key role in 3D video processing because it can be used to:

- **monitor delivered quality**: 3D perceptual degradation is possibly introduced during the process of video capturing, transmitting, and synthesizing resource. Monitoring the delivered quality gives the service provider the ability to adjust allocation strategies to meet the requirements of QoE,
- **evaluate performance**: a quality assessment provides a means to evaluate the perceptual performance of 3D capturing, processing, transmitting, and synthesizing systems,
- **optimize 3D video processing procedure**: a system can be designed to either satisfy a specific maximal perceptual distortion with minimal resource allocation or minimize the possible perceptual distortion with a proper perceptual quality assessment metric.

Image and video quality assessments have been research topics for the past few decades. 3D videos extend the concept of 2D videos by adding the extra depth for the stereoscopic perception of the 3D world. Thus, the quality assessment of 3D videos should be closely related to the concepts of 2D videos and image quality assessment methods. Thus, this section will first review several important aspects and techniques in image and video quality assessment. Then, several current available 3D video quality assessments will be discussed.

7.2.1 Subjective Evaluations

Since humans are the ultimate judge of the 3D contents delivered, subjective studies are generally used for 3D system development in choosing the algorithms for the system pipeline, optimizing the system parameters or developing objective quality assessments. In this section, a short review is given, and then two commonly used methods are introduced.

Generally the subjective studies can be categorized as:

1. **Psychoperceptual approaches**
   In 1974, ITU-R BT.500 [20] was published by the International Telecommunication Union (ITU) as the recommendation for conducting psychoperceptual studies focusing on television pictures. The recommendation was adjusted for evaluating stereoscopic content to become ITU-R BT.1438 [21]. These ITU recommendations focus on measuring subjective and human perceptual quality. The evaluation is either based on pair comparisons of stimuli to judge the perceived differences, or on single-stimulus methods of rating the stimuli independently. Psychoperceptual approaches generally create preference orders of the stimuli for understanding the impact of parameters on human perceptual video quality.
2. **User-centered approaches**
   The user-centered approaches expand subjective quality evaluation toward the human behavioral level. Quality of perception (QoP) [22] can link the viewers' overall acceptance of the presented content and their ability to understand the information contained in the content. However, QoP does not discover the quality acceptance threshold. Studies [23, 24] discover the acceptance threshold based on Fechner's method of limits and use a bi-dimensional measure to combine retrospective overall quality acceptance

and satisfaction. The results of the study reveal the identification of the acceptance threshold and a preference analysis of the stimuli. Generally, the studies of evaluation are conducted in a controlled environment but quality evaluation in the context of use has become more important for 3D systems. Therefore, research [25, 26] has tried to close the gap using so-called quasi-experimental settings which represent a new concept to conduct experiments without full control over potential causal events.

3. **Descriptive quality approaches**

   These methods focus on discovering quality factors and/or their relationship to quality preferences. As demonstrated in [27], the result of several predefined variables should not be viewed as subjective quality measurements, and the study should be open in order to understand underlying quality factors. The approaches used are different from the first two categories. Interviews [27] and other studies such as the sensory profiling approaches [28] are used to discover quality factors that the users experience. Radum et al. [29] adapted the concept to study the perception of still images and Strohmeier et al. [30] applied the free choice profiling approach [31] to study the perception of audiovisual and stereoscopic videos.

These three different categories of subjective quality methods have different research focuses. Psychoperceptual studies [20, 21, 32] are highly controlled and they focus on the quality preferences. User-centered studies [22–24] expand the evaluation to the actual use of the system. Descriptive studies [27–29] try to discover the factors that affect viewers' perceptual quality. Jumisko et al. [23] provided an overview of existing psychoperceptual, user-center, and descriptive evaluation methods and their applications in stereoscopic video quality studies. However, in order to do a proper quality evaluation which can study the quality as a whole according to users, the system, and context of use, a 3D quality research must create a framework considering all the mentioned aspects in three categories.

7.2.1.1   Open Profiling Quality (OPQ)

OPQ [33–35] is a subjective method for 3D quality assessment and is a method which can evaluate the quality preferences and elicit the idiosyncratic quality factors. OPQ adapts free choice profiling to do quantitative psychoperceptual evaluation. The goals of the method are:

1. to find out how good the perception quality is,
2. to discover the perception factors,
3. to build a relation between user preferences and quality factors,
4. to provide researchers a simple and naive test methodology.

Researchers can use OPQ to study the parameters and attributes for quality assessments. In other words, it is up to researchers to find out what viewers perceive as quality factors.

1. **Procedure**

   Strohmeier et al. [34, 35] described the procedure of OPQ in detail. Based on the recommendations [20], a psychoperceptual evaluation is conducted for participants to evaluate the acceptance and satisfaction with the overall quality. Free choice profiling [31] is adapted to conduct a sensory profiling evaluation. This profiling allows participants to use their own vocabulary for the evaluation of overall quality. As shown in Figure 7.6, the main steps are as follows:

(a) An introduction of quality elicitation is given.
(b) Participants discover the factors based on their own vocabularies which are preferably adjectives.
(c) Participants refine their final vocabularies to identify the factors that are unique and can be precisely identified by the researchers.
(d) After refinement, the participants score these factors as they are presented with the stimuli one after another for stimulus evaluation.

Figure 7.7 shows the outline of traditional psychoperceptual quality evaluation. The main difference is that the OPQ splits the second step of the traditional psychoperceptual quality evaluation into two steps: attribute finding and attribute refinement.

2. **Analysis**

After applying OPQ, a quantitative data set and sensory data set are generated. Analysis of variance is applied to the quantitative data for a preference ranking. Then, generalized procrustes analysis (GPA) is applied to the sensory data to create a low-dimensional perceptual model which shows the principal components separating the test items and correlating with idiosyncratic factors. With further analysis of the model, deeper insight can be obtained to explain the quality preferences shown in the quantitative data. Finally, external preference mapping [36] is applied to link the preference and the perception model, that is, quality factors.

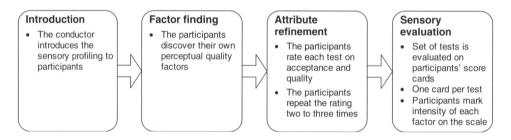

Figure 7.6   The flow diagram of the main steps executed in the process of OPQ.

Figure 7.7   The flow diagram of the general steps conducted in psychoperceptual quality evaluation.

7.2.1.2   User-centered Quality of Experience

Because we are evaluating the produced quality of 3D dynamic and heterogeneous contexts in consumer services, conventional quality evaluation methods are questionable. In order to conduct evaluation, a quasi-experimental evaluation and novel tools for the evaluation procedure are required for conducting research in quality evaluation outside controlled laboratory conditions. User-centered quality of experience [37, 38] is for quality evaluation in the natural circumstances. Generally, the context used in the study can be described in terms of:

1. **macro,** that is a high-level description of the contexts, for example, describing the context capturing a certain type of scenes under certain conditions,
2. **micro,** that is a situational description, for example, describing the context in a second-by-second manner.

The quality evaluation in the context of use requires a hybrid data-collection and analysis procedure. This method is composed of the following three phases:

1. **Planning Phase**
   Fundamentally, this phase analyzes macro information of the contexts and their characteristics. The following describes the two main steps:
   (a) Select the contexts based on the research requirements: Because the length of experiments must be reasonable, only a certain number of contexts can be presented. The chosen contexts should be the most common and diverse to gather the heterogeneity of extreme circumstances. The content used in stereoscopic quality assessments can be categorized as:
       i. physically, which mainly focuses on the place where the 3D devices are watched such as at home or in a hall [39–44],
       ii. temporally, which mainly focuses on the length of the 3D contents [39, 40, 44, 45] and the time when watching events happen [43],
       iii. socially, which mainly focuses on the social interactions which vary from solo-viewing [40, 42] to co-viewing [39–40, 42],
       iv. task-orientedly, technically, and informatively, which mainly focuses on the degree of attention needed to achieve the viewer's goal such as high concentration [40] and low concentration [39, 42, 45].
   (b) Analyze the characteristics of chosen contexts: A semantic description and more detailed and systematic analysis must be given to the chosen context in order to understand what the right conditions are for the experiment to take place. For example, usability study of mobile 3DTV conducted in [37] uses CoU-MHCI form [46] to characterize the chosen contexts and to list the potential threads to causal interference as discussed in [25]. Instructions to the participants and operators are written in order to avoid the mono-operation bias. A pilot test can also help the researchers to check the relevance of selected situations and testing equipment and algorithms. Finally, back-up plans are needed to deal with changes that happen during the experiments.

2. **Data-collection Phase**

The data-collection phase contains the following six parts:

(a) **Quality evaluation task:** A simple evaluation method is used to rate the preference of overall quality after applying each stimulus using a simple evaluation task, because it is desirable to know whether the presented quality reaches an acceptable threshold for the usage of the consumer technologies [23]. Generally, the main challenge in this task is to maximize the range of contexts and minimize the evaluation obstruction.

(b) **Structured observation by the conductor:** During the evaluation procedure, the conductor instructs the participants and observes and records the situations and conditions of the evaluation procedures with the aid of a semi-structured observation form such as [47, 37].

(c) **Work-load assessment of quality evaluation:** After each evaluation task, the overall experiences of the evaluation in terms of mental demand, physical demand, time pressure, effort, frustration, and performance are investigated with a questionnaire such as NASA-TLX [48].

(d) **Interview about quality of used contexts:** An interview about experiences and impressions of quality in the context is conducted by the conductor during the time between contexts. The interview should be collected naturally and casually to get the first impressions of quality in the context.

(e) **Interview about experiences of quality:** Following contextual evaluations, the conductors conduct broader semi-structured interview about the experiences of the quality context and quality. The importance of the interview is mainly for discovering the experiences of perceived quality and requirements for good perception.

(f) **Situational data-collection audio-video recording of the experiment:** The entire experimental process is recorded with video cameras and microphones [49].

Parts (a) to (e) describe the macro-level data-collection tools in a context while part (f) targets the micro-level analysis of context.

3. **Analysis Phase**

First, the collected data is analyzed separately and then the analyzed results are integrated as:

(a) **characteristics of center of use (CoU):** This focuses on identifying central values of the actual characteristics of contexts of use to count participants' CoU.

(b) **contextual influences on quality:** This focuses on statistically analyzing the influence of used context on quality requirements and workload.

(c) **linkage between the interview:** This focuses on linking the contextual quality experience with the interview data about experience of contexts and situational audio-video recordings based on data-driven frameworks.

7.2.2 2D Image and Video QoE Measurement

Since the content is ultimately consumed by humans and the quality of these video contents affects the perception of viewers, the subjective assessment of the image and video quality is needed and preferred. However, the subjective methods are generally expensive and time-consuming and require good knowledge and deep efforts to collect meaningful ratings from a group of subjects. Furthermore, the subjective assessment methods cannot be applied to all images and videos of interest. Therefore, an automatic algorithm, which is objective and not affected by mood, expectation, past experience, or other factors inherent in human subjects, is required to better achieve the goal of evaluation described previously. The goal of an objective perceptual metric uses a number to represent the probability that a human eye can detect the distortions of an image or video or the difference between two images or videos. Alternatively, a map can be used to represent the probability of a distortion detected on that pixel of an image or video or the difference between two images or videos. Wang et al. [50] and Winkler et al. [51] categorized objective metrics according to the amount of information required from the reference image or video to evaluate the degree of distortions:

- **Full-reference (FR) metrics** require the entire original image or video as the reference for quality evaluation. The requirement is generally fulfilled in compression, restoration, enhancement, and reproduction applications in the server side. The goal of FR algorithms is to evaluate the fidelity of the test or distorted video compared to the reference video. This category is still the main focus and thus most algorithms discussed in this section belong to this category.
- **Reduced-reference (RR) metrics** extract a fixed number of features from the reference image or video and use them as reference to evaluate the quality of the image or video. Generally, the algorithm is used to evaluate the efficiency of streaming and broadcasting applications because the full reference image or video is not available in the client side. The representative researches are [50, 52–57].
- **No-reference (NR) metrics** or blind algorithms attempt to evaluate the quality of an image or video without any other reference information. Generally, it is designed to detect the distortions generated by specific applications such as blocking (typically generated in the process of discrete cosine transform), ringing, and blurring. Several NR algorithms have been proposed to evaluate the contrast, sharpness, color saturation, and presence of noise in an image or video. However, NR-based methods still remain difficult problems to combine all these affecting factors into a meaningful metric [58].

Furthermore, the quality assessments can also be categorized according to the types of operation conducted.

1. **Pixel-based metrics**
   These metrics are probably the earliest and most commonly used quality metrics because of their simplicity. The representatives are the mean square error (MSE) and the peak signal-to-noise ratio (PSNR) difference metrics. $f(\overline{p})$ and $g(\overline{p})$ are the values of an image pixel at location $\overline{p}$ for the image f and g, where $\overline{p} = (x, y)$. The MSE can be computed as:

$$MSE(f, g) = \frac{1}{N} \sum_{\overline{p}} \left[f(\overline{p}) - g(\overline{p}) \right]^2, \tag{7.40}$$

where N is the total number of pixel in the images. PSNR can be computed as:

$$PSNR(f, g) = 10 \log_{10} \frac{E^2}{MSE(f, g)}, \tag{7.41}$$

where E is the maximum value that an image can have in this representation. For example, $E = 255$ for 8-bit gray-scale image. Both PSNR and MSE can be directly applied to a 2D video by accumulating the error in all pixels in all frames, and a 3D video by accumulating errors in all pixels of both views in all frames. However, the most arguable issue of using MSE and PSNR is that they do not directly reflect the perception of human eyes. Thus, the number computed cannot truly reflect the real perceived distortions of images or videos.

2. **Human vision system based metrics**

Psychophysics has modeled the human vision system as a sequence of processing stages which are described by a set of mathematical equations. Human vision system (HVS) based metrics evaluate the quality of an image or video based on these sets of mathematical models. These metrics first compute the threshold of distortion visibility and then apply the thresholds to normalize the error between the test and reference content to get a perceptual metric. In order to compute the threshold of distortion visibility, different aspects in the visual processing procedure must be considered, such as luminance response, contrast, spatial frequencies, and orientations; HVS based metrics then attempt to model these aspects into different HVS processing stages that induce different observed visibility thresholds. Generally, an HVS based image quality assessment system consists of a set of blocks shown in Figure 7.8a. To address the additional time domain information brought by a video, there is an extra block for temporal processing in the HVS based video quality assessment, as illustrated in Figure 7.8b. The following gives a short description of each block.

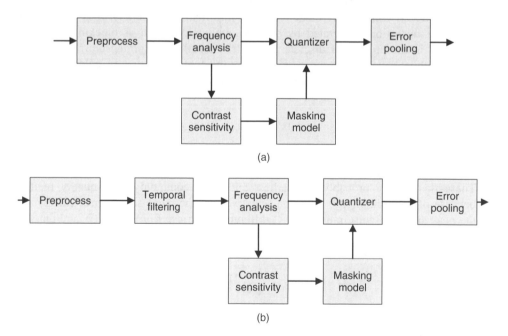

(a)

(b)

Figure 7.8 (a) HVS-based image quality assessment blocks. (b) HVS-based video quality assessment blocks.

- **Preprocessing**: The preprocessing step generally comprises two substeps: calibration and registration. The calibration process is used to remove the color and viewing bias by applying a mapping algorithm from values to units of visual frequencies or cycles per degree of visual angle. It was proposed in [59–61] that the input parameters include the viewing distance, physical pixel distance, fixation depth, eccentricity of the images in the observer visual field, and display related parameters. Registration establishes the point-to-point correspondence between the test and reference images or videos. Without this step, misaligned pairs will introduce shifting in the pixel domain or in the selected coefficient values and degrade the system performance.

- **Frequency analysis**: The HVS responds differently to different spatial frequencies and orientations and therefore this stage fundamentally simulates HVS spatial component response: neurons in the brain respond selectively to spatial signal components with particular frequencies and orientations by using frequency transformation to transform an image or video into components having different color channels with different spatial frequencies and orientations.

- **Contrast sensitivity**: The contrast sensitivity function (CSF) characterizes the frequency response of HVS and is also called the modulation transfer function (MTF). The action of CSF can be simulated by the response of a set of bandpass filters. Since the spatial frequencies are measured in the units of cycles per degree of visual angle, the viewing distance affects the visibility of details at a particular frequency. Quality metrics generally define a minimum viewing distance where distortion is maximally detectable and evaluate the distortion metric at that point. The contrast sensitivity denotes the amount of change in a flat mid-gray image in each frequency that can be detected. Sometimes it is also called just noticeable difference (JND).

- **Luminance masking**: An eye's perception of lightness is not a linear function of the luminance. Sometimes this phenomenon is called light adaptation or luminance masking because the luminance of the original image signal masks the distortions of the distorted images. The effect is generally computed along with other masking effect in the masking block [62].

- **Contrast masking**: Psychophysical experiments generally use an assumption of simple contents. However, natural scenes contain a wide range of frequencies and different scale contents. In addition, the HVS is a nonlinear system and the CSF cannot completely describe the behavior of the response for any arbitrary input. Therefore Robson et al. [63] and Leggel et al. [64] proposed that contrast masking refers to the reduction in detection of an image component under the presence of other image components with a similar spatial location and frequency content.

- **Error pooling**: The final process is to combine all errors from the output of different psychophysical models into a single number for each pixel of the image or video or a single number for the entire image or video.

- **Temporal filtering**: Videos contain a sequence of images and have different effects on the detection of image components. Generally, a spatiotemporal filter is separable along the spatial and temporal dimensions. Temporal filters use linear low-pass and bandpass filters to model two early visual coretex processing mechanisms. The temporal filtering utilizes a Gabor filter. Furthermore, the CSF is measured as a nonseparable function of spatial and temporal frequencies using psychophysical experiments.

In the following we will summarize several quality assessment models including the visible differences predictor (VDP), the Sarnoff JND vision model, the Teo and Heeger model, visual signal-to-noise ratio (VSNR), moving pictures quality metric (MPQM), perceptual distortion metric (PDM), peak signal-noise-ratio-based on human visual system metric (PSNR-HVS), and modified peak signal-noise-ratio based human visual system (PSNR-HVS-M).

(a) **Visible difference predictor (VDP)**: The VDP is developed for high quality image systems [59]. Frequency analysis is done with a variation of the cortex transformation. Contrast sensitivity uses the CSF which models luminance masking or amplitude nonlinearities using a point-by-point nonlinearity, and contrast masking is done with two alternative methods: local contrast and global contrast. To account for the complex content in a natural image, an experimental result of masking is used to help the masking. Error pooling is done with a map which represents the computational result of the probability of discriminating the difference in each pixel between the reference and testing image.

(b) **Sarnoff JND vision model** [60]: The algorithm applies preprocessing steps to consider the viewing distance, fixation depth, and eccentricity of the observers' visual field. Burt et al. [65] proposed to use Laplacian pyramid for frequency analysis. Freeman et al. [66] used two Hilbert transform pairs for computing the orientation of the signal. The contrast sensitivity is normalized by the CSF for that position and pyramid level. A transducer or a contrast gain control model is used to model the adaptation of response to the ambient contrast of the stimulus. A Minkowski error between the responses of the test and reference images is computed and converted to the distance measurement using a psychometric function. The measurement represents a probability value for the discrimination of the test and reference image.

(c) **Teo and Heeger model** [67]: Frequency analysis is done with the steerable pyramid transform in [68] which decomposes the image into several spatial frequency and orientation bands. In addition, it combines the contrast sensitivity and contrast masking effects into a normalization model to explain baseline contrast sensitivity, contrast masking, and orientation masking that occur when the orientations of the target and the mask are different. The error pooling uses the Minkowski error which is similar to Sarnoff JND.

(d) **Visual signal-to-noise ratio (VSNR)** [69]: VSNR is different from those methods discussed previously in three aspects:

   i. VSNR computational models are derived from the results of psychophysical experiments on detecting visual distortions in natural images.
   ii. VSNR is designed to measure the perceived contrast of supra-threshold distortion not just a threshold of visibility.
   iii. VSNR is also designed to capture a mid-level property of the HVS known as global precedence when comparing to capturing low-level processes in the visual system.

Basically, the preprocessing considers the effect of viewing conditions and display characteristics. Frequency analysis uses the decomposition of an M-level discrete wavelet transform using the 9/7 bi-orthogonal filters. The average contrast signal-to-noise ratios (CSNR) is computed as a threshold to detect distortions in the transformation. VSNR applies the contrast constancy using RMS to scale the error for using a measurement of the perceived distortion, d_{pc}. Contrast constancy is that the perceived change in supra-threshold range generally depends much less on spatial frequency than those predicted by the CSF. The HVS has the preference of integrating edges in a coarse-to-fine scale fashion. A global contrast precedence model is used to compute the detected contrast distortion magnitude, d_{gp}. Error pooling is the linear combination of d_{pc} and d_{gp}.

(e) **Moving pictures quality metric (MPQM)** [70]: Frequency analysis uses a Gabor filter bank. The temporal filtering mechanism uses a combination of a bandpass filter and a low-pass filter. Furthermore, the contrast sensitivity function uses a non-separable function of spatial and temporal frequencies built from psychophysical experiments.

(f) **Perceptual distortion metric (PDM)** [71]: Frequency analysis uses the steerable pyramid, and temporal filtering uses two infinite impulse response (IIR) filters to model the low-pass and bandpass mechanisms [72].

(g) **Peak signal-noise-ratio-based on human visual system metric (PSNR-HVS)** [73]: PSNR-HVS computes PSNR with consideration of the peculiarities of the human visual system (HVS). Past studies show that the HVS is more sensitive to low frequency distortions rather than to high frequency on. In addition, the HVS is also sensitive to contrast and noise. DCT can provide the de-correlation and the correlation information to the visual perception and, therefore, the PSNR-HVS can be computed as:

$$PSNR_{HVS} = 10 \log_{10} \frac{255^2}{MSE_E}, \tag{7.42}$$

where MSE_E is computed when considering the HVS characteristics in the following manners:

$$MSE_E = K \sum_{i=1}^{W/8} \sum_{j=1}^{H/8} \sum_{m=1}^{8} \sum_{n=1}^{8} \left(\left(F_{ij}[m,n] - F_{ij}^e[m,n] \right) C[m,n] \right)^2, \tag{7.43}$$

where W and H are the width and height of the image respectively, $K = 1/WH$ is a normalization constant, F_{ij} are 8×8 DCT coefficients of the 8×8 image block whose left upper corner locates at $[8i, 8j]$, $F_{ij}[m, n]$ is the coefficient whose location is at m and n inside the block of F_{ij}, F_{ij}^e is the DCT coefficients of the corresponding block in the reference image, and C is the matrix of the correcting constants [73].

(h) **Modified peak signal-noise-ratio-based on human visual system metric (PSNR-HVS)**: Ponomarenko et al. [74] extend PSNR-HVS to take the CSF into account and use 8×8 DCT basis functions to estimate between-coefficient contrast masking effects. The model can compute the maximal distortion of each DCT coefficient which is not visible due to the between-coefficient masking. The masking degree at each coefficient $F_{ij}[m, n]$ depends on its power and the human eye sensitivity to the DCT basis function based on the means of the CSF:

$$E_W = \sum_{m=1}^{8} \sum_{n=1}^{8} F_{ij}^2[m, n] C[m, n], \tag{7.44}$$

where $F_{ij}[m, n]$ is the DCT coefficient which is the same as the one used in PSNR-HVS, $C[m, n]$ is a correcting constant calculated using the CSF and computed from normalizing quantization table used in JPEG [75]. The algorithm assumes that two sets of DCT coefficients, F_{ij} and G_{ij}, are visually undistinguished if $E_W(F_{ij} - G_{ij}) < max(E_W(F_{ij})/16, E_W(G_{ij})/16)$, where $E_W(F_{ij})/16$ models a masking effect. Edge presence can reduce the masking effect in the analyzed image block D. Divide the 8×8 image D into four 4×4 sub-blocks D_1, D_2, D_3, and D_4. PSNR-HVS-M proposes that the strength of this masking effect is proportional to the local variance $Var(D)$:

$$E_m(D) = \frac{E_w(D)\,\delta(D)}{p} \tag{7.45}$$

$$\delta(D) = \frac{\sum_{i=1}^{4} Var(D_i)}{4Var(D)},$$

where the normalizing factor $p = 16$ has been selected experimentally, $Var(D)$ is the variance of all the DCT coefficients in the 8×8 block D and $Var(D_i)$ is the variance of all the DCT coefficients in the 4×4 sub-block D_i. And the error metrics can be computed as:

$$PSNR_{HVS-M} = 10\log_{10}\frac{255^2}{MSE_M}, \tag{7.46}$$

where MSE_M is computed as

$$MSE_M = K\sum_{i=1}^{W/8}\sum_{j=1}^{H/8} E_m\left(F_{i,j} - F_{i,j}^e\right). \tag{7.47}$$

3. **Structure based or feature based metrics**
   Since the HVS is strongly specialized in learning about scenes through extracting structural information, it can be expected that the perceived image quality can be well approximated by measuring structural distortions between images.
   The algorithms extract features computed from the reference and test images or videos and then compare the extracted features for measuring the quality of the test video. Feature based approaches form the bases of several no-reference quality assessments which are discussed in [55]. Depending on how structural information and structural distortions are defined, there are several different quality assessments:

   (a) **The structural similarity (SSIM) index**: Wang et al. [76] observed that the luminance of the surfaces on an object is the product of the illumination and the reflectance but is independent of the structures of the object. As a result, during the analysis of perception, it is better to separate the influence of illumination from the structural information of the object. Intuitively, the illumination change should have a main impact on the variation of the local luminance and contrast but such variation should not have a strong effect on the structural perception of the image. Therefore, SSIM is set up to compute the image quality based on the structural information in the following steps:

   i. The mean intensity of each image is computed as the luminance.
   ii. A luminance comparison function is then defined with the mean intensity, and the standard deviation of each patch is computed to define the contrast of that patch.

iii. The value in each pixel is normalized with its own standard deviation for structural comparison.

As a result, the SSIM index is computed as a combination of the three comparison functions: luminance, contrast, and structure. The structure term is the most important term in SSIM and should not be affected by the luminance and contrast change. Error pooling is done with a weighted linear combination of all SSIM indices.

(b) **The perceptual evaluation of video quality (PEVQ)** [77–80]: PEVQ is developed based on the perceptual video quality measure (PVQM) [78]. From the reference and test videos for perceptual analysis, these algorithms compute three indicators: an edginess indicator, a temporal indicator, and a chrominance indicator. The edginess indicator gives the information of the structural differences between the reference and test videos and is to compare the edge structure between the reference and test videos where the edge structure is approximated using the local gradients of the luminance of the frames in the videos. The temporal indicator defines the amount of movement or change in the video sequence and is computed as a normalized cross-correlation between adjacent frames of the video. The chrominance indicator provides the perceived difference in chrominance or color between the reference and test videos and is computed similarly to the contrast masking procedure. Finally, these indicators are combined into a mapping for measuring the visual quality of the test video.

(c) **The video quality metric (VQM)** [81]: The VQM contains the following processing steps:

i. Preprocessing steps calibrate the reference and test sequences, align them spatially and temporally, extract valid regions from the videos, and obtain the gain and offset correction [81, 82].

ii. Features are extracted from spatiotemporal subregions of the reference and test videos. The VQM computes seven parameters from the feature streams. Four of the seven parameters are based on features extracted from the spatial gradient of the luminance in the videos. Another two components are computed from the chrominance components. The number of spatial and temporal details affects the perceptibility of temporal and spatial impairments in a video. The final parameter is computed as the product of a contrast feature that measures the number of spatial details and a temporal feature for temporal details.

iii. A spatiotemporally local quality parameter is computed using one of the following three comparison functions that emulate the perception of impairments: a Euclidean distance, a ratio comparison and a log comparison. The three comparison functions in VQM have been developed to account for visual masking properties of videos.

iv. Error pooling computes a single quality score using spatial pooling and temporal pooling functions. The spatial pooling functions are defined with the mean, standard deviation, and worst-case quantile defined in statistics [83]. The temporal pooling functions are defined with the mean, standard deviation, worst-case quantile and best-case quantile of the time history of the videos.

4. **Information theoretic approaches**

Information theoretic quality assessments view the quality as an information fidelity problem rather than a signal fidelity problem. An image or video is sent to the receiver through a channel with limited communication ability and therefore distortions are introduced into the receiving information. The input to the communication channel is the reference image or video, and the output of the receiving channel is the test image or video and visual quality is measured as the amount of information shared between the reference and test images or videos. Thus, information fidelity approaches exploit the relationship between statistical information and perception quality. The core of the fidelity analysis is statistical models for signal sources and transmission channels. Images and videos whose quality needs to be assessed are the captured images or videos of the 3D visual environments or natural scenes, and researchers have developed complex models to capture the key statistical features of natural images or videos which are a tiny subspace of the natural signals. There are several commonly available theoretic information metrics which model the natural images with the Gaussian scale mixture (GSM) model in the wavelet domain.

(a) **The information fidelity criterion (IFC)** [84] uses the general transmission distortion model whose reference image or video is the input and whose test image or video is yielded from the output of the channel, and the mutual information between the reference image and test image is modeled by GSM to quantify the information shared between the test image and the reference image.

(b) **The visual information fidelity (VIF) measure** [85] adds an additional HVS channel model to the IFC. Both the reference image and the test image are passed through the HVS in the fidelity analysis to quantify the uncertainty that the HVS adds to the signal that flows through the HVS. Two aspects of information are used to analyze the perceptual quality by modeling with GSM. The two aspects are the information shared between the test and the reference, and the information in the reference.

5. **Motion modeling based methods**

Image quality assessments model the spatial aspects of human vision including spatial contrast masking, color perception, response to spatial frequencies and orientations, and so on. In addition to spatial distortions, Yuen et al. [16] showed that videos also suffer temporal distortions including ghosting, motion blocking, motion compensation mismatches, mosquito effect, and so on. And human eyes are more sensitive to temporal jerkiness. Human eyes are very sensitive to motion and can accurately judge the velocity and direction of an object motion in a scene because these abilities are critical for survival. Motion draws the visual attention and affects spatiotemporal aspects of the HVS such as reduced sensitivity to fine spatial detail in fast moving videos. Those quality assessments discussed so far do not capture these spatiotemporal aspects or model the importance of motion in human visual perception. Using motion models should be a significant step toward the ultimate goal of video quality assessments which match human perception of videos. Seshadrinathan et al. [86] propose a framework called the MOtion based Video Integrity Evaluation (MOVIE) index that evaluates spatial, temporal, and spatiotemporal aspects of distortions in a video. The spatial, temporal, and spatiotemporal aspects are evaluated motion qualities along computed motion trajectories and can be computed in the following steps [86, 87]:

(a) A Gabor filter decomposes the reference and test videos into spatiotemporal band-pass elements.
(b) The motion of the video is estimated from the reference video using optical flow [88].
(c) A spatial quality measure can be computed as an error index between the bandpass reference and distorted Gabor channels, using models of the contrast masking property of visual perception.
(d) A temporal quality measure can be computed using the motion information computed in the second step above.
(e) An overall video score is computed using the spatial and temporal quality scores.

7.2.3   3D Video HVS Based QoE Measurement

As discussed previously, metrics are important for the development and evaluation of image and video coding. Therefore, a proper metric can also help the development and evaluation of 3D stereoscopic techniques in the process of capturing, transmitting, and rendering. This section first describes the direct extension of the 2D metrics to 3D stereoscopic images and videos. The limitations of 2D-based 3D metrics will be discussed later. Finally, true 3D metrics are discussed.

7.2.3.1   Extend 2D Metrics to Evaluate 3D Images

Since quality metrics play important roles in 3D technology, 3D quality metrics has been a hot research topic in recent years. Early research starts with 2D metrics to incorporate 3D information into the error metrics. An FR 3D quality metric consists of a monoscopic quality component and a stereoscopic quality component [89] as shown in Figure 7.9.

The monoscopic component based on a structural similarity metric accounts for the perceptual similarity and the trivial monoscopic distortions induced in the 2D image processing such as blur, noise, and contrast change The stereoscopic component based on a multiscale algorithm uses a perceptual disparity map and a stereo similarity map to describe the perceptual degradation of binocular depth cues only. The metrics are verified using subjective tests on distorted stereo images and coded stereo sequences.

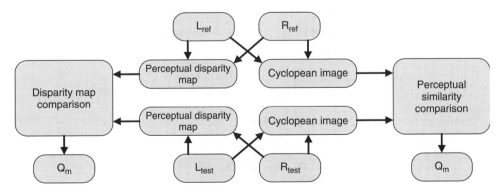

Figure 7.9   Block diagram of the 3D quality metric [90].

There are several other 2D to 3D metrics proposed and these include the following metrics:

1. Hewage et al. [91] compare the results of subjective tests with the 2D VQM score of stereoscopic videos encoded with a depth-image-based representation. The comparisons show that the scores have high correlation with both the overall perception of image quality and depth perception from the subjective studies. This shows the possibility of using VQM for evaluating 3D images.
2. Benoit et al. [92] propose to enhance SSIM for depth maps using a local approach for the measure of the disparity map distortion in order to extend 2D metrics to 3D perceptual metrics. A block diagram of the local approach for SSIM is given in Figure 7.10.
3. Gorley et al. [93] propose stereo band limited contrast (SBLC) for evaluating stereoscopic images using two-view conventional video streams. The metric first uses the scale invariant feature transform (SIFT) [94] to extract and match the feature points in the left and right views. Then, RANdom SAmple Consensus (RANSAC) [95] is applied to these features for searching the matching regions between the left and right views. The matching regions are used to calculate HVS sensitivity to the contrast and luminance impairments. Finally, the HVS sensitivity is used for the perceptual score.

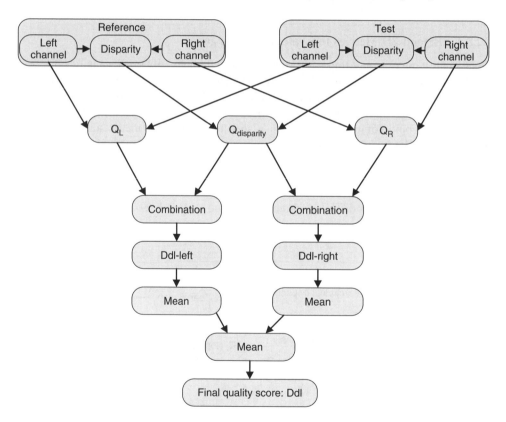

Figure 7.10   Block diagram of the proposed 3D metric using local approach for SSIM [92].

4. Shao et al. [96] propose a metric for the quality of stereo images encoded in the format of depth-image-based representations. The metric consists of two parts: the color and the sharpness of edge distortion (CSED) measurement. Color distortion is a fundamental 2D measurement for the comparison in luminance between the reference image and test image. The sharpness of edge distortion is calculated based on the edge distortion in the test image weighted with the depth in the original image. Both measurements are combined by a weighting average of both measurements to give the score as the quality metric of the stereo image.

5. Yang et al. [97] propose a method to measure the quality of stereo images encoded in the format of image-based representations using the 2D image quality metrics in the stereo sense. The image quality is calculated as the mean of PSNRs of the left and right images respectively, and the stereoscopic evaluation is then adjusted according to the absolute difference between stereo images.

6. Lu et al. [98] propose a metric for mixed-resolution coding 3D videos using a spatial frequency dominance model. A weighted sum of differences and imparities in spatial frequencies between the test image or video and the reference image or video is calculated to represent the perceptual quality.

7.2.3.2   Why 2D Metrics Fail for 3D Images

The simplest scenario to extend 2D metrics to 3D metrics is to calculate the mean of 2D metrics from the two views independently, which is used as the stereoscopic perceptual score. The assumption for this scenario is that impairments in each view have equal effect on the perception of stereo videos but this assumption fails in many cases. This is similar to the condition when using the mean quality over all individual frames in a video because the video metric cannot reflect the effects in temporal masking and thus separate evaluations in both views fail to predict the inter-view masking effects in stereoscopic vision. Although the difference between two views of a point in the scene is an important depth cue for the HVS and the HVS can fuse this difference into a single 3D image, artifacts in both views may introduce a contradiction in binocular depth cues and cause serious distortions in 3D stereoscopic perception. Several different theories discuss the effects of impairments on the HVS perception but generally also believe that the view perceived by one eye may suppress the view perceived by the other eye instead of fusing the contradictory cues. This phenomenon is called binocular suppression theory which illustrates the masking and facilitation effects between the images perceived by each eye [99]. This is similar to the temporal masking effects in video. The subjective study in mixed-resolution coding [100] shows that the overall perceived quality is closer to the quality of the better channel instead of the mean of the quality of both views. Furthermore, the content in the video also affects the 3D perceptual quality. The extended 2D metrics fail to accurately measure the 3D quality metrics because they fail to model the perception of human stereoscopic vision. There are two important properties which must be considered when designing a 3D quality metric:

1. The model should consider the quality of the cyclopean image and binocular disparity of the scene separately. The degradation in the cyclopean image is perceived as 2D distortions and the degradation in the binocular disparity is perceived as 3D distortions.

2. Because the HVS perceives the fused results instead of individual artifacts in each channel, the cyclopean and binocular perception of the distortions may affect each other but the effect is generally nonlinear as shown in the following ways:

   (a) Pictorial depth cues are important for the depth perception. In addition there are masking and facilitation effects between depth cues coming from the two perception models. Therefore, the perception quality of binocular disparity is affected by the cyclopean image perception. Past studies [101, 102] show that motion parallax and stereopsis are considered more important depth cues over monocular depth cues such as shadows, texture, and focal depth. Furthermore, blur is perceived mainly as a "2D" distortion and affects the cyclopean image rather than binocular disparity. The subjective studies [101] also verify that the quality of the cyclopean image might have some distortions and the perception of depth might still be perceived perfectly under minor distortion. However, as the cyclopean quality drops further beyond minor distortions, the accuracy of depth perception drops accordingly. The results correspond to the study results [33, 30] which claim that the depth effect only contributes to the quality perception when there is little compression. This effect suggests that there is an influence of 2D artifacts over the 3D perception.

   (b) Cyclopean perception is affected by the scene depth. The masking in the cyclopean view during image fusion may relieve the artifacts on the cyclopean perception. Therefore, the cyclopean image perception is affected by the perception quality of the binocular disparity. The stereoscopic depth modifies the perception of image details. Boev et al. [101] and Kunze et al. [33] show that equivalent information loss of image fidelity in videos is perceived very differently in 2D and 3D videos. The subjective studies [101] show that the binocular disparity affects the cyclopean image perception in two different ways depending on changes in local or global binocular disparity. Generally, local binocular disparity affects the convergence of the eye and in turn determines which image regions are fused together in the cyclopean image and this therefore has an effect on the region of the cyclopean image comparison and on distortion detection. Global binocular disparity changes the perceived volume of the 3D scene. A larger variance of disparities in the stereoscopic pair generates the perception of a more spacious scene. Thus, Kunze et al. [33] showed that the presence of depth affects the perception of the image quality.

According to these observations, 3D stereoscopic perception metrics, as shown in Figure 7.11a should be designed in the following steps:

1. Extract the cyclopean image and binocular disparity from both the test video and reference video.
2. Evaluate the quality scores separately in each format according to the first property discussed above.
3. Design a measurement function to compute the final metric using the quality score in each format when taking into account mutual influences in both channels according to the observation of the second property discussed above.

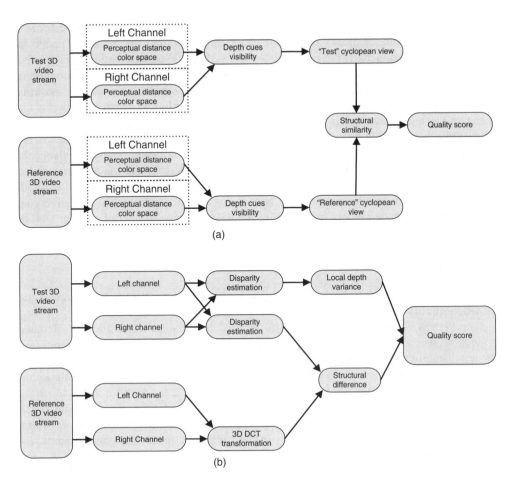

Figure 7.11   Image processing channel for 3D quality estimation: (a) comprehensive model for offline processing, (b) simplified model optimized for mobile 3D video.

Traditional optimized 2D video quality metrics can be used for comparing the quality of the cyclopean images. However, adequate knowledge about the mutual effects of the cyclopean image and binocular disparity on the perception of each other is required. Proper subjective tests have to be designed for these investigations, too. The following will present a set of metrics based on the steps discussed in the previous paragraphs.

7.2.3.3   Real HVS 3D Video Metrics

Subjective studies [101, 103] show that binocular fusion and binocular difference are two important prospects in binocular disparity. The original binocular disparity model can be simplified to focus on binocular fusion and depth extraction processes and compute contrast sensitivity in the frequency domain as shown in Figure 7.11b. The quality score is computed by comparing two DCT video streams. The binocular convergence is performed by searching for similar blocks in the left and right views, and the binocular fusion in lateral geniculate nucleus (LGN) is modeled by a 3D-DCT transformation over similar blocks in the left and right views. DCT simplifies the computation and comparison among patches in different spatial frequency and orientation for estimating the pattern masking and CSF. The perception of depth is estimated by calculation of disparity between the views in the test video stream with the help of local depth variance. Direct comparison of disparity between the test video stream and the reference video stream induces errors in metrics estimation and cannot reflect the perception of depth. Thus the algorithm compares the cyclopean distortion between the test video stream and the reference video stream but only computes the depth perception in the test video stream, and the depth is used as a weight for the output score because binocular depth is only a relative cue. The disparity variance matters most and is calculated on a local area of angular size of one degree corresponding to the area of foveal vision. Larger disparity variance generally represents more obviously perceived depth. The following are three different methods for considering these effects:

1. **3D Peak signal-noise-raito based on human visual system (PHVS-3D) stereoscopic video quality metrics**

   The PHVS-3D metric [103] is given in Figure 7.12. The test video and the reference video consist of a stereo-pair view. The depth perception from two views is manifested as a disparity map. Both the test video and the reference video are fed in to compute the disparity map between the corresponding left and right video streams. The algorithm runs the assessment on blocks. As shown in Figure 7.12, for each reference block A_0 in the left view of the test video stream, the algorithm locates the matching block B_0 in the left view of the reference video stream and the most similar blocks which are A_1 in the left view and A_2 and A_3 in the right view in the test video streams. B_0 is used to locate the most similar blocks which are B_1 in the left view and B_2 and B_3 in the right view in the reference video stream. All similar blocks are located in a 3D structure and all blocks are transformed to the 3D-DCT domain. All 3D-DCT transformed blocks are corrected with luminance masking and the contrast sensitivity function. The mean square error between the 3D-DCT test block and the reference

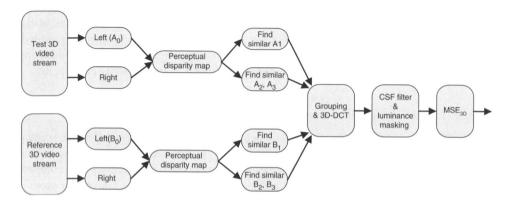

Figure 7.12   Flow chart of the PHVS-3D quality assessment model.

concentration of most energy are weighted with a masking table [74]. Other layers are weighted with coefficients computed from the energy distribution of the block. The PHVS-3D can be computed as:

$$PHVS_{3D} = 10 \log_{10} \frac{255^2}{MSE_{3D}} \tag{7.48}$$

$$MSE_{3D} = \frac{16}{W \times H} \sum_{i=1}^{W/4} \sum_{j=1}^{H/4} MSE\left(A_{ij}^D, B_{ij}^D\right) C_{4\times4}^2 Mask,$$

where W and H are the width and height of the image, A_{ij}^D is the first layer of $4 \times 4 \times 4$ 3D-DCT coefficients indexed at the left-top corner of location $[4i, 4j]$ in the reference image, B_{ij}^D is the corresponding one in the test image, $C_{4\times4}$ is a correcting constant determined by the CSF [73] and $Mask$ is the contrast masking correction constant [74].

2. **PHSD 3D video quality metrics**

Figure 7.14 shows another stereo assessment method which extends the concept of PHVS-3D [103]. The disparity maps are first computed from the test image and reference image. The mean square error (MSE) of the difference between the reference disparity map and test disparity map is calculated and denoted as MSE_d, and the local disparity variance of the reference is also computed to model the depth perception. A similar 3D-DCT transform to that used in PHVS-3D is applied to the test and reference images. Both 3D-DCT transformed structures are modified to consider the effect of the contrast sensitivity function. The MSE of the difference in the 3D-DCT coefficients is computed to represent the cyclopean perceptual difference in the DCT domain and is denoted as MSE_{bs}. The local disparity variance of the reference image is used to scale MSE_{bs} according to the ability of detecting distortions on flat areas or

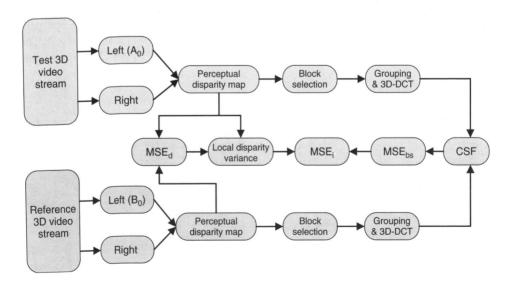

Figure 7.14 Flow chart of the PHSD-3D model.

block is computed for measuring the stereoscopic video quality. The following are the key elements for execution of this algorithm:

(a) **Finding the block-disparity map**: The disparity (or parallax) is shown as the difference between the left view and the right view of the same 3D point in the scene, and the value is generally inversely proportional to the depth of the point, as discussed in Chapter 2. Generally the disparity is computed using a stereo matching algorithm, as discussed in Chapter 4. The dense disparity map between the left view and the right view is computed using the block matching algorithm [104] with a block size of 9×9.

(b) **Block selection and 3D-DCT transform**: The DCT basis method can de-correlate data and achieve a highly sparse representation and thus is used to model two HVS processes:

   i. The binocular fusion process [105]
   ii. The saccades process which is pseudo-random movement of the eyes for processing spatial information [106]

   The DCT basis consists of all these similar blocks stacked together and can be used to explore the similarity across views and in the spatial vicinity. The similar blocks to the base blocks A_0 and B_0 in the left view and right view from the test and reference videos are found by using block matching (BM). BM searches the left view and right view to find the best matched block in the left view and two similar blocks in the right view as shown in Figure 7.13. A_0 is the base block and A_1 is the similar block in the left view. A_d is the corresponding block with a disparity of d. A_2 and A_3 are the best matching blocks to A_0 in the search region of A_d. $A = A_0, A_1, A_2, A_3$ and $B = B_0, B_1, B_2, B_3$ are respectively the four blocks in the reference stereoscopic image and test stereoscopic image. Then 3D-DCT is applied to A and B respectively. Jin et al. [103] chose a 4×4 block size and a 28×28 searching region for this metric.

(c) **Modified MSE**: The metric extends PSNR-HVS [73] and PSNR-HVS-M [74] to compute a modified MSE for considering contrast masking and also between-coefficients contrast masking of DCT basis functions in a block size of 4×4. The coefficients of the top layer in the $4 \times 4 \times 4$ 3D-DCT block which represents the

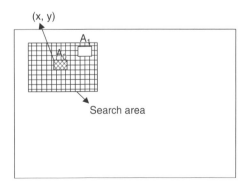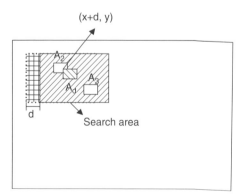

Figure 7.13   An example of block selection in stereoscopic image.

pronounced-depth regions. The detail of the key steps for the algorithm are presented in the following:

(a) **Local disparity variance**: PHSD-3D suggests that the disparity should be normalized with the disparity range of the target display. Boev et al. [107] and Hoffman et al. [108] proposed that the disparity range represents the comfort zone and is defined in terms of *cm* or the number of pixels for the target display with respect to the Percival's zone of comfort [108]. The disparity is normalized as:

$$R_{ij} = \frac{r_{ij}}{(D_{max} - D_{min})} \tag{7.49}$$

$$D_{ij} = \frac{d_{ij}}{(D_{max} - D_{min})},$$

where r_{ij} and d_{ij} are the estimated disparity at the location $[i, j]$ in the test image and reference image respectively, D_{max} and D_{min} are the minimum and maximum disparities of the comfort zone in number of pixels. The MSE of the global disparity differences between the reference disparity map and test disparity map is computed as:

$$MSE_d = \frac{1}{\#\Omega} \sum_{i,j \in \Omega} (R_{ij} - D_{ij})^2, \tag{7.50}$$

where Ω is the domain which contains all the pixels in the entire image whose disparity can be confidently estimated, that is, the pixel in the left can find its corresponding pixel in the right, and $\#\Omega$ is its cardinality. Those pixels from the left that cannot find corresponding pixels in the right are marked as holes and are excluded from the estimate.

The local disparity variance is computed inside a $W_f \times H_f$ block where W_f and H_f are used to approximate the size of the fovea projected to the screen in the typical viewing distance, and the fovea block is identified by its center pixel index. For example, the proper block size for a mobile 3D display may be chosen as 28×28. The local variance can be computed as:

$$\sigma_d^2 (i, j) = \frac{1}{\#\Omega_{ij} - 1} \sum_{m,n \in \Omega_{i,j}} (u (i, j) - R_{ij} (i, j))^2, \tag{7.51}$$

where $u(i, j)$ is the mean disparity calculated over $\Omega_{i,j}$ inside the fovea block $[i, j]$ and $\Omega_{ij} \in \Omega$ are those pixels whose disparity can be estimated confidently inside the fovea block at $[i, j]$. The local variance value models the variation of depth around the central 4×4 block around the pixel $[i, j]$ and can be used to correct the visual impairment induced by binocular disparity.

(b) **Assessment of visual artifacts in a transform-domain cyclopean view model**: After applying 3D-DCT transformation at a pixel $[i, j]$ as described previously, the 3D-DCT coefficients are passed through a block which models the CSF and masking effects at that pixel in the following manner:

$$MSE_{bs} (i, j) = \frac{1}{64} \sum_{m,n=1}^{4} \sum_{k=0}^{3} w_k T_{mn}^2 (U_{mnk} (i, j) - V_{mnk} (i, j))^2, \tag{7.52}$$

where $U = U_{mnk}(i, j)$, m, $n = 1 \cdots 4$, $k = 0 \cdots 3$ and $V = V_{mnk}(i, j)$, m, $n = 1 \cdots 4$, $k = 0 \cdots 3$ are the $4 \times 4 \times 4$ DCT coefficients at the pixel $[i, j]$ for the test and reference image respectively, w_n is the weight of the nth layer and T_{mn} is the CSF masking coefficient which represents the masking effect for each layer and is scaled down by a factor determined by the energy distribution for each transform layer.

(c) **Weighting with local disparity variance**: Subjective studies [103] show that the distortions are more obvious in the flat regions than in pronounced-depth regions such as edges when the distortion is low. However, when the distortion is high, the presence of depth did not affect the perceived quality. Therefore, the metric makes two assumptions:

  i. The high disparity region represents the place where the depth is highly pronounced.
  ii. The structural distortions are less visible in highly depth-pronounced regions if the distortions are below a threshold.

The local disparity variance $\sigma_d^2(i, j)$ should correct the perceptual error estimation $MSE_{bs}(i, j)$ at $[i, j]$ as follows:

$$MSE_{3dbs}(i, j) = MSE_{bs}(i, j) \frac{1}{1 + \dfrac{\alpha \sigma_d^2(i, j)}{MSE_{bs}(i, j)}} \tag{7.53}$$

Then, MSE_i of the image is calculated as the average of MSE_{3dbs} over all pixels.

(d) **Composite quality measure**: The overall assessment should be a combination of MSE_i and MSE_d and then transformed from error to PSNR-type measurement:

$$MSE_H(k) = (1 - \varepsilon) MSE_i + \varepsilon MSE_d \tag{7.54}$$

$$PHSE = 10 \log_{10} \frac{255^2}{MSE_H}$$

7.2.3.4 Feature-based 3D Video Quality Evaluation

Although a feature-based method already takes image structure into account, a 3D feature-based method should be 3D model aware. Figure 7.15 illustrates the possible stages of stereoscopic vision for a 3D feature-based metric. The view of a scene is first collected by each eye through the photo receptors on the retina. The processing in the retina is responsible for the luminance masking, color processing and contrast sensitivity as discussed in Section 7.2. Then the information is passed to the LGN, which mainly focuses on binocular masking and extraction of binocular depth cues. Then the single and fused information is sent to the V_1 visual center in the cortex. V_1 is responsible for the spatial decomposition and spatial masking with different spatial frequencies and orientations. Finally, temporal masking follows. In addition, a small part of the visual information is directly fed to the V_1 cortex without being processed in LGN according to the binocular suppression theory and anatomical evidence. The depth perception occurs in the higher and later processes after V_1. Thus the process shown in Figure 7.16 which simulates the process in Figure 7.15 makes possible masking and facilitation effects between depth cues.

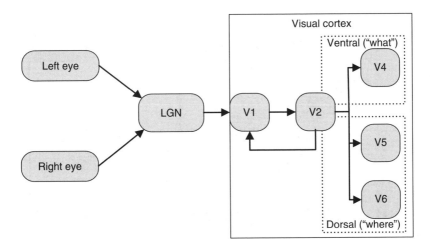

Figure 7.15   Modeling of the stereoscopic HVS in 3D vision process.

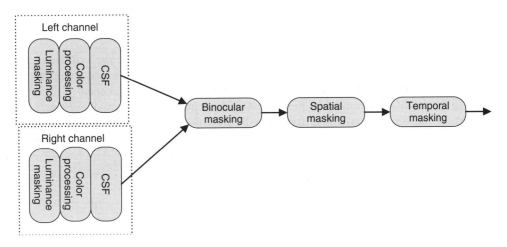

Figure 7.16   Modeling of the stereoscopic HVS using image processing channel realizing the 3D vision process.

The presence and strength of one type of depth cue might suppress or enhance the perceptibility of another. This makes the process of estimating depth cues and binocular masking together necessary.

When the expected artifacts are limited and the amount of computation for metrics is also constrained, feature-based quality estimation is more suitable than HVS-based quality estimation. Figure 7.17 shows a model-aware feature-based 3D quality metric. The inputs are two 3D video streams: test and reference. First, each video is transformed into a perceptual color space using methods such as S-CIELAB [109] and ST-CIELAB [110]. Then, the visibility of depth cues and the suppression among different depth cues are calculated and recorded as 3D quality factors. An optional block such as [59, 71] can

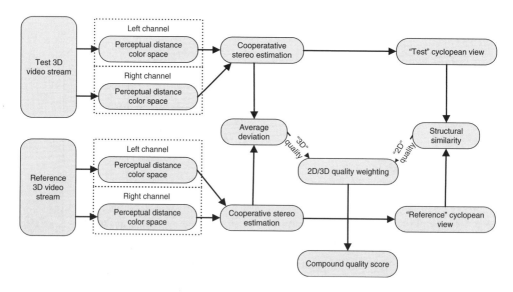

Figure 7.17 Image processing channel for feature-based quantity estimation.

be used to estimate the temporal integration and masking. Finally, the derived cyclopean view and perceptual disparity map are formed from the cyclopean view and compared by a structural similarity metric, which estimates CSF and perceptual salience of different areas in the visual content to form the indicator of 2D quality. Good structural similarity algorithms include [58] which is based on local statistics and [89] which uses adaptive scales. At the end, the final quality measure should be computed using a nonlinear weighting function to combine the 2D and 3D quality measurements:

$$Q_{total} = Q_{2D} + Q_{3D} \qquad (7.55)$$
$$k = f_{depth} Q_{3D}$$
$$l = f_{cue} Q_{3D},$$

where f_{depth} describes the influence of binocular disparity over the cyclopean perception and f_{cues} describes the influence of cyclopean distortions over the depth perception.

7.2.4 Postscript on Quality of Assessment

Although video quality assessment on traditional 2D video has been an active research topic and has reached a certain level of maturity [111], 3D video quality assessment is still in its early stages and remains an open research direction (see an early survey of 3D perceptual evaluation [3]). The works [112, 113] extend the well-established 2D video quality measurement methods for 3D scenarios and indicate that certain 2D measurements on the left and right view can be combined together to evaluate the 3D stereoscopic quality. However, in many cases a stereo video exhibits different characteristics from 2D video systems and provides dramatically dissimilar viewing experiences such as the perception of accommodation, binocular depth cues, pictorial cues, and motion parallax. Moreover, the compression/rendering approach also affects the quality assessment scheme. More customized quality assessment methods are expected to address the uniqueness of different codecs [114].

For free viewpoint video systems, the quality assessment can be additionally quantified as the structure error in reproducing the appearance of a scene, because the human visual system (HVS) is good at perceiving structural and temporal details in a scene, and errors in features or geometric structure are prominent. The accuracy of a synthesized image is quantified as the registration error with respect to a reference image using the 90th percentile measure of Hausdorff distance [18]. This framework provides a single intuitive value in terms of pixel accuracy in view synthesis to evaluate free viewpoint 3D video system. However, the quality metrics for stereoscopic and free viewpoint video systems are still open problems and active research topics.

7.3   QoE Oriented System Design

When using 3D displays to simulate the binocular perception of a complex real scene, the 3D display must carefully regenerate all standard depth cues such as binocular disparity, occlusion, motion, and shading. In other words, the geometric information presented to two eyes from the scene and the displays must be the same. However, researches and experience [115–123] suggest that the depth delivered by the 3D display generally appears unattended or exaggerated relative to the real scene. These flattened or exaggerated effects may create unnatural conflicts for binocular fusion and cause visual fatigue. When designing a QoE oriented system, they are important factors to consider. In the following, we give a short description of the influence of accommodation and blur on binocular fusion, depth perception, and visual fatigue.

7.3.1   Focus Cues and Perceptual Distortions

Works in [124–127] show the evidence that the depth perception is generated as a minimum-variance estimate from depth cues. Works in [128, 129] propose that if the noise at each cue is independent and modeled as Gaussian distribution, the perceived depth can be expressed as the minimum-variance estimate:

$$\hat{Z} = \sum_i w_i Z_i \quad \text{where} \quad w_i = \frac{\sigma_i^{-2}}{\sum_j \sigma_j^{-2}}, \tag{7.56}$$

where Z_i is the relative depth to a reference point specified by cue i and σ_i is the standard deviation of depth estimation using that cue. Generally, the 3D displays provide the following cues:

1. **Capture cues**: these cues represent the depth cues captured by the cameras and set by the graphics engineers.
2. **Screen cues**: these cues are delivered by the display to create the relative depth of the screen rather than the intended depth. Motion parallax is one of them. Motion parallax is induced by the relative movements between the head and the display device and

visible pixelization due to the discrete nature of the display device. However, motion parallax is only a minor cause fatigue and discomfort. According to the works in [116, 119, 130, 162, 122], focus cues are more important because they may be the cause of visual discomfort and viewer fatigue, and they are also hard to eliminate [131]. There are two different forms of focus cues:

(a) **Blur gradient in the retinal image**: As shown in the top left and bottom left of Figure 7.18, retinal blur varies consistent with changes in scene depth when watching real scenes. Works in [132–137] discussed the effect that objects at the vergence distance look sharp and look blurred at farther or nearer than the vergence distance. However, the focal distance for a 3D display is the same, and the reconstructed stereoscopic images is sharp when eyes focus on the screen as shown in the top right and bottom right of Figure 7.18. Consequently, the lack of blur gradient make the screen look flattened.

(b) **Accommodation**: Mon et al. [138] and Wallach et al. [139] show that when eyes watch a real scene, the lens muscles change focal power to minimize blur for the fixated part of the scene. However, when watching the captured scenes, the focal distance does not change, the lens muscles do not change and they lose the depth cues of muscle adjustment (as shown in Figure 7.18).

When the estimation of depth from each cue is unbiased, (7.56) can be written as:

$$\hat{Z} = w_{sim} Z_{sim} + w_{foc} Z_{foc}, \tag{7.57}$$

where Z is relative depth, Z_{foc} is the depth estimated from focus cues and Z_{sim} is the depth induced by other cues, and w is the same in (7.56).

7.3.1.1 Focus Cues, Fusion, and Stereopsis

When we want to sharply focus on an object, the eyes must be accommodated close to the focal distance of the object. Works in [140, 141] show that the depth of focus – the range of acceptable distance difference to the focal distance – is generally about ± 0.3 diopters. Works in [142, 143] show that the tolerance range for accommodation is 15–30 arcmin and is called Panum's fusional area. An accommodative error induces blur to the view and reduces the stereoacuity [144, 145]. Julesz et al. [146] show that vergence errors over this range cause a breakdown in binocular fusion and the formation of stereopsis. Blakemore et al. [147] show that smaller vergence errors induce measurable reduction in stereo-acuity. Therefore, reasonably accurate accommodation and vergence is necessary to generate accurate stereopsis. The relationship between the range of acceptable vergence distances (Panum's area) and the accommodation and convergence distance are shown in Figure 2 in [108]. Works in [148–150] demonstrate that the acceptable range can be divided into two zones: the zone of clear single binocular vision and Percival's zone of comfort which are also shown in Figure 2 in [108]. Works in [151, 152] show that accommodation and vergence responses are normally coupled. The coupling can be helpful because focal and vergence distances are almost always the same no matter where the viewer looks, as shown in the top left of Figure 7.18. However, 3D displays disrupt the normal correlation between focal and vergence distance as shown in the bottom left of

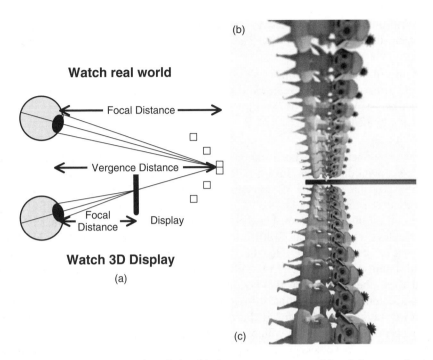

Figure 7.18 This demonstrates the relationship between vergence and focal distance when watching the real scene and the captured videos on conventional 3D displays [108]. The top left shows the situation when both eyes watch a real scene and focus on the point of interest. The vergence distance is the distance to the point of interest, that is, the convergence distance discussed in Section 7.1. Vergence response is the process of adjusting the focus and view line of both eyes to the point. Focal length is the distance to the point. Accommodative response adjusts the accommodated distance to allow both eyes to search the proper information. The top middle three characters in the right show when the viewer is accommodated to the point, the characters on the top in the right appear on the retinal image looks blurred relative to the point of interest. The bottom left shows the situation when both eyes watch a conventional 3D display to simulate the process of focusing on the point of interest. Vergence distance is still the distance to the point. But the focal length become the distance to the display. When the viewer is accommodated to the point, all characters in the bottom of the virtual scene appearing on the retinal image looks equally sharp.

Figure 7.18. Therefore, the stereo-acuity should be reduced when compared to watching the real scenes and the time to do binocular fusion should increase in 3D display.

7.3.2 *Visual Fatigue*

Fatigue, an important factor of QoE, is rather complicated from one perspective, visual fatigue refers to a decrease in performance of the HVS, which can be objectively measured, but its subjective counterpart, visual discomfort is hard to quantify. In [153], three subjective classes of methods, including explorative studies, psychophysical scaling, and questionnaires, and three classes of objective measurements, including optometric instrument-based measurement, optometric clinically based measurements, and brain activity measurements, are studied to understand the relationship of visual fatigue and distortion in stereoscopic perception. The results show that fatigue is caused by:

1. anomalies of binocular vision;
2. dichotic errors, such as geometrical distortions between the left and right images;
3. conflict between vergence of eye movement and accommodation;
4. excessive binocular parallax.

Several experiments have been conducted by [108] to study the influence of focus cues on perceptual distortions, fusion failures, and fatigue. Several groups of researchers [154–158] show that watching 3D contents for a long time induces fatigue and discomfort. Several groups of researchers [154, 157–159] show that fatigue and discomfort are generally caused by the dissociation between vergence and accommodation that is required in such displays. Howard et al. [160], Morgan [149], and Percival [161] show that Percival's zone of comfort represents the set of vergence and accommodative responses without discomfort. Ukai et al. [159] and Wann et al. [162] demonstrate that in order to fuse and focus the contents on the 3D display, the viewer must counteract the normal vergence-accommodation coupling for real scenes, and the effort involved is believed to cause viewer fatigue and discomfort. Furthermore, accommodation and vergence cannot be set independently to arbitrary values because a change in vergence innervation affects accommodation and vice versa. This vergence-accommodation coupling can help a person identify a stereoscopic stimulus more quickly, increase stereo-acuity, reduce the distortions in perceived depth, and reduce the viewer's fatigue and discomfort. The study [108] also provides a methodology to set up the experiment to examine the relationship between stereoscopic properties and physiological symptoms.

References

1. D. Strohmeier, S. Jumisko-Pyykkö, and K. Kunze. "New, Lively, And Exciting Or Just Artificial, Straining, And Distracting: A Sensory Profiling Approach To Understand Mobile 3D Audiovisual Quality".In: *Proceedings of VPQM 2010, The Fifth International Workshop on Video Processing and Quality Metrics (VPQM 2010)*, pp. 1–12, 2010.
2. A. Boev, D. Hollosi, and A. Gotchev. "*Classification of stereoscopic artefacts*". Technical Report D4.3, MOBILE3DTV, 2008.
3. L. Meesters, W. IJsselsteijn, and P. Seuntiens. "A survey of perceptual evaluations and requirements of three-dimensional TV". *IEEE Transactions on Circuits and Systems for Video Technology*, vol. 14, no. 3, pp. 381–391, March 2004.
4. I. P. Howard. *Binocular vision and stereopsis*. Oxford University Press, New York, 1995.
5. A. Woods, T. Docherty, and R. Koch. "*Image Distortions in Stereoscopic Video Systems*". In: *Stereoscopic Displays and Applications*, 1993.
6. V. Petrov and K. Grebenyuk. "*Optical correction of depth plane curvature image distortion*". In: *Proceedings of SPIE*, May 2007.
7. S. Pastoor. "Human factors of 3D displays in advanced image communications". *Displays*, vol. 14, no. 3, pp. 150–157, 1993.
8. H. Yamanoue, M. Okui, and F. Okano. "Geometrical analysis of puppet-theater and cardboard effects in stereoscopic HDTV images". *Circuits and Systems for Video Technology, IEEE Transactions on*, vol. 16, no. 6, pp. 744–752, June 2006.
9. K. Shimono, W. J. Tam, C. Vázquez, F. Speranza, and R. Renaud. "Removing the cardboard effect in stereoscopic images using smoothed depth maps". In: *Proc. SPIE*, pp. 75241C, 2010.

10. A. Smolic, P. Kauff, S. Knorr, A. Hornung, M. Kunter, M. Mueller, and M. Lang. "Three-Dimensional Video Postproduction and Processing". *Proceedings of the IEEE*, vol. 99, no. 4, pp. 607–625, April 2011.

11. S. Pastoor. "3D-television: A survey of recent research results on subjective requirements". *Signal Processing: Image Communication*, vol. 4, no. 1, pp. 21–32, 1991.

12. B. Mendiburu. *D TV and 3D Cinema: Tools and Processes for Creative Stereoscopy*. Focal Press, Elsevier, 2011.

13. F. Zilly, M. Muller, P. Eisert, and P. Kauff. *"The Stereoscopic Analyzer: An image-based assistance tool for stereo shooting and 3D production"*. In: *th IEEE International Conference on Image Processing (ICIP)*, 2010, pp. 4029–4032, September 2010.

14. S. Daly, R. Held, and D. Hoffman. "Perceptual Issues in Stereoscopic Signal Processing". *IEEE Transactions on Broadcasting*, vol. 57, no. 2, pp. 347–361, June 2011.

15. C. van Berkel and J. A. Clarke. "Characterization and optimization of 3D-LCD module design". In: *Proceedings of SPIE*, pp. 179, 1997.

16. M. Yuen and H. R. Wu. "A survey of hybrid MC/DPCM/DCT video coding distortions". *Signal Process.*, vol. 70, pp. 247–278, November 1998.

17. F. Zilly, J. Kluger, and P. Kauff. "Production Rules for Stereo Acquisition". *Proceedings of the IEEE*, vol. 99, no. 4, pp. 590–606, April 2011.

18. J. Starch, J. Kilner, and A. Hilton. "Objective Quality Assessment in Free-Viewpoint Video Production". In: *DTV Conference: The True Vision–Capture, Transmission and Display of 3D Video*, 2008, pp. 225–228, May 2008.

19. A. Boev, A. Gotchev, and K. Egiazarian. "Stereoscopic artifacts on portable auto-stereoscopic displays: what matters?" In: *Proceedings of the Fourth International Workshop on Video Processing and Quality Metrics Consumer Electronics, VPQM* 2009, pp. 1–6, 2009.

20. ITU-R. BT.500-11. *"Methodology for the Subjective Assessment of the Quality of Television Pictures"*. International Telecommunication Union Std., 2002.

21. ITU-R. BT.1438. *"Subjective assessment of stereoscopic television pictures"* Internation Telecommunications Union Std., 2000.

22. G. Ghinea and J. P. Thomas. "QoS impact on user perception and understanding of multimedia video clips". In: *Proceedings of the sixth ACM international conference on Multimedia*, pp. 49–54, 1998.

23. S. Jumisko-Pyykkö, V. K. M. Vadakital, and M. M. Hannuksela. "Acceptance Threshold: A Bidimensional Research Method for User-Oriented Quality Evaluation Studies". *International Journal of Digital Multimedia Broadcasting*, vol. 2008, 2008.

24. J. D. McCarthy, M. A. Sasse, and D. Miras. "Sharp or Smooth? Comparing the Effects of Quantization vs. Frame Rate for Streamed Video". In: *In CHI 04: Proceedings of the SIGCHI conference on human factors in computing systems*, pp. 535–542, ACM Press, 2004.

25. W. R. Shadish, T. D. Cook, and D. T. Campbell. *Experimental and quasi-experimental designs for generalized causal inference*. Cengage Learning, 2 Ed., 2001.

26. J. L. Wynekoop and N. L. Russo. "Studying system development methodologies: an examination of research methods". *Information Systems Journal*, vol. 7, No. 1, pp. 47–65, 1997.

27. S. Jumisko-Pyykkö, J. Häkkinen, and G. Nyman. "Experienced quality factors: qualitative evaluation approach to audiovisual quality". In: *Proceedings of SPIE*, pp. 6507M, 2007.

28. H. Stone and J. Sidel. *Sensory Evaluation Practies*. 3rd ed. *Food Science and Technology*. International Series, 2004.

29. J. Radun, T. Leisti, J. Häkkinen, H. Ojanen, J.-L. Olives, T. Vuori, and G. Nyman. "Content and quality: Interpretation-based estimation of image quality". *ACM Trans. Appl. Percept.*, vol. 4, no. 4, pp. 2:1–2:15, February 2008.

30. D. Strohmeier. *Wahrnehmungsuntersuchung von 2D vs. 3D Displays in A/V-Applikationen mittels einer kombinierten Analysemethodik*. PhD thesis, DiplomarbeitDiploma Thesis, Ilmenau University of Technology, Germany, 2007.

31. A. A. Williams and S. P. Langron. "The use of free-choice profiling for the evaluation of commercial ports". *Journal of the Science of Food and Agriculture*, vol. 35, No. 5, pp. 558–568, 1984.

32. I.-T. P.911. *"Subjective audiovisual quality assessment methods for multimedia application"*. International Telecommunications Union Std., 1998.

33. K. Kunze, G. Tech, D. Bugdayci, M. O. Bici, D. Strohmeier, and S. Jumisko-Pyykkö. *"Results of quality attributes of coding, transmission, and their combinations"*. Technical Report D4.3, MOBILE3DTV, 2010.

34. D. Strohmeier, S. Jumisko-Pyykkö, and K. Kunze. "Open profiling of quality: a mixed method approach to understanding multimodal quality perception". *Adv. MultiMedia*, vol. 2010, pp. 3:1–3:17–, January 2010.

35. D. Strohmeier and G. Tech. "Sharp, bright, three-dimensional: open profiling of quality for mobile 3DTV coding methods". In: *Proceedings of SPIE*, pp. 7542–75420T, 2010.

36. J. A. McEwan. "Preference mapping for product optimization". In: T. Naes and E. Risvik, Eds., *Multivariate analysis of data in sensory science*, pp. 71–102, Elsevier, 1996.

37. S. Jumisko-Pyykkö and U. Timo. "Objective quality assessment method of stereo images". In: *Proceedings of the SPIE*, pp. 7542–, January 2010.

38. S. Jumisko-Pyykköö and T. Utriainen. "A Hybrid Method for Quality Evaluation in the Context of Use for Mobile (3D) Television". *Multimedia Tools and Applications*, vol. 55, pp. 1–41, 2010.

39. Y. Cui, J. Chipchase, and Y. Jung. "Personal television: a qualitative study of mobile TV users". *Lecture Notes in Computer Science*, vol. 4471, pp. 195–204, 2006.

40. S. Jumisko-Pyykkö, M. Weitzel, and D. Strohmeier. "Designing for user experience: what to expect from mobile 3D TV and video?". In: *Proceedings of the 1st international conference on Designinginteractive user experiences for TV and video*, pp. 183–192, 2008.

41. J. Mäki. "*Finnish mobile TV results*". Tech. Rep., Research International Finland, 2005.

42. K. O'Hara, A. S. Mitchell, and A. Vorbau. "Consuming video on mobile devices". In: *Proceedings of the SIGCHI conference on human factors in computing systems*, pp. 857–866, 2007.

43. V. Oksman, V. Ollikainen, E. Noppari, C. Herrero, and A. Tammela. "Podracing: experimenting with mobile TV content consumption and delivery methods". *Multimedia Systems*, vol. 14, no. 2, pp. 105–114, 2008.

44. C. Sädergórd. "Mobile television technology and user experiences". Tech. Rep., Report on the Mobile TV Project, 2003.

45. V. Oksman, E. Noppari, A. Tammela, M. Mäkinen, and V. Ollikainen. "News in Mobiles. Comparing text, audio and video". Tech. Rep., VTT Tiedotteita, 2007.

46. S. Jumisko-Pyykkö and T. Vainio. "Framing the context of use for mobile HCI". *International Journal of Mobile Human–Computer Interaction (IJMHCI)*, vol. 2, pp. 1–28, 2010.

47. S. Jumisko-Pyykkö and T. Utriainen. "*Results of the user-centred quality evaluation experiments*". Technical Report D4.4 v2.0, MOBILE3DTV, 2010.

48. S. G. Hart and L. E. Stavenland. "Development of NASA-TLX (Task Load Index): Results of empirical and theoretical research". In: P. A. Hancock and N. Meshkati, Eds., *Human Mental Workload*, Chap. 7, pp. 139–183, Elsevier, 1988.

49. A. Oulasvirta and S. Researcher. "Flexible Hardware Configurations for Studying Mobile Usability". *Science and Technology*, vol. 4, no. 2, pp. 93–105, 2009.

50. Z. Wang and A. C. Bovik. *Modern Image Quality Assessment*. Morgan & Claypool, San Rafael, CA, 2006.

51. S. Winkler. "Chapter 5: Perceptual Video Quality Metrics–A review". 2006. *In:* Digital Vides Image Quality and Perceptual Coding, CRC Press, Boca Raton, FL.

52. A. Bovik and S. Liu. "DCT-domain blind measurement of blocking artifacts in DCT-coded images". In: *IEEE International Conference on Acoustics, Speech, and Signal Processing, 2001. Proceedings. (ICASSP '01)*. pp. 1725–1728 vol.3, 2001.

53. S. Liu and A. Bovik. "Efficient DCT-domain blind measurement and reduction of blocking artifacts". *IEEE Transactions on Circuits and Systems for Video Technology*, vol. 12, no. 12, pp. 1139–1149, December 2002.

54. C.-M. Liu, J.-Y. Lin, K.-G. Wu, and C.-N. Wang. "Objective image quality measure for block-based DCT coding". *IEEE Transactions on Consumer Electronics*, vol. 43, no. 3, pp. 511–516, August 1997.

55. H. Sheikh, A. Bovik, and L. Cormack. "No-reference quality assessment using natural scene statistics: JPEG2000". *IEEE Transactions on Image Processing*, vol. 14, no. 11, pp. 1918–1927, November 2005.

56. K. Tan and M. Ghanbari. "Frequency domain measurement of blockiness in MPEG-2 coded video". In: *Proceedings. 2000 International Conference on Image Processing*, 2000, pp. 977–980 vol. 3, 2000.

57. Z. Wang, A. Bovik, and B. Evan. "Blind measurement of blocking artifacts in images". In: *Image Processing*, 2000. Proceedings. 2000 International Conference on, vol. 3, pp. 981–984 2000.

58. Z. Wang, L. Lu, and A. C. Bovik. "Video quality assessment based on structural distortion measurement". *Signal Processing: Image Communication*, vol. 19, no. 2, pp. 121–132,2004.

59. S. Daly. "The visible differences predictor: An algorithms for the assessment of image fidelity". In: *Digital images and human vision*, Cambridge, MIT Press, 1993.

60. J. Lubin and D. Fibush. "Sarnoff JND vision model". ANSI T1 Standards Committee 1997.

61. T. Pappas and D. Neuhoff. "Least-squares model-based halftoning". *IEEE Transactions on Image Processing*, vol. 8, no. 8, pp. 1102–1116, August 1999.

62. A. B. Watson. "DCT quantization matrices visually optimized for individual images". *Proceedings of SPIE*, vol. 1913, no. 3, pp. 202–216, 1993.

63. J. Robson and N. Graham. "Probability summation and regional variation in contrast sensitivity across the visual field". *Vision Research*, vol. 21, no. 3, pp. 409–418, 1981.

64. G. E. Legge and J. M. Foley. "Contrast masking in human vision". *J. Opt. Soc. Am.*, vol. 70, no. 12, pp. 1458–1471, 1980.

65. P. Burt and E. Adelson. "The Laplacian Pyramid as a Compact Image Code". *Communications, IEEE Transactions on*, vol. 31, no. 4, pp. 532–540, April 1983.

66. W. Freeman and E. Adelson. "The design and use of steerable filters". *IEEE Transactions on Pattern Analysis and Machine Intelligence*, vol. 13, no. 9, pp. 891–906, September 1991.

67. P. Teo and D. Heeger. "Perceptual image distortion". In: *Image Processing, 1994. Proceedings. ICIP-94., IEEE International Conference*, pp. 982–986 vol. 2, November 1994.

68. E. Simoncelli, W. Freeman, E. Adelson, and D. Heeger. "Shiftable multiscale transforms". *IEEE Transactions on Information Theory*, vol. 38, no. 2, pp. 587–607, March 1992.

69. D. Chandler and S. Hemami. "VSNR: A Wavelet-Based Visual Signal-to-Noise Ratio for Natural Images". *IEEE Transactions on Image Processing*, vol. 16, no. 9, pp. 2284–2298, September 2007.

70. C. J. V. D. B. Lambrecht and O. Verscheure. "Perceptual quality measure using a spatiotemporal model of the human visual system". *Signal Processing*, vol. 2668, pp. 450–461, 1996.

71. S. Winkler. "A perceptual distortion metric for digital color video". In: *Proceedings of the SPIE Conference on Human Vision and Electronic Imaging*, pp. 175–184, 1999.

72. R. E. Fredericksen and R. F. Hess. "Temporal detection in human vision: dependence on stimulus energy". *J. Opt. Soc. Am.*, vol. 14, pp. 2557–2569, 1997.

73. K. Egiazarian, J. Astola, N. Ponomarenko, V. Lukin, F. Battisti, and M. Carli. "New full-reference quality metrics based on HVS". *CD-ROM Proceedings of the Third International Workshop on Video Processing and Quality Metrics for Consumer Electronics* VPQM-06, pp. 1–4, Jan 2006.

74. N. Ponomarenko, F. Silvestri, K. Egiazarian, M. Carli, J. Astola, and V. Lukin. "On between-coefficient contrast masking of DCT basis functions". *In: CD-ROM Proceedings of the Third International Workshop on Video Processing and Quality Metrics for Consumer Electronics* VPQM-07, pp. 1–4, January 2007.

75. G. K. Wallace. "The JPEG still picture compression standard". *Commun. ACM*, vol. 34, no. 4, pp. 30–44, April 1991.

76. Z. Wang and A. Bovik. "A universal image quality index". *IEEE Signal Processing Letters*, vol. 9, no. 3, pp. 81–84, March 2002.

77. M. Barkowsky, J. Bialkowski, R. Bitto, and A. Kaup. "Temporal registration using 3D phase correlation and a maximum likelihood approach in the perceptual evaluation of video quality". In: *IEEE 9th Workshop on Multimedia Signal Processing, 2007. MMSP* 2007, pp. 195–198, oct. 2007.

78. A. P. Hekstra, J. G. Beerends, D. Ledermann, F. E. de Caluwe, S. Kohler, R. H. Koenen, M. E. S. Rihs, and D. Schlauss. "PVQM–A perceptual video quality measure. Signal Proc. Image Commun.". *Signal Processing: Image Communication*, vol. 17, pp. 781–798, June 2002.

79. M. Malkowski and D. Claen. "Performance of Video Telephony Services in UMTS using Live Measurements and Network Emulation". In: *Proceedings of IST Mobile Summit 06*, pp. 5, Junuary 2006.

80. Opticom. "Opticom". Available: http:www.opticom.de/technology/pevq-video-quality-testing.html 2011.

81. M. Pinson and S. Wolf. "A new standardized method for objectively measuring video quality". *IEEE Transactions on Broadcasting*, vol. 50, no. 3, pp. 312–322, September 2004.

82. I.-T. Rec.J.144. "*Objective perceptual video quality measurement techniques for digital cable television in the presence of a full reference*". International Telecommunications Union Std., 2004.

83. P. J. Huber. *Robust statistics*. Wiley, New York, pp. 308–, 1981.

84. H. Sheikh, A. Bovik, and G. de Veciana. "An information fidelity criterion for image quality assessment using natural scene statistics". *IEEE Transactions on Image Processing*, vol. 14, no. 12, pp. 2117–2128, December 2005.

85. H. Sheikh and A. Bovik. "Image information and visual quality". *IEEE Transactions on Image Processing*, vol. 15, no. 2, pp. 430–444, February 2006.

86. K. Seshadrinathan and A. Bovik. "A Structural Similarity Metric for Video Based on Motion Models". In: *IEEE International Conference on Acoustics, Speech and Signal Processing*, 2007. *ICASSP 2007*, pp. I–869–872, April 2007.

87. K. Seshadrinathan. *Video quality assessment based on motion models*. PhD thesis, University of Texas at Austin, 2008.

88. D. J. Fleet and A. D. Jepson. "Computation of component image velocity from local phase information". *Int. J. Comput. Vision*, vol. 5, pp. 77–104, September 1990.

89. A. Boev, A. Gotchev, K. Egiazarian, A. Aksay, and G. Akar. "Towards compound stereo-video quality metric: a specific encoder-based framework". In: *Image Analysis and Interpretation, 2006 IEEE Southwest Symposium on*, pp. 218–222, 2006.

90. A. Boev, A. Foi, K. Egiazarian, and V. Katkovnik. "Adaptive scales as a structural similarity indicator for image quality assessment". *In: Proceedings of the Second International Workshop on Video Processing and Quality Metrics for Consumer Electronics, VPQM* 2006, pp. 1–4, Jan. 2006.

91. C. Hewage, S. Worrall, S. Dogan, and A. Kondoz. "Prediction of stereoscopic video quality using objective quality models of 2-D video". *Electronics Letters*, vol. 44, no. s16, pp. 963–965, 31 2008.

92. A. Benoit, P. L. Callet, P. Campisi, and R. Cousseau. "Quality assessment of stereoscopic images". In: *EURASIP Journal on Image and Video Processing, special issue on 3D Image and Video Processing*, pp. 1–13, 2008.

93. P. Gorley and N. Holliman. "Stereoscopic image quality metrics and compression". *Stereoscopic Displays and Applications XIX*, vol. 6803, no. 1, pp. 680305, 2008.

94. D. Lowe. "Object recognition from local scale-invariant features". In: *The Proceedings of the Seventh IEEE International Conference on Computer Vision* 1999, pp. 1150–1157 vol. 2, 1999.

95. M. A. Fischler and R. C. Bolles. "Random sample consensus: a paradigm for model fitting with applications to image analysis and automated cartography". *Commun. ACM*, vol. 24, no. 6, pp. 381–395, June 1981.

96. H. Shao, X. Cao, and G. Er. "Objective quality assessment of depth image based rendering in 3DTV system". In: *DTV Conference: The True Vision–Capture, Transmission and Display of 3D Video*, 2009, pp. 1–4, May 2009.

97. J. Yang, C. Hou, Y. Zhou, Z. Zhang, and J. Guo. "*Objective quality assessment method of stereo images*". In: *DTV Conference: The True Vision–Capture, Transmission and Display of 3D Video*, 2009, pp. 1–4, May 2009.

98. F. Lu, H. Wang, X. Ji, and G. Er. "Quality assessment of 3D asymmetric view coding using spatial frequency dominance model". In: *DTV Conference: The True Vision–Capture, Transmissionand Display of 3D Video*, 2009, pp. 1–4, May 2009.

99. H. Asher. "Supression theory of binocular vision". *Brit. J. Ophtamology*, vol. 37, pp. 37–49, 1953.

100. P. Seuntiens, L. Meesters, and W. Ijsselsteijn. "Perceived quality of compressed stereoscopic images: Effects of symmetric and asymmetric JPEG coding and camera separation". *ACM Trans. Appl. Percept.*, vol. 3, pp. 95–109, April 2006.

101. A. Boev, M. Poikela, A. Gotchev, and A. Aksay. "*Modelling of the stereoscopic HVS*". Technical Report D5.3, MOBILE3DTV, 2010.

102. S. Ohtsuka and S. Saida. "Depth perception from motion parallax in the peripheral vision". In: *Proceedings., 3rd IEEE International Workshop on Robot and Human Communication, 1994. RO-MAN '94 Nagoya*, pp. 72–77, July 1994.

103. L. Jin, A. Boev, S. Jumisko-Pyykkö, T. Haustola, and A. Gotchev. "*Novel Stereo-Video Quality Metric*". Technical Report D5.5, MOBILE3DTV, 2011.

104. J. G. Daugman. "Two-dimensional spectral analysis of cortical receptive field profiles". *Vision Research*, vol. 20, no. 10, pp. 847–856, 1980.

105. A. B. Watson. "The cortex transform: rapid computation of simulated neural images". *Comput. Vision Graph. Image Process.*, vol. 39, pp. 311–327, September 1987.

106. I. Daubechies and W. Sweldens. "Factoring wavelet transforms into lifting steps". *Journal of Fourier Analysis and Applications*, vol. 4, pp. 247–269, 1998.

107. A. Boev and A. Gotchev. "Comparative Study of Autos tereoscopic Displays for Mobile Devices". *In: Proceedings of SPIE* 7881A, pp. 1–12, May 2011.

108. D. Hoffman, A. Girshick, K. Akeley, and M. Banks. "Vergence–accommodation conflicts hinder visual performance and cause visual fatigue". *Journal of Vision*, vol. 8, pp. 1–30, 2008.

109. X. Zhang and B. A. Wandell. "A spatial extension of CIELAB for digital color-image reproduction". *Journal of the Society for Information Display*, vol. 5, no. 1, pp. 61–63, 1997.

110. X. Tong, D. J. Heeger, and C. J. Van den Branden Lambrecht. "Video quality evaluation using ST-CIELAB". *In: Proceedings of SPIE* 3644, pp. 185–196, August 1999.

111. K. Seshadrinathan, R. Soundararajan, A. Bovik, and L. Cormack. "Study of Subjective and Objective Quality Assessment of Video". *IEEE Transactions on Image Processing*, vol. 19, no. 6, pp. 1427–1441, June 2010.

112. C. Hewage, S. Worrall, S. Dogan, S. Villette, and A. Kondoz. "Quality Evaluation of Color Plus Depth Map-Based Stereoscopic Video". *IEEE Journal of Selected Topics in Signal Processing*, vol. 3, no. 2, pp. 304–318, April 2009.

113. S. Yasakethu, C. Hewage, W. Fernando, and A. Kondoz. "Quality analysis for 3D video using 2D video quality models". *IEEE Transactions on Consumer Electronics*, vol. 54, no. iss4, pp. 1969–1976, November 2008.

114. L. Stelmach, W. J. Tam, D. Meegan, and A. Vincent. "Stereo image quality: effects of mixed spatio-temporal resolution". *IEEE Transactions on Circuits and Systems for Video Technology/*, vol. 10, no. 2, pp. 188–193, March 2000.

115. B. T. Backus, M. S. Banks, R. van Ee, and J. A. Crowell. "Horizontal and vertical disparity, eye position, and stereoscopic slant perception". *Vision Research*, vol. 39, pp. 1143–1170, 1990.

116. D. Buckley and J. P. Frisby. "Interaction of stereo, texture and outline cues in the shape perception of three-dimensional ridges.". *Vision Research*, vol. 33, pp. 919–933, 1993.

117. S. H. Creem-Regehr, P. Willemsen, A. A. Gooch, and W. B. Thompson. "The influence of restricted viewing conditions on egocentric distance perception: Implications for real and virtual indoor environments". *Perception*, vol. 34, pp. 191–204, 2005.

118. S. R. Ellis, S. Smith, A. Grunwald, and M. W. McGreevy. "Direction judgement error in computer generated displays and actual scenes". In: S. R. Ellis, Ed., Pictorial communication in virtual and real environments*, pp. 504–526*, Taylor & Francis, Inc., 1991.

119. J. P. Frisby, D. Buckley, K. A. Wishart, J. Porrill, J. Garding, and J. E. Mayhew. "Interaction of stereo and texture cues in the perception of 3-dimensional steps". l*Vision Research*, vol. 35, pp. 1463–1472, 1995.

120. J. P. Frisby, D. Buckley, and P. A. Duke. "Evidence for good recovery of lengths of real objects seen with natural stereo viewing". *Perception*, vol. 25, pp. 129–154, 1996.

121. C. S. Sahm, S. H. Creem-Regehr, W. B. Thompson, and P. Willemsen. "Throwing versus walking as indicators of distance perception in similar real and virtual environments". *ACM Trans. Appl. Percept.*, vol. 2, no. 1, pp. 35–45, 2005.

122. S. J. Watt, K. Akeley, M. O. Ernst, and M. S. Banks. "Focus cues affect perceived depth". *Journal of Vision*, vol. 5, no. 7, pp. 834–862, 2005.

123. P. Willemsen, A. A. Gooch, W. B. Thompson, and S. H. Creem-Regehr. "Effects of stereo viewing conditions on distance perception in virtual environments". *MIT Press Journal*, vol. 17, no. 1, pp. 91–101, 2008.

124. J. Burge, M. A. Peterson, and S. E. Palmer. "Ordinal configural cues combine with metric disparity in depth perception". *Journal of Vision*, vol. 5, no. 5, pp. 534–542, 2005.

125. J. M. Hillis, S. J. Watt, M. S. Landy, and M. S. Banks. "Slant from texture and disparity cues: Optimal cue combination". *Journal of Vision*, vol. 4, no. 12, pp. 967–992, 2004.

126. R. A. Jacobs. "Optimal integration of texture and motion cues to depth". *Vision Research*, vol. 39, no. 9, pp. 3621–3629, 1999.

127. D. C. Knill and J. A. Saunders. "Do humans optimally integrate stereo and texture information for judgments of surface slant?" *Vision Research*, vol. 43, no. 20, pp. 2539–2558, 2003.

128. W. G. Cochran. "Problems arising in the analysis of a series of similar experiments.". *Supplement to the Journal of the Royal Statistical Society*, vol. 4, pp. 102–118, 1937.

129. Z. Ghahramani, D. M. Wolpert, and M. I. Jordan. "Computational models of sensorimotor integration". In: P. G. Morasso and V. Sanguineti, Eds., *Self-organization, computational maps, and motor control*, pp. 117–147, Amsterdam: North-Holland, 1997.

130. K. Ukai and P. A. Howarth. "Visual fatigue caused by viewing stereoscopic motion images: Background, theories, and observations". *Displays*, vol. 29, no. 2, pp. 106–116, 2008.

131. K. Akeley, S. J. Watt, A. R. Girshick, and M. S. Banks. "A stereo display prototype with multiple focal distances". *ACM Trans. Graph.*, vol. 23, no. 3, pp. 804–813, August 2004.

132. H. Kuribayashi, Y. Ishigure, S. Suyama, H. Takada, M. Date, K. Ishikawa, and H. Toyohiko. "Effect on depth perception by a blur in a depth-fused 3-D display.". *Journal of the Institute of Image Information and Television Engineers*, vol. 60, pp. 431–438, 2006.

133. J. A. Marshall, C. A. Burbeck, D. Ariely, J. P. Rolland, and K. E. Martin. "Occlusion edge blur: A cue to relative visual depth.". *Journal of the Optical Society of America A, Optics, Image Science, and Vision*, vol. 13, pp. 681–688, 1996.

134. G. Mather and D. R. Smith. "Depth cue integration: Stereopsis and image blur". *Vision Research*, vol. 40, pp. 3501–3506, 2000.

135. G. Mather and D. R. Smith. "Blur discrimination and its relation to blur-mediated depth perception". *Perception*, vol. 31, pp. 1211–1219, 2002.

136. G. Mather. "The use of image blur as a depth cue". *Perception*, vol. 26, pp. 1147–1158, 2005.

137. R. P. OShea, D. G. Govan, and R. Sekuler. "Blur and contrast as pictorial depth cues". *Perception*, vol. 26, pp. 599–612, 1997.

138. M. Mon-Williams, J. R. Tresilian, and A. Roberts. "Vergence provides veridical depth perception from horizontal retinal image disparities". *Experimental Brain Research*, vol. 133, pp. 407–413, 2000.

139. H. Wallach and C. M. Norris. "Accommodation as a distance-cue". *American Journal of Psychology*, vol. 76, pp. 659–664, 1963.

140. F. W. Campbell. "The depth of field of the human eye". *Journal of Modern Optics*, vol. 4, pp. 157–164, 1963.

141. W. N. Charman and H. Whitefoot. "Pupil diameter and depth-of-field of human eye as measured by laser speckle". *Optica Acta*, vol. 24, pp. 1211–1216, 1977.

142. K. N. Ogle. "An analytical treatment of the longitudinal horopter, its measurement and application to related phenomena, especially to the relative size and shape of the ocular images". *Journal of the Optical Society of America*, vol. 22, pp. 665–728, 1932.

143. C. Schor, I. Wood, and J. Ogawa. "Binocular sensory fusion is limited by spatial resolution". *Vision Research*, vol. 24, pp. 661–665, 1984.

144. J. V. Odom, G. M. Chao, and M. Leys. "Symmetrical refractive error elevates stereo thresholds". *Investigative Ophthalmology & Visual Science*, vol. 33, pp. 1375–1375, 1992.

145. G. Westheimer and S. P. McKee. "Stereoscopic acuity with defocused and spatially filtered retinal images". *Journal of the Optical Society of America*, vol. 70, pp. 772–778, 1980.

146. B. Julesz. *Foundations of cyclopean perception*. University of Chicago Press, Chicago, 1971.

147. C. Blakemore. "The range and scope of binocular depth discrimination in man.". *The Journal of Physiology*, vol. 211, pp. 599–622, 1970.

148. G. A. Fry. "Further experiments on the accommodation convergence relationship". *American Journal of Optometry*, vol. 16, pp. 125, 1939.

149. M. W. Morgan. "The clinical aspects of accommodation and convergence". *American Journal of Optometry and Archives of American Academy of Optometry*, vol. 21, pp. 183–195, 1944.

150. B. J. Rogers and M. F. Bradshaw. "Binocular judgments of depth, size, shape and absolute distance V Is the same d used for all judgments.". *Investigative Ophthamology & Visual Science*, vol. 36, pp. S230–S230, 1995.

151. E. F. Fincham. "The accommodation reflex and its stimulus.". *British Journal of Ophthalmology*, vol. 35, pp. 381–393, 1951.

152. T. G. Martens and K. N. Ogle. "Observations on accommodative convergence; especially its nonlinear relationships". *American Journal of Ophthalmology*, vol. 47, pp. 455–463, 1959.

153. M. Lambooij, W. IJsselsteijn, M. Fortuin, and I. Heynderickx. "Visual Discomfort and Visual Fatigue of Stereoscopic Displays: A Review". *Journal of Imaging Science and Technology*, vol. 53, no. 3, pp. 030201, 2009.

154. M. Emoto, T. Niida, and F. Okano. "Repeated vergence adaptation causes the decline of visual functions in watching stereoscopic television". *Journal of Display Technology*, vol. 1, pp. 328–340, 2005.

155. Y. Takaki. "Novel 3D display using an array of LCD panels". In: *Proceedings of SPIE*, pp. 1–8, September 2003.

156. H. Takada. "The progress of high presence and 3D display technology. The depth-fused 3-D display for the eye sweetly". *Optical and Electro-Optical Engineering Contact*, vol. 44, pp. 316–323, 2006.

157. J. P. Wann and M. Mon-Williams. "Measurement of visual after-effects following virtual environment exposure". In: M. Stanney, Ed., *Handbook of virtual environments: Design, implementation, and applications*, pp. 731–749, Lawrence Erlbaum Associates, 2002.

158. S. Yano, M. Emoto, and T. Mitsuhashi. "Two factors in visual fatigue caused by stereoscopic HDTV images". *Displays*, vol. 25, no. 25, pp. 141–150, 2004.

159. K. Ukai. "Visual fatigue caused by viewing stereoscopic images and mechanism of accommodation". In: *In Proceedings of the First International Symposium on University Communication*, pp. 176–179, 2007.

160. I. P. Howard and B. J. Rogers. *Seeing in depth*. University of Toronto Press, 2002.

161. A. S. Percival. *The prescribing of spectacles*. J. Wright, 1920.

162. J. P. Wann and M. Mon-Williams. "Health issues with virtual reality displays: what we do know and what we don't". *SIGGRAPH Comput. Graph.*, vol. 31, no. 2, pp. 53–57, May 1997.

8

3D Video over Networks

8.1 Transmission-Induced Error

The transmission of video over a communication channel adds to the challenges associated with source compression, those arising from the errors that inevitably would be introduced in the channel. The presentation in Chapter 6 should have conveyed, among others, the message that while some channels are more benign, introducing errors less frequently than others, all channels do introduced errors. Therefore, when considering the quality of the communicated video from an end-to-end perspective, the experienced distortion will not only be due to the compression operation, but also due to channel errors. To differentiate these two types of distortions, we will be calling the former "source encoding distortion" or "source compression distortion", and the latter "channel-induced distortion" or "transmission-induced distortion".

Of course, channel errors will introduce a channel-induced distortion to the end-to-end video quality, but the magnitude of this distortion usually depends on several variables, such as the source encoding method used on the source, the error pattern introduced by the channel, the importance of the affected information from the human perception perspective, and so on. Indeed, practical video encoders frequently need to make use of and combine multiple techniques in order to achieve good compression performance. As a result, the bit stream at the output of a source encoder may be formed by different components, each having been generated by one of the data compression techniques. For example, in the bit stream at the output of a video encoder it is possible to find data related to the motion vectors obtained from using motion compensation, data related to a frame image or prediction error texture, which may result from differential encoding followed by entropy coding, data used to mark different parts in the bit stream, or headers carrying important metadata about the bit stream. The data being of different types, it is natural to see that channel errors will have different impacts on the source reconstruction quality for different parts of the source encoded bit stream. That is, while an error in one part of the bit stream may add a little distortion to the source reconstruction, an error of the same magnitude may have a devastating effect when affecting a different part of the bit stream.

The effects that the channel errors may have on the reconstruction quality of a source may differ depending on the importance of the parts affected or on the sensitivity of those

3D Visual Communications, First Edition. Guan-Ming Su, Yu-Chi Lai, Andres Kwasinski and Haohong Wang.
© 2013 John Wiley & Sons, Ltd. Published 2013 by John Wiley & Sons, Ltd.

parts to channel errors. One example of highly important parts within a source encoder bit stream are headers. The headers usually contain information that is indispensable for configuring the decoder. If this information is corrupted, then it simply may not be possible to decode a frame or a group of frames. In other cases, it may be that certain parts of the compressed video bit stream contain information that has been encoded with techniques that, while being more efficient, are more sensitive to channel errors. Sometimes this may happen due to the inherent structure of the encoded bit stream. For example, if using variable-length entropy coding, channel errors will have a more significant effect when affecting earlier bits. This is because all the succeeding bits will need to be discarded. In other cases, the higher sensitivity of a part of the compressed video bit stream may be due to using an encoding technique that is naturally more sensitive. This situation may occur, for example, when part of the information has been encoded using differential encoding, as is frequently the case with motion vectors. Because in differential encoding, one source encoded sample may depend on several previous samples, an error that is introduced for the reconstruction of a sample would affect several successive samples. We illustrate this point with the following simple example. Assume that a portion of a bit stream is encoding samples from a first order autoregressive Gaussian source x_n (n being the discrete time index) that behaves according to:

$$x_n = \rho x_{n-1} + w_n, n = 1, 2, \ldots,$$

where w_n is the noise sequence, modeled as a discrete-time, zero-mean Gaussian random process with unit variance, and ρ controls the correlation between two successive samples. Since any given sample is correlated with the previous sample, it is natural to consider using differential encoding to compactly represent the samples x_n. A simplified form of the differential encoder and decoder is shown in Figure 8.1, for reference purposes. It can be seen how the encoder quantizes the error between the input sample and its value predicted from previous samples. In this case, the prediction can be implemented using a

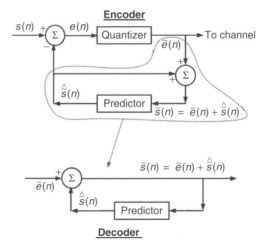

Figure 8.1   Block diagram for differential encoder and decoder.

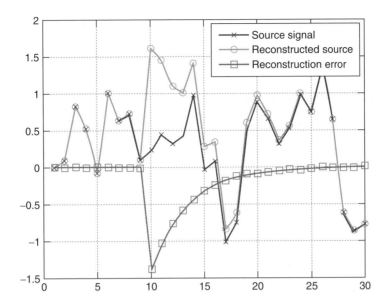

Figure 8.2 The effect of channel errors on a differentially encoded first order autoregressive Gaussian source. Channel errors are introduced only with the tenth transmitted error data.

linear predictor that is just a one-tap prediction filter, with its only coefficient being $a_o = \rho$. That is, the linear predictor is an FIR filter with input–output difference equation, [1],

$$y_n = \rho x_{n-1}.$$

It can be seen in Figure 8.1 that the transmitted data is in fact the quantized error between the input sample and its predicted value.

In this illustrative example, we now suppose that the channel introduces errors that only affect the tenth transmitted data. This data is subject to a binary symmetric channel with bit error rate of 10%. Figure 8.2 shows the impact of this error. As can be seen, before the tenth sample, when there have not been any channel errors, the reconstruction of the source follows the source quite faithfully. When the errors are introduced in the tenth transmitted data, the difference between the source and its reconstruction becomes large. This effect is, of course, as expected; but the higher sensitivity of differential encoding becomes evident as the error in the tenth transmitted data also affects the following samples through the prediction and differential methods used in the kernel of the decoder. The difference between the input source and its reconstruction decays slowly following the damped time constant given by the coefficient of the first order linear prediction filter. Of course, if it was possible to have errors with any of the transmitted data, not just the tenth one, the difference between the input source and its reconstruction would be significant at all times (see the example in Figure 8.3 with all transmissions going through a binary symmetric channel with bit error rate 0.1%).

The effect of channel errors on the reconstructed video also depends on the different importance of the compressed parts of the source or of the bits in the compressed video bit stream. The above-mentioned case of variable-length entropy coding is one example

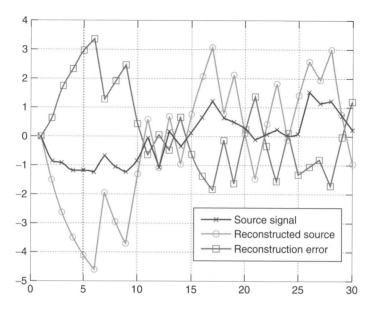

Figure 8.3 The effect of channel errors on a differentially encoded first order autoregressive Gaussian source when all the transmitted data is subject to a binary symmetric channel with bit error rate 0.1%.

of the different importance for the bits in the bit stream. The case of compressing source information that is not equally important is crucial in video communication because it occurs often. Indeed, in video compression the unequal importance of the samples can be related to the different human subjective perception of sample distortion. We illustrate this case with an example using a simplified JPEG image compression scheme. The use of image compression here is only because it lends itself to an example that can be illustrated in a printed medium such as this book, but the observations are equally applicable to video compression. In this case we consider the source encoding and decoding of the image in Figure 8.4 using an eight-by-eight block discrete cosine transform (DCT) followed by quantization using the same quantization matrix and procedure followed in the JPEG image compression standard.

The result of encoding and decoding without channel errors is shown in Figure 8.5, with the reconstructed image on the left and the corresponding pixel-by-pixel squared error on the right. For reference purposes, the measured peak signal-to-noise ratio (PSNR) in this case was 35.3 dB.

In terms of the block-based DCT technique used in JPEG and in this example, the DC coefficient is more important not only in terms of distortion associated with errors in this coefficient, but also in terms of human perception of the image quality. Figure 8.6 shows the same image after affecting the DC coefficients through a binary symmetric channel with bit error rate of 50% (this value of bit error rate is rather exaggerated in practical terms, but appropriate for this example). The figure shows the reconstructed image on the left and the corresponding pixel-by-pixel squared error on the right. In this case, the measured PSNR was 25.5 dB, a value that is also evident from the clearly distorted result in the figure.

Figure 8.4 Original image to be encoded and decoded using a simplified JPEG technique.

Figure 8.5 The recovered image from Figure 8.4, after encoding and decoding. On the left, the reconstructed image and on the right the corresponding squared error.

Figure 8.6 The recovered image from Figure 8.4, after encoding and decoding when the DC coefficients of the block DCT transforms are transmitted through a binary symmetric channel with bit error rate 50%. On the left, the reconstructed image and on the right the corresponding squared error.

Figure 8.7 The recovered image from Figure 8.4, after encoding and decoding the coefficients with coordinates (1,1) of the block DCT transforms, are transmitted through a binary symmetric channel with bit error rate 50%. On the left, the reconstructed image and on the right the corresponding squared error.

The DC coefficient is the most important one, and the rest of the coefficients are not as important. Figure 8.7 shows the same image, after affecting the coefficients with coordinates (1,1) by the same binary symmetric channel with bit error rate of 50% as was used for the DC coefficients. The figure shows the reconstructed image on the left and the corresponding pixel-by-pixel squared error on the right. In this case, the measured PSNR was 34.7 dB, roughly 0.5 dB less than the case with no channel errors. In this case, the errors are so difficult to perceive that the figure that shows the pixel-by-pixel squared error becomes indispensable. In this figure, it can be seen that the biggest distortion is introduced in areas of the original image with some edges in the texture, for example the edges of the seashell-shaped roof of Sydney's opera house.

In multi-view video, there are cases where in the output bit stream from the video compressor it is possible to recognize two parts: one containing color and texture information, and another containing video depth information. This organization is useful in certain applications where the color information can be used to provide backwards compatibility with legacy 2D video systems. It was observed in [2] that the channel errors have a more negative effect in terms of distortion over the color information and less of a negative effect on the video depth information.

In general, the modeling of channel-induced distortion for multi-view video sequences is a complex task. This is because the encoding–decoding process depends on the application of a number of techniques but, more importantly, because the use of differential encoding in both the time domain and between different views creates error propagation effects with complex interrelations in the time and in the inter-view dimensions. The modeling of channel-induced distortion for multi-view video was studied in [3]. In this case, the source encoder exploits the correlation in time and between views. Specifically, denoting by $M(s, t)$ the frame from view s at time t, most of the views are assumed to encode a frame using differential encoding from the previous frame in time, $M(s, t - 1)$, and in the view domain, $M(s - 1, t)$. The only exception to this encoding structure is a view, identified as "view 0", which starts a group of pictures (GoPs) with an intra-predicted frame, encoded independently of any other frame, and follows with frames that are encoded using differential encoding only in the time domain.

Having introduced the encoding model and basic notation, it is possible to illustrate the complexity involved with the modeling of channel-induced distortion with multi-view video. Suppose that a frame $M(s, t)$ is affected by errors during transmission. For this frame it will be necessary to estimate the effects of the errors. Yet, the errors will propagate to frames $M(s + 1, t)$, $M(s + 2, t)$, ..., $M(s + S, t)$, assuming that there are S views, and to frames $M(s, t + 1)$, $M(s, t + 2)$, ..., $M(s, t + T)$, assuming that there are T frames in a GoPs. The propagation of the errors will depend on such factors as the nature of the prediction done during differential encoding, how errors are concealed, and so on. Furthermore, for as much as the previous case assumes the presence of errors in a single frame $M(s, t)$, in practice these errors will occur in multiple frames, creating a complex pattern of interweaved error propagation effects.

To model channel-induced distortion, the work in [3] starts by assuming that the presence of an error in a frame that leads to the loss of a packet results, in turn, in the loss of the complete frame. Also, analytical studies for very simple source and channel coding schemes and video communication simulations all point toward an end-to-end distortion model where the frame source encoding distortion, $D_s(s, t)$, and the frame channel-induced distortion, $D_c(s, t)$, are uncorrelated. Therefore, the end-to-end distortion can be written as:

$$D(s, t) = D_s(s, t) + D_c(s, t).$$

Modeling the channel-induced distortion implies focusing only on the term $D_c(s, t)$.

Let P be the probability of losing a packet and, consequently, also the probability of losing a frame. For a given frame $M(s,t)$, the mean channel-induced distortion follows from the channel-induced distortion when frame $M(s,t)$ is lost, $D_L(s,t)$, and the channel-induced distortion when frame $M(s,t)$ is not lost but is being affected by error propagation from a previous-time or previous-view frame, $D_{NL}(s,t)$:

$$D_c(s,t) = (1 - P) D_{NL}(s,t) + P D_L(s,t).$$

Inter-predicted frames usually switch between macroblocks encoded inter- or intra-prediction. The decision on whether to use one or the other mode is based on an estimation of the resulting distortion. When the frame $M(s,t)$ was not lost, the channel-induced distortion is for the most part due to the propagation of errors that affected a previous frame. These errors may also affect the portion of the frame that is encoded using intra-prediction, as there is a correlation through the decision on whether or not to use intra-prediction, but it has been observed that this effect is negligible. As a consequence, if the average proportion of macroblocks encoded using intra-prediction is Q, the channel-induced distortion in this case can be written as:

$$D_{NL}(s,t) = (1 - Q)\left[V\lambda_b D_c(s, t - 1) + (1 - V)\lambda_a D_c(s - 1, t)\right],$$

where V is the percentage of proportion of macroblocks using differential encoding in the time domain, and λ_b and λ_a are values related with the error-introduced distortion rate of decay while an error propagates when using differential encoding on the view and the time domain, respectively. The two values λ_b and λ_a are intended to capture the gradual decrease in the value of the propagating distortion due to the filtering operation embedded within the prediction in differential encoding, as illustrated with the simple example in Figure 8.2.

When a packet is lost, it is assumed in [3] that this also creates the loss of a frame. Consequently, the study of the channel-induced distortion when a frame $M(s,t)$ is lost also needs to consider how to replace the lost information. This technique, called "error concealment", will be studied in more detail later in this chapter. In the case of the study in [3], the concealment of lost information is implemented in a very simple way, by replacing the lost frame with a copy of the frame in the previous view or time. If the proportion of frames replaced using a copy of the previous frame in time is U, the channel induced distortion when a frame is lost can be written as:

$$D_L(s,t) = U D_{LT}(s,t) + (1 - U)D_{LV}(s,t),$$

where $D_{LT}(s,t)$ is the average distortion when replacing a lost frame with the previous frame in time and $D_{LV}(s,t)$ is the average distortion when replacing a lost frame with the frame in the previous view.

The model for $D_{LT}(s,t)$ is essentially the same as when considering a single-view video and can be written as:

$$D_{LT}(s,t) = D_{TEC}(s,t) + \mu_b D_c(s, t - 1).$$

This expression splits the distortion $D_{LT}(s,t)$ into two terms. The first term, $D_{TEC}(s,t)$, is the distortion due to replacing a lost frame with the previous temporal frame. The second term, $\mu_b D_c(s, t-1)$, characterizes the distortion due to transmission errors, where μ_b is the value modeling the gradual decay in error-introduced distortion when using differential encoding. The value of μ_b may differ from λ_b because in principle the predictors may be operating with different data.

With similar arguments, the distortion $D_{LV}(s, t)$ can be written as:

$$D_{LV}(s, t) = D_{VEC}(s, t) + \mu_a D_c(s-1, t),$$

where it is possible to recognize the same two terms, with analogous variables and functions, as in the expression for $D_{LT}(s, t)$.

Since $D_c(s, t) = (1-P)D_{NL}(s, t) + P\, D_L(s, t)$, it is now possible to combine all the different components of the channel-induced distortion shown above to get:

$$D_c(s, t) = \left[(1-P)(1-Q)\,V\lambda_b + PU\mu_b\right]D_c(s, t-1)$$
$$+ \left[(1-P)(1-Q)(1-V)\lambda_a + P(1-U)\mu_a\right]D_c(s-1, t)$$
$$+ P\left[U D_{TEC}(s, t) + (1-U)D_{VEC}(s, t)\right].$$

As can be seen, the channel-induced distortion depends on the distortion performance delivered by the error concealment scheme being used, and the distortion from previous temporal and view frames. The degree to which the channel-induced distortion from previous frames decreases over time depends on the values $[(1-P)(1-Q)V\lambda_b + PU\mu_b]$ and $[(1-P)(1-Q)(1-V)\lambda_a + P(1-U)\mu_a]$ for the time domain and previous view domain. These values depend on the statistics of the video sequence and characteristics of the video encoder.

As a summary of this section, we note that errors introduced during transmission of compressed video will have an effect on end-to-end distortion that will be combined with the distortion already introduced during the video compression stage. The magnitude of the channel error effect will depend on several factors related to the communication process itself. In the rest of this chapter we will be focusing on channel-induced errors and their effect on end-to-end distortion. We will discuss techniques to reduce the sensitivity to errors, to recover from them, and to efficiently protect against them.

8.2 Error Resilience

In this section we will be discussing error resilience techniques. As we shall see over the rest of this chapter, it is sometimes difficult to make a clear demarcation as to whether a particular technique is an error resilience technique or rather belongs to one of the other types of techniques to be discussed in later sections. For the purpose of keeping an ordered presentation, we will consider error resilience those that introduce certain structure and techniques within the transmitted 3D video bit stream that reduces or limits the negative effects of channel errors on the recovered video.

One approach to provide larger error resilience to an encoded 3D video bit stream is to modify the compression procedure or the resulting compressed bit stream to aid in the recovery from errors or to provide a level of embedded redundancy in the encoding of information. This approach is contrary to the goals for signal compression, which aims at eliminating as much redundancy as possible from the source. Consequently, it is expected that the changes associated with added error resilience would result in the source encoder having less compression efficiency. This may not necessarily be a bad outcome since the measure of quality for 3D video has to be of an end-to-end nature, meaning with this that it has to include both distortion due to compression and distortion introduced in the communication channel. A good error resilience technique should trade a moderate or small increase in distortion from signal compression for a larger reduction in channel-induced distortion, with the overall result of achieving a lower end-to-end distortion.

An error resilience technique based on modifying the calculation of motion vectors was presented in [4]. The technique presented in this work is based on the observation that motion information from color and depth shows a high correlation. As such, the technique is applicable to the compression of 3D video based on separate motion-compensated differential encoding for the color and depth components. Error resilience is introduced by, instead of generating two correlated sets of motion vectors, generating one combined motion vector set resulting from the motion estimation jointly using the color and depth information. This is implemented by using an algorithm that searches for the best position to estimate motion by minimizing the cost function:

$$C\left(x, y\right) = SAD_{Color}\left(x, y\right) + SAD_{Depth}\left(x, y\right) \frac{\max\left(SAD_{Color}\right)}{\max\left(SAD_{Depth}\right)} + MV_{Cost},$$

where $C(x,y)$ is the cost associated with the motion vector with coordinates (x,y), $SAD_{Color}(x,y)$ is the sum of absolute differences (SAD) of color information when the selected motion vector is the one with coordinates (x,y), $SAD_{Depth}(x,y)$ is the SAD of depth information when the selected motion vector is the one with coordinates (x,y), SAD_{Color} is the matrix for color information with the SAD value for each coordinate within the search window, SAD_{Depth} is the same as SAD_{Color} but for depth information, and MV_{Cost} is the cost of the selected motion vector, which depends on the number of bits needed to transmit the differentially encoded motion vectors.

As a result of the joint motion estimation, the motion vectors transmitted for the color information and for the depth information are the same. This characteristic is used to improve the error concealment operation as the motion vectors received in the color stream can be used to conceal packet lost in the depth stream and vice versa. Since the motion vectors determined in this joint manner are not as closely matched to the motion vectors that would be obtained from independent motion estimation for the color and depth components, the compression efficiency of the resulting 3D video compressor is less than what would be achieved with a separate motion estimation procedure on the color and depth components. Nevertheless, as shown in [4], the end-to-end quality results, measured as PSNR as a function of packet loss rate, is better than a 3D video compression system with independent motion estimation by close to 1 dB. The only exception to the improvement in end-to-end performance is for sequences with low motion because for these sequences the penalty in compression efficiency due to the joint motion estimation is the largest.

Another technique for error resilience based on using the redundancy in the source encoder is given in [5]. The intrinsic characteristics of 3D video offers new opportunities for the exploitation of the redundancy within the source. Indeed, when considering a group of successive frames from multiple views it is possible to recognize three types of correlation between frames:

- temporal: the correlation between frames of the same view which are close by in time,
- disparity: the correlation between frames of different views occurring at the same time; this is also called inter-view correlation,
- mixed: the correlation between frames of different views occurring close by in time.

These types of correlation are important in 3D video coding because they can be leveraged through prediction for differential encoding or estimation for added error resilience. The names given to the different types of correlation are also used for the prediction and estimation using it. In this way, we can talk for example of a disparity prediction or a temporal estimation.

The 3D video encoder designed in [5] adds error resilience to the compressed bit stream by including for one view frame two descriptions: one that could be seen as the usually present one, obtained from exploiting disparity correlation on I-frames with exploiting temporal correlation on P-frames, and a second one that is obtained from disparity prediction on all frames and that adds error resilience (see Figure 8.8). As can be seen in the figure, the structure of the encoder also recognizes two layers: a base layer, which is the representation of one view from which the representation of the second view is derived, and an enhancement layer which is the representation of the second view. Error resilience is introduced in the enhancement layer only, because its generation depends on the information in the base layer. As a brief side comment, we note that this technique can also be seen as an instance of multiple description coding, a technique that will be discussed later in this chapter.

The redundant disparity-based description that is added to the compressed bit stream provides error resilience by providing an alternative information source that can be used

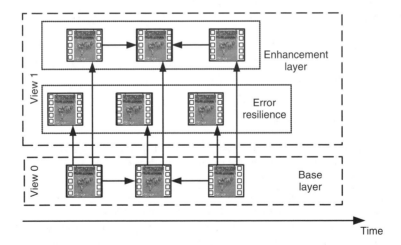

Figure 8.8 Frame interdependencies for an error resilient 3D video encoder by adding an extra representation using disparity correlation as in [5].

during decoding when certain parts of the compressed video stream are lost during transmission. As such, if a temporally predicted part of a frame from view 1 is lost, most of the lost information can be recovered from the corresponding disparity-predicted data and the use of error concealment techniques (to be discussed in the next section). Also, if both the temporally predicted and its corresponding disparity-predicted part of a frame in view 1 are lost, the potential error propagation that would occur due to the use of differential encoding could be stopped by discarding the correlated temporally predicted information and replacing it with the corresponding disparity-predicted data. Error propagation would be stopped in this case because the disparity-predicted data is not correlated with the lost information from view 1 but, instead, is correlated with the received information from view 0.

As is to be expected, when adding redundancy into the source encoder operation, the efficiency in compressing 3D video is reduced with this scheme. In fact, the compression performance results reported in [5] show quality losses, measured as PSNR, between 1 and 2 dB. Nevertheless, as pointed out earlier, the advantages of error resilience become clear when considering the end-to-end distortion and not just distortion due to compression. When evaluating end-to-end PSNR the results in [5] show quality improvement of up to 3 dB with high packet loss rates of 20%. The results also show that when the packet loss rate is relatively low, below around 7%, an equivalent scheme without error resilience has better end-to-end quality. This is obviously because at packet loss rates that are relatively low, the major component in end-to-end distortion is due to the source compression, so there is no advantage to be gained by using error resilience under these operating conditions. In fact, the metric that determines what should be considered as a large or small packet loss rate is the relation between source compression and channel-induced distortion. In the range of operating conditions where source compression distortion accounts for the majority of end-to-end distortion, the packet loss rate, and the channel effects for any general consideration, is considered to be low. When the end-to-end distortion has a major component due to transmission impairments, the packet loss rate, or the channel impairments in general, are large. Finally, recall that when using differential encoding, as is the case with most video encoders, when the channel introduces an error, the error propagates over the correlated encoded information. As illustrated in Figure 8.2, this error may eventually die off at a rate that is given by the prediction filter characteristics. The results in [5] also show how the use of error resilience damps the error propagation from using differential encoding.

8.3 Error Concealment

There are numerous techniques with the goal of preventing the occurrence of channel-induced errors, reducing the sensitivity of the compressed video stream to these errors, or recovering from errors, but the reality is that errors will eventually be introduced by channel impairments. This section discusses techniques that allow the decoder to conceal and limit the effects of these errors on the reconstructed video.

The general idea for error concealment is to replace part of a missing frame with an estimate of it. This involves using other parts of the video sequence that are correlated with the missing one and possibly combining it with other available information so as to obtain the best possible estimate for replacing the missing part of the video. Figure 8.9

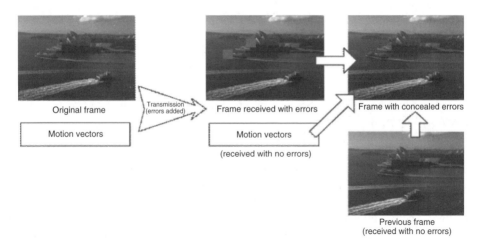

Original frame

Motion vectors

Transmission (errors added)

Frame received with errors

Motion vectors (received with no errors)

Frame with concealed errors

Previous frame (received with no errors)

Figure 8.9 Illustration of error concealment in legacy single-view video, replacing lost macroblocks with the motion-compensated macroblocks from the previous frame received with no errors.

illustrates what is perhaps the best case scenario for error concealment in legacy single-view video. In this example, two macroblocks of a frame have errors after decoding and need to be discarded. Fortunately, we assume that the motion vectors for the frame with errors and the previous frame are received with no errors. In this case, the discarded macroblocks can be replaced by using the correctly received motion vectors to estimate the lost macroblocks by doing motion compensation from the previous frame.

Multi-view video offers more options for correlated information that can be used to do error concealment. In addition to the possibilities already present in single-view video, using spatial and temporal correlation plus motion vector information, multi-view video also offers the disparity correlation between different views. However, having more options presents the challenge of choosing the best one. That is, one problem of interest with multi-view error concealment is what received data that is correlated with the lost information to use to achieve the best error concealment results. This problem is addressed in [6] by presenting the following simple procedure:

(a) Denote as $l_1, l_2, \ldots, l_L$ the lost macroblocks in a frame from view v at time index n.
(b) Denote as $p_1, p_2, \ldots, p_L$ the macroblocks in the same spatial position in the frame from view v at time index $n-1$.
(c) Denote as $s_1, s_2, \ldots, s_L$ the macroblocks in the same spatial position in the frame from view v at time index $n-2$.
(d) Denote as $m_1, m_2, \ldots, m_L$ the macroblocks in the same spatial position in the frame from view w at time index $n-1$.
(e) Calculate

$$\text{SSD}_{ps} = \sum_{i=1}^{L} \Delta_{psi},$$

where Δ_{psi} is the squared differences between the pixels in macroblocks p_i and s_i.

(f) Calculate

$$\text{SSD}_{pm} = \sum_{i=1}^{L} \Delta_{pm_i},$$

where Δ_{pm_i} is the squared differences between the pixels in macroblocks p_i and m_i.

(g) Evaluate whether $\text{SSD}_{ps} \leq \text{SSD}_{pm}$, in which case the macroblocks $l_1, l_2, \ldots, l_L$ are replaced by $p_1, p_2, \ldots, p_L$.

(h) When $\text{SSD}_{ps} > \text{SSD}_{pm}$ the macroblocks $l_1, l_2, \ldots, l_L$ are replaced by $m_1, m_2, \ldots, m_L$.

In most 3D video compression algorithms one of the views is encoded as a single-view video sequence, that is, using temporal motion compensation, while the other view is encoded using both temporal motion compensation and other-view disparity differential encoding. Then, while the first view does not depend on another view for encoding and decoding, the second view does. This is a key difference that influences how error concealment can be implemented. This issue is addressed in [7]. In this work, it was assumed that the left view is encoded using only temporal motion compensation and that the right view is encoded using both temporal motion compensation and disparity differential encoding with respect to the left view.

The first error concealment case studied in [7] is when the right view is received with errors and the left view is received correctly. Here, the problem may have two stages. The first part of the problem is how to replace motion and disparity vectors if they had been lost due to channel-introduced errors. If this is the case, the motion and disparity vectors are replaced by selecting candidate replacement vectors as those that had been correctly received and are from regions in the affected frame that neighbor the area where the information was lost. Each candidate replacement vector has associated a possible replacing macroblock from the reference frame from which the vector is derived and that can be used for error concealment. The next task is to select one replacement macroblock. This is accomplished by choosing the candidate replacement macroblock with the minimum absolute difference between the external boundary of the lost macroblock in the current frame and the internal boundary of the replacing macroblock in the reference frame.

Nevertheless, the presentation in [7] successfully argues against performing error concealment by simply replacing one lost macroblock with another macroblock (this is, in fact, the simple idea illustrated in Figure 8.9). This is because the effects of motion or view disparity do not affect all pixels in a macroblock in the same way. With this observation in mind, the improvement proposed in [7] is based on an "overlapped block motion and disparity compensation" (OBMDC) operation that replaces each pixel in the lost macroblock with a weighted combination of pixels in the same location but from more than one replacement macroblock, using the expression:

$$p_{\text{lost}}(x, y) = \frac{w_1 p^*(x, y) + w_2 \sum_v p_{\text{cent}}(x, y) + w_3 \sum_{\tilde{v}} p_{\text{cent}}(x, y)}{w_1 + \sum_v w_2 + w_3 \sum_{\tilde{v}} w_3},$$

where $p_{\text{lost}}(x, y)$ is the new replacement pixel at coordinates (x, y), $p^*(x, y)$ is the pixel at the same coordinates associated with the previously selected best vector (that is, the pixel that belongs to the macroblock with the minimum absolute difference between the external boundary of the lost macroblock in the current frame and the internal boundary of the replacing macroblock in the reference frame), $p_{cndt}(x, y)$ is a pixel from one of the other candidate macroblocks (which was not selected as best), v refers to pixels in the same view as the one with errors, $\bar{v}$ refers to the other view, and w_1, w_2, and w_3 are the weights chosen so that $w_1 > w_2 > w_3$. Note that the choice $w_1 > w_2 > w_3$ implies that the previously chosen best macroblock still retains a higher weight, followed by macroblocks in the same block and lastly macroblocks in the other view. In [7], w_1, w_2, and w_3 are chosen equal to 5, 4, and 3, respectively.

Recall next that in [7] it is assumed that the left view acts as reference for encoding the right view using disparity differential encoding. As a consequence, the presence of lost or discarded macroblocks in the left view adds the challenge of error propagation in the right view also. In [7], it is argued that the best approach to tackling this issue is to perform error concealment on the left view and then decode the right view using the concealed macroblocks from the left view.

In addition to losses at the level of a number of macroblocks, it is possible that channel impairments may lead toward the loss of a frame. In this case, it is necessary to apply error concealment techniques at the frame level. In [8] the problem is approached for a 3D video compressor that encodes the information into a color and a depth component. For the purpose of implementing the error concealment technique, the encoder is modified to operate using a "shared motion vectors" mode. This mode, which in fact can be considered an instance of error resilience encoding, does motion estimation and calculation of motion vectors only for the color component of the encoded video. The resulting motion vectors are used of course to encode the color information but they are also used to encode the depth information. With this configuration, when a color frame is lost, the motion vectors can be recovered and the lost frame concealed by using a correctly received depth frame. Conversely, when a depth frame is lost, it can be concealed by using the received shared motion vectors and a correctly received corresponding color frame. The results presented in [8] show that the use of shared motion vectors has a relatively small impact on the source encoder coding efficiency since it introduces a penalty of around 1 dB in the PSNR. At the same time, the resulting frame loss concealment scheme has a performance of 3 dB or better for most operating conditions when compared to a frame replacement solution.

For the case of multi-view video sequences, [9] discusses three different error concealment techniques and a method to choose the best one to use. The first technique, identified as "temporal bilateral error concealment" (TBEC) uses a temporally correlated previous and subsequent frame to estimate the motion vector. By assuming that the motion vector in the video was constant during the time elapsed between the previous and the subsequent frame, the motion vector is estimated to be equal to that derived from the motion estimation using the previous and subsequent frames. Having estimated a motion vector, the concealed pixel is the average between the motion compensated pixels in the previous and subsequent frames. Note that the main limitation of this scheme is the assumption that the motion vector stays invariant in the time elapsed between the previous and subsequent frames. Consequently, this error concealment technique will perform better, the less motion is present in the video sequence.

The TBEC error concealment technique can be further extended to the particular correlated information offered by multi-view video. This technique, called "inter-view bilateral error concealment" (IBEC) estimates the disparity vector by using the view to the left and to the right of the one to be concealed. The technique is based on the assumption that the cameras for each view are located in a parallel configuration, with the objects in the video at a sufficient distance that the disparity vectors can be assumed constant between the views to the left and to the right of the one to be error-concealed. With this assumption, the disparity vector is estimated to be equal to the disparity vector derived from the disparity estimation using the views to the left and to the right. Having estimated a disparity vector, the concealed pixel is the average between the disparity-compensated pixels from the views to the left and to the right. Note that the main limitation of this scheme is the assumption that the disparity vector stays invariant between the views to the left and to the right. As such, this technique does not work well when there are objects that are occluded in some of the three views being considered and not in the rest.

The third error concealment technique, discussed in [9], is called "multi-hypothesis error concealment" (MHEC), and is reminiscent of the scheme discussed above from [7] where candidate replacement vectors are selected from those that had been correctly received and are from the same regions in the affected frame. In the case of I-views and P-views, the candidate vectors are those from the previous and subsequent frames, and in the case of B-views the candidate vectors are selected also from the previous and subsequent frames and, in addition, the views to the left and to the right of the one that is the target for concealment. Each candidate replacement vector has associated a possible replacing block from the reference frame from which the vector is derived and that can be used for error concealment. In the MHEC technique, the candidate replacement blocks with the two smallest sum of absolute differences (SAD) are used to replace the lost block using the relation:

$$\mathbf{B} = w\mathbf{B}_1 + (1 - w)\mathbf{B}_2,$$

where $\mathbf{B}$ is the replacement block, $\mathbf{B}_1$ is the candidate block with the smallest SAD, $\mathbf{B}_2$ is the candidate block with the second smallest SAD and w is the applied weight (with possible values between 0 and 1) which was chosen equal to 2/3. In the case of this error concealment technique, it is necessary to bear in mind that the selection of the two best replacement blocks becomes unreliable when the reference frames have different motions or disparities.

From the above discussion, it is possible to see that the three techniques discussed in [9] follow well-established principles but also are limited in their performance under some operating conditions. Consequently, the last challenge to address in the error concealment technique in [9] is which of the three error concealment techniques to use in each case. This is decided by computing for each of the three techniques the cost function:

$$C\left(\mathbf{x}_1, \mathbf{x}_2\right) = SAD\left(\mathbf{x}_1\right) + SAD\left(\mathbf{x}_2\right) + \lambda\left(\|\mathbf{x}_1^2\| + \|\mathbf{x}_2^2\|\right),$$

where λ is a weighting factor and $\mathbf{x}_1$ and $\mathbf{x}_2$ are, respectively, the motion vector and the negative of the motion vector used in TBEC, the disparity vector and the negative of the disparity vector used in IBEC, and the blocks $\mathbf{B}_1$ and $\mathbf{B}_2$ for the MHEC technique. Once the cost function has been computed for the three techniques, the one with lowest result is the one chosen.

8.4 Unequal Error Protection

As mentioned earlier in this chapter, in a video communication system, the output of the source encoder is a bit stream that usually has different parts and a great deal of structure. Within the bit stream, headers and markers separate frames and group of frames. But even beyond this structure, there is a structure within the source encoded bit stream corresponding to a single frame. Within this portion of the bit stream it is usually possible to recognize different parts corresponding to the different outputs from the source encoder operation. For example, it will usually be possible to recognize a part composed of entropy-coded information resulting from the compression of a frame texture, if it is an intra-predicted frame, or resulting from the compression of a motion compensated prediction error frame if the frame is not intra-predicted. Within the source encoded bit stream for non-intra-predicted frames it will be possible to find, for example, another part containing the motion vector information, which is frequently encoded using differential encoding.

In essence, the different parts of the compressed video bit stream result in different reconstruction distortion after being affected by channel errors. To reduce the likelihood of these errors happening, it is necessary to add forward error control (FEC) to the compressed video bit stream. This implies adding redundant bits that will help identify and correct some errors. Since these added redundancy bits will increase the bit rate required to transmit the video, they bring the problem of how much error protection redundancy to add. Adding enough redundancy so as to have the strong error correcting code required by those parts of the bit stream that yield the most distortion would result in an inefficient excess of redundancy for the other parts. Adding redundancy matched to the average error-related distortion performance between all the parts of the bit stream is both excessive for the parts that need little error protection and insufficient for the parts that need the most error protection. Of course, adding a small amount of redundancy, such as that usually needed by most of the parts of the bit stream, may be cheap in terms of transmission bit rate increase but would result in severe distortion of those few parts requiring a lot more error protection. In summary, the best approach in terms of striking the best tradeoff between distortion performance and added error control redundancy is to assign different levels of error protection to the different parts of the source encoded bit stream, according to the impact that the channel errors on that part would have on the end-to-end distortion. This assignment of different error protection to different parts of the source encoded bit stream is a technique called "unequal error protection" (UEP).

With 3D video, different frames have different importance, depending on their temporal dependency and the effects that their loss or corruption produces. For example, I-frames are the most important of all frames because their loss will propagate error into the reconstruction of all dependent P-frames. Also, if P-frames from a view, say, the right view, are used to predict and differentially encode the other view, then it is more important for these frames to be received with no errors. These observations, common to 3D video, naturally lend themselves to a UEP error protection scheme design. This is the problem approached in [10], where both a rate-distortion optimized and a UEP protection scheme are designed for a 3D video codec derived from the H.264 codec. A simplified block diagram, showing the configuration for this video codec is shown in Figure 8.10.

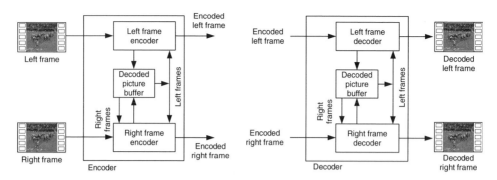

Figure 8.10 Simplified block diagram for the H.264-based 3D video encoder and decoder from [11].

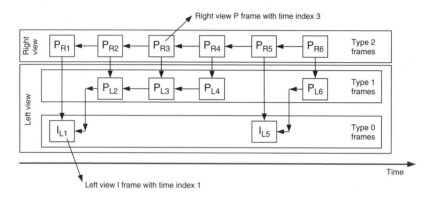

Figure 8.11 Frames types and their interdependency for the H.264-based 3D video encoder and decoder from [11].

Figure 8.10 shows a typical configuration for a video codec that outputs I-frames and P-frames, implemented with the H.264 codec, but now expanded to provide 3D functionality by adding a decoded picture buffer that allows differential encoding of one view based on the other view. The interdependency of the different frames is shown in Figure 8.11. The figure introduces, for ease of discussion, a classification of frames into three different types. Frames of different types have different importance. As such, frames of type 0 are the most important ones because their loss affects all P-frames from both views. Frames of type 1 (left view, P-frames) are second in importance because their loss affects P-frames from both views. Frames of type 2 (right view, P-frames) are the least important ones because their loss only affects other frames of the same type.

As mentioned, the design in [10] follows two main steps. In the first step, the video encoding rate is calculated for the three types of frames using as a criterion the minimization of the overall distortion subject to total rate limitations. This step of the design is the well-known problem of using knowledge of the rate-distortion (RD) source codec curve to do bit rate allocation so as to minimize distortion. The different twist to this problem is the presence of the different views from the 3D view. Nevertheless, considering the different views is not too different from considering the different predictive types of frames in 2D video. To solve this design problem, it is necessary to derive first the RD curve. In [10], this is done by extending the model for 2D RD curves. Consequently, the RD curve for a type 0 frame is found to be:

$$D_0 = \frac{\theta_0}{R_0 + R_{c0}} + D_{c0},$$

where D_0 is the distortion of a type 0 frame when encoding at a rate R_0. The variables θ_0, R_{c0} and D_{c0} are coded-specific adjustment values for the model that need to be calculated through simulations and curve fitting. Similarly, the RD curve for a type 1 frame is:

$$D_1 = \frac{\theta_1}{R_1 + C_1 R_0 + R_{c1}} + D_{c1},$$

where D_1 is the distortion of a type 1 frame when encoding at a rate R_1, and θ_1, C_1, R_{c1}, and D_{c1} are the adjustment variables that need to be computed to match the model to the codec performance. Note that the RD curve for a type 1 frame depends also on the rate used for type 0 frames, making explicit the need of type 0 frames in the encoding and decoding of type 1 frames. Finally, and reasoning in the same way, the RD curve for a type 2 frame is:

$$D_2 = \frac{\theta_2}{R_2 + C_2 R_0 + C_3 R_1 + R_{c2}} + D_{c2},$$

where D_2 is the distortion of a type 2 frame when encoding at a rate R_2, and θ_2, C_2, C_3, R_{c2}, and D_{c2} are the adjustment variables that need to be computed to match the model to the codec performance. Knowing the RD performance from the three types of frames allows calculating the total RD model:

$$D_T = D_0 + D_1 + D_2$$

$$= \frac{\theta_0}{R_0 + R_{c0}} + \frac{\theta_1}{R_1 + C_1 R_0 + R_{c1}} + \frac{\theta_2}{R_2 + C_2 R_0 + C_3 R_1 + R_{c2}} + D_{cT},$$

where $D_{cT} = D_{c0} + D_{c1} + D_{c2}$. With this intermediate result it is now possible to write the rate allocation design problem:

$$\min_{R_0, R_1, R_2} D_T,$$

$$\text{subject to } R_0 + R_1 + R_2 = (1 - p) R_{CH},$$

where p is the proportional increase in bit rate due to the added redundancy and R_{CH} is the total bit rate supported for transmission over the channel. One of the advantages of the model used for DR function is that the design problem can be solved using simply the Lagrange multiplier method. The result is the optimal allocation of encoding rate to each type of frame. In the above formulation, one possible debatable assumption is whether the total distortion can actually be assumed to be equal to the sum of distortions from each frame type $D_T = D_0 + D_1 + D_2$. As it turns out, it is possible to make this assumption in this case, as results presented in [10] show that the result from the Lagrange multiplier based rate assignment is very close to the optimal solution.

The 3D video codec in this case retains many of the characteristics and structure of the H.264 video codec because it was implemented as an adaptation from it. In particular, the output from the encoder is organized into data packets called the "network abstraction layer" (NAL). Losing a NAL unit during transmission means losing a number of macroblocks from a type 0, type 1, or type 2 frame. Yet, as discussed earlier, the effect of losing a NAL unit is more important when the NAL unit contains macroblock data from a type 0 frame rather than from a type 1 frame and even less important if the macroblock contains data from a type 2 frame. Therefore, a UEP scheme that considers this effect will achieve a more efficient redundancy allocation. In [10] this is done by first calculating the average distortion linked with losing a NAL unit associated with each of the three frames types. For NAL units associated with type 0 frames, the average distortion D_{L0} is the mean squared difference between the original macroblocks and their replacement using spatial error concealment. For NAL units associated with type 1 and type 2 frames, the average distortions D_{L1} and D_{L2} are the mean squared difference between the original macroblocks and their replacement using temporal error concealment. With this result, the UEP design problem consists of distributing redundancy between the three frame types. Formally, this can be written as:

$$\min_{p_0,\, p_1,\, p_2} \left\{ D_0 P_0 \frac{R_0}{(1-p)R_{CH}} + D_1 P_1 \frac{R_1}{(1-p)R_{CH}} + D_2 P_2 \frac{R_2}{(1-p)R_{CH}} \right\},$$

$$\text{subject to } p_0 R_0 + p_1 R_1 + p_2 R_2 = p R_{CH},$$

where p_0, p_1, and p_2 are the proportion of the bit rate allocated to frame types 0, 1, and 2, respectively, used for redundancy. Also, P_0, P_1, and P_2 are the loss probability for frame types 0, 1, and 2, respectively, and which depend on the FEC technique used and the channel conditions and parameters. Note that in the expression for the problem formulation:

$$\frac{R_0}{(1-p)R_{CH}}$$

is the probability that a NAL unit is associated with a type 0 frame,

$$\frac{R_1}{(1-p)R_{CH}}$$

is the probability that a NAL unit is associated with a type 1 frame, and

$$\frac{R_2}{(1-p)R_{CH}}$$

is the probability that a NAL unit is associated with a type 2 frame. The constraint $p_0 R_0 + p_1 R_1 + p_2 R_2 = p R_{CH}$ in the UEP design formulation expresses that the combined redundancy from NAL units associated with all the frame types should equal the total transmitted redundancy.

The error protection in [10] is implemented using systematic Raptor codes, [12]. With this setting, the UEP scheme shows 3–8 dB improvement in PSNR when compared to the equivalent scheme with no UEP (the redundancy is distributed evenly among the three types of frames) and is approximately 4 dB away from the PSNR performance with no channel errors.

8.5 Multiple Description Coding

Multiple description coding is a source compression technique where the bit stream at the output of the encoder instead of having the usual single coded representation of the source, it now has multiple representations. For example, Figure 8.12 illustrates the particular case of a dual description encoder and decoder, where the number of descriptions is two. Encoding using multiple description coding also has the property that during decoding, each description can be decoded independently of the others, each resulting in a reconstruction of the source that can be considered to have a baseline quality. At the same time, the decoder can combine multiple descriptions (in principle, those that had been received with no errors in a communication setting) and obtain a reconstruction of the source with better quality than the baseline obtained from individual descriptions. Multiple description codecs are usually used in communication scenarios where each description can be communicated through a different link, independent of the others. In this way, each description will be affected through channel impairments that are independent of the others. With multiple description coding, receiving only one description is all that is required to recover a description of the source of usually fair quality. If more than one description is received, they can be combined at the decoder to obtain a reconstruction of the source with better quality. It is because of this operation that multiple description coding is often used for transmission diversity schemes at the physical layer. These transmission diversity schemes achieve through different means transmission paths that are independently affected by channel impairments.

Multiple description (MD) codecs were first studied in the context of rate distortion theory. The rate distortion performance of MD codecs was first studied by Ozarov, [13]. Succeeding works studied the use of MD codecs for communications over parallel channels [14, 15]. Also, as mentioned earlier in this chapter, MD coding can be straightforwardly applied in error resilience schemes where the bit stream at the output of the source encoder contains embedded redundancy. In this case, the particular approach seen with MD coding aims at making it possible to recover at least a representation of the source with basic quality. This relation between MD coding and error resilience has resulted in many research works studying this application, such as those in [16, 17].

Within MD codecs, the dual description ones are of particular interest because their simpler configuration has allowed for better understanding of its theoretical performance limits, measured through the rate-distortion (RD) function. In principle, there is no limitation to prevent each description being encoded at a different rate. Therefore, let R_{D1}

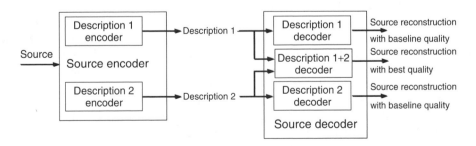

Figure 8.12 A dual description encoder and decoder.

and R_{D2} be the source encoding rates for the first and second description, respectively. At the receiver, if either of the two descriptions is decoded independently of the other, the achievable DR function follows the same performance as for single description coding:

$$D_{D1}\left(R_{D1}\right) = 2^{-2R_{D1}},$$

$$D_{D2}\left(R_{D2}\right) = 2^{-2R_{D2}}.$$

When the two descriptions are combined and decoded together, the achievable DR function is equal to:

$$D_M\left(R_1, R_2\right) = \frac{2^{-2(R_{D1}+R_{D2})}}{\sqrt{\left(1 - 2^{-2R_{D1}}\right)\left(1 - 2^{-2R_{D2}}\right)}},$$

in the low distortion case defined when $D_{D1} - D_{D2} - D_M < 1$ and equal to:

$$D_M\left(R_1, R_2\right) = 2^{-2(R_{D1}+R_{D2})},$$

in the high distortion case.

Of all the possible sources, video, be it single or multi-view, offers perhaps the largest and best example of the use of multiple description coding. For example, a simple implementation of a dual description 2D video codec can split the input video stream into odd and even numbered frames, obtaining two video sequences with half the frame rate as the input sequence. Then, the encoder compresses each of the two video sequences independently of the other, generating two coded descriptions. At the receiver, if only one of the descriptions is received unaffected by channel impairments, the decoder can still output a reconstruction of the original video sequence of lower quality because either the output video will be of half frame rate or it would have the original frame rate but with the missing frames being estimated through interpolation of the frames in the single recovered description. If, instead, both descriptions can be decoded at the receiver, it will be possible to recover a video sequence with the same quality as the original. Nevertheless, note that the compression efficiency of this dual description video codec will not be as good as the one for an equivalent single description video codec. This is because the motion estimation and differential encoding of the half frame rate sequence is not as efficient as that for the full rate sequence.

Multi-view and 3D video present more opportunities for multiple description coding than those found in 2D video. Two possible multiple description 3D video coding schemes are presented in [18]. The first, illustrated in Figure 8.13, is a direct extension of the even-odd frame split described above for 2D video. The only difference in this case, besides the obvious one of now having two views, is that the descriptions are fully complementary of each other. That is, while description 1 encodes the even-numbered frames, with an I-frame on the right view and disparity prediction encoding on the left view, description 2 has the I-frame on the left view and disparity prediction on the right view.

The second multiple description 3D video coding scheme presented in [18] is illustrated in Figure 8.14. This scheme includes more sophisticated processing than the previous one. As shown in Figure 8.14, both descriptions encode all frames. While description 1 encodes the left view using disparity prediction, description 2 encodes the right view

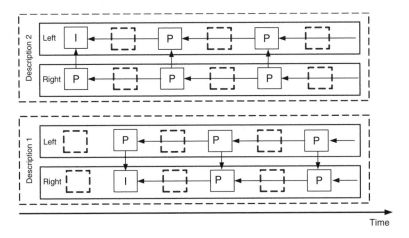

Figure 8.13 Frame interdependencies for a dual description 3D video codec with descriptions based on odd-even frame separation.

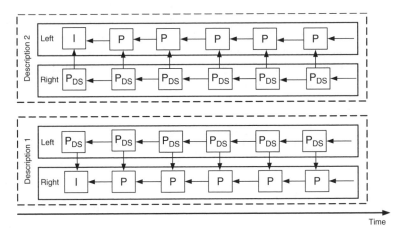

Figure 8.14 Frame interdependencies for a dual description 3D video codec based on downsampling the disparity-predicted frames in each description.

using disparity prediction. Furthermore, in each description the frames of the views being encoded using disparity prediction are also downsampled. The operation of downsampling a video frame consists in performing a two-dimensional low-pass filtering, followed by decimation of the frame. The decimation is implemented by keeping only every other pixel in the frame being decimated. The end result is that the downsampled frame has a lower, or coarser, spatial resolution. Usually, with each downsampling pass, the spatial resolution is halved. In [18], the implemented downsampling factors were two and four, meaning that the implementation of the downsampling followed one and two passes, respectively. For this scheme, the results presented in [18] show that the quality when only being able to decode a single description is still acceptable. The penalty in extra bits used during encoding depends on the level of encoded video sequence disparity correlation. When the disparity correlation is small, the number of extra bits used in this dual description scheme is also small and, of course, the number of extra bits used in this dual description scheme is large when the disparity correlation is large.

Some of the 3D video codecs used in the schemes earlier in this chapter result in compressed video bit streams containing two components: color information and depth information. A multiple description coding scheme based on this type of codec is presented in [19]. The approach taken can be seen as a combination of the different techniques already discussed in this section. First, a dual description codec can be implemented by separating the odd and even frames into two descriptions, each with their corresponding color and depth components. Next, in order to reduce the extra bits added by the embedded redundancy in multiple descriptions, downsampling can be applied to the color and depth components of the descriptions. Here there are multiple possible options and combinations onto which component to apply decimation. For example, decimation could be applied to only the depth components of both descriptions or it could be applied to the depth components of both descriptions and to the color information in alternate frames from the descriptions. The downsampled component can be transmitted to reduce the number of transmitted frames or it is also possible to introduce another form of multiple description by including in the coded bit stream both the non-downsampled and the downsampled component. Because for 3D video reconstruction quality purposes, color information is more important than depth information, it is preferable to transmit an extra description of downsampled color information before doing so for depth information. As a matter of fact, in [19] a good number of different combinations are tried. The most complete case is where, for each of the two descriptions, even and odd numbered frames, both downsampled and non-downsampled depth and color components are transmitted. A less complete, but more efficient, configuration is where for each of the two descriptions, even and odd numbered frames, both the downsampled and non-downsampled depth and only the downsampled color components are transmitted. A variation of this configuration is where, for each of the two descriptions, even and odd numbered frames, both the downsampled and non-downsampled depth and only the non-downsampled color components are transmitted. The performance results discussed in [19] for these schemes show that when the channel impairment consists of relatively low packet loss rate, the overhead in extra transmitted bits due to multiple descriptions is a performance penalty that results in a loss of quality of approximately 2 dB. But, when channel impairments are in the form of a relatively large packet loss rate, the multiple descriptions provide better end-to-end quality.

8.6 Cross-Layer Design

As discussed in Chapter 6, network protocols are organized in what is a called a "layered architecture". In this architecture, the different functions and services needed for end-to-end communication of information, 3D video in our case, are divided into stacked layers. At the transmitter side, upper layers of the stack pass on information to the layer immediately below and lower layers of the stack provide services to the layer immediately above. The key concept to note in the layered protocol stack architecture is that layers pass on information and provide services only to those contiguous layers immediately below and above a given layer. In a cross-layer approach, this concept is replaced by the idea that layers can exchange information and provide services between noncontiguous layers. This idea of cross-layering still maintains the modularity of layers seen in a layered architecture. Another interpretation for a cross-layer approach where modularity is lost, consists in merging multiple layers into a single one.

One application of cross-layer design for the wireless communication of 3D video is studied in [20]. In this case, cross-layering is proposed for the very interesting application, very much relevant to 3D video, where for the foreseeable future 3D video services will have to maintain backwards compatibility with 2D services. This is because during the period of mass-market deployment of 3D services and viewing devices, a good proportion of users will still be using devices that are only useful for 2D content. Consequently, a user with a 2D video viewing device should be able to see the limited content in 2D by extracting it from the backward-compatible 3D video stream. Within this setting, it is likely that the 2D video-transmitted information will be more important than the 3D one, for two reasons. The first reason is that initially a majority of users will still be using 2D devices and therefore the 2D video content would be more important because it would be reaching a larger audience. At the same time, the 2D video information could be considered as more important because it may be needed to recover the 3D video content (which is the case shown in Figure 8.11 when considering that frames types 0 and 1 form a 2D video sequence and the addition of frames of type 2 expand the video content to 3D). Also, 2D video may be considered more important because it can be seen as a lower quality service that a 3D receiver could switch to when some problem prevents the correct reception of video in 3D (this particular approach could also be studied in the context of the multiple description framework, as discussed in the previous section). Consequently, the work in [20] aims at designing a cross-layer scheme that assigns different physical layer resources to different parts of the encoded video. As such, the scheme in [20] allocates power and number of subcarriers for WiMAX transmission, differentiating between assignment for the more important color information (which applies also to 2D video) and for the less important video depth information (which is needed only for 3D video). One point of note in this work is that the presentation in [20] considers the design case of unequal error protections instead of one of cross-layer design. As presented in this chapter, unequal error protection refers to the allocation of different amount of FEC redundancy to different parts of the compressed 3D video stream, while the work in [20] is a case of cross-layer design.

Another design that uses a cross-layer technique linking the physical layer with the application layer to improve the quality of received 3D video transmitted over a wireless medium is the work in [21]. This is another case where the goal of the design is to efficiently allocate network resources by providing differentiated link quality for the more important color information and less important depth information appearing as two parts of the compressed video bit stream. The salient feature of the physical layer resource allocation is that in this case the problem is that of assigning different types of relay and relay signal processing operation to the color and video depth components of the bit stream to be transmitted. As shown in Figure 8.15, the transmission of information is not done through a direct transmission between source and destination, but instead through the use of a relay located between the source and destination.

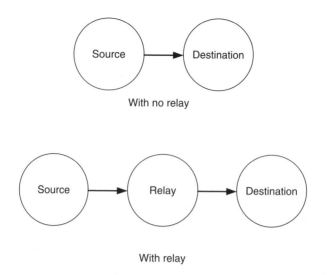

Figure 8.15 Communication with and without the use of a relay.

The operation of the relay in [21] follows the ideas within the paradigm of cooperative communications. Cooperative communications is a technique that is itself derived from studies on the relay channel [22] and presented in [23–25]. It is based on the broadcast nature of wireless channels where a transmitted signal can be overheard by other network nodes, called "relays", and instead of traditionally treating the signal as interference and discarding it, it is processed at the relay, and retransmitted to the destination. The relays can be classified into different types depending on the processing done with the signal to be relayed. The two simplest and most popular types are amplify-and-forward (AF), where the relay simply amplifies the received signal and retransmits it, and decode-and-forward (DF), where the relay is capable of decoding the received signal, checking for errors, and if received correctly, re-encoding and retransmitting it.

Research on user cooperation has presented evidence that the use of these techniques is capable of improving the quality of the wireless link. At the same time, the use of a relay in the context of cooperative communications presents a tradeoff between received signal quality and transmit bit rate or other related metrics. This is because with the use of a relay it is necessary to allocate part of the resources that are usually used only for the transmission between the source and the destination – channel allocation, transmit bit rate, time slot duration, etc. – for the transmission from the relay to the destination. This is an important issue, especially when transmitting sources of information with the characteristics of 3D video. An analysis of this issue, for generic real-time multimedia sources can be found in [26]. The results here show that in a majority of cases, DF cooperation exhibits better performance than AF cooperation.

The work in [21] addresses the issues of allocating resources to the relay transmission and the difference in performance between AF and DF relaying. It does so by assigning the more important transmission of color information to the best of the group of relays that can perform DF operation, and by assigning the less important transmission of video

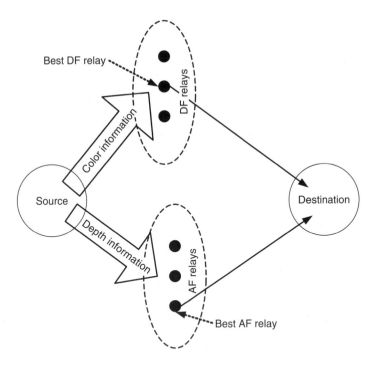

Figure 8.16   Transmission of 3D video information using two groups of relays.

depth information to the best of the group of relays that cannot perform DF operation and, thus, are available to operate using AF relaying. This operation is shown in Figure 8.16.

The configuration of relays into two separate groups allows for the scheduling of transmissions, and the needed resources, as shown in Figure 8.17. As can be seen, the transmission of information is divided into phases. During the odd numbered phases the source is sending information and the best of the AF relays is sending video depth information to the destination. During the even numbered phases the source sends video depth information and the best of the DF relays sends the color information to the destination. Note that in practice, a DF relay cannot retransmit video depth information because doing so would require it to be receiving and transmitting at the same time, an operation that presents significant technical challenges due to the large difference between the powers of the two signals involved. For the same reason, an AF relay cannot transmit color information (an operation that would not be efficient anyway because the performance would not be as good as that achieved with a relay from the DF group). Also note that in order to allocate resources for the transmission of the relays, the time duration needed to transmit frames needs to be divided into two phases. Nevertheless, the separation of the relaying operation into the staggered transmission of two relays from two different groups does not require the use of any extra resources, and the only penalty is a small half-frame delay incurred during the transmission from the AF relay to the destination. Of course, the operation of the system is based on the assumption that the transmission from the source is not interfering with the reception at the destination.

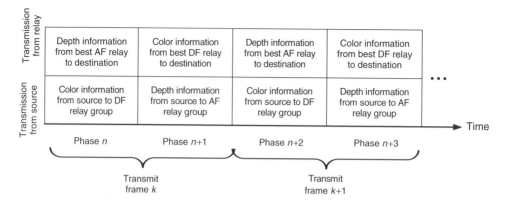

Figure 8.17   Transmission schedule for source and relays.

The main difference between AF and DF operation is that for the latter it is necessary to successfully decode at the relay the transmitted information from the source. Then, the criteria used to allocate a relay to DF or AF is that the relays in the DF group are those with a channel from the source good enough that the decoding of the transmitted information is highly likely. Those relays for which the channel from the source is not as good are assigned to the AF group. This criterion also accounts for why DF relaying shows better performance. Once the groups of relays are set, it is necessary to choose the best relay within each group. This is done by choosing the relay within each group yielding the largest signal-to-noise ratio at the destination. This value depends on the quality of the channels between the source and the relay and between the relay and the destination.

References

1. W. A. Pearlman and A. Said, *"Digital Signal Compression, Principles and Practice"*, Cambridge University Press, 2011.
2. B. Kamolrat, W. A. C. Fernando, M. Mark, A. Condos, "Joint source and channel coding for 3D video with depth image – based rendering", *IEEE Transactions on Consumer Electronics*, vol. 54, no. 2, pp. 887–894, May 2008.
3. Y. Zhou, C. Hou, W. Xiang, and F. Wu, "Channel Distortion Modeling for Multi-View Video Transmission Over Packet-Switched Networks", *IEEE Transactions on Circuits and Systems for Video Technology*, vol. 21, no. 11, pp. 1679–1692, November 2011.
4. D. V. S. X. De Silva, W. A. C. Fernando, S. T. Worrall, "3D Video communication scheme for error prone environments based on motion vector sharing", *3DTV-Conference: The True Vision – Capture, Transmission and Display of 3D Video (3DTV-CON)*, pp. 1–4, 7–9 June 2010.
5. M. B. Dissanayake, D. V. S. X. De Silva, S. T. Worrall, W. A. C. Fernando, "Error resilience technique for multi-view coding using redundant disparity vectors", *2010 IEEE International Conference on Multimedia and Expo (ICME)*, pp. 1712–1717, 19–23 July 2010.
6. Y. Zhou, C. Hou, R. Pan, Z. Yuan, and L. Yang, "Distortion analysis and error concealment for multi-view video transmission", in Proceedings of the IEEE International Symposium on Broadband Multimedia Systems and Broadcasting (BMSB), pp. 1–5, 24–26 March 2010.
7. X. Xiang, D. Zhao, Q. Wang, X. Ji, and W. Gao, "A Novel Error Concealment Method for Stereoscopic Video Coding", in Proceedings of the IEEE International Conference on Image Processing (ICIP), vol. 5, pp. V-101-V-104, 16–19 September 2007.

8. C. T. E. R. Hewage, S. Worrall, S. Dogan, and A. M. Kondoz, "Frame concealment algorithm for stereoscopic video using motion vector sharing", in Proceedings of the IEEE International Conference on Multimedia and Expo, pp. 485–488, 23–26 June 2008.

9. K. Song, T. Chung, Y. Oh, and C.-S. Kim, "Error concealment of multi-view video sequences using inter-view and intra-view correlations", *Journal of Visual Communication and Image Representation*, vol. 20, no. 4, May 2009, pp. 281–292.

10. A. Serdar Tan, A. Aksay, C. Bilen, G. Bozdagi Akar, and E. Arikan, "Rate-distortion optimized layered stereoscopic video streaming with raptor codes", *Packet Video 2007*, pp. 98–104, 12–13 November 2007.

11. C. Bilen, A. Aksay, and G. Bozdagi Akar, "A multi-view video codec based on H.264", in *Proceedings of the IEEE Conference on Image Processing (ICIP)*, 8–11 October, Atlanta, USA, 2006.

12. M. Luby, M. Watson, T. Gasiba, T. Stockhammer, and W. Xu, "Raptor codes for reliable download delivery in wireless broadcast systems", in *Proc. of IEEE CCNC*, pp. 192–197, 8–10 January, 2006.

13. L. Ozarov, "On a source coding problem with two channels and three receivers", *Bell Sys. Tech. Journal*, vol. 59, no. 10, pp. 1909–1921, December 1980.

14. M. Alasti, K. Sayrafian-Pour, A. Ephremides, and N. Farvardin, "Multiple Description Coding in Networks with Congestion Problem", *IEEE Transaction on Information Theory*, vol. 47, no. 1, pp. 891–902, March 2001.

15. J. N. Laneman, E. Martinian, G. W. Wornell, and J. G. Apostolopoulos, "Source-Channel Diversity for Parallel Channels", *IEEE Transaction on Information Theory*, vol. 51, no. 10, pp. 3518–3539, October 2005.

16. V. K. Goyal, "Multiple description coding: compression meets the network", *IEEE Signal Processing Magazine*, vol. 18, no. 5, pp. 74–93, September 2001.

17. A. R. Reibman, H. Jafarkhani, M. T. Orchard, and Y. Wang, "Performance of Multiple Description Coders on a Real Channel", in Proceedings of the International Conference on Acoustics, Speech and Signal Processing (ICASSP), vol. 5, pp. 2415–2418, 1999.

18. A. Norkin, A. Aksay, C. Bilen, G. Akar, A. Gotchev, and J. Astola, "Schemes for Multiple Description Coding of Stereoscopic Video", in Multimedia Content Representation, Classification and Security, vol. 4105, pp. 730–737, Springer Berlin/Heidelberg, 2006.

19. H. A. Karim, C. Hewage, S. Worrall, and A. Kondoz, "Scalable multiple description video coding for stereoscopic 3D", *IEEE Transactions on Consumer Electronics*, vol. 54, no. 2, pp. 745–752, May 2008.

20. C. T. E. R. Hewage, Z. Ahmad, S. T. Worrall, S. Dogan, W. A. C. Fernando, and A. Kondoz, "Unequal Error Protection for backward compatible 3-D video transmission over WiMAX", in *Proc. IEEE International Symposium on Circuits and Systems, ISCAS 2009.*, pp. 125–128, 24–27 May 2009.

21. I.K. Sileh, K.M. Alajel, Wei Xiang, "Cooperative Relay Selection Based UEP Scheme for 3D Video Transmission over Rayleigh Fading Channel", *in Proceedings of the 2011 International Conference on Digital Image Computing Techniques and Applications (DICTA)*, pp. 689–693, 6–8 December 2011.

22. T. M. Cover and A. A. El Gamal, "Capacity theorems for the relay channel", *IEEE Transactions on Information Theory*, vol. 25, no. 9, pp. 572–584, September 1979.

23. A. Sendonaris, E. Erkip, and B. Aazhang, "User cooperation diversity, part I: System description", *IEEE Transactions on Communications*, vol. 51, no. 11, pp. 1927–1938, November 2003.

24. J. N. Laneman and G. W. Wornell, "Distributed space-time coded protocols for exploiting cooperative diversity in wireless networks", *IEEE Transactions on Information Theory*, vol. 49, no. 10, pp. 2415–2525, October 2003.

25. J.N. Laneman, D.N.C. Tse, and G.W. Wornell, "Cooperative diversity in wireless networks: Efficient protocols and outage behavior", *Transactions on Information Theory*, vol. 50, no. 12, pp. 3062–3080, December 2004.

26. A. Kwasinski and K. J. R. Liu, "Source-Channel-Cooperation Tradeoffs for Adaptive Coded Communications", *IEEE Transactions on Wireless Communications*, vol. 7, no. 9, pp. 3347–3358, September 2008.

9

3D Applications

Developing 3D stereoscopic applications has become really popular in the software industry. 3D stereoscopic research is advancing fast due to the commercial need and the popularity of 3D stereoscopic products. Therefore, this chapter will give a short discussion of commercially available and advanced technologies for application development. The discussed topics include glass-less two-view systems, 3D capturing and displaying systems, two-view gaming systems, mobile 3D systems and perception, and 3D augmented reality systems.

9.1 Glass-Less Two-View Systems

The popularity of 3D movies has broken the ice of the 3D industry and pushed 3D technologies into commercial products and applications including 3D movies, 3D videos, 3D games, and 3D augmented surgery systems. It is not convenient for consumers to watch the 3D contents due to the requirement to wear 3D glasses when using commercially available 3D display devices. Therefore, a glass-less two-view 3D system would relieve this inconvenience. The first glass-less two-view 3D technology, the "parallax barrier" technology, was developed by Frederic E. Ives as early as 1901. It is a general belief that the quality and price of glass 3D display devices would be better than that of glass-less 3D display devices because delivering proper visual information to each eye in open space is a very hard problem. Despite of the cost and technical limitations, glass-less display devices can still be used in several 3D applications including 3D mobile smartphones, 3D portable game consoles, and 3D augmented surgery systems. This is because wearing a pair of 3D glasses may distort the view of objects in the world when smartphones and portable game consoles are used in public and not in a private space.

Stereoscopy delivers respective views of the scene to the left eye and right eye on one single display device. A glass-less two-view 3D display system, which is called autostereoscopy, must be able to deliver stereoscopic content to each eye respectively

---

3D Visual Communications, First Edition. Guan-Ming Su, Yu-Chi Lai, Andres Kwasinski and Haohong Wang.
© 2013 John Wiley & Sons, Ltd. Published 2013 by John Wiley & Sons, Ltd.

without wearing pairs of glasses. Fundamentally, autostereoscopic technologies can be divided into two categories:

1. **Spatially multiplexed systems**: each eye sees its respective image or video in different parts of the display device at the same time.
2. **Temporally multiplexed systems**: each eye sees its respective image or video on the same display device at different moments of time.

Details about autostereoscopy are discussed in Chapter 3. The following will only summarize those commercially available autostereoscopic systems.

9.1.1 Spatially Multiplexed Systems

Spatially multiplexed devices are widely used for portable 3D devices including Nintendo 3DS and HTC EVO 3D. There are mainly two technologies: parallax barrier and lenticular. The parallax barrier technology depends on a set of barriers to deliver the correct visual information to the left eye and right eye respectively. The lenticular technology depends on a set of micro lens to adjust the angle of lights from the LCD panel to deliver respective visual information to the left eye and right eye. As a result, the parallax barrier technology has better control over the delivery to each eye but the 3D content can only be nicely watched within a small range of viewing angles and from a few plausible viewing positions. Furthermore, the perceived resolution and brightness of the content is low, too. The main advantage of the lenticular technology is the perceived brightness of the content, but the perceived resolution is also low and the amount of perceived artifacts is high. Furthermore, the cost of the lenticular technology is higher than the parallax barrier technology. As a result, smartphones, 3D cameras, and portable game consoles mainly choose the parallax barrier technology to deliver 3D images and videos to users because it is the cheapest autostereoscopic technology to deliver 3D content with acceptable quality. Details of these two technologies are discussed in Chapter 3.

9.1.2 Temporally Multiplexed Systems

Active 3D-glass display devices use an LCD panel at a refresh rate of 120 Hz and 240 Hz to deliver correct visual information to one eye by actively and alternately blocking the view of the other eye. Similarly, the temporally multiplexed technology as shown in Figure 9.1 uses two sets of directional backlight sources to deliver the respective visual information to each eye alternately. The set of left-eye light sources are turned on and the set of right-eye light sources are turned off in order to deliver the left-eye visual information. Then, the set of left-eye lights are turned off and the set of right-eye lights are turned on in order to deliver the right-eye visual information. As a result, users can watch 3D images and videos with correct visual information delivered to each eye alternately. The perceived resolution of the content is high for the temporally multiplexed technology but the 3D content can only be comfortably watched within a small range of viewing angles and at a few plausible viewing positions. Furthermore, the perceived brightness and refresh rate of the content is low, too. Generally, the technology is also used mostly on small display devices.

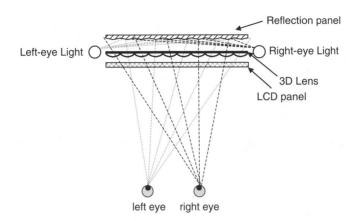

Figure 9.1 This illustrates the concept of a temporally-multiplexed glass-less system. A set of left-eye light sources distribute the respective visual information only to the left eye in one time slot and a set of right-eye light sources distribute the respective visual information only to the right eye in another time slot.

9.2   3D Capture and Display Systems

Chapter 4 discussed 3D content construction techniques. These constructed 3D contents can be represented in different formats including the conventional stereo video (CSV) format, the mixed resolution stereo (MRS) format, and video plus depth (V+D) format. Figure 9.2 shows an example of using CSV, MRS, and V+D to represent a 3D image. The three formats also use two different ways to capture the real world: one is to capture the real world with two sensors where one represents the left eye and the other represents the right eye. The other is to capture the real world with one traditional sensor and one depth sensor. In the following, we give a short description of two-sensor capturing systems and color-depth-sensor capturing systems.

On 22 July 2009, Fujifilm announced its FinePix Real 3D System which is a complete 3D solution to capture, edit, and display stereoscopic images and videos. The first device in the system is a digital 3D camera called the FinePix Real 3D W1. There are two CCD sensors on the camera to capture the world in stereoscopic images or videos. An autostereoscopic 3D LCD is integrated into the camera to preview the possible shots and watch the captured images and videos. The previewing ability allows users to adjust the 3D effect of images and videos interactively. The second device is a digital 3D viewer, FinePix REAL 3D V1, which is also implemented with autostereoscopic display technologies to see and edit the captured stereoscopic images and videos. For general consumers, Fujifilm provides a total solution from 3D contents shooting to 3D contents viewing. Furthermore, Fujifilm continues to improve its 3D cameras' capture and display abilities and announced its FinePix Real 3D W3 in 2011. Panasonic, Sony, and JVC have also launched their own stereo camera projects and announced their own 3D cameras which are Panasonic TM-750, Sony HDR-TD20V, and JVC GS-TD1. In addition to buying a new 3D cameras, users can also choose to attach an auxiliary 3D lens to certain cameras for capturing 3D contents. For example, Panasonic has released an auxiliary 3D camera lens, Lumix Micro G Microsystem, for their G/GF series cameras.

Figure 9.2 The top two images record Chiang Kai-Shek Memorial Hall with the left view image and right view image. The middle two images record Chiang Kai-Shek Memorial Hall with the full-resolution left view image and half-resolution right view. The bottom two images record Chiang Kai-Shek Memorial Hall with the left view image and corresponding depth map of the left view.

In addition to 3D cameras, Maya which is a famous 3D animation software, also provides 3D camera functions (as shown in Figure 9.3) to create pairs of stereo cameras in the virtual 3D environment. Designers could first create a pair of stereo cameras for rendering the virtual scene in the stereoscopic images. Then, they can adjust properties of the pair of cameras. For example, the interaxial separation, which is the distance between

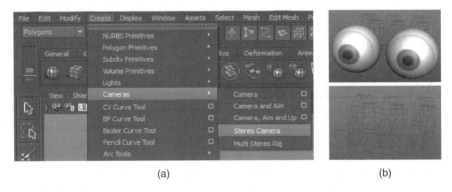

(a)   (b)

Figure 9.3   (a) The user interface to initiate the stereoscopic camera setting for animation creation. (b) The exemplar camera setting condition.

(a)   (b)

Figure 9.4   (a) An anaglyph image rendered by the camera setting using the Autodesk Maya system. (b) The capturing condition and scene for the left 3D stereoscopic image.

two eyes, can be adjusted to give different depth perception. Figure 9.4 is an illustration of an exemplar stereo scene created by Maya.

According to the discussion in Chapter 5, video plus depth is a popular choice for transmission. Therefore, a depth map or "disparisty map" must be constructed or captured along with the color map. For those videos which were shot in 2D, the corresponding depth map for each frame must be created. This process is called 2D-3D conversion, and is discussed in Chapter 4. However, automatic 2D-3D conversion algorithms are still not mature enough to convert just any 2D images and videos. Therefore, manually creating the depth map for each frame in those 2D videos is still the only robust algorithm. Wang et al. [1] provide an interactive interface called Stereobrush to use strokes of different depth values to construct all possible layers with different depth values. The application allows users to construct the depth map for each frame efficiently and effectively.

Manual depth map construction is generally used in the movie industry to transform 2D movies to 3D, but this post-processing procedure is still tedious work for general consumers. Therefore, more and more depth capturing devices are being introduced and developed to generate a depth map of the world. When combining a color sensor and a depth sensor, the video plus depth 3D contents can be directly constructed without any post-processing procedure. The most famous and popular one is Kinect which is designed to be a new user interface to control game characters. Kinect provides not only intuitive control of elements in the 3D gaming environment but also abilities to capture 3D video plus depth contents. Therefore, Kinect has become a popular human–computer interaction device in the worldwide and therefore a large number of applications have been developed. For example, Kinect can be used to assist surgeons to check the conditions inside the patient and help them visualize the twists, turns, and branches of the aorta for navigating catheters inside the blood vessels during the surgical procedure. This surgical procedure has successfully been conducted in Guy's and St Thomas's hospitals in London. Benko et al. [2] propose Mirage Table which uses Kinect as a control in an AR application to directly interact with the virtual object in the 3D environment. Developing other types of human–computer interaction based on Kinect is still a hot research topic. Additionally, the precision of real-time video plus depth capturing devices is still limited. Mechanically and algorithmically improving the precision is also another popular research topic.

9.3 Two-View Gaming Systems

Video games need reality and exciting components to attract customers. Therefore, new technologies are developed and easily accepted by the video game community. Since people see the world with their own two eyes, 3D stereoscopic techniques can provide an extra sense of presence. These 3D techniques become new attraction points for the video game industry. Furthermore, stereoscopy gives developers the ease of picking up things that look fake. Depth is important for correct perception of the virtual world, and setting the depth of the virtual scene properly is critical to the success of a game. The stereoscopic development environment can provide an extra tool for developers to check and correct visual defects by giving proper depth cues in the game before they are even used in a game during the development procedure. According to our discussion in Chapter 2, 3D polygonal meshes are the fundamental representations for games. As shown in Figure 9.5, applications deliver stereoscopic content to the customers by the following steps:

1. Applications issue geometry-based rendering commands to the graphics card.
2. The graphics card generates the frames for the left and right views through a stereo-scopic pipeline which can be one of two possible forms as shown in Figure 9.6.
3. The two views are sent to the 3D vision-ready display units and the 3D-ready display delivers the interlaced images to the left eye and right eye separately.
4. Pairs of stereoscopic glasses help customers extract each view separately and the customer's brain can reconstruct the 3D perception of the scene from these views.

There are mainly two possible rendering pipelines for generating stereoscopic views as shown in Figure 9.6.

1. **Rendering the scene twice**
   The polygonal meshes of the 3D world are fed into the original graphics pipeline with two camera settings to represent the left view and right view respectively. The scene must run through the entire pipeline twice to render frames for the left view and right view. Therefore, the rendering process requires twice the amount of rendering time when compared to rendering a monocular view for a single 3D stereoscopic view and the resulting frame rate is approximately half of the original one.

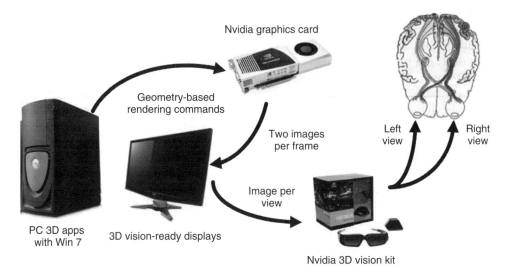

Figure 9.5   The 3D game content delivery procedure.

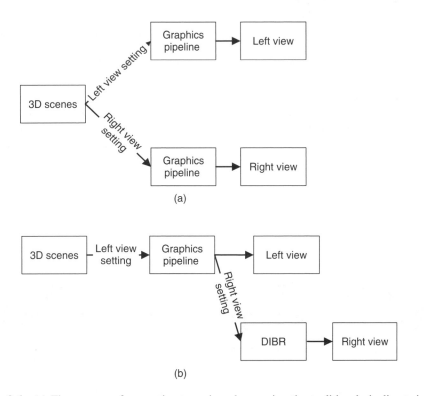

Figure 9.6   (a) The process of generating two views by running the traditional pipeline twice for each view respectively. (b) The process of generating two views by running the traditional pipeline once for the left view and DIBR once for the right view.

2. **Rendering once with DIBR**

   A depth map is the byproduct of a traditional graphics pipeline because the z-buffer algorithm is the default visibility algorithm. Therefore, depth-image-based rendering (DIBR) can be added after the original rendering to generate the stereoscopic view of the scene at little cost. There are two extra advantages for this category. As discussed in Chapter 2, DIBR also decouples the rendering process and the displaying process to give players the ability to adjust their preferred disparity setting. The extra DIBR process can be naturally extended for free-view gaming systems.

   NVidia, which is one of main manufacturers and developers of graphics processing units (GPUs), saw the commercial possibility of 3D stereoscopic technologies and started to develop 3D stereoscopic hardware and software for new 3D applications. The company revealed the NVidia 3D Vision Pro to incorporate with their manufactured graphics cards as solutions for delivering the highest quality and the most advanced 3D stereoscopic environment. The 3D environment enables designers, engineers, digital artists, and scientists to see and share their work in true 3D. As shown in Figure 9.7, there are four components needed:

1. **Graphics processing units (GPUs)**

   A GPU is the core technology, which provides realism of the virtual world to players in modern games technology. The 3D stereoscopic games require even more computational resources from the graphics hardware and thus a proper GPU is necessary for 3D stereoscopic games. For example, the newest version of NVidia GeForce, Quadro and Tesla GPUs can be used.

2. **3D vision-ready display**

   The rendering results must be displayed on a device for the player to see and interact. Currently, glass-less autostereoscopic monitors are only commercially available on mobile devices and not for LCD monitors, televisions, or projectors. Therefore, the commercially available 3D display devices generally require a pair of glasses to watch 3D content. Pairs of active shutter glasses provide better control and visual quality and thus, pairs of active shutter glasses should be the main choice for 3D stereoscopic games. Therefore, the fundamental requirement for 3D vision-ready displays is that the refresh rate must be over 120 Hz to prevent the lag problem of temporally multiplexed 3D-glass display devices.

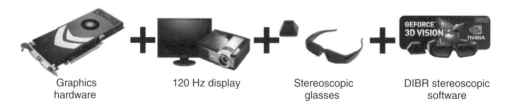

| Graphics | 120 Hz display | Stereoscopic | DIBR stereoscopic |
| hardware | | glasses | software |

Figure 9.7   The devices and software required for 3D gaming.

3. **Stereoscopic glasses**
   3D movies can be seen through a pair of red–cyan glasses or polarized glasses because of the price, but the artifacts are generally more serious than with a pair of active shutter glasses. Therefore, it is recommended to use pairs of active shutter glasses for achieving better stereoscopic perception.
4. **Stereoscopic drivers**
   Stereoscopic 3D games require programmers to set up the viewing conditions for each eye in every frame. The setting procedure is cumbersome. A good 3D driver should provide an intuitive and automatic control to set the 3D stereoscopic viewing conditions.

Setting proper depth of the world is one of the important tasks for designing a 3D stereoscopic video game. Therefore, here are several issues related to depth setting which must be considered before developing a 3D stereoscopic game.

1. Depth setting represents the maximum stereo separation.
2. Stereo separation is the distance of a given object as shown in the left view image and the right view image.
   - Maximum stereo separation should be equal to the distance between the two pupils of a person which is roughly about 2.5 inches.
   - Some people may feel uncomfortable with a large amount of stereo separation and thus the default value is generally set to 15% of the maximum stereo separation.
   - Most users will raise it to a higher value after their eyes become used to the 3D stereo contents.
   - If the stereo separation of an object is equal to 0, the object appears at the screen depth.
   - Distant objects have separation quickly approaching maximum, which is a function of $1/D$ where D is the depth of the object.
3. Generally, the 3D viewing system should provide a convergence control to set the depth for the zero stereo separation, $screen_{depth}$.

In addition, the developer also would like to maximize the 3D stereoscopic experience of players when playing games. The following are several hints to enhance the experience:

1. Place objects at their correct depths.
   - Since our eyes use multiple cues to determine the distance from the eye to an object, the rendering of objects must be consistent in these depth cues to deliver the right depth perception.
   - Occlusion is only a weak depth cue but it generally provides the relative distance to the viewer. If object A is obscured by object B, it is a strong hint that object A is further away.
   - When stereo separation contradicts with other depth cues, eyestrain and headache will result.

For example, the skybox is a common technique used in a game. A skybox is generally rendered at the beginning of the rendering process without using the z-buffer visibility algorithm. Therefore, some random D value which is unrelated to the rest of the scene is assigned to the drawing. This D value may induce issues in depth perception of the scene. Therefore, when rendering skybox or other far-away background objects, their D values must be set to a value which is larger than the D value of the rest of objects in the scene.

2. Maximum stereo separation is about 2.5 inches which is roughly 100–200 pixels in a common game setting. Stereo separation is a function of $1/D$ and can quickly approach the maximum value.

3. According to the experience, the D range between $screen_{depth}$ and $screen_{depth} \times 100$ can generate a vivid 3D effect. Therefore, try to fit as many scene objects within this range as possible.

4. Set $screen_{depth}$ to the maximum possible value (using "convergence adjustment") to enhance the 3D effect. However, the process must make sure that objects are inside the screen and do not come out of the screen and get clipped by the screen sides.

9.4   3D Mobile

Due to keen competition in the smartphone market, companies try their best to equip their phones with different interesting functions to attract consumers. 3D technology is one of them. Thus, there are at least two 3D smartphones available commercially: LG Optimal and HTC EVO 3D. The main attraction points provided by these two phones are to capture and display 3D contents using a stereoscopic pair of cameras and an autostereoscopic display. Thus, a short description of HTC EVO 3D is given as a representative of current 3D mobile systems. Later, a discussion about the perception in mobile 3D display devices is also given.

9.4.1   HTC EVO 3D

In addition to the original features provided by HTC smartphones, HTC EVO 3D has been equipped with 3D stereoscopic features including 3D gaming, 3D photo and video capture, 3D photo and video viewing, and an easy 2D-to-3D switch. This smartphone can capture the world in 3D stereoscopic images and videos and the 3D stereoscopic images and videos can be viewed on the screen without the need for glasses. There are a few feature points for HTC EVO 3D:

- **Screen**: The screen is bright and clear. Although EVO 3D can capture and display 3D stereoscopic images or videos, none of the widgets runs in 3D. Currently, there is only one 3D app available in the store. Lack of 3D applications and content is still the main issue for 3D technologies. There is a 2D-3D switch which allows users to operate the phone in 2D mode.
- **Camera**: The stereoscopic pair of cameras is one of the specific feature points of HTC Evo 3D. When opening the capturing app, there is a button to switch between the 2D and 3D capturing modes. The phone should be held at the position of about the length of an arm to get a proper stereoscopic view of the world. When the phone is further

away from the scene, the 3D effect is not obvious. When the phone is too close to the scene, the captured 3D content becomes ghosted and error-prone. At the right distance, the 3D effect is vivid and gives viewers a perfect 3D stereoscopic sense of the scene.

- **Video**: HTC Evo 3D becomes a powerful mobile 3D video camera that is able to shoot clean movies. The recommended 3D videos have a resolution up to 720p. The shooting videos are clean and the 3D effect can be more convincing if the foreground objects and background are on two obviously distinct depth planes. In the 3D video capturing mode, MPO or JPS file formats are available. A grid option helps the user line up distant and near objects in the frame.
- **Media**: Content is important for the popularity of a device. 3D content editing needs a proper medium to show the intermediate and final results. HTC Evo 3D provides a simple means for users to watch their own 3D content. It also provides functions to make their own 3D images and movies. Those 3D videos and photos must look convincing and interesting. YouTube provides a simple means to get 3D videos. Users can search for "YT3D" to find hundreds of 3D videos and EVO 3D allows users to watch them directly.
- **More 2D applications and less 3D applications**: Although HTC Evo 3D has the stereoscopic pairs of cameras and 3D autostereoscopic display, it does not provide any interesting 3D user interface out of its 3D abilities. For example, the phone cannot have the 3D profiles of the user's friends popping out on the screen when browsing through contacts. It does not provide 3D tele conference between two Evo 3D phones. The messaging system still uses traditional 2D methods without any 3D effects. Generally, 3D hardware advances much faster than 3D software. Therefore, it is easy to put the 3D hardware into a system but the corresponding applications and features are hard to come by to make the 3D system popular. Because HTC Evo 3D does not try to use as many 3D features as possible, it is hard to make 3D mobile phones popular.

Headaches and eye strain may be induced after watching 3D stereoscopic content for over 30 minutes.

9.4.2 Mobile 3D Perception

Because smartphones have become popular and mobile services are an important business, more advanced services are developed to fulfill the expectation of users. 3D services can use depth perception to enhance the naturalness of the displayed content and give viewers the feeling of being there [3–5]. Autostereoscopic displays provide the 3D effect without the need of glasses or other extra devices as discussed in Chapter 3 and also Section 9.1. Humans perceive the 3D world using a combination of different visual depth cues. Details about possible depth cues are discussed in Chapter 7. Depth cues are generally classified as binocular depth cues that need both eyes to perceive and monocular depth cues that can be perceived by a single eye. The perception of the binocular depth cues is independent of that of monocular depth cues [6]. Additionally, the depth range perceived by a viewer is highly accurate but quite narrow [7]. The process of perceiving depth is delicate and vulnerable to artifacts. The aim of mobile autostereoscopic 3D displays is to enhance the realism for viewers by giving extra depth perception. Because these autostereocopic technologies are still not mature, artifacts are induced in the delivery process. How the depth perception is affected by the delivery of binocular depth cues and monocular cues is important for the proper usage of mobile 3D autostereoscopic displays. Motion parallax and stereopsis are considered as the most important depth cues [8–10]. Binocular depth cues get better ratings on the accuracy and speed of depth perception than monocular cues do. Additional monocular depth cues (shadows, texture, focal depth) do not lead to better depth perception. This phenomenon might be an implication of the supremacy of stereopsis over monocular depth cues on portable displays. Furthermore, even though users do not have any reason to make an assumption of constant object size, the size is generally used as a depth cue for them. For example, when texture depth cues are not reliable, the size may be used as a strong auxiliary cue for depth judgment. This phenomenon also confirms the theory [8, 11–13] that the importance of depth cues can be seen as a weighted combination of the presented cues, based on their reliability in each situation. However, focal depth cues seem to get a low ranking in accuracy, efficiency, and acceptance. This finding may seem to be surprising and may be a topic for further exploitation. To summarize the above, binocular depth cues outperform the monocular ones in efficiency and accuracy on portable autostereoscopic displays. Additionally, an interesting topic for further exploitation would be how much monocular cues–such as strong perspective lines, textures and sizes–can facilitate the depth estimation task.

Another interesting issue is how compression artifacts affect depth perception. When few compression artifacts are induced in a 3D video, the depth perception contributes to the quality perception on mobile 3D autostereoscopic displays [14]. But when compression artifacts become noticeable, artifacts induced by compression seem to significantly affect depth perception on both the correctness of depth estimation and the depth estimation speed [8]. Especially, the depth estimation speed can be affected even by slight blockedness induced by compression. When the quality has few defects, the depth might be still perceived perfectly but when the defects increase, the accuracy of depth perception becomes affected further. The time needed to estimate the depth and the correctness of the depth estimation has a negative correlation. This indicates that if the depth estimation can be finished fast, the depth estimation results seem to be also most likely correct. The kind of effects on 3D videos can be easily understood: if lower quality affects the efficiency of depth perception, the binocular HVS might not have enough time to create a plausible 3D effect for objects. The binocular HVS is very vulnerable to losing the depth effect if artifacts are present.

3D stereoscopic technologies have been introduced into mobile devices and it is important to have proper content and applications to make 3D mobile devices popular. Therefore, researchers are trying to push 3D movies onto the 3D mobile devices. Motivation to use a mobile TV is to kill time while waiting, or to get hold of up-to-date news while on the move [15]. Therefore, users of mobile TV services prefer short clips such as news, music videos, YouTube videos and sports programs [16]. In contrast, motivation to use 3DTV is to be entertained and therefore realism and the feeling of being there [17, 18] seem to be the killer experiences. And the users normally expect to watch movies with special 3D effects [19] to experience the new feeling of presence and to explore the content sufficiently [20]. For the context of usage, 3DTV is used for entertainment in environments such as 3D cinemas and would like to use shared views, and the main situations for the usage of mobile TV are at work during breaks, while commuting, at home to create privacy, and in waiting or waste-time situations [15, 21, 22]. And additionally users would like to have private viewing conditions and sometimes use shared viewing like co-view during lunch or just to share funny stories or clips [15, 21]. These differences would also reflect the difference in requirement of merging 3DTV and mobile TV into mobile 3DTV.

Mobile TV fundamentally offers the entertainment for users to kill time or to get informed or to watch TV while being on the move. Mobile 3DTV adds a higher interest to mobile TV in the content through raised realism, atmosphere, and emotional identification using the stereoscopic 3D technologies. The 3D representation of the content also increases the realism and naturalness of the content and contributes to a raised feeling of being inside the content or being present at it, according to user experience research [19]. A few guidelines from consideration of users, systems, and contexts are given for designing mobile 3DTV systems and services [23]:

1. **User**
   - Mobile 3DTV must offer a program to satisfy users with different motivations in different contexts.
   - Mobile 3DTV needs to fulfill the needs for entertainment and information so that viewers can relax, spend time, and learn through mobile 3D services.
   - Mobile 3DTV should provide increased realism and naturalness of content and the feeling of being there when compared to 2D systems.
   - Mobile 3DTV needs to minimize simulator sickness and increase the excitement and fun of 3D for high viewing comfort.

2. **System and Service**
   - Mobile 3DTV should provide 3D video contents which can satisfy the need for information and entertainment to reflect the added values of 3D.
   - Mobile 3DTV should offer interactive content such as 3D games to fully exploit the potential of 3D stereoscopic technologies.
   - Mobile 3DTV must have a display device with a size of 4–5 inches or at least over 3 inches.
   - Mobile 3DTV should offer both monomodal (audio or visual only) and multimodal (audiovisual) presentation modes as well as fluent shifts between these modes and 2D/3D visual presentation.
   - Mobile 3DTV must offer an easy manipulation interface for service navigation and 3D content handling.
   - Mobile 3DTV should provide functions to save, send, receive, and capture 3D content.
   - Mobile 3DTV should provide the same requirements as for 2D mobile services, such as long battery life, high storage capacity, spontaneous access to all preferred or needed services or multiple network connection interfaces.
   - Mobile 3DTV should have simple and clear payment models to finance the service.

3. **Context**
   - Mobile 3DTV contents can be watched in public and private locations as well as outdoors and indoors. These locations probably include public transport, parks, cars, cafes, waiting rooms, as well as the home.
   - Mobile 3DTV contents are primarily designed for private viewing, but shared viewing may be needed.

• Duration of viewing 3D content generally depends on the usage context. The duration can vary from a short period of time in waiting situations to a long period of time during journeys.

The contextual situations affect the usage of mobile 3DTV. Video services for mobile phones are basically used for entertainment for a short period of free time and thus short entertainment and information programs should be popular and attractive for mobile 3DTV services.

9.5 Augmented Reality

Computer graphics provides a virtual environment (VE) to immerse a user into a synthetic environment but a user cannot actually see the world around him or her. Augmented reality (AR), a variation on VE, allows the user to see parts of the world with virtual objects added into the real world. Therefore, AR supports reality with the appearance of both real and virtual objects rather than replacing reality. AR also provides a middle ground between VE (completely synthetic) and telepresence (completely real) [24, 25]. AR can enhance the perception of a user to helps them perform real-world tasks with the assistance of the virtual objects. AR is defined by Azuma [26] as a system that has the following three characteristics:

1. combine real and virtual objects and scenes
2. allow the interaction with the real and virtual objects in real time
3. register interactions and objects in the 3D world

The fundamental functions provided by an AR system are the ability to add and remove objects to and from a real world and to provide haptics. Current research focuses on adding virtual objects into a real environment and blending virtual and real images seamlessly for display. However, the display or overlay should be able to remove and hide the real objects from the real world, too. Vision is not the only sense of a human. Hearing, touch, smell and taste are other senses which are also important hints for interaction with the scene. Especially touch can give the user the sense of interaction with the objects. Therefore a proper haptic sense should be generated and fed to the user for proper interaction. Accordingly, a AR system should consist of the following three basic subsystems:

1. **Scene generator**
   Compared to VE systems which replace the real world with a virtual environment, AR uses virtual images as supplements to the real world. Therefore, only a few virtual objects need to be drawn but realism is not required in order to provide proper interaction. Therefore, adding virtual objects into the real world using a scene generator is the fundamental function for proper AR interactions. However, seamlessly compositing virtual objects into the real world is not the critical issue for AR applications.
2. **Display device**
   Because the composited images must be delivered to the user through a display device, the display device is important for an AR system. But the requirement of a display device for an AR system may be less stringent than that of a VE system because

AR does not replace the real world. For example, the image overlay in Section 9.5.1 shows the composition of the patient's head and the MRI scanned brain virtual image. The quality of the overlay image may not reach the pleasant entertainment level but it provides useful information for the surgeon.

3. **Tracking and sensing**

In the previous two cases, AR had lower requirements than VE, but the requirements for tracking and sensing are much stricter than those for VE systems. Proper alignment of the virtual objects in the real world is important to provide the correct and necessary information for achieving the user's goal. Without that, AR is only a nice-looking application. Tracking and sensing can also be viewed as a registration problem. In order to have virtual objects registered correctly in the real world, the real world must be constructed or analyzed for the AR system. But 3D scene reconstruction is still a difficult problem. Therefore, tracking and sensing is still the key to pushing AR applications to another level.

A basic design decision in building an AR system is how to accomplish the task of combining real and virtual objects on the same display device. Currently there are two techniques to achieve this goal:

1. **Optical augmented display**

As shown in Figure 9.8, an optical augmented display system can let the user see the real world by placing optical combiners in front of the user. These combiners are partially transmissive, so that the user can look directly through them to see the real world. The virtual objects can be composited onto the display by reflection. Later, the medical visualization image overlay system can illustrate this concept.

2. **Video augmented display**

As shown in Figure 9.9, a video augmented display system does not allow any direct view of the real world. A single video camera, or a set of cameras, can provide the view of the real world. The virtual images generated by the scene generator are superimposed on the real world. The composite result is then sent to the display device for a visual perception of the augmented world. There is more than one way to composite the virtual images with the real world video. The blue screen composition algorithm is one of them. The algorithm uses a specific color, say green, to identify the non important part of the virtual images and then composition replaces the non important part with the corresponding part of the real world video. The overall effect is to superimpose the virtual objects over the real world. Another composition algorithm can use depth information to help place the virtual object in the proper location according to the related depth information. The virtual object can be composited into the real world by doing a pixel-by-pixel depth comparison. This would allow real objects to cover virtual objects and vice versa. Therefore, reconstructing the depth of the world is critical for proper AR interaction and view synthesis of the 3D stereoscopic view. Later, the mobile AR system can illustrate this concept.

Currently, there are several different possible applications including medical visualization, maintenance and repair, annotation, robot path planning, entertainment, and military aircraft navigation and targeting. Since 3D applications are the focus of this section, we

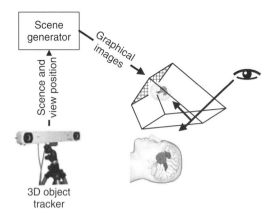

Figure 9.8   The optical augmented display system concept. The subject is direct under the transmissive display device. There is a tracking device to tracking the real world for registration of the virtual object. The scene generator generates the virtual objects. The virtual objects are then composited onto the transmissive display.

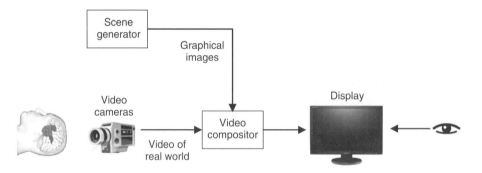

Figure 9.9   The video camera captures the real world. The 3D tracker tracks the real world for registration. The scene generator generates virtual objects. The compositor combines the real world video with the virtual object using the registration information from the 3D tracker.

would like to focus on two applications of augmented reality. Other parts will be neglected and interesting readers can refer to [26] for more details.

9.5.1 Medical Visualization

Currently, minimally invasive surgical techniques are popular because they reduce the destruction of the tissues of a patient which gives faster recovery and a better cure. However, these techniques have a major problem that the reduction in the ability to see the surgical location makes the process more difficult. AR can be helpful in relieving this problem. AR first collects 3D datasets of a patient in real time using non invasive sensors like magnetic resonance imaging (MRI), computed tomography scans (CT), or ultrasound imaging. Then, these collected datasets are input to the scene generator to create virtual images. The virtual images are superimposed on the view of the real patient. This effectively gives a surgeon "X-ray vision" inside the patient, which would be very helpful during minimally invasive surgery. Additionally, AR can even be helpful in the traditional surgery because certain medical features are hard to detect with the naked eye but easy to detect with MRI or CT scans and vice versa. AR can use the collected data sets to generate accantuated views of the operation position and target tissues to help surgeons precisely remove the problematic tissues and cure the disease. AR might also be helpful for guiding tasks which need high precision, such as displaying where to drill a hole into the skull for brain surgery or where to perform a needle biopsy of a tiny tumor. The information from the non invasive sensors would be directly displayed on the patient to show exactly where to perform the operation. There are several AR medical systems proposed in [27–32].

As shown in Figure 9.10, Liao et al. [33] proposed a 3D augmented reality navigation system which consists of an integral videography (IV) overlay device, a 3D data scanner

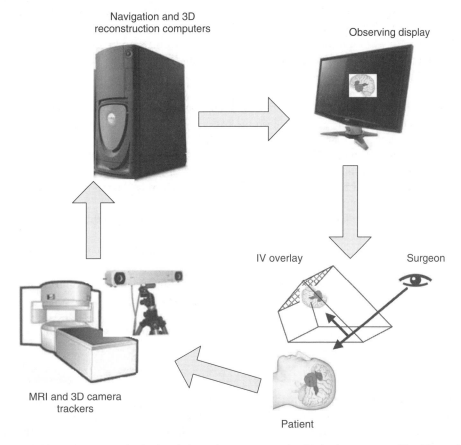

Figure 9.10 MRI scans the brain of the patient to create the 3D brain structure. The 3D tracker uses test patterns to register the patient's location. The computer collects MRI scanned images and tracking information to place the virtual object at the proper location on the image overlay. The doctor can directly see both the helping image and the patient.

(MRI), a position tracking device and computers for image rendering and display. The IV overlay device [33–36] is constructed with autostereoscopic techniques for 3D stereoscopic perception and is aligned with a half-silvered mirror to display the 3D structure of the patient to the doctor. The half-silvered mirror reflects an autostereoscopic image on the IV display back to the surgeon. Looking through this mirror, the surgeon sees the IV image formed in the corresponding location in the body. The spatially projected 3D images are superimposed onto the patient via the half-silvered mirror. Using this image overlay with reconstructed 3D medical images, a surgeon can "see through" the patient's body while being exactly positioned within the patient's anatomy. This system potentially enhances the surgeon's ability to perform a complex procedure. To properly align the MRI virtual images with the patient body, the system use a set of spatial test patterns to calibrate the displayed IV image and a set of fiducial markers for registering 3D points in space. A set of anatomic or fiducial markers (more than four markers located in different planes) is used to track the position of the patient's body. The same markers can be detected by MRI and localized in the position sensor space by computing their 3D coordinates. This procedure enables theoretical registration of the reflected spatial 3D image in conjunction with the target object.

Surgical safety is important and critical and thus the following gives a complete workflow for checking the safety and precision of MRI-guided surgery using an IV image overlay:

1. The spatial position of the IV must be calibrated preoperatively with a designed pattern.
2. Sterile fiducial markers are placed on the patient's body. The images of the target area on the patient's body are scanned by open MRI.
3. The markers and images are used to perform intraoperative segmentation and patient-to-image registration.
4. The IV images are rendered and transferred to the overlay device for superimposing with the image captured from the patient.
5. The IV image is updated according to the registration results, and the alignment of the overlay image with the patient is verified.
6. The surgical treatment can be guided with the help of the IV image overlay to adjust the position and orientation of the instrument.
7. After finishing the treatment, the patient is scanned by the MRI to confirm whether the entire tumor was resected or the target was punctured.

The procedure can be repeated until the evaluation of the surgery is successful.

9.5.2 Mobile Phone Applications

With the advance of a modern smartphones and the rapid adoption of wireless broadband technologies, AR has moved out of the lab and into the real world and become feasible in consumer devices. Although smartphones are not ideal platforms for AR research, they provide several useful functions as a successful platform for AR. The AR applications on mobile devices basically follow the video-augmented-display techniques to deliver the augmented sense to the users. However, the AR applications are still not as popular as the researchers expect a decade ago for the following two reasons. First, the currently available technology cannot reach the expectations of all consumers. The imagination and pop culture have made customers believe that immersive 3D and smart object technologies can deliver fantastic interaction to them but current technology is only half way there and thus the gap is still beyond the expectation. Second, immersive 3D technologies are impressive but there is little real life usage of them. For example, smart lamps and desks do not fit our current lifestyles, meet our needs, or provide any perceived benefit. Through careful observation, three technologies are the key in the past AR technologies. The first is "vision" which means the predominance of displays, graphics, and cameras, and the effects of these on the human visual system. The second is "space" which means the registration of objects physically and conceptually in the real world for creating a convincing AR. The final aspect is the technology which needs special techniques and equipment to be made for AR systems which makes the process expensive and hard to be accepted by the general public. Therefore, with limited success in smartphones, the AR applications should focus on the emergent technology available. However, for future applications, three aspects should be extended: vision becomes perception, space becomes place, and technologies become capabilities [37].

1. **Vision becomes perceptions**

   AR has always focused on the perception and representations in the hybrid space consisting of real and virtual objects. Although traditionally the focus has always been visual representations, there is more perception for AR to let the human comprehend the hybrid space rather than vision alone. Information perceived should give the user the distinct characteristics of the hybrid space for some kinds of human activities. One simple example is tabletop AR games [37] which work very well technically and are published with new generations of handheld gaming devices such as the Nintendo 3DS. However, AR research should go beyond the demonstration of what we might use AR for and begin to focus more explicitly on understanding the elements of perception and representation that are needed to accomplish each of these tasks. According to the tasks, AR designers and researchers understand how to blend and adapt information with the technologies available to help users accomplish their goal. This will be critical for the success of AR.

2. **Space becomes place**

   Currently, smartphone users tend to store and access information on the cloud and the cloud has made the computing placeness disappears. For example, you can no longer guarantee that a researcher is at home or in an office when simulating complex phenomena. The distinctive characteristic of AR is its ability to define a hybrid space but there is more to creating a place than the space itself. A place is a space with meaning. HCI researchers have used this same distinction to argue that seemingly inconsequential elements, such as furniture and artwork, are actually vital to effective collaboration and telepresence technologies [38] because they help create a sense of place that frames appropriate behaviors. It is also a distinction that can help us adapt AR research for the future. Mobile computing would like to have web-based services that are inherently built for location awareness and context awareness. Fundamentally, the kinds of captured data and the ways to structure and access the data need to evolve accordingly. The main challenge is to determine what data is relevant, how to collect data, when to retrieve data, and how to represent data when finishing retrieval. These are fundamental questions to understand humans rather than technologies.

3. **Technologies become capabilities**

In the past, AR researchers focused their efforts on developing expensive and cumbersome equipment to create a proper AR interaction environment [39–41]. The environments are built for specific tasks or scenarios and the defects of such schemes are that the systems are expensive and hard to standardize. Although smartphones make AR popular, they are not explicitly designed for AR and not ideal for delivering AR content. A large number of smartphone applications provide AR by overlaying text on the magic window. This text is used to view the physical world with no more than the sensors built into the device (compass, GPS, accelerometers, gyroscopes). However, this AR helping scheme also has its limitations. The future generation of smartphone systems must create new AR interaction and application models to meet the expectation of users. These new models must present AR information in the real space around the user and this in turn requires the information to be aligned rigidly with their view of the physical space. Precise alignment requires the fusion of sensor information with vision processing of camera-captured videos [42, 43], which is beyond the capabilities of current technologies.

From these observations, 3D technologies can push mobile technologies to another level. First, the autostereoscopic display device can provide more precise perception of the world to the viewer. Second, video-plus-depth is an important content delivery scheme in 3D technologies The delivered depth map can be used to create better registration of virtual objects for AR applications. Therefore, 2D-3D reconstruction is the key for the success of 3D and AR technologies.

9.5.2.1 Nintendo 3DS System

Nintendo 3DS is a portable game console produced by Nintendo. It is the first 3D stereoscopic game console device released by a major game company. The company claims that it is a mobile gaming device where "games can be enjoyed with 3D effects without the need of any special glasses". The system was revealed at the E3 show in Los Angeles in June 2010 and released in Japan on 26 February 2011, in Europe on 25 March 2011, in North America on 27 March 2011 and in Australia on 31 March 2011. The console is the successor of the handheld systems which are the primary competent of Sony's PlayStation Portable (PSP). In addition, the system would like to explore the possibility of motion-sensing elements and 3D vision display for portable devices. The following are several important specification of the system:

- Graphics processing unit (GPU): Nintendo 3DS is based on a custom PICA200 graphics processor from a Japanese start-up, Digital Media Professionals (DMP). The company has been developing optimized 2D and 3D graphics technologies which support OpenGL ES specifications which primarily focus on the embedded market.
- Two screens: 3DS has two screens. Both screens are capable of displaying a brilliant 16.77 million colors. The top screen is the largest selling point for this device to provide gamers a spatial feeling and depth of objects through the parallax barrier technology. 3D effect gives gamers the ability to find and aim objects more easily to enhance the game experience. The excellent 3D effects have a limited zone to perceive them.

Outside the optimal zone, the perception of depth will distort and artifacts will show up. Therefore the 3DS provides a 3D view controller which allows users to adjust the intensity of the 3D display to fine tune the level of depth. Although the adjustment can relieve partial 3D problems, there are still several other issues: the players may experience eye strain or discomfort when they perceive the 3D effect; generally, most users will feel discomfort after an extended play session.

- Connectivity: Currently, the system only support a 2.4 GHz 802.11 Wi-Fi connectivity with enhanced security WPA2. Mobile connectivity is not provided in this device.
- Motion sensor and gyro sensor: Gyro sensors and motion sensors have become the default devices in smartphones because they provide different means for human–machine interaction. These devices can track the motion and tilt of the machine for a game to react with the user's control. They may provide a portable control for new and unique gameplay mechanics.
- 3D cameras: There are two cameras on the outside of the device. The cameras are synchronized to take a set of stereoscopic images. In addition, there is a camera on the top screen facing the player which is used to take 2D images and shoot 2D videos. All three cameras have a resolution of 640×480 pixels (0.3 megapixels). The two outer cameras simulates human eyes to see the world in 3D vision and allow for the creation of 3D photos. These 3D photos can be shown in a similar manner to the 3D game on the stereoscopic screen.
- 3D videos: In addition to 3D games and photos, the stereoscopic screen also has the ability to show 3D videos.
- Augmented reality games: The sense of AR can be enhanced by the 3D stereoscopic pair of cameras and motion sensor and gyro. The 3DS system uses the outer cameras and AR cards to have a video game able to unfold in the real world such as on your kitchen table or the floor of your living room. Generally, the AR cards are placed on a region in the real world and the camera will read the card and initiate the game stages and characters right before your eyes.

This naked-eye 3D vision-based screen can provide new gaming experiences to the players but there are still 3D artifact issues needing to be solved. Furthermore, a "killer app" for the usage of 3D vision is still need to get the console overwhelmingly by accepted gamers.

References

1. O. Wang, M. Lang, M. Frei, A. Hornung, A. Smolic, and M. Gross. "StereoBrush: interactive 2D to 3D conversion using discontinuous warps". In: *Proceedings of the Eighth Eurographics Symposium on Sketch-Based Interfaces and Modeling*, pp. 47–54, 2011.
2. H. Benko, R. Jota, and A. D. Wilson. "MirageTable: Freehand Interaction on a Projected Augmented Reality Tabletop". In: *In Proc. of ACM CHI*, pp. 1–10, 2012.
3. W. Ijsselsteijn, H. de Ridder, R. Hamberg, D. Bouwhuis, and J. Freeman. "Perceived depth and the feeling of presence in 3DTV". *Displays*, vol. 18, no. 4, pp. 207–214, 1998.
4. H. Ridder. "Naturalness and image quality: Saturation and lightness variations in color images of natural scenes". *The Journal of Imaging Science and Technology*, vol. 40, no. 6, pp. 487–493, 1996.
5. D. Strohmeier and G. Tech. "Sharp, bright, three-dimensional: open profiling of quality for mobile 3DTV coding methods". In: *Proc. SPIE*, pp. 7542–75420T, 2010.
6. B. Julesz. "*Foundations of Cyclopean Perception*". MIT Press, 1971.

7. H. B. Barlow, C. Blakemore, and J. D. Pettigrew. "The neural mechanism of binocular depth discrimination". *Journal of Physiology*, vol. 193, no. 2, pp. 327–342, 1967.

8. M. Mikkola, A. Boev, and A. Gotchev. "Relative importance of depth cues on portable autostereoscopic display". In: *Proceedings of the 3rd workshop on mobile video delivery*, pp. 63–68, 2010.

9. M. Nawrot. "Depth from motion parallax scales with eye movement gain". *Journal of Vision*, vol. 3, pp. 841–851, 2003.

10. S. Ohtsuka and S. Saida. "Depth perception from motion parallax in the peripheral vision". In: *Proceedings of the 3rd IEEE International Workshop on Robot and Human Communication*, 1994. *RO-MAN '94 Nagoya*, pp. 72–77, July 1994.

11. E. Johnston, B. Cumming, and A. Parker. "Integration of depth modules: Stereopsis and texture". *Vision Research*, vol. 33, no. 5–6, pp. 813–826, 1993.

12. D. Knill and J. Saunders. "Do humans optimally integrate stereo and texture information for judgments of surface slant?" *Vision Research*, vol. 43, no. 24, pp. 2539–2558, 2003.

13. M. Young, M. Landy, and L. Maloney. "A perturbation analysis of depth perception from combinations of texture and motion cues". *Vision Research*, vol. 33, no. 18, pp. 2685–2696, 1993.

14. K. Kunze, G. Tech, D. Bugdayci, M. O. Bici, D. Strohmeier, and S. Jumisko-Pyykkö. *"Results of quality attributes of coding, transmission, and their combinations"*. Technical Report D4.3, Mobile3DTV, 2010.

15. Y. Cui, J. Chipchase, and Y. Jung. "Personal TV: A qualitative study of mobile TV users". In: *EuroITV 2007*, Springer, 2007.

16. H. Knoche and J. McCarthy. "Mobile Users' Needs and Expectations of Future Multimedia Services". In: *Proceedings of WWRF12*, 2004.

17. W. IJsselsteijn. "Understanding Presence". In: *Proceedings of the AIIA*, p. 1, 2001.

18. M. Slater. "A Note on Presence Terminology". *Presence Connect*, vol. 13, no. 3, 2003.

19. J. Freeman and S. E. Avons. "Focus Group Exploration of Presence through Advanced Broadcast Services". In: *In Proc. SPIE*, pp. 3959–3976, 2000.

20. J. Hakkinen, T. Kawai, J. Takatalo, T. Leisti, J. Radun, A. Hirsaho, and G. Nyman. "Measuring stereoscopic image quality experience with interpretation based quality methodology". In: *Proceedings of the SPIE*, pp. 68081B–68081B–12, 2004.

21. K. O' Hara, A. S. Mitchell, and A. Vorbau. "Consuming video on mobile devices". In: *Proceedings of the SIGCHI conference on Human factors in computing systems*, pp. 857–866, 2007.

22. V. Oksman, E. Noppari, A. Tammela, M. Mäkinen, and V. Ollikainen. "Mobile TV in Everyday Life Contexts–Individual Entertainment or Shared Experiences?" In: *InteractiveTV: a Shared Experience*, pp. 215–225, 2007.

23. D. Strohmeier, S. Jumisko-Pyykkö, S. Weitzel, and M. Schneider. *"Report on user needs and expectations for mobile stereo-video"*. Technical Report D4.1 v1.0, Mobile3DTV, 2008.

24. P. Milgram and F. Kishino. "A Taxonomy of Mixed Reality Virtual Displays". *EICE Transactions on Information and Systems E77-D*, vol. 9, pp. 1321–1329, 1994.

25. P. Milgram, H. Takemura, A. Utsumi, and F. Kishino. "Augmented Reality: A Class of Displays on the Reality-Virtuality Continuum". In: *SPIE Proceedings volume 2351: Telemanipulator and Telepresence Technologies*, pp. 282–292, 1994.

26. R. Azuma. "A Survey of Augmented Reality". *Presence*, vol. 16, pp. 355–385, 1997.

27. M. Bajura, H. Fuchs, and R. Ohbuchi. "Merging virtual objects with the real world: seeing ultrasound imagery within the patient". *SIGGRAPH Comput. Graph.*, vol. 26, no. 2, pp. 203–210, 1992.

28. W. Grimson, G. Ettinger, S. White, P. Gleason, T. Lozano-Perez, W. Wells, and R. Kikinis. "Evaluating and validating an automated registration system for enhanced reality visualization in surgery". In: *Computer Vision, Virtual Reality and Robotics in Medicine*, pp. 1–12, 1995.

29. W. Grimson, G. Ettinger, S. White, T. Lozano-Perez, I. Wells, W.M., and R. Kikinis. "An automatic registration method for frameless stereotaxy, image guided surgery, and enhanced reality visualization". *Medical Imaging, IEEE Transactions on*, vol. 15, no. 2, pp. 129–140, 1996.

30. J. Mellor. "Realtime Camera Calibration for Enhanced Reality Visualization". In: *Proceedings of Computer Vision, Virtual Reality and Robotics in Medicine (CVRMed '95) Conference*, pp. 471–475, Springer-Verlag, 1995.

31. P. Mellor. *Enhanced Reality Visualization in a Surgical Environment*. Master's thesis, MIT, 1995.

32. A. State, D. T. Chen, C. Tector, A. Brandt, H. Chen, R. Ohbuchi, M. Bajura, and H. Fuchs. "Case Study: Observing a Volume Rendered Fetus within a Pregnant Patient". In: *Proceedings of the 1994 IEEE Visualization Conference*, pp. 364–368, 1994.

33. H. Liao, T. Inomata, I. Sakuma, and T. Dohi. "3-D Augmented Reality for MRI-Guided Surgery Using Integral Videography Autostereoscopic Image Overlay". *Biomedical Engineering, IEEE Transactions on*, vol. 57, no. 6, pp. 1476–1486, 2010.

34. M. Blackwell, C. Nikou, A. M. Digioia, and T. Kanade. "An image overlay system for medical data visualization". In: *Proceedings of the 1998 Medical Imaging Computing and Computer Assisted Intervention Conference (MICCAI '98)*, 1998.

35. K. Massamune, A. Deguet, H. Mathieu, R. H. Taylor, E. Balogh, J. Zinreich, L. Fayad, G. Fischer, and G. Fichtinger. "Image Overlay Guidance for Needle Insertion in CT Scanner". *IEEE Transaction on Biomedical Engineering*, vol. 52, no. 8, pp. 1415–1424, 2005.

36. G. Stetten and V. Chib. "Overlaying Ultrasound Images on Direct Vision". *Journal of Ultrasound in Medicine*, vol. 20, no. 3, pp. 235–240, 2001.

37. Y. Xu, E. Barba, I. Radu, M. Gandy, R. Shemaka, B. Schrank, B. MacIntyre, and T. Tseng. "Pre-patterns for designing embodied interactions in handheld augmented reality games". In: *IEEE International Symposium on Mixed and Augmented Reality–Arts, Media, and Humanities (ISMAR-AMH), 2011*, pp. 19–28, October 2011.

38. S. Harrison and P. Dourish. "Replaceing space: the roles of place and space in collaborative systems". In: *Proceedings of the 1996 ACM conference on computer supported cooperative work*, pp. 67–76, 1996.

39. G. Abowd, C. Atkeson, J. Hong, S. Long, R. Kooper, and M. Pinkerton. "Cyberguide: A mobile context-aware tour guide". *Wireless Networks*, vol. 3, pp. 421–433, 1997.

40. S. Feiner, B. MacIntyre, T. Höllerer, and A. Webster. "A touring machine: Prototyping 3D mobile augmented reality systems for exploring the urban environment". *Personal Technologies*, vol. 1, pp. 208–217, 1997.

41. B. Schilit, N. Adams, R. Gold, M. Tso, and R. Want. "The PARCTAB mobile computing system". In: *Proceedings of the Fourth Workshop on Workstation Operating Systems*, 1993, pp. 34–39, October 1993.

42. J. W. Lee, S. You, and U. Neumann. "Tracking with Omni-Directional Vision for Outdoor AR Systems". In: *Proceedings of the 1st International Symposium on Mixed and Augmented Reality*, p. 47, 2002.

43. G. Reitmayr and T. Drummond. "Going out: robust model-based tracking for outdoor augmented reality". In: *ISMAR 2006. IEEE/ACM International Symposium on Mixed and Augmented Reality*, 2006. pp. 109–118, October 2006.

10

Advanced 3D Video Streaming Applications

10.1 Rate Control in Adaptive Streaming

Streaming 3D video over communication networks for real-time application has many challenges. One of these is how to utilize the current limited network resources to achieve the best perceived 3D video quality. Besides, the bandwidth provided by the network may vary from time to time. For the best received quality, the streaming applications need to dynamically perform rate control to adjust the encoding rate at the encoder side to fit in the current network status and maintain the playback smoothness at the decoder side. However, different coding tools and modes can be selected to meet the same target bit rate but result in different perceived quality. Although the encoder can resort to the full search methodology by trying all possibilities for best tradeoff, this kind of solution is often NP hard and/or very time consuming, thus not practical for real-time applications. It is desired to have a fast selection method for near-optimal solutions to reduce the computation complexity at the encoder side. In this section, we will address both the rate control and the mode decision issue in the 3D video streaming applications.

10.1.1 Fundamentals of Rate Control

A generic 3D video streaming framework is shown in Figure 10.1. The encoder located at the transmitter side will adjust the coding parameters to control the bit rate according to the latest estimated network bandwidth and optional error control message through receiver's feedback. The decoder located at the receiver side equips a decoder buffer to smooth out the network jitter and the bit rate fluctuation owing to different coding parameters being selected by the encoder. The main objective of the decoder buffer is to ensure that the playback is as smooth as possible. As we can see from Figure 10.1, there are two common constraints that the encoder needs to follow so that the playback at the decoder side can be smooth. The first constraint is that the bit rate sent from the transmitter should not exceed the capacity of the underlying networks at any time instant.

3D Visual Communications, First Edition. Guan-Ming Su, Yu-Chi Lai, Andres Kwasinski and Haohong Wang.
© 2013 John Wiley & Sons, Ltd. Published 2013 by John Wiley & Sons, Ltd.

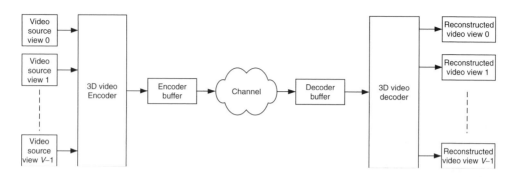

Figure 10.1   Framework of 3D video streaming.

Without any buffering mechanism deployed at the transmitter side, those out-of-capacity bits will be dropped out and cause decoding problems at the decoder side as video streams exhibit strong decoding dependency. The second constraint is the fullness of the decoder buffer: it should neither underflow, which causes playback jitter, nor overflow, which drops bits which causes video quality degradation and error propagation.

Given the aforementioned constraints, the encoder needs to adjust the encoding parameter such that the perceived video quality is as high as possible. A well-known rate control method for traditional 2D video is defined in MPEG-2 test model 5 (TM5) [1]. Basically, TM5 rate control follows a top-down hierarchical approach and consists of three steps: (1) target bit allocation at frame level by addressing the picture complexity in the temporal domain; (2) rate control at macro-block (MB) level by addressing the buffer fullness; (3) adaptive quantization to refine the decision made in step (2) by addressing the varying texture complexity in the spatial domain. The bit allocation is assigned by a complexity model according to different inter/intra type: I, P, or B. Consider the scenario that the channel bandwidth is R bits per second (bps) and the picture refresh rate is F. An N-frame group of pictures (GOP) consists of N_I I-frames, N_P P-frames, and N_B B-frames: $N = N_I + N_P + N_B$.

In the first step, the encoder allocates bits to N frames within a GOP with N frames such that the overall number of bits consumed in one GOP is NR/F. The complexity model assumes that the number of bits for one frame multiplied by its quantization scale remains around a constant, and has the following expressions:

$$X_I = S_I Q_I, \ X_P = S_P Q_P, \ \text{and} \ X_B = S_B Q_B, \tag{10.1}$$

where X, S, and Q represent the complexity, number of bits for one frame, quantization scale, respectively, and the subscript denotes the different picture type. The complexity is first initialized before the encoding as:

$$X_I = \frac{160 \cdot R}{115}, X_P = \frac{60 \cdot R}{115}, \ \text{and} \ X_B = \frac{42 \cdot R}{115}. \tag{10.2}$$

After encoding the first frame for each type, the complexity model of each picture type in (10.1) is updated according to both the average chosen quantization scale and the number of bits consumed.

To provide consistent perceived video quality across different picture types, empirical studies suggest that it can be achieved by setting a constant ratio between different quantization scales. In other words:

$$Q_I = K_I Q, Q_P = K_P Q, \text{ and } Q_B = K_B Q, \tag{10.3}$$

where the value of K_I, K_P and K_B are suggested to be 1.0, 1.0, and 1.4 in TM5. Bringing in (10.3) to (10.1), the number of bits for each picture type can be rewritten as:

$$S_I = \frac{X_I}{K_I Q}, S_P = \frac{X_P}{K_P Q}, \text{ and } S_B = \frac{X_B}{K_B Q}. \tag{10.4}$$

Note that the targeted total number of bits allocated in a GOP is to achieve NR/F:

$$N_I S_I + N_P S_P + N_B S_B = NR/F. \tag{10.5}$$

The number of bits for I type, S_I, can be derived as follows. By rearranging (10.4), S_P and S_B can be represented by S_I:

$$Q = \frac{X_I}{K_I S_I}, S_P = \frac{X_P}{K_P Q} = \frac{X_P K_I}{K_P X_I} S_I, \text{ and } S_B = \frac{X_B K_I}{K_B X_I} S_I. \tag{10.6}$$

By combining (10.6) and (10.5), we arrive at:

$$S_I = \frac{NR/F}{N_I + \dfrac{N_P X_P K_I}{K_P X_I} + \dfrac{N_B X_B K_I}{K_B X_I}}. \tag{10.7a}$$

Similarly, we can have S_P and S_B as:

$$S_P = \frac{NR/F}{N_P + \dfrac{N_I X_I K_P}{K_I X_P} + \dfrac{N_B X_B K_P}{K_B X_P}}, \tag{10.7b}$$

and

$$S_B = \frac{NR/F}{N_B + \dfrac{N_I X_I K_B}{K_I X_B} + \dfrac{N_P X_P K_B}{K_P X_B}}. \tag{10.7c}$$

After allocating bits in the frame level, in the second step, the bits are allocated in the MB level by adjusting the reference quantization scale for each MB with the consideration of buffer fullness. For the jth MB, the reference quantization scale, Q_j, is computed as:

$$Q_j = \frac{31 \cdot d_j}{r}, \tag{10.8}$$

where d_j is the decoder buffer fullness, and r is a reaction parameter defined as $r = 2R/F$.

It is often noticed that the spatial complexity within a frame is not a constant and varies from one region to another, depending on the local texture and activities. The activity factor, act_j, is obtained by first calculating the variances of all luminance 8×8 blocks within one 16×16 MB, selecting the minimum variance among all candidates, and adding a constant value, one, to the selected minimum variance. The activity measurement will be normalized as:

$$N_{act,j} = \frac{2 \cdot act_j + ave\_act}{act_j + ave\_act},$$ (10.9)

where ave_act is the average act_j in the previous picture. For the first frame, ave_act is set to 400. The final used quantization scale will be refined by addressing the local activity measurement, $N_{act,j}$, and can be calculated as:

$$Q_j = \min\{Q_j \cdot N_{act,j}, 31\}.$$ (10.10)

The rate control method in MPEG-4 verification model (VM) is an extension of MPEG-2 TM5 but with a more precise complexity model [2]. Denote the number of bits for one frame as S and the number of bits for nontexture information, such as header and motion vectors as H, and the mean of absolute difference (MAD) computed using motion-compensated residual for the luminance component as M. The R–D curve is described by a quadratic model:

$$\frac{S - H}{M} = \frac{a_1}{Q} + \frac{a_2}{Q^2},$$ (10.11)

where a_1 and a_2 are the first and the second order coefficients and can be estimated on-line via the least squared solution.

A similar top-down bit allocation strategy from GOP-level, picture level, to uniform slice level is adopted in H.264 JM software (JVT-G012) [3]. Note that H.264 does not define a picture as a pure I/P/B-frame type since a frame can contain I/P/B slices. The complexity model (X_I, X_P, and X_B) used in MPEG-2 and MPEG-4 is replaced by the concept of signal deviation measure σ for each frame in H.264 codec. The signal deviation measure will be updated by the first order polynomial predictor from the MAD of the previous stored picture. The main goal of the GOP level rate control is to control the deviation of the quantization parameters in a small range from one GOP to another, such that the video quality fluctuation is maintained under an unnoticeable level. The decoder buffer occupancy should be checked to avoid overflow and underflow. There are two stages in the picture-level rate control: pre-encoding and post-encoding. The pre-encoding stage is to calculate the required quantization parameter for each picture, and the post-encoding stage is to refine the quantization parameters for each uniform slice or MB unit by the given allocated bit rate. The quadratic R-D model (10.11) is used. At the MB-level, a rate distortion optimization (RDO) strategy is deployed by formulating the rate control problem as minimizing the overall distortion subjected to a given target bit rate by selecting the coding method. The general RDO process is constructed as follows. Denote s_k as the kth coding block and $\mathbf{s} = [s_0, s_1, \ldots, s_{K-1}]$ is the collection of all coding blocks in one MB. Denote m_k as the selected mode in the kth coding block and $\mathbf{m} = [m_0, m_1, \ldots, m_{K-1}]$ is the collection of all coding modes in one MB. The distortion and the bit rate are functions of selected coding modes and they can be represented as $D(\mathbf{s},\mathbf{m})$ and $R(\mathbf{s},\mathbf{m})$, respectively. With a maximal bit rate budget, R, the optimization problem is formulated as:

$$\min_{\mathbf{m}} D(\mathbf{s}, \mathbf{m})$$ (10.12)

$$\text{s.t. } R(\mathbf{s}, \mathbf{m}) \leq R.$$

This constrained optimization problem can be reformulated as an unconstrained optimization by introducing a Lagrange multiplier, λ. The objective function becomes:

$$J(\mathbf{s}, \mathbf{m}|\lambda) = D(\mathbf{s}, \mathbf{m}) + \lambda R(\mathbf{s}, \mathbf{m}). \tag{10.13}$$

With a given λ, we can have a corresponding optimal solution of (10.13). The optimal solution of (10.12) is achieved when the selected λ results in $R(\mathbf{s}, \mathbf{m}) = R$. For simplicity, the overall distortion function within an MB is assumed as independently summed from each coding block. The objective function can be decomposed into K small functions and can be solved individually.

$$J(\mathbf{s}, \mathbf{m}|\lambda) = \sum_{k=0}^{K-1} J(s_k, m_k|\lambda) = \min_{\mathbf{m}} \sum_{k=0}^{K-1} D(s_k, m_k) + \lambda R(s_k, m_k). \tag{10.14}$$

More specifically, the formulation in JM H.264 is to optimize the following cost function by selecting the optimal coding mode under a given quantization parameter, Q_P, and the value of associated λ_{MODE}:

$$J_{MODE}(s_k, m_k|Q_p, \lambda) = D_{REC}(s_k, m_k|Q_p) + \lambda_{MODE} R_{REC}(s_k, m_k|Q_p), \tag{10.15}$$

where MODE can be the intra-prediction mode or the inter-prediction mode. Let $s(x, y, t)$ be the original pixel value with coordinate (x, y) at frame t and let A be the collection of coordinates for all pixels in the considered coding block. Depending on whether intra or inter mode is selected, the distortion and the λ_{MODE} are calculated differently.

For intra mode, the distortion, D_{REC}, is measured as sum of squared difference (SSD) as follows:

$$SSD = \sum_{(x,y)\in A} |s(x, y, t) - s_{INTRA}(x, y, t)|^2, \tag{10.16}$$

where $s_{INTRA}(x, y, t)$ is the pixel value after intra mode coding.

For inter mode, the distortion measurement, D_{REC}, is calculated as the displaced frame difference (DFD):

$$DFD = \sum_{(x,y)\in A} |s(x, y, t) - s_{INTER}(x - m_x, y - m_y, t - m_t)|^p, \tag{10.17}$$

where (m_x, m_y) is the motion vector pair, $s_{INTER}(x - m_x, y - m_y, t - m_t)$ is the pixel value after inter mode coding, and p as the coding parameter to choose different order of distortion.

λ_{MODE} is suggested from the experiment as follows:

$$\lambda_{MODE} = 0.85 \times 2^{(Q_p - 12)/3} \tag{10.18}$$

Depending on the chosen order of inter-mode distortion measurement, λ_{INTER} has a different expression:

$$\lambda_{INTER} = \begin{cases} \sqrt{\lambda_{MODE}} & p = 1 \\ \lambda_{MODE} & p = 2 \end{cases} \tag{10.19}$$

10.1.2 Two-View Stereo Video Streaming

The rate control for two-view stereo video rate control can be extended from previous discussed methods according to the adopted stereo video codec. For the individual view coding, which encodes left view and right view with two independent video encoders, one could deploy the joint multi-program rate control method commonly used in multiuser scenario [4, 5]. Although the bit streams are encoded independently in the individual view coding scenario, the underlying resources, such as bit stream buffers and allocated transmission channels, can be merged together and jointly utilized to achieve higher multiplexing gain. Besides, the encoder can further explore the diversity gain exhibited from different content complexity via (10.1) or (10.11) in both views, and allocate bits to each view accordingly.

For the frame-compatible stereo video streaming, one could deploy and extend the commonly used single-program rate control method. Note that each picture in the frame-compatible stereo video contains two downsampled views. Advanced rate control methods to address different characteristics of these two different downsampled views can be used for better visual quality. For example, if TM5 rate control method is used, the average spatial activity measurement, ave_act, used in (10.9) may need to have two variables to track regions in two different views. For the full-resolution frame-compatible stereo video streaming, the codec has one base layer and one enhancement layer. The enhancement layer has decoding dependency on the base layer. The scalability and dependency often bring a penalty on coding efficiency [6]. Given a total bit budget for both layers, different rates assigned to the base layer and enhancement layer will result in different perceived quality in the base layer only and in the base layer plus enhancement layer. A balanced bit allocation between two layers can be performed for different video quality requirements from the baseline half-resolution experience and enhanced full resolution experience.

As discussed in Chapter 5, the binocular suppression theory suggests that the video qualities measured by objective metrics, such as PSNR, in both views do not have a strong correlation to the perceived stereo video experience. Based on this observation, the bit allocated in the dominant view can be higher than that of the non-dominant view.

10.1.3 MVC Streaming

The MVC codec encodes one more dimension to incorporate different camera views. A group of GOP (GGOP) from multiple views is often constructed first. A straightforward method for MVC rate control is to start the bit allocation from this GGOP level. After allocating bits to each view, one could employ the common 2D video rate control scheme to handle the frame level and the MB level. In [7], the bit budget allocation for each view is based on the view complexity measured by the correlation between the base view and the predicted views. Denote $I(x,y,v)$ as the (x,y) pixel located at the v-th view and the dimension for each view is $W \times H$. The correlation between view v and base view 0 is calculated as:

$$C(v) = \frac{\sum_{x=0}^{W-1} \sum_{y=0}^{H-1} (I(x, y, v) - \bar{I}(v))(I(x, y, 0) - \bar{I}(0))}{\sqrt{\sum_{x=0}^{W-1} \sum_{y=0}^{H-1} (I(x, y, v) - \bar{I}(v))^2} \sqrt{\sum_{x=0}^{W-1} \sum_{y=0}^{H-1} (I(x, y, 0) - \bar{I}(0))^2}},$$

$$(10.20)$$

where

$$\bar{I}(v) = \frac{1}{WH} \sum_{x=0}^{W-1} \sum_{y=0}^{H-1} I(x, y, v). \tag{10.21}$$

The correlation will be normalized as:

$$w(v) = \frac{C(v)}{\sum_{k=0}^{M-1} C(k)}. \tag{10.22}$$

Given a total bit rate, R, for one MVC stream, the rate allocated to view v, R_v, will be:

$$R_v = w(v)R. \tag{10.23}$$

The correlation-based bit allocation will assign more bits to the views with higher similarity to the base view, thus the summed distortion over all views is minimized. When equal video quality among all views becomes a requirement, one can modify the weighting factors, $\{w(v)\}$, by assigning more bits to the views with lower correlation. In that regard, the system's objective becomes to maximize the minimal video quality among all views [8].

An RDO approach can also be adopted in the MVC streaming rate control by searching the quantization parameter in each view [9]. Similar to the independent optimization methodology used in H.264 optimization, the optimization problem can be decoupled to several subproblems and solved independently via a trellis expansion.

10.1.4 MVD Streaming

In the MVD coding, some views are not encoded in the bit streams and need to be synthesized from neighboring texture videos and depth maps. Therefore, the visual quality of the synthesized view, D_v, depends on the quality of the reconstructed texture videos and depth maps from the neighboring coded real views. The distortions of those coded real views depend on the selected quantization parameters. One can simplify the problem to reduce the range of parameters set by assuming that both neighboring coded real views use the same quantization parameter to achieve similar perceptual quality. Denote Q_t and Q_d as the selected quantization parameter for the texture video and depth map in both neighboring views, respectively. Then, D_v can be expressed as a function of Q_t and Q_d, namely, $D_v(Q_t, Q_d)$. The required bit rate in the texture video, R_t, and the depth map, R_d, can be also expressed as functions of quantization parameter Q_t and Q_d. In other words, the rate functions are $R_t(Q_t)$ and $R_d(Q_d)$. The major issues in MVD streaming are how to distribute bits to the texture videos and depth maps, given a total rate constraint, R, so that the perceived video quality at the desired viewing position(s) is optimized. One can formulate the bit allocation in MVD streaming application to optimize the synthesized view's distortion by selecting the optimal Q_t and Q_d in both neighboring real views subject to the rate constraint, R:

$$\min_{\{Q_t, Q_d\}} D_v(Q_t, Q_d) \tag{10.24}$$

$$\text{s.t. } R_t(Q_t) + R_d(Q_d) \le R.$$

A full-search method can be conducted to find the optimal encoding parameters in both texture and depth video at the cost of higher computation complexity [10]. The full-search is performed on the 2D distortion surface constructed by one dimension along the texture video bit rate and another dimension along the depth map bit rate. Although the optimal solution can be found from a full search methodology, the computation complexity is often very high. A distortion model for the synthesized view is often desired such that the computation complexity can be simplified [11].

Since the synthesized view is often generated from a linear combination of neighboring real views, the distortion of the synthesized view can be modeled as a linear combination of the distortion from texture image and depth image belonging to both neighboring left view and right view [12]:

$$D_v = \alpha_L D_t^L + \alpha_R D_t^R + \beta_L D_d^L + \beta_R D_d^R + \gamma, \tag{10.25}$$

where D_t^L, D_t^R, D_d^L, and D_d^R represent the compression distortion for the reconstructed left view texture video, right view texture video, left view depth map, and right view depth map, respectively. α_L, α_R, β_L, β_R, and γ are the model parameters and need to be estimated.

Since the video's encoded rate and distortion are functions of the selected quantization parameters, the encoded rate for texture, R_t, and depth, R_d, in both neighboring coded views can be modeled as functions of the corresponding quantization step as follows:

$$R_t(Q_t) = \frac{a_t}{Q_t} + b_t \text{ and } R_d(Q_d) = \frac{a_d}{Q_d} + b_d, \tag{10.26}$$

where a_t, b_t, a_d, b_d are the rate-quantization model parameters and need to be empirically estimated. The distortion for texture, D_t, and depth, D_d, in both neighboring coded views can be modeled as functions of corresponding quantization step:

$$D_t(Q_t) = m_t Q_t + n_t \text{ and } D_d(Q_d) = m_d Q_d + n_d, \tag{10.27}$$

where m_t, n_t, m_d, n_d are the rate-quantization model parameters and need to be empirically estimated. With the assumption that the content in both neighboring coded views is similar, the distortion in the neighboring views is very similar by using the same quantization parameter. Therefore, the distortion in the synthesized view, D_v, can be further simplified and modeled as a function of Q_t and Q_d in both views.

Having those models, problem (10.24) can be reformulated as:

$$\min_{\{Q_t, Q_d\}} (\mu Q_t + v Q_d + C) \tag{10.28}$$

$$\text{s.t. } \frac{a_t}{Q_t} + b_t + \frac{a_d}{Q_d} + b_d \leq R.$$

Standard optimization methods, such as the Lagrangian multiplier method, can be applied to solve Q_t and Q_d.

With a model to describe the rate-quantization and distortion-quantization relationship, one can apply it to the MVD rate control. In [13], the rate control is conducted via a top-down approach by first assigning a bit rate for each real view, then allocating bits between texture video and depth map in each view, and finally conducting frame level rate allocation. In the frame level rate allocation, the quantization parameter is adjusted to satisfy the decoder buffer fullness requirement. Similar to most rate control methods, the distortion-rate-quantization model needs updating after a frame is encoded.

When the number of views becomes large in the MVD case, one may choose to transmit fewer coded views to save on bit rate. In this scenario, several intermediate views need to be synthesized between two neighboring coded views from the bit streams. An important question is how to select the most important views to be encoded in the streams and leave other views to be synthesized at the rendering stage so the overall distortion from all views are minimized subject to a target bit rate. As the distance between these two neighboring coded views is large, the selected quantization parameters will be different to address different content complexity owing to different viewpoints. Under this condition, the distortions in these two neighboring coded views are not similar. Consider a synthesized view at a virtual viewpoint having a distance ratio to the left coded view and the right coded view as $k/(1-k)$, where $0 \leq k \leq 1$, the distortion of this synthesized view can be modeled as a cubic function with respect to the viewing position between two coded real views [14].

$$D_v(k) = c_0 + c_1 k + c_2 k^2 + c_3 k^3. \tag{10.29}$$

The parameters c_0, c_1, c_2, and c_3 can be estimated from curve fitting technology such as least squared solution by sampling a small number of virtual views and synthesizing the view to measure the distortion. With this more general model, we can formulate a more generalized problem to minimize the overall distortion in all coded views and the synthesized views subject to the rate constraint by: (1) selecting which views to code and which views to synthesize and (2) choosing the quantization parameters for texture video and depth map in the coded view. The optimal solution can be found using the 3D trellis algorithm.

10.2 Multi-View Video View Switching

The multi-view video application provides an interactive and immersive viewing experience. The viewer can switch their viewpoints and watch the events from different angles for their greatest interest. On the other hand, the required bandwidth to provide such viewing experiences through online streaming is very high. In fact, for the multi-view streaming scenario, a user watches only two views at each time instant and normally these two views will be watched for a certain time duration. As illustrated in Figure 10.2, a user watches view 1 and view 2 at time instance t, and switches to view 2 and view 3 at time instance $t+1$. From a bandwidth utilization point of view, it is inefficient to transmit all views to the end user since the user only consumes two views. The bandwidth problem will become worse when there are multiple users requesting multiple view services from one server simultaneously. Although MVC provides an efficient way to compress multiple views into one single bit stream compared to other coding schemes, the required bandwidth is still large. Besides, owing to the inter-view prediction adopted in MVC, the decoding processor needs higher computation complexity and memory access to decode all encoded views but to display only two interested views.

One solution to alleviate the aforementioned bandwidth issue and computation complexity is to encode each view independently (i.e., without exploiting the inter-view prediction) and transmit each encoded view in one IP multicast channel [15], as illustrated

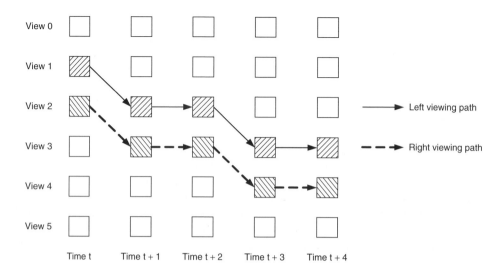

Figure 10.2 Illustration of view switching in interactive multi-view video streaming.

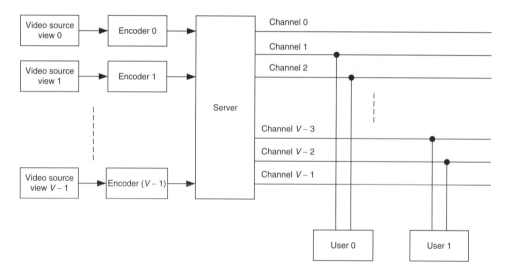

Figure 10.3 Individual view encoding and streaming in multi-view video streaming.

in Figure 10.3. In the considered scenario, there are V view video sources. Each view is encoded by its own encoder and transmitted through its own IP multicast channel. The server is responsible for the subscriptions of the selected views from multiple users. Each user can subscribe to the desired views by joining the corresponding IP multicast channels. For example, user 0 subscribes to channel 1 and channel 2 to watch video from view 1 and view 2; and user 1 subscribes channel $V - 3$ and channel $V - 2$ to watch video from view $V - 3$ and view $V - 2$. Later on, when user 0 wants to switch the interested view to view $V - 3$ and view $V - 2$, they inform the server to leave the multicast channel 1 and 2 and join the new channel $V - 3$ and $V - 2$. Note that, owing to the decoding dependency exhibited from motion compensated video codec, the view switching can only be conducted when the new selected views reach the next I or IDR frame. There is a tradeoff for the frequency of I or IDR frame usage. From coding efficiency point of view, the encoder prefers to use fewer I-frames as they consume a higher bit rate than P/B-frames. From the view switching point of view, users may prefer to have more I-frames to allow finer granularity of view switching point. The view-switching latency in this IP multicasting framework consists of the channel switching time, the time duration to sync up to the latest I-frame, and initialization time for decoder bit stream buffering. The system should carefully choose the corresponding parameters such that the view-switching latency is within users' tolerance.

To reduce the view-switching latency, one can deploy a layered codec structure in this system [16]. The framework is depicted in Figure 10.4. In the server side, each view is spatially down-sampled and all downsampled views are encoded using an MVC codec to construct the base layer (BL). Then, each reconstructed view from BL will be spatially upsampled and the difference between the original view and the spatially upsampled version is encoded as enhancement layer (EL) independently. In this way, the BL contains the basic quality for all V views and the stream is transmitted through a dedicated channel. The enhancement layer for each view will be transmitted separately through its own channel. When users subscribe to the BL channel, they can watch all views but with a lower visual quality. When a user is interested in some particular views, they can join the enhancement layer channel(s) for better visual quality. For example, when the user 0 wants to watch view 1 and view 2, they can subscribe to three channels, namely, BL, EL-1 and EL-2. When user 0 wants to switch view to view $V - 3$ and view $V - 2$, the user can inform the server of their preference to quit channel EL-1 and EL-2 and join EL $V - 3$ and EL $V - 2$. During the view switching transition, though the enhancement

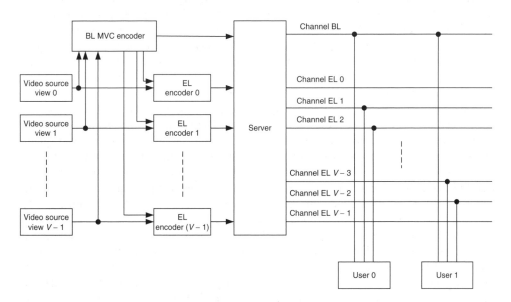

Figure 10.4   Illustration of scalable MVC streaming.

layer links are not set up, the user can still watch the base layer with the basic quality. Thus, the interruption of playback fluency caused by the view switching is minimized.

The other approach to tackling the view switching problem is to use the SP-frame provided in H.264 standard [17]. The SP-frame is introduced to enable efficient switching between video streams encoded in multiple different bit rates to adapt to varying channel bandwidth for offline stored video programs (discussed in Chapter 5). Assume that one user wants to switch stream from A to stream B with different bit rate at time instance $t - 1$. In the server side, a SP-frame from stream A to stream B is constructed at time instance t to utilize temporal prediction from stream A and results in an identical reconstruction at the final reconstructed frame as the one in stream B at time instance t. Then, the user can switch to stream B after time instance t and keep decoding the stream without any decoding drifting. Similarly, one can deploy SP-frames in the view switching scenario [18]. Each view is encoded independently without inter-view prediction, and the SP-frames are encoded at the possible view switching points. Since the SP-frame uses temporal prediction, its coding efficiency is higher than I-frames and can help to reduce the required bandwidth during the view switching period compared to using I-frame. Besides, users can switch their desired views whenever an I-frame or an SP-frame is available, which provides much higher interactivity and lower switching delay.

Although the SP-frame provides the potential to alleviate the bandwidth problem in view switching, the required storage in the server side may pose a challenge, especially when the number of views and/or the desired view switching points is large. For each view, to allow random view switching from one view to all other views, we need to prepare the $V - 1$ SP-frames. For a V-view video sequence, there are $V(V - 1)$ SP-frames needed at each particular view switching point. A tradeoff between the bandwidth consumption and the storage requirement should be made to achieve the system's objectives [19].

When the multi-view video streaming server has higher computation power, the interactive multi-view video can be encoded online according to users' real time feedback for minimal view-switching latency with moderate bandwidth requirement via a modified MVC coding structure [20]. Assuming that the end user is only allowed to switch view to immediately neighboring views, the encoder will encode only the video frames along the predicted viewing paths based on the historical users' feedback, as shown in Figure 10.5. The actual encoding structure depends on the frequency of the user's feedback and the speed of view switching.

In the wireless network, bit streams experience bit corruption and packet loss and they need a certain level of error protection mechanism. Depending on the channel conditions between the server and the mobile users, some users may suffer bad perceived quality and some users may have very good video quality. Besides the adoption of forward error coding to overcome the distortion introduced in the communication system, one could also build a reliable local channel among peers and request the packets from peers which experience good channel conditions from the server side. As illustrated in Figure 10.6, user 0 experiences good channel condition in the subscribed channels and can play back view 1 and view 2 smoothly. User 1 subscribes to channel 0 and channel 1 and experiences bad channel condition. User 0 and user 1 can set up a local channel and relay data from user 0 to user 1. As we notice that user 1 has one different view from user 0 and this unsubscribed view 0 can be rendered by the DIBR technology from view 1 [21]. To deploy this DIBR-based error recovery, each channel should transmit both the texture and the depth map information.

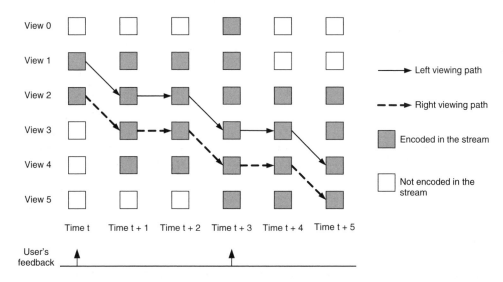

Figure 10.5 Predicted viewing frames in the left and right view according to user's feedback.

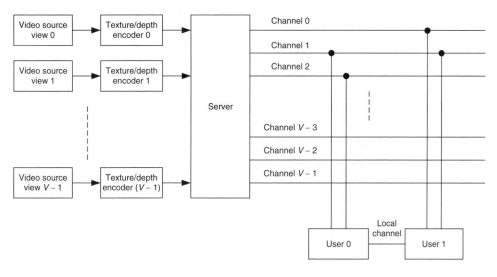

Figure 10.6 Peer-to-Peer assisted multi-view streaming for view repairing.

10.3   Peer-to-Peer 3D Video Streaming

The server–client streaming paradigm has its limitation owning to the bandwidth bottle-neck and is not scalable to support a large group of end users. The problem will become worse for the multi-view video streaming service. It has been demonstrated that the peer-to-peer (P2P) video streaming can significantly alleviate the computation load and bandwidth requirement experienced in a centralized video streaming system. Basically,

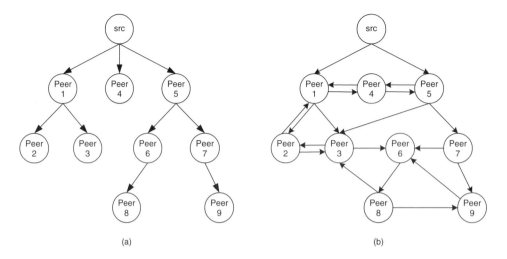

(a)   (b)

Figure 10.7 Peer-to-peer streaming approaches (a) tree-based, (b) mesh-based.

the P2P streaming system can be categorized into two different approaches: tree-based approach and mesh-based approach, as illustrated in Figure 10.7.

The tree-based approach will construct a structured network in a tree topology. The server will serve as the root of the tree and each peer will play both the role of the parent and child node. The video delivery path is built by starting from the server and relaying the streams by peers through the connected nodes, which can provide a low latency video delivery, and thus is suitable for video broadcasting. The advantage of this approach is a shorter join time for a new peer since there is no peer discovery phase needed during the initialization. However, the peer leaving will bring extra handling for the tree reorganization, especially for a peer serving as a parent node who needs to link its parent and child node together to avoid leaving its child out of the tree. In addition, since each parent node is responsible for its child node, the required outbound bandwidth for each peer has higher requirement.

The mesh-based approach is to build an unstructured network where each peer connects to multiple peers. The video delivery path is set up in both ways between each pair of peers, and therefore the concept of parent node and child node is blurred in this network. The mesh-based approach requires extra time for peer discovery when a peer wants to join the streaming service. Therefore, the target application for mesh-based approach is the video-on-demand service. The requirement of the outbound bandwidth is not as high as the tree-based since each peer only needs to contribute a portion of the video data for its neighboring peer. Because the connectivity of mesh-based approach is higher than the tree-based solution, the mesh-based approach will suffer fewer problems when a peer chooses to quit the current video service.

Since the multi-view video streaming requires high bandwidth consumption, deploying a multi-view video service in a distributed and cooperative fashion is expected to alleviate these problems. A simple solution for multi-view video over P2P networks can be constructed by encoding each view independently (i.e., no inter-view prediction) and transmit each view along each independent P2P streaming delivery path. Owing to the distributed nature of P2P networks, users will experience a longer waiting delay for view synchronization by leaving the current video delivery path completely and requesting to join a new video delivery path when the view switching is requested. A proper design of joint/quit protocol and peer management is needed to reduce the waiting latency [22–24].

One way to alleviate the long view-switching latency is to construct the two-layer overlay architecture, which takes advantage of the MVC coding structure and consists of cross-view overlay and intra-view overlay [25]. As illustrated in Figure 10.8, the cross-view overlay delivers the global I-frames as they are needed for every view and the intra-view overlay transmits both the required B/P-frames in each view and the referenced B/P-frames from neighboring views. In other words, users in the same cross-view overlay may watch different views and users in the same intra-view overlay watch the same view. Each user should join these two overlay trees. During the normal playback within one view, each user receives the required video bit streams for the required I/P/B-frames from these two trees. When one user wants to switch from view 1 and view 2, the node will send notification to both overlay neighbors. Some intra-view neighbors who contribute the most content to the user will become this node's new neighbor in the cross-view overlay. The cross-view neighbors who play back view 2 become this node's new intra-view neighbors and send the local and referenced B/P-frames for view 2 to this user. By doing so, the view-switching latency can be reduced.

The multi-view bit streams may experience bit corruption or packet lost during transmission. Multiple description coding (MDC) is already shown as an effective solution to overcome those transmission problems. A video program encoded in MDC format consists of multiple descriptions, and each description can be decoded independently and rendered to provide a basic visual quality. The more descriptions the decoder successfully receives and decodes, the better final visual quality the end user will observe. Therefore, MDC streams are useful in a distributed environment to provide progressive quality refinement. Bringing MDC technology into a P2P network, each end user will have the basic video quality with receiving at least one description from his/her peer. When the degree of connectivity from other peers increases or inbound channel bandwidth becomes larger, the end user can receive more descriptions for higher visual quality. This is different from the traditional single description method in which the end user waits for all segments

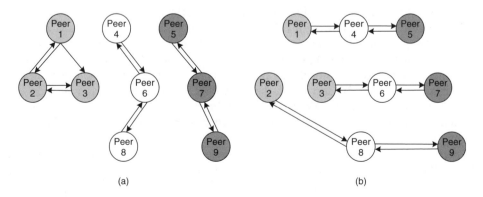

(a)   (b)

Figure 10.8 Two-layer overlay architecture (a) intra-view overlay, (b) cross-view overlay.

from all peers to arrive to start a smooth playback, especially for real-time streaming scenario. Further improvement on the final reconstructed 3D video quality via MDC is expected when the bit streams are transmitted through a lossy channel condition [26].

Precise synchronization for left view and right view also is a key factor to determine the success of a 3D P2P streaming service. To achieve the best 3D viewing experience, the left view and the right view video frames should be available for rendering at the targeted time instant after the playback starts. Having one view missing will downgrade the 3D viewing to 2D viewing; and having two views missing will result in playback jitter. An intuitive way to achieve perfect synchronization is to pack the left and right views that have the same display timestamp together in the same P2P segment. However, this will increase the required bandwidth between peers and cannot fully utilize the distributed manner in P2P streaming. A proper design for receiving each view separately from different peers can improve the playback performance. The scheduler can be further formulated as an optimization problem and solved via binary quadratic programming [27].

10.4 3D Video Broadcasting

When considering services that broadcast 3D video content, it is natural to expect that these services will be designed with the constraint of maintaining backwards compatibility with legacy video services that do not provide 3D rendering. As such, this is a consideration that has influenced most of the systems available today for broadcasting 3D video.

On a broad view, broadcasting 3D video involves the capture of 3D video information, its encoding into a usually compressed representation, the transport over a network, and the reception of the 3D video. All of these components have been described throughout this book, so in this section we will focus on describing how they are applied to different system configurations for 3D broadcasting.

The first element of the broadcasting system to look at is the video encoder. Here, the approaches heavily rely on the use of modified MPEG-2 and H.264 codecs. One approach [28] is to encode the left view using a standard MPEG-2 encoding. This part of the video bit stream is considered as a base layer and can be decoded by non-3D video receivers. To provide a 3D video service, the right view is encoded as an enhancement layer and transmitted as a second component of the video stream. In the ATTEST (Advanced Three-Dimensional Television Systems Technologies) project, the encoding of 3D video was done following a video-plus-depth representation using the H.264/AVC codec. Interoperability with legacy systems not capable of representing 3D video is maintained, in this case through the availability of a 2D video description within the transmitted stream. This approach has the advantage that the transmission of additional information to provide 3D service, in the form of a video depth description, adds only a relatively small overhead. Indeed, as reported in [28], the video depth information can be compressed at rates of 200–300 kbps, which amounts to roughly 10% of a typical 3 Mbps 2D broadcast-quality video.

Transmission of broadcast 3D video can be done using a number of transport methods also available with different degrees of modifications for the transmission of legacy 2D video. One such case is transmission using the infrastructure for broadcasting 2D digital television. Being used in Europe, Australia and good proportions of Asia and Africa, the DVB (Digital Video Broadcast) standard is the most widely used standard for broadcasting

2D digital TV in the World. Depending on the application, there are different variations to the DVB standard [29]. The DVB-T, DVB-S, and DVB-C are applied to the digital broadcasting of, respectively, terrestrial, satellite, and cable television. The three variations of the standard share the use of an outer Reed–Solomon (204,188) FEC code and an inner punctured convolutional code. After the FEC blocks, and following an interleaving operation, DVB-T transmits using OFDM where each subcarrier can carry QPSK, 16-QAM, or 64-QAM-modulated symbols. Differently from DVB-T, DVB-S transmits using QPSK or BPSK and DVB-C uses 16-QAM, 32-QAM, 64-QAM, 128-QAM, or 256-QAM. In addition to these three variants, there is also the DVB-H standard for broadcasting digital video to handheld devices [30].

The DVB-H adapts the DVB standard for the transmission of digital video over the much more error-prone environment found in mobile communications. This is done by maintaining the final stage of data transmission using DVB-T but, at the transmitter side, the video encoder and other possible higher network layers (i.e., transport and network layers) are fed into an MPE-FEC (multi-protocol encapsulation – forward error control) module before going through the stages for DVB-T transmission. The function of the MPE-FEC module is to add extra error protection for the transmission over the more challenging wireless channel. A study of this system was presented in [31] where the extra error correcting in the MPE-FEC module is implemented with a Reed–Solomon code. The results from the study show that the MPE-FEC adds the needed extra level of protection against errors but for channels that are very degraded it is also necessary to implement unequal error protection techniques.

It is also commonplace to add in the transmission chain of 3D video the processing steps for transmission over IP networks. With IP-encapsulated 3D video, the delivery of the service can be done using server unicast to a single client, server multicast to several clients, peer-to-peer (P2P) unicasting, or P2P multicasting. For transmission of 3D video over IP networks, the protocol stack can be organized as RTP/UDP/IP. This is the most widely used configuration today because UDP is needed for applications that have timing constraints for the transmitted video, but it faces the problem that UDP does not provide congestion control functionality. Transmission of video using protocols that provide congestion control is especially useful due to the large volume of traffic that are expected in relation to video services. Consequently, a new protocol, called "datagram congestion control protocol" (DCCP), was published in 2006 [32] as an alternate to UDP that provides congestion control functionality. One of the congestion control methods provided by DCCP calculates a transmit rate using the TCP throughput equation (which depends on an estimated round trip time for the connection). This congestion control method provides a smooth transmit rate, with slow changes over time, and is also fair to other TCP traffic streams with which it needs to coexist on the Internet. DCCP also provides a congestion control mechanism that behaves similarly to the Additive Increase, Multiplicative Increase method used in TCP.

10.5   3D Video over 4G Networks

As discussed in Chapter 6, fourth generation mobile networks provide a number of important improvements from the preceding 3G networks [33]. Among other improvements, 4G is capable of delivering connections at very high data rates (with target speeds of 100 Mbps or better). Circuit switching will not be supported in 4G networks, as they will be entirely based on an all-IP architecture. Consequently, it is expected that a major part of the total traffic will be from different IP-based multimedia services, such as voice over IP and video streaming. To support the large variety of services over the same IP architecture, 4G systems provide different mechanisms such as differentiated classes of service for varied quality of service (QoS) support and improved security to the end users. Recall from Chapter 6 that, depending how strict is the classification of a mobile system into the "4G" category, the two main 4G standards can be considered to be 3GPP LTE (long term evolution) and IEEE802.16e or their respective evolutions LTE-A (long term evolution – advanced) and IEEE 802.16m WiMAX (sometimes called WiMAX 2). Also, recall from Chapter 6 that, in broad terms, both families of standards share many similarities. Both standards are based on OFDM technology with low latency (e.g., by defining a 10 ms frame in LTE). The use of OFDM presents advantages in terms of high bit rate data transmission (due to the good performance in multipath environments) and results in a flexible implementation that allows the standards to be easily adapted to operate over different system bandwidths. Indeed, the flexibility provided by OFDM also allows for developers to more easily design products for one of the family using as starting point intellectual property, such as software libraries, already developed for products based on the other family of standards. The low latency helps enhance channel estimation in high Doppler scenarios, which enables the use of a number of techniques that improve transmission speed. In addition, both families of standards support time-division multiplexing (TDM) and Frequency-division multiplexing (FDM) uplink/downlink duplexing, incorporate multiple transmit and receive antenna technology (MIMO), adaptive modulation and coding (AMC), and hybrid automatic repeat-reQuest (ARQ) for flexible and efficient error correction.

A study of 3D video transmission over WiMAX was reported in [34]. The study is limited to the physical layer of IEEE 802.16e Mobile WiMAX and compared 3D video encoded into two separate left-right views at 3 Mbps each and using a color-plus-depth scheme with 4.8 Mbps allocated to color and 1.2 Mbps allocated to depth information. The work studies different setting for the AMC feature in WiMAX so as to deliver the total 6 Mbps required by the test video sequences. Mobility was considered in the study as the channel model was the ITU Vehicular A for a user traveling at 60 km/h. As a result of the study, it was observed that 3D video streams encoded using the two-view (left and right) method yielded better PSNR results than the color-plus-depth method. The measured difference in PSNR was between 1 and 5 dB.

The higher bit rate and lower latency that can be achieved with 4G technology are going to be key enablers to transmit 3DTV services and also new features such as view switching/selection or multi-view applications. At the same time, this will bring new challenges and considerations to the design of schedulers and resource allocation mechanisms. The 4G standards do not specify algorithms for resource allocation. Therefore, an important area for research and development is to design techniques to allocate resources for video transmission that exploit the flexibility offered by OFDM in terms of wireless spectrum resource assignments. For example, in [35], subcarriers are allocated and the encoding rates of multiple scalable video programs are calculated so as to meet quality, fairness, and efficiency goals by using the frequency, time, and multiuser diversity offered by the OFDM system. Another example of resource allocation for video transmission over 4G networks is the work in [36]. This work studies, as an application of a novel video frame synthetic generator, three scheduling algorithms for the allocation of WiMAX slots. A WiMAX slot consists on one subcarrier assignment lasting for a number of OFDM symbols. The three discussed scheduling algorithms are:

- earliest deadline first (EDF): the scheduler examines the packet at the head of each queue from flows requesting service and schedules first the one with the earliest deadline,
- deficit round robin (DRR): the scheduler allocates in a WiMAX frame those packets that meet a fair share criterion; the fair share criterion is derived from the queue length and the modulation and coding level as an indicator of the channel conditions,
- earliest deadline first with deficit round robin (EDF-DRR): the scheduler sorts the packets in order of earliest deadline and then applies the DDR criteria to make the final scheduling decision.

In [36] it is shown through simulations that EDF is the most unfair of the three scheduling algorithms and that DDR is approximately as fair as EDF-DDR but also has better performance for mobile video traffic.

As explained in Chapter 6, the use in all 4G standards of different variants of OFDM, leads to the need to allocate wireless medium access resources within a time–frequency grid, where the time dimension is given by the successive transmitted symbols, and the frequency dimension is given by different subcarriers allocation. A scheduler for time–frequency resource allocation in LTE is studied in [37]. This scheduler departs from the popular Proportional Fairness choice because it is argued that although it is possible to achieve long-term fairness in the resource allocation, there are no guarantees for delay-constrained real-time video services. In contrast, the scheduler in [37] takes a two-pronged approach where on one side a weighted round-robin (WRR) algorithm allocates time–frequency resources, and on the other side a cross-layer approach is used to perform AMC and choose source coding parameters based on channel conditions. Furthermore, the weights for the WRR algorithm, that determine the share of resources for a given call, is given as a linear combination of three weights, one incorporating the channel quality, a second considering the QoS constraint for an application and the third introducing an element of fairness that measures the historical average data rate.

As mentioned earlier, the resource allocation mechanism has not been specified in the 4G standard. Therefore, 4G system designers need to devise techniques that are able to couple the design of schedulers and resource allocation mechanisms with the QoS-related mechanisms defined within the standard. Both family of standards, LTE and WiMAX, support multimedia services by providing several QoS mechanisms [38]. Specifically, 4G standards include mechanisms to establish connections with different scheduling types and priorities, which support, for example, traffic with guaranteed maximum and minimum traffic rate. Also, the standards include different mechanisms that allow the uplink scheduler at the base station to learn the status of the buffers at the mobiles.

References

1. ISO-IEC/JTC1/SC29/WG11/N0400. Test model 5, April 1993. Document AVC-491b, Version 2.
2. H.-J. Lee, T. Chiang, and Y.-Q. Zhang, "Scalable rate control for MPEG-4 video", *IEEE Trans. on Circuits and Systems for Video Technology*, vol. 10, no. 6, pp. 878–894, June 2000.

3. Z. Li, F. Pan, K. P. Lim, G. Feng, X. Lin, and S. Rahardja, "Adaptive basic unit layer rate control for JVT", JVT-G012, Joint Video Team of ISO/IEC MPEG & ITU-T VCEG 7th Meeting: March 2003.

4. L. Wang and A. Vincent, "Bit allocation and constraints for joint coding of multiple video programs", *IEEE Transactions on Circuits and Systems for Video Technology*, vol. 9, no. 6, September 1999, pp. 949–959.

5. G.-M. Su and M. Wu, "Efficient bandwidth resource allocation low-delay multiuser video streaming", *IEEE Trans. on Circuits and Systems for Video Technology*, vol. 15, no. 9, pp. 1124–1137, September 2005.

6. J.-R. Ohm, "Advances in Scalable Video Coding", *Proceedings of the IEEE*, vol. 93, no. 1, January 2005. pp. 42–56.

7. T. Yan, P. An, L. Shen, Q. Zhang, and Z. Zhang, *"Rate control algorithm for multi-view video coding based on correlation analysis"*, Symposium on Photonics and Optoelectronics, 2009.

8. G.-M. Su, Z. Han, M. Wu, and K. J. R. Liu, "A scalable multiuser framework for video over OFDM networks: fairness and efficiency", *IEEE Trans. on Circuits and Systems for Video Technology*, vol. 16, no. 10, October 2006, pp. 1217–1231.

9. J. H. Kim, J. Garcia, and A. Ortega, "Dependent bit allocation in multi-view video coding", *IEEE International Conference on Image Processing*, vol. 2, pp. 293–296, 2005.

10. Y. Morvan, D. Farin, and P. H. N. de With, "Joint depth/texture bit allocation for multi-view video compression", in Proc. 26th PCS, November 2007, pp. 265–268.

11. Y. Liu, Q. Huang, S. Ma, D. Zhao, and W. Gao, "Joint video/depth rate allocation for 3D video coding based on view synthesis distortion model", Signal Process.: Image Commun., vol. 24, no. 8, pp. 666–681, September 2009.

12. H. Yuan, Y. Chang, J. Huo, F. Yang, and Z. Lu, "Model-Based Joint Bit Allocation Between Texture Videos and Depth Maps for 3D Video Coding", *IEEE Trans. on Circuits and Systems for Video Technology*, vol. 21, no. 4, pp. 485–497, April 2011.

13. Y. Liu, Q. Huang, S. Ma, D. Zhao, W. Gao, S. Ci, and H. Tang, "A novel rate control technique for multi-view video plus depth based 3D video coding", *IEEE Trans. on Broadcasting*, vol. 57, no. 2, June 2011, pp. 562–571.

14. G. Cheung, V. Velisavljevic, and A. Ortega, "On dependent bit allocation for multi-view image coding with depth-image-based rendering", *IEEE Trans. on Image Processing*, vol. 20, no. 11, November 2011, pp. 3179–3194.

15. J.-G. Lou, H. Cai, and J. Li, "Interactive multi-view video delivery based on IP multicast", Advances in Multimedia, vol. 2007, article ID 97535.

16. E. Kurutepe, M. R. Civanlar, and A. M. Tekalp, "Client-driven selective streaming of multi-view video for interactive 3DTV", *IEEE Trans. on Circuits and Systems for Video Technology*, vol. 17, no. 11, November 2007, pp. 1558–1565.

17. M. Karczewicz and R. Kurceren, "The SP- and SI-frames design for H.264/AVC", *IEEE Trans. on Circuits and Systems for Video Technology*, vol. 13, no. 7, pp. 637–644, Jul. 2003.

18. K.-Ki. Lai, Y.-L. Chan, and W.-C. Siu, "Quantized transform-domain motion estimation for SP-frame coding in viewpoint switching of multi-view video", *IEEE Trans. on Circuits and Systems for Video Technology*, vol. 20, no. 3, March 2010, pp. 365–381.

19. G. Cheung, A. Ortega, and N.-M. Cheung, "Interactive streaming of stored multi-view video using redundant frame structures", *IEEE Trans. on Image Processing*, vol. 20, no. 3, March 2011, pp. 744–761.

20. Z. Pan, Y. Ikuta, M. Bandai, T. Watanabe, *"User dependent scheme for multi-view video transmission"*, IEEE International Conference on Communications, 2011.

21. Z. Liu, G. Cheung, V. Velisavljević, E. Ekmekcioglu, and Y. Yusheng Ji, "Joint source channel coding for WWAN multi-view video multicast with cooperative peer-to-peer repair", Packet Video Workshop, 2010, pp. 110–117.

22. J. Kim, K. Choi, H. Lee, and J. W. Kim, "Multi-view 3D video transport using application layer multicast with view switching delay constraints", 3DTV Conference, 2007, pp. 1–4.

23. E. Kurutepe and T. Sikora, "Feasibility of multi-view video streaming over P2P networks", 3DTV Conference, 2008, pp. 157–160.

24. E. Kurutepe and T. Sikora, "Multi-view video streaming over P2P networks with low start-up delay", IEEE International Conference on Image Processing 2008, pp. 3088–3091.

25. Z. Chen, L. Sun, and S. Yang, "Overcoming view switching dynamic in multi-view video streaming over P2P network", 3DTV Conference, 2010, p. 1–4.

26. S. Milani, M. Gaggio, and G. Calvagno, *"3DTV streaming over peer-to-peer networks using FEC-based noncooperative multiple description"*, IEEE Symposium on Computers and Communications, 2011, pp. 13–18.

27. Y. Ding and J. Liu, *"Efficient stereo segment scheduling in peer-to-peer 3D/multi-view video streaming"*, IEEE International Conference on Peer-to-Peer Computing 2011. pp. 182–191.

28. G. B. Akar, A. M. Tekalp, C. Fehn, and M. R. Civanlar, "Transport Methods in 3DTV – A Survey", *IEEE Transactions on Circuits and Systems for Video Technology*, vol. 17, no. 11, pp. 1622–1630, November 2007.

29. U. H. Reimers, "DVB – The Family of International Standards for Digital Video Broadcasting", *Proceedings of the IEEE*, vol. 94, no. 1, pp. 173–182, January 2006.

30. G. Faria, J. A. Henriksson, E. Stare, and P. Talmola, "DVB-H: Digital Broadcast Services to Handheld Devices", *Proceedings of the IEEE*, vol. 94, no. 1, pp. 194–209, January 2006.

31. A. Aksay, M. Orgu z Bici, D. Bugdayci, A. Tikanmaki, A. Gotchev, and G. B. Akar, "A study on the effect of MPE-FEC for 3D video broadcasting over DVB-H", in *Proceedings of the 5th International ICST Mobile Multimedia Communications Conference (Mobimedia)*, 2009.

32. E. Kohler, M. Handley, and S. Floyd, "Datagram Congestion Control Protocol (DCCP)", IETF Request for Comments 4340 (RFC-4340).

33. H. Wang, L. Kondi, A. Luthra, S. Ci. *4G Wireless Video Communications*, John Wiley & Sons, 2009.

34. D. V. S. X De Silva, E. Ekmekcioglu, O. Abdul-Hameed, W. A. C. Fernando, S. T. Worrall, and A. M. Kondoz, "Performance evaluation of 3D-TV transmission over WiMAX broadband access networks", in *Proc. 5th International Conference on Information and Automation for Sustainability (ICIAFs)*, pp. 298–303, 17–19 December 2010.

35. G.-M. Su, Z. Han, M. Wu, and K. J. R. Liu "A Scalable Multiuser Framework for Video over OFDM Networks: Fairness and Efficiency". *IEEE Transactions on Circuits and Systems for Video Technology*, 2006; 16(10): 1217–1231.

36. A. K. Al-Tamimi, C. So-In, and R. Jain. "Modeling and resource allocation for mobile video over WiMAX broadband wireless networks". *IEEE Journal on Selected Area in Communications*, 2010; vol. 28 no. 3, pp. 354–365.

37. H. Luo, S. Ci, S. Wu, J. Wu, H. Tang, "Quality-driven cross-layer optimized video delivery over LTE". *IEEE Communications Magazine*, vol. 48 no. 2 pp. 102–109, 2010.

38. M. Alasti, B. Neekzad, J. Hui, R. Vannithamby, "Quality of service in WiMAX and LTE networks", *IEEE Communications Magazine*, vol. 48 no. 5 pp. 104–111, 2010.

Index

2D to 3D conversion, 7, 56, 85, 293
3D artifacts, 205–220
3D content capturing, 85
3D content creation, 85
3D display, 63
3D gaming system, 295–8
3D mobile, 298–302
3D modeling, 5–6
3D multi-view generation, 125–6
3D quality of experience, 9–10
3D representation, 5–6
3D scanner, 29, 38
3D scene modeling, 85
3D-DCT, 241
3DVC, 167

accommodation, 63, 248
active 3D-glass display, 290
adaptive modulation and coding (AMC), 11, 191
additive white Gaussian noise (AWGN), 177
ad-hoc network, 193
Advanced Video Coding (AVC), 129
aliasing, 77, 81
all-IP architecture, 200, 330
alpha matting, 56
amplify-and-forward (AF), 284
anaglyph, 65
angular disparity, 64
angular intra-prediction, 141

animation framework extension (AFX), 165–6
application layer, 174
approximating scheme, 35–6
arbitrary slice order (ASO), 140
arithmetic coding, 136
asymmetric motion partition (AMP), 141
asymmetric stereo video coding, 142–3
asymmetries in stereo camera rig, 216–17
augmented reality, 302–9
autofocus processing, 91
automatic 2D-to-3D conversion (a3DC), 103–11
automatic repeat request (ARQ), 173
automultiscopic, 79
autostereoscopic display, 9, 71–8
autostereoscopy, 289

banding artifact, 218
base layer (BL), 323
basis function, 32
B-frame, 137
bilateral filter, 153
binarization process, 136
binary bin, 136
binary format for scenes (BIFS), 165
binary phase shift keying (BPSK), 176
binocular depth cue, 64, 205
binocular rivalry, 217
binocular suppression theory, 7, 142, 318

3D Visual Communications, First Edition. Guan-Ming Su, Yu-Chi Lai, Andres Kwasinski and Haohong Wang.
© 2013 John Wiley & Sons, Ltd. Published 2013 by John Wiley & Sons, Ltd.

block matching (BM), 241
blocky artifact, 136, 218
blur gradient, 248
blurring artifact, 218
broadband channel, 181
B-slice, 137

capture cues, 247
cardboard effect, 215–16
cave automatic virtual environment
    (CAVE), 71
center of use (CoU), 226
channel, 175
channel code rate, 175
channel delay spread, 181
channel encoder, 174
channel-induced distortion, 259
checkerboard format, 7, 145
chromatic aberration, 217
circuit switching, 171
circular polarization, 69
coding block, 141
coding unit (CU), 137, 141
coherence bandwidth, 181
coherence time, 188
color bleeding artifact, 218
color cues, 64
color dispersion, 77
color matching function, 66
color rivalry, 68
color separation, 77
colorimetric asymmetry, 217
comoplementary decimation, 146
complexity model, 314
compression artifact, 218
context adaptive binary arithmetic coding
    (CABAC), 135–6
context adaptive variable length coding
    (CAVLC), 135–6
contrast masking, 229
contrast sensitivity, 229
conventional stereo video (CSV), 291
converence point, 206
cooperative communications, 14, 284
coordinate transform, 207
corner cutting, 35

corner-table mesh, 26
corona artifact, 164
correlation, 318
crossed disparity, 206
crossed parallax, 207
cross-layer design, 12, 282
crosstalk, 73, 82, 217
curve fitting, 321

data-driven animation, 20
data link layer, 173
datagram congestion control protocol
    (DCCP), 329
DCT compression artifact, 218–19
deblocking filter, 130
deblocking process, 136
decimation, 146, 281
decode-and-forward (DF), 284
decoding drift, 324
de-correlation transform, 130
deficit round robin (DRR), 331
defocus cues, 63
depth camera, 88
depth cue, 205
depth from focus and defocus, 103–4
depth from geometric cues, 103
depth from motion, 104–5
depth from planar model, 103
depth from shading, 104
depth-image-based rendering (DIBR), 148
depth image-based representation, 6, 18,
    51–7
depth map bleeing, 219
depth map ringing, 219
depth offset, 156
depth-plane curvature, 212
depth ringing, 219
depth video camera, 5
descriptive quality, 223
diagonal scan, 141
DIBR-based error recovery, 324
diplopia, 206
discrete cosine transform (DCT), 133
disparity, 87
disparity compensation, 157
disparity correlation, 269

disparity estimation, 160
disparity map, 6
displaced frame difference (DFD), 317
displacement map, 33
distortion-quantization, 320
distributed source coding, 14
divergent parallax, 207
Doppler shift, 188
Doppler spectrum, 188
Doppler spread, 188
double flash, 70
downsampling, 281
drifting artifact, 139
dual LCD panel, 78
Digital Video Broadcast (DVB), 328
DVB-C, 329
DVB-H, 329
DVB-S, 329
DVB-T, 329

earliest deadline first (EDF), 331
earliest deadline first with deficit round
     robin (EDF-DRR), 331
edge, 24
edge collapse, 30
edge-preserving, 153
end-to-end 3D visual ecosystem, 3–5
end-to-end distortion, 265
enhancement layer (EL), 323
eNodeB, 195
entropy coding, 129–130, 135–6
error concealment, 5, 8, 270
error protection, 324
error resilience, 267
evolved packet core (EPC), 195, 200
evolved universal terrestrial radio access
     network (E-UTRAN), 195
Exp-Golomb coding, 135
external preference mapping, 224
extraordinary vertex, 36
extrinsic matrix, 162

face, 24
face-vertex mesh, 25
false contouring artifact, 218
false edge artifact, 218

fast binary arithmetic coding, 136
fast fading, 188
fatigue, 249
feature based metrics, 232–3
feature-based 3D QA, 244–6
femtocell, 12
film-type patterned retarder
     (FPR), 69
FinePix Real 3D System, 291
finite impulse response (FIR), 136
flat-fading channel, 181
flexible macroblock order (FSO), 140
focus cues, 63, 247
focus value (FV), 91
forward error control (FEC), 8, 324
frame-compatible, 7
frame-compatible stereo video streaming,
     318
free viewpoint video, 166
free-viewpoint 3DTV (FVT), 9
frequency-selective channel, 181
full-reference (FR) metrics, 227
full-resolution frame-compatible, 146–8
full-resolution frame-compatible stereo
     video streaming, 318

Gaussian kernel, 153
generalized procrustes analysis (GPA),
     224
geometric cues, 63
geometry-based modeling, 6, 85–6
geometry-based representation, 17,
     22–43, 166
glass-less two-view systems, 289
global Illumination, 21, 32
global system for mobile communications
     (GSM), 194
google street, 48
Grammian matrix, 67
graphics pipeline, 31
group of GOP (GGOP), 318
group of pictures (GOP), 137

H.264, 129
H.264/MPEG-2 multiview profile, 143
half-edge mesh, 27
half-resolution frame-compatible, 144–6

Hardamard transform, 134
head tracking, 79
header, 172
hierarchical B-frame, 138, 159
high efficiency video coding (HEVC),
    129, 140–142
high-speed uplink packet access
    (HSUPA), 195
hill-climbing focusing, 94
hole, 150, 219
hole-filling algorithm, 150
hologram, 83–4
holographic 3DTV, 9
horizontal disparity, 64
Horopter circle, 206
HTC EVO 3D, 298–9
Huffman coding, 135
human vision system based metrics,
    228–32
human visual system (HVS), 9, 63, 205–6
hybrid modeling, 6, 85, 87

IEEE 802.16–WiMAX, 202
I-frame, 137
image-based modeling, 6, 85–6
image-based representation, 18, 43–51,
    166
individual view coding, 142–3
information fidelity criterion (IFC), 234
information theoretic QA, 234
instantaneous decoder refresh (IDR), 137
integer DCT transform, 134
integral image, 75
integral videography (IV) overlay, 305
intensity cues, 64
interactive 2D-to-3D conversion, 111
interference, 177
inter-frame prediction, 130
interocular distance, 205
interpolating scheme, 35–6
inter-symbol interference (ISI), 183
inter-view bilateral error concealment
    (IBEC), 273
inter-view correlation, 269
inter-view prediction, 143
intra-frame prediction, 130–132

intrinsic matrix, 162
IP multicast, 321
IPv4, 174
IPv6, 174
IS-95, 194
I-slice, 137

joint multi-program rate control, 318
just-noticeable threshold (JNT), 143

Karhunen-Loeve transform
    (KLT), 133
key frame extraction, 116
key-framed animation, 20
keystone distortion, 211
Kinect, 88, 293–4

Lagrange multiplier, 317, 320
large-scale propagation effect, 177
largest coding unit (LCU), 140
lattice artifacts, 217–18
layer depth image (LDI), 54–6
layered depth video (LDV), 7, 163–5
least squared, 321
lenticular lens, 9, 75–8, 80, 290
light field, 49–50
linear polarization, 69
local illumination, 21, 31–2
logical link control, 173
log-normal fading, 178
long-term evolution (LTE), 11, 194
long term evolution-advance (LTE-A),
    194, 201
luma-based chroma prediction, 141
lumigraph, 49–50
luminance masking, 229

macroblock (MB), 137
magnification factor, 215
M-ary phase shift keying (MPSK), 176
mean of absolute difference (MAD),
    132–3, 316
mean square error (MSE), 227
medical visualization, 304
medium access control, 173
mesh compression and encoding, 29–31

mesh-based, 326
Mirage Table, 294
mismatch compensation, 158
mixed resolution stereo (MRS), 291
mixed-resolution, 7, 269
mixed-resolution video coding, 143
mode decision algorithm, 160
modulation, 175
monocular depth cue, 63–4, 205
mosquito noise, 219
motion compensation, 133
motion compensation mismatch, 219
motion confusion, 70
motion estimation, 132–3
motion judder artifact, 219
motion modeling based QA, 235–6
motion parallax, 64, 79, 247–8
motion vectors, 95–6, 268
moving pictures quality metric (MPQM), 231
MPEG-2 test model 5 (TM5), 314
MPEG-4 Part 10, 129
MPEG-4 verification model (VM), 316
MPEG-A, 166
MPEG-C Part 3, 150
MPEG-FTV, 167
multi-band filter, 68
multicarrier modulation, 196
multi-hypothesis error concealment (MHEC), 274
multimedia application format (MAF), 166
multipath channel, 179
multiple description coding (MDC), 8, 269, 327
multiple description (MD) coding, 279
multiple texture technique, 48–50
multiple view coding (MVC), 156–160
multiple view image, 50
multiple-input and multiple-output (MIMO), 11
multiuser video communications, 13
multi-view camera, 88
multi-view correspondence, 87
multi-view matching, 6, 87
multi-view system, 78–83

multi-view video coding (MVC), 1, 7, 146
multi-view video plus depth (MVD), 7, 160–163
MVC streaming, 318–19
MVD streaming, 319–21

Nakagami fading, 190
narrowband channel, 181
negative parallax, 207
network abstraction layer (NAL), 278
network layer, 174
non-square quad-tree transform (NSQT), 141
non-uniform rational B-spline surface (NURBS), 32–4
no-reference (NR) metrics, 227
N-view video camera, 5

object classification, 120–121
object orientation, 119
object segmentation, 117–19
object thickness, 119
occlusion, 5, 50, 64
occlusion-based, 9, 71–5, 79
octree, 41
open profiling quality (OPQ), 223–4
optical augmented display, 303
orthogonal frequency division multiplexing (OFDM), 11, 196
orthogonal projection, 65
over-under format, 7, 145

packet, 172
packet switching, 172
Panum's fusional area, 206
parallax, 209
parallax barrier, 9, 71–5, 79–80, 289–290
parallel camera configuration, 207–8
parallel stereoscopic camera, 207
path loss, 177–8
path loss exponent, 178
patterned retarder (PR), 69
peak signal-to-noise ratio (PSNR), 227
peer-to-peer (P2P), 13

peer-to-peer streaming, 325–8
perceptual distortion metric (PDM), 231
perceptual evaluation of video quality
    (PEVQ), 233
Percival's zone of comfort, 248
P-frame, 137
PHSD-3D, 242–4
PHVS-3D, 240–242
physical layer, 173
physically-based animation, 21
picket-fence effect, 217–8
pixel-based metrics, 227–8
platelet, 154
plenoptic function, 43–6, 86, 166
point-based modeling, 6
point-based representation, 37–9
polarization multiplexing, 9, 69
polygonal mesh, 24–32
positive parallax, 207
power delay profile, 180
prediction, 129
prediction path, 129
prediction unit (PU), 141
primary color system, 65
progressive mesh, 30
projection matrix, 162
pseudoscopic, 73
P-slice, 137
PSNR-HVS, 231
PSNR-HVS-M, 231–2
psychoperceptual, 222
puppet-theater effect, 213–5

quad-edge mesh, 27
quad-lateral filter, 154
quadratic model, 316
quadrature amplitude modulation (QAM),
    176
quadrilateral, 24
quad-tree, 140
quad-tree decomposition, 155
quality accessment (QA), 220
quality of expeience (QoE), 3, 220
quality of perception (QoP), 222
quality of sevice (QoS), 11
quantization, 129, 130

quantization parameter (QP), 134
quantization step size, 134
quaternary phase shift keying (QPSK),
    176
Quicktime VR, 47–8

radial distortion, 217
radiosity, 32
rate control, 313
rate distortion optimization (RDO), 316
rate-quantization, 320
ray marching, 42–3
Rayleigh fading, 189
ray-tracing, 32
real-time transport protocol (RTP), 329
recontruction path, 129
reduced-reference (RR) metrics, 227
redundant slice, 140
reference picture buffer, 137
refraction-based, 9, 75–8, 79
relay, 283
reproduction magnification factor, 215
residual, 129
residual quad-tree (RQT), 141
retinal disparity, 206
RGB, 130
ringing artifact, 218

Sarnoff JND vision model, 230
scalable MVC streaming, 323
scalable video coding (SVC), 146
scene geometric structure, 117
scheduling, 331
screen cues, 247–8
semantic object, 117
semantic rule, 122
shadow fading, 178
shape-from-silhouette, 86
shared motion vectors, 273
shear distortion, 212–3
shutter glasses, 70
side-by-side format, 7, 145
single carrier-frequency division multiple
    access (SC-FDMA), 200
single texture technique, 47–8
size maganification factor, 215

slanted multi-view display, 80
slice, 137
slice group, 140
slow fading, 188
small-scale propagation effect, 177
SNR asymmetry, 143
source encoder, 174
source encoding distortion, 259
spatial asymmetry, 142–3
spatial light modulator (SLM), 83
spatial monocular depth cue, 63–4
spatial multiplexing, 71
spatial redundancy, 130
spatial scalability, 146
spatially multiplexed systems, 290
spatial-temporal monocular depth cues, 64
spectral absorption function, 66
spectral density function, 65
splating, 39
spot focus window, 92
staircase artifact, 218
stereo band limited contrast (SBLC), 236
Stereobrush, 293
stereo camera, 87
stereo camera rig, 216
stereo correspondence, 87
stereo matching, 87
stereoscopic artifact, 10
stereoscopic display, 65–71
store-and-forward, 172
structural similarity (SSIM) index, 232–3
structure based metrics, 232–3
structure from motion (SfM), 89
subdivision surface representation, 34–7
subpixel, 77
subpixel motion estimation, 133
sum of squared difference (SSD), 317
surface-based modeling, 6
surface-based representation, 17, 23–37
sweet spot, 71
switching I (SI)-slice, 139
switching P (SP)-slice, 139, 324
synchronization, 328

temporal asymmetry, 143
temporal bilateral error concealment
    (TBEC), 273

temporal correlation, 269
temporal random access, 157
temporal redundancy, 132
temporal scalability, 146
temporally multiplexed systems, 290
Teo and Heeger model, 230
texture-based representation, 18, 43–51
texturing techniques, 27
tile, 141
tiling artifact, 218
time multiplexing, 9, 69–71
time-of-flight, 88
toed-in camera configuration, 207–8
toed-in stereoscopic camera, 207
transform, 129
transform unit (TU), 141
transmission artifact, 219
transmission control protocol (TCP), 174
transmission-induced distortion, 259
tree-based, 326
triangle, 24
trilateral filter, 153–4
triple flash, 70
two-layer overlay, 327
two-view stereo video streaming, 318

uncrossed disparity, 206
uncrossed parallax, 207
unequal error protection (UEP), 5, 8, 275
uniform scattering environment, 188
universal mobile telecommunications
    system (UMTS), 194
user datagram protocol (UDP), 174, 329
user-centered, 222
user-centered quality of experience,
    225–6

vector Huffman coding, 136
vergence angle, 64
vergence-accommodation coupling, 250
vertex, 24
vertex insertion, 35
vertex split, 30
vertex-vertex mesh, 25
video augmented display, 303
video broadcasting, 326, 328

video plus depth (V+D), 1, 7,
    148–56, 291
video quality metric (VQM), 233
video structure analysis, 116
video-on-demand, 326
Vieth-Muller circle, 206
view switching, 321–5
view switching latency, 323
view synthesized artifact, 219–220
view-dependent texture, 49
viewing zone, 71
view-switching, 157
view-switching latency, 327
view-synthesis prediction (VSP), 162
virtual environment (VE), 302
virtual reality, 71
virtual reality model language (VRML),
    165
visible difference predictor (VDP), 230
visual discomfort, 10
visual fatigue, 10
visual hull, 86
visual information fidelity (VIF), 234

visual signal-to-noise ratio (VSNR), 230
volume-based modeling, 6
volume-based representation, 17,
    40–43
voxel, 40
voxelization, 41

wavefront parallel processing, 141–2
wavelength division multiplexing, 9,
    65–8
wedgelet, 154
weighted prediction, 133
wideband-CDMA, 194
Wiener-Ziv coding, 14
WiMAX, 11
winged-edge mesh, 27

YCbCr, 130

Z-buffer-basd 3D surface recovering,
    98–100
zero parallax, 207
zigzag, 135